The Brutality
of Nations

THE BRUTALITY OF NATIONS

by Dan Jacobs

PARAGON HOUSE PUBLISHERS

New York

First paperback edition, 1988

Published in the United States by

Paragon House Publishers
90 Fifth Avenue
New York, NY 10011

Library of Congress Cataloging-in-Publication Data

Jacobs, Dan.
The brutality of nations.

Bibliography: p.
Includes index.
1. Nigeria—History—Civil War, 1967-1970—Civilian
relief.   2. Nigeria—History—Civil War, 1967-1970—
War work—Red Cross.   3. International relief—Nigeria—
Political aspects.   I. Title.
DT515.836.J33   1988   966.9′05   87-7235
ISBN 1-55778-104-4 (pbk.)

The Indian saw the Englishman function only as an official with all the inhumanity of the machine and with all the passion of a vested interest trying to preserve itself. How different was the behavior of a person acting as an individual and obeying his own impulses from his behavior as an official or a unit in the army! The soldier, stiffening to attention, drops his humanity and, acting as an automaton, shoots and kills inoffensive and harmless persons who have done him no ill. So also, I thought, the police officer who would hesitate to do an unkindness to an individual would, the day after, direct a lathee charge on innocent people. He will not think of himself as an individual then, nor will he consider as individuals those crowds whom he beats down or shoots.

JAWAHARLAL NEHRU, *"Toward Freedom"*

In a hundred years, how will the world judge the rulers of 1969, who permitted these horrors?

MONSEIGNEUR JEAN RODHAIN

The Brutality
of Nations

Prologue

On the morning of October 12, 1968, a cable arrived on the thirty-eighth floor of the United Nations Secretariat, the office of Secretary General U Thant. It had been stamped twice: the time and date received and "For Action" by Undersecretary General José Rolz-Bennett, Thant's deputy. The cable was from Dr. Herman Middelkoop, the Dutch missionary doctor in charge of relief operations in Biafra for the World Council of Churches.

Biafra had been blockaded for seventeen months, and by June of that year the shortage of protein foods had begun to take its toll. The smallest children, with their growing bodies, starved first. For months, the people of the world had been shaken and angered by photographs and scenes on television of Biafran children—skeletal bodies, swollen joints and bellies, the profound sadness of their faces and the reproachful stare of their eyes.

Now, in October, after months of this, Dr. Middelkoop, a man not given to overstatement, cabled:

FOR SECRETARY GENERAL UN FROM WCC REFUGEE RELIEF BIAFRA. DEAR MR. THANT. ESTIMATED DEATH FROM STARVATION IN MONTH OF JULY 6,000 PER DAY, AUGUST 10,000 PER DAY, SEPTEMBER 12,000 PER DAY. PRESENT SITUATION HOLDS OR DECREASING SLIGHTLY WITH PRESENT LEVEL OF RELIEF FLIGHTS. HOWEVER UNLESS IMMEDIATE CEASE FIRE MONTH OF DECEMBER COULD SEE DEATH RATE UNITS OF 25,000 PER DAY. CARBOHYDRATES LIKELY TO BE EXHAUSTED IN NEXT SEVEN WEEKS. BIAFRA WILL BE COMPLETELY WITHOUT FOOD. ACUTE MASS STARVATION UNAVOIDABLE. ANSWER DOES NOT LIE WITH RELIEF ORGANIZATIONS. ANSWER LIES WITH END OF WAR.

The estimates of death were not made up for propaganda purposes.

Every Wednesday a committee headed by Dr. Clyne Shepherd, a gentle Scotsman, met at Middelkoop's hospital in Umuahia. Relief workers came from all parts of Biafra to discuss the medical situation, each bringing with him a census of the number of deaths in his area during the past week. They had buried many of the small bodies with their own hands. Cabinetmakers had been kept busy day and night for months making the tiny coffins—now they were running out of wood. So Middelkoop's estimate of some twelve thousand dying each day was more accurate than any other information available.

The public, however, did not know of this dire prediction by one of the most responsible and best-informed officials in Biafra. Days went by, and no action was planned. Then someone at the UN decided that what was at stake outweighed the niceties of correct bureaucratic behavior. A copy of the cable found its way to Lloyd Garrison, the *New York Times* correspondent who had covered the Nigerian-Biafran war from both sides. Knowing Dr. Middelkoop, his integrity and avoidance of sensationalism, Garrison recognized the full significance of the cable. He wrote a comprehensive story, drawing upon other relief sources as well. It appeared in the *Times* of Sunday, October 20.

Following Garrison's story was a brief item:

THANT HAS NO MESSAGE

United Nations, N.Y., October 19—Secretary General Thant said through a spokesman today that he had not received any recent message from Dr. Middelkoop concerning starvation rates in Biafra.

As Nigerian troops overran the Biafran enclave in the early days of 1970, the Paris newspaper *Le Monde* commented: "Even if the capitulation of Biafra means for millions of Ibos an easing of that calvary they have endured for thirty months—and one would like to be more convinced of it—this conflict will remain one of the most somber pages in all human history."

Three million died. Or was it two million? This gets us into what diplomats at the time called "the numbers game." Recently a diplomat as responsible as anyone for this tragedy told me he thought only one hundred thousand had died. In fact, he said, the British High Commissioner's Office in Lagos had done a survey after the war and compiled only fifty thousand missing.

In our scientific age it is necessary to quantify if we are to make a statement like "Biafra was the greatest human catastrophe since World War II." If there is no precise statistic, it is difficult to compare Biafra with other recent human disasters: Indochina, the southern Sudan, Bangladesh, Burundi, the Sahel and Ethiopian famines, Uganda, Kampuchea (Cambodia), the African drought.

However, the sheer horror of children starving—or being deliberately starved—made this one of the most emotional events of our time. A few months after it began, there arose confusion as to who was at fault and what could be done about it, as to who was blocking food relief and causing the starvation. Nigeria, by imposing the blockade? Or was Nigeria entirely prepared to allow food to go in by daylight flights or a land corridor? Biafra, because General Ojukwu insisted on unreasonable conditions for entry of relief, as he needed the starvation to sustain the world's compassion and support for Biafran independence?

The public could not follow the complex negotiations and get to the bottom of who was blocking food shipments. They did not know what to believe. They only knew the starvation continued—getting worse, getting better, getting worse again. The confusion and anguish sapped their emotions. The ordeal became too protracted; they turned away, finding it too painful to continue to watch, helpless to do anything.

Those involved in relief, trying to get food and medical care to people on both sides of the fighting, knew who was blocking their efforts. Those in official positions who knew did not speak out to inform the public. Those of us who tried found our efforts thwarted as effectively as were attempts to get food to the starving. Just how this was being done was not clear.

After the war ended, I began to talk with officials of governments and international relief agencies and to gather documents. As I pieced them together, trying to learn what had actually happened, an unexpected level of the archeological dig emerged. I went to a National Security Council staff man and said: "The British did this."

"Oh, of course," he responded. "The British orchestrated the whole thing."

As we shall see, the British government had to cover up the fact that the Nigerians were starving the Biafrans—and killing them by every other means they could, such as bombing crowded marketplaces. The British were providing arms to the Nigerian government in what was becoming an increasingly bloody war. Critics in Parliament threatened to halt the arms supply. The Nigerians had brought the Soviet Union in on their side and warned that if the British supply was cut off, they would turn to the Soviets.

A great deal was at stake for the British. Not only were they deeply involved in their former colony—with important commercial interests in the newly independent, most populous nation of Africa—but under the territory with which the Biafrans were attempting to secede lay one of the most promising oil deposits in the world.

Most of those who became aware of Biafra's starving children in the early summer of 1968 knew little of this history or politics. Nor was it known that British diplomats had already set in motion an effective propaganda-diplomatic ploy aimed at concealing from their critics in Parliament what was actually happening. The State Department's Bureau of African Affairs, other foreign offices, and the secretary general of the United Nations, in order to take the pressure off themselves, joined in sustaining this campaign over the following twenty months.

What made this doubly reprehensible is that the British—in "muddling through"—chanced upon using the International Committee of the Red Cross (ICRC) as their chosen instrument to conceal that it was the Nigerians who were obstructing the relief agencies. In doing so, they gravely damaged this humanitarian organization. Officials of the Red Cross would later say: "Nothing like this had ever happened to us before."

We shall see how in the second year of starvation ("stepped in so far that . . . returning were as tedious as go o'er"), the British and Nigerians came to use the Geneva Convention intended to protect civilians in war to block relief instead, so as to starve the Biafrans into submission. For, after the Nigerians had shot down a Red Cross plane in broad daylight, "the hawks were in the ascendance in Lagos" (as diplomats began saying), and the British carried on an extended campaign of "daylight flights into Uli" aimed both at keeping the ICRC from ever flying again and at curtailing the airlift still being operated by church relief agencies.

Finally, the strategy succeeded: Biafra collapsed, its soldiers too weakened to stand and fight. The conquered people, by now in the worst nutritional condition of any in medically recorded history, needed food urgently. The "hawks" set about methodically to prevent relief from reaching them, the cover-up continued for a while longer.

And the story does not end there. For the Red Cross requested that governments improve the world's ability to provide humanitarian assistance in civil wars. Only one article of the Geneva Conventions applied, and it had proven wholly inadequate. The Red Cross could not aid civilians when their own government wanted them dead and other nations acquiesced or actively colluded.

So the ICRC attempted to strengthen the Geneva Conventions in "conflicts not of an international character." There was great resistance to this in the meetings of government representatives; leadership of the opposition came from two countries which had themselves a short time before been killing large numbers of people they claimed as their own citizens—Pakistan and Iraq. As a result, the Red Cross did not gain the added authority it sought to aid civilians in wars such as Nigeria-Biafra.

Many of the twists and turns of events described here can be understood only in terms of these rather abstruse conventions—in peacetime, a subject for debate among scholars of international law in their learned journals; in wartime, literally a matter of life or death for people scarcely aware of the conventions' existence. There was really no question that the humanitarian conventions applied in the Nigeria-Biafra situation; the proof of this will be seen in the way the Nigerian and British governments and the United Nations secretary general set about to thwart their application.

It was simply not true, as Secretary General Thant said time and again, that this was an internal matter of a sovereign nation. No one should have known it better than he: this was the very question the United Nations had dealt with, unanimously and effectively, in the aftershock of the Nazis' "final solution of the Jewish problem." Raphael Lemkin, one of those in the forefront of the effort to prevent a recurrence of such mass murder, put it at the time: "The question arose whether sovereignty goes so far that a government can destroy with impunity its own citizens and whether such acts of destruction are domestic affairs or matters of international concern."

Twice the United Nations had decided, unanimously, in the negative, and created new international law converting the moral right of humanitarian intervention into a legal right—the Convention for the Prevention and Punishment of Genocide. Could it have been invoked in the Nigerian situation? Was Nigeria "deliberately inflicting on the group conditions of life calculated to bring about its physical destruction in whole or in part"? The UN intended, in creating the convention, that the world act not just to punish the guilty after all the victims are dead but "to prevent" such acts as well. How did an event of such proportions as the death by starvation of millions of noncombatants escape at least inquiry by the United Nations?

In an anarchic world, large numbers of human beings can be ground up in the machinations of great powers. It is not enough to shrug and say that there have always been wars, that siege and starvation have always been legitimate weapons of war. Wars have become, in this century, infinitely more destructive of uninvolved, innocent citizens—noncombatants. During recent decades we have seen develop between the great powers an arms competition exporting the most modern weapons of war to underdeveloped countries, making it possible for them to wage a kind of warfare against their neighbors or their own people that they could never support with their own resources.

Though there seems little prospect that we will soon find a way to put an end to wars, we had at least embarked upon a course of seeking to limit their destructiveness, of devising international agreements barring wholesale atrocities against civilian populations. Where are we heading when governments to which we look for humanitarian leadership make themselves parties to the abrogation of these international conventions instead of insisting on their observance?

May–September 1968

Chapter 1

In the refugee camps and villages of Biafra, the hair of every fourth child was turning reddish-gold. The Red Cross and missionary doctors and the Irish priests and nuns who had stayed with their flocks as the Nigerian Army pressed the Biafrans back into a smaller and smaller redoubt had seen the starvation coming for months. They had been doing what they could to provide relief. By May, however, the problem had grown to proportions beyond their limited means.

Dr. Clyne Shepherd, a medical missionary from Edinburgh, wrote officials of the World Council of Churches in Geneva requesting further supplies and went on to describe what he and others in Biafra were beginning to encounter every day: "There are many gruesome stories about refugees. My experience of a few hours ago is by no means the worst. A nurse brought in two dying women . . . one with dysentery and the other with anemia and pneumonia. This led to the discovery that the 400 people in their camp had had no solid food for four days. Their only sustenance since the beginning of the week had been the four bags of milk delivered by ourselves. I was able to hand over to the accompanying nurse some baby food and egg powder, which had arrived yesterday. . . ."

Heinrich ("Harry") Jaggi, a Swiss businessman in Nigeria, had been pressed into service as the Red Cross delegate in Biafra. He radioed headquarters in Geneva: "The refugee problem is now increased to such an extent that there are no longer words to describe it. Thousands upon thousands of fleeing civilians have moved toward the center. . . . Men, women and children dying along the road due to exhaustion or starvation."

Urgent appeals began coming in to the international relief agencies in New York, Geneva, Rome:

FULLY ONE THIRD POPULATION NOW REFUGEES IN SMALL LAND AREA. THOUSANDS REDUCED TO ONLY ONE MEAL A WEEK. ALARM-

ING INCREASE IN DEATHS FROM STARVATION. IMMEDIATE MASSIVE
ASSISTANCE NEEDED TO AVERT CATASTROPHE. ESSENTIAL THAT
PRESSURE BE BROUGHT TO BEAR ON GOVERNMENTS TO LIFT
BLOCKADE.

Infants and small children need proportionately more protein than
adults for their rapidly growing bodies. Their hair turning reddish-gold
indicated kwashiorkor, the disease of protein malnutrition. (Its name
comes from a West African word meaning "the sickness the child develops
when another child is born"; that is, when the infant is taken off the breast
and fed the same starchy foods the parents eat.) These children would
soon die if they did not get protein.

Always one of the most densely populated places in Africa, now with
an additional one and a half million refugees, Biafra had been cut off
from its customary sources of protein—fish from the sea and Lake Chad,
beef from the plateau to the north, stockfish from Iceland and Norway.
Blockade of the area had begun even before Biafran secession from Nigeria a year before. Following massacres in other regions of Nigeria, Ibos
had fled back to their homeland in the east of the country and finally
concluded they could find no security living among the other tribes of the
nation.

They proclaimed their independence as the Republic of Biafra, a
short time later the Federal Military Government of Nigeria (FMG) attacked with what army it had, and the Biafrans defended themselves with
what army they could muster. Now the Nigerian army—enlarged, supplied with British arms and ammunition—had driven the Biafrans back
into a besieged enclave, dwindling in land area, crowded with displaced
people.

In London, in the House of Commons, Conservative Reginald Maudling
asked the British foreign secretary "whether he will reconsider policy on
this point, particularly now when dangers of massive slaughter appear to
be brooding over the scene. . . ."

Sir Alec Douglas-Home, the Shadow Cabinet foreign minister, also
raised a question about the government's policy: ". . . Both sides of the
House have perhaps felt that the Government has not quite appreciated
up to now that a final and terrible massacre of the Ibos would be intolerable and that, if that situation came about, it would be even more in-
supportable to think that this had been achieved with the help of British
arms. . . ."

It was becoming awkward for members of the government to defend the sending of arms to Nigeria. One by one, Czechoslovakia, the Netherlands, France, and Belgium had halted their supply of weapons to an increasingly bloody conflict. Early in the war, after Britain had declined to provide planes and bombs, Nigerian officials had traveled to Moscow to conclude a deal. Soon an advance party of twenty-six Soviet military advisers arrived in the capital city of Lagos, followed by flights of air freighters bearing MiG jet fighters to Kano airport in the north. Now the MiGs and Ilyushin bombers, flown by Egyptian Air Force pilots, coursed up and down over the Biafran countryside, strafing open-air markets, bombing wherever people congregated as well as large buildings such as hospitals.

Bringing in the Soviet Union provided the Nigerians with leverage should there be any wavering in British support. Chief Anthony Enahoro, a government commissioner who became roving spokesman for Nigeria in other countries, wrote a letter to each of the M.P.s at the time of the parliamentary debate during which Maudling and Douglas-Home posed their questions, warning that a halt to British arms shipments would "prolong the war," "alienate the vast majority of Nigerians," and "compel the Federal government to turn to other sources of supply."

Prime Minister Harold Wilson and members of his Labour government maintained their outward composure, taking up the argument as well as any Tory might, maintaining as offensives waxed and waned that British arms supplies "amounted to about 15 per cent by value of Nigeria's arms purchases." They persisted in this throughout the remaining eighteen months of the conflict as the Nigerian Army grew in size—and it was an army using up inordinate amounts of ammunition.

The British military adviser in the Lagos embassy wrote in a secret report (which fell into the hands of a journalist in the closing days of the war, to the embarrassment of the British government) that Nigerian "units regard a vast expenditure of small arms ammunition—the basic weapon being fully automatic—as a substitute for their acute shortage of leaders at the lower level. . . . It is the cacophony of automatic weapons, with most bullets flying harmlessly into the trees, which carries the Nigerian soldiers forward. It has been said that the Nigerian Army in the advance is the best defoliant agent known. . . ."

Only many months later, as the conflict drew to a close, did one of the government's critics discover that throughout the war the *Nigerian Trade Summary* had been publishing the "Total Value of Arms Imported into Nigeria by Country of Origin." Far from being fixed at a level of 15 percent "by value," British supplies had gone sharply upward: the Nigerians received from London more than three-quarters of their arms and ammunition in 1968, and in the following year they became almost wholly dependent on Britain for the arms with which they were waging ground warfare.

This could not be known during the spring and summer of 1968 as Parliament debated whether to continue supplying arms to Nigeria. The *Manchester Guardian* commented: "There is a disingenuousness about some aspects of British policy which verges on the sinister." Prime Minister Wilson assured Commons that the supply "has been limited to the normal arms we have supplied in the past." Nigerian troops were attacking, driving the Biafrans back. Wilson stated: "There has been no special provision for the needs of war." The *Guardian* commented: "Yet it is known that, with or without the special provision, the supply of British arms to Nigeria has multiplied many times since the war started."

Anticipating such questions as those raised by Maudling and Douglas-Home, the government had prepared a policy statement for the debate on Nigeria. Michael Stewart had not had great experience in international affairs before becoming foreign secretary; he previously had been concerned mainly with education. The statement he now read to Congress seemed to make a government pledge: "If we make the supposition that it were the intention of the Federal Government not merely to preserve the unity of Nigeria but to proceed without mercy either with the slaughter or the starvation of the Ibo people . . . then the arguments which justified the policy we have so far pursued would fall, and we would have to reconsider, and more than reconsider, the action we have so far taken. . . ."

In other countries of Europe, in the United States and Canada, Biafra had not yet been noticed. During the months of mid-1968, a succession of dramatic events came one after another, capturing public attention.

Mounting protests over United States involvement in Vietnam and the shock of the Tet offensive brought Lyndon Johnson to announce he would not seek reelection as president. Little more than a week later, the murder of Martin Luther King, Jr. in Memphis roused blacks across the nation to a fury of rioting and burning of their own neighborhoods—smoke rose over many of America's cities.

Students at Columbia University, protesting about a local civil rights issue, seized college buildings, stirring students in other countries around the world to revolt—some later to become revolutionaries and urban guerrillas. Those battling riot police on the "Boul' Mich" and at other French universities eventually brought Charles de Gaulle to resign the presidency and return to his village of Colombey-les-Deux-Eglises.

A young Palestinian refugee shot Senator Robert Kennedy at his moment of triumph in the California primary, removing him from the presidential race. Democrats turned to Vice-President Hubert Humphrey at their national convention in Chicago, further angering Vietnam protesters in the streets outside who became caught up in a "police riot."

The Dubček government in Czechoslovakia, attempting to create "communism with a human face," provoked brutal Soviet suppression; Warsaw Pact armies invaded, and a shocked world watched young Czechs defy Soviet tanks with their bodies.

In Britain, as early as June, a few people began forming a "Save the Biafrans Committee"—but government policy had already been set.

The United Nations Children's Fund (UNICEF) and the International Committee of the Red Cross (ICRC) had been trying since the previous autumn to gain access to what, diplomatically, was still the Eastern Region of Nigeria. The international community did not officially recognize Biafra as a nation; by late spring 1968, diplomatic recognition had come only from four African countries. In order to provide food and medical care for people in Biafra, UNICEF and the ICRC, as international agencies dependent on governments, had first to negotiate permission from the Nigerian government.

One of UNICEF's representatives in Lagos, himself an African, went to a Nigerian government ministry to ask permission to provide relief to civilians in the war-stricken area. The Nigerian official said emphatically, "We want no food going to the rebels." The representative explained, carefully, that UNICEF did not want to help "rebels"—it was the UN Children's Fund, it only wanted to provide food and medical assistance to small children. The Nigerian official responded, "The son of a snake is a snake."

To officials of international agencies who came to Lagos seeking permission to provide relief, General Yakubu Gowon, the Nigerian head of state, seemed a genuinely humanitarian man, willing to allow assistance to the Biafrans. He was a young officer, however, inexperienced in politics, catapulted into the role of head of state by a coup d'état two years before, surrounded by more experienced political men and permanent civil servants, not all of whom shared his willingness to allow humanitarian relief for the "rebels." He did not control the government entirely—he was not even first among equals in the collegial group running Nigeria. Nor did his writ extend far into the countryside. Around the periphery of Biafra, where it mattered, military commanders operated like warlords; for food to enter the blockaded area by land or upriver, it would have to pass through their satrapies.

UNICEF and the Red Cross believed they had obtained authorization from the Nigerian government at the end of December 1967 to fly relief into Biafra, but a series of disagreements between the Biafrans and Nigerians barred the start of flights in January, February, and March of 1968. Finally, the head of the Nigerian Red Cross, Sir Adetokunbo Ademola, intervened and gained grudging permission in April. The wording of the government's note is revealing: ". . . If the International Committee of the Red Cross (ICRC) persists in sending supplies by air at their own risk to the rebel-held areas, they may do so." While assuring the ICRC that all possible precautions would be taken "to avoid incidents," the note added, "However, the ICRC is required to issue a statement absolving the Federal Military Government from all responsibility in this regard."

Eleven Red Cross flights transported one hundred tons of UNICEF powdered milk and five million vitamin capsules into Biafra, while the two relief agencies—to maintain their impartiality—supplied a like amount on the Nigerian side of the lines. Soon, however, the Federal Military Government declared the authorization "null and void," saying that the April note applied only to the airport at Port Harcourt. That field had now fallen into FMG hands as the Nigerian Third Marine Commando Division pushed up from the coast, compressing Biafra into a smaller area and creating another six hundred thousand refugees.

The ICRC sent out an "SOS Biafra" to national Red Cross societies in sixty-five countries, stating that the means available were totally inadequate to meet the situation; they in turn began asking assistance from their governments—food, planes, ships.

The Red Cross then took an unorthodox action, intervening in peace negotiations convened in Kampala, Uganda, under the auspices of the Commonwealth Secretariat. The former ICRC delegate in West Africa, Georg Hoffmann, sought an extensive lifting of the blockade, "in accordance with the letter and spirit of the Geneva Conventions," to allow passage of relief.

"What are you doing here?" Nigerian Commissioner Enahoro asked Hoffmann. "This is political here." Chief Enahoro declined to talk with the ICRC official, saying, "You can only deal with Lagos."

Hoffmann's attempted intervention coincided with requests by governments—in response to the Red Cross "SOS"—for "exact" information from their embassies in Lagos on the situation in Nigeria and Biafra. The Nigerians were furious. They charged that the Red Cross, by its appeal for them to lift the blockade, "will find it difficult to convince skeptics that it is not allowing itself, perhaps unwittingly through political naïveté, to be used as a tool of the rebel propaganda."

The Red Cross delegate came to Lagos. General Gowon proposed that relief supplies "be airlifted to Enugu, Port Harcourt or any other airports under Federal control and thence by road to an agreed point in rebel-held territory." This was not new. Three months earlier, as the ICRC persisted in efforts to gain authorization to fly, the FMG had offered an alternative—the road from the former Biafran capital, Enugu, now in Federal hands, to Awgu, still in Biafran territory. Biafran leaders could not take the proposal seriously. Fierce fighting was going on as the Nigerian First Division drove down this Enugu-Awgu road, the invasion route into the Ibo heartland from the north. For convoys of relief trucks to travel this highway into Biafran territory, the Biafrans would have had to open up their defenses.

Besides, they intended to fight their way back up the road from Awgu to recapture their capital, Enugu. It had symbolic importance to them: they continued to dateline their dispatches "Enugu" as if they were still in possession of the city. When they had rejected the Enugu-Awgu land route earlier, in February, the Nigerians had established that it was unacceptable to the Biafrans.

Now the Federal Military Government offered the land corridor again. The statement noted that Biafran leaders refused "to accept any relief supplies which are not sent directly to them," referring to flights to the airfield in Biafra. The next sentence proposed a relief route that did not go directly to them but required airlifting to the smaller airfield at Enugu, then transport by truck through the combat lines, opening up Biafran defenses.

The FMG cabled the statement to its ambassadors in various countries with the following instructions:

GRATEFUL BRING TO KNOWLEDGE OF YOUR HOST GOVERNMENT AND GIVE MAXIMUM PUBLICITY. EMPHASIZE OUR GOVERNMENT'S GENUINE CONCERN FOR THE SUFFERING MASS OF IBOS AND THE OBSTRUCTIONS PLACED IN THE WAY OF THE ICRC BY THE REBEL LEADERS WHO WISH TO EXPLOIT HUMANITARIAN CONSIDERATIONS FOR POLITICAL ENDS.

Chapter 2

There had been no Nigeria before this century. Trading companies, pushing inland from the coast at the end of the nineteenth century, appealed to London for aid against the French. The British soldier sent out, Frederick (later Lord) Lugard, consolidated British rule over some two hundred fifty tribes. Lady Lugard later named the colony "Nigeria." It was not even united until 1914.

Forty-six years later, given its independence, Nigeria was a nation in name only. Like many others in Africa formed to suit the convenience of colonial trading interests, it faced the problem of absorbing dissimilar peoples. Its three main tribes—Ibos, Hausa-Fulani, and Yorubas—are as different, say, as Israelis, Saudi Arabians, and Hungarians. Their languages are different, their outlooks and ways of life are different, their religions are different.

The Hausa-Fulani in the north are Moslem, ruled by emirs, and arrested in some earlier, feudalistic, slow-moving period. Their talent for administration lent itself to the British style of "indirect rule." Working through the emirs, a small number of colonial officers could control the vast territories of the northern region. The Yorubas are a sophisticated people who reached the peak of their civilization a century or two ago. Most are animists, though some are Moslems and Christians.

The Ibos, from being nearly primitive in the last century, had become a people who placed their highest premium on education. Converted to Christianity by Catholic, Anglican, and Presbyterian missionaries, they took up self-improvement with such enthusiasm that, by the 1960s, the Ibos had the highest percentage of doctors, lawyers, professors, physicists, teachers, and other trained and educated people of any tribe in Africa. They had been the most ardent advocates of a united Nigeria. Upon independence in 1960, an Ibo became the first president. They moved out of their own tribal area in the Eastern Region and worked and lived among other peoples in Nigeria. A dynamic, progressive, and ambitious people, they moved quickly into good jobs, acquired government positions, and began businesses.

There were many political problems during those first years of independence, not all involving Ibos. The British were still deeply engaged in the new country—commerce, businesses, as civil servants. While outwardly they had granted Nigeria independence, they still maintained a measure of concealed "indirect rule" through the Hausas, who played a major role in the federation. The Yorubas and Ibos deeply resented this influential position of the less educated, more rural North. To put these tribes—and some two hundred others—together, give the place a name, then finally proclaim it a nation and keep trying to hold it together when it kept splitting apart in two or three directions, was to create not a federation but potential civil war.

The Hausa-Fulani were reluctant to remain in a united Nigeria—it was expected that the split would come between the North and the South. However, the breakdown of the federation began with a series of coups d'état. The first, in January 1966, was provoked by the issue of corruption in the new country. There were Ibos among the young army officers who set about to end the corruption and it came to be spoken of as an "Ibo plot." They ended up in jail, later killed, and there was no connection between them and another Ibo, General Ironsi, commander of the army, who put down the coup. What remained of the government asked Ironsi to run the country.

In the coup, two Moslem leaders were killed: the prime minister of Nigeria, Sir Abubakar Tafawa Balewa, and the Sardauna of Sokoto, spiritual head as well as premier of the North. Even without these killings, there might have been violence against Ibos—incidents bordering on pogroms had taken place even under British rule. But the coup provided the detonating device, giving the renewed violence in the Moslem North the force of a *jihad*, which had high-level organization and direction. The word around Nigeria: "One million Ibos must die to avenge the death of the Sardauna."

Another coup and further massacres would soon follow. No one was more aware of these events or more conscious of the inherent instability of the Nigerian Federation than British diplomats in Lagos and the Commonwealth Office in Whitehall. (The Commonwealth Office had been the Colonial Office until a few years before, with all the implications that has for it as an institution.) "They had already lost a couple of federations, you know," a journalist in London put it. "They really wanted to make this one work. There were people at all different levels of the British government who were personally committed to saving this one and making it work."

When war finally came, it broke out at the same time as the Six-DayWar in the Middle East; Federal troops invaded Biafra on the day the Suez Canal was closed. Britain, in shaky financial condition since the loss of its empire, faced being cut off from its main sources of oil and from considerable future revenue. Recent explorations suggested there might be as much petroleum in eastern Nigeria as in the whole of the Middle East. Oil companies from a number of countries were seeking to exploit this newfound potential, but the major producer, long on the scene, was Shell-BP. British Petroleum was in large part owned by the British government. While it is always contended that Her Majesty's Government leaves the operation of BP to management, no one has ever suggested that government officials and BP officials do not talk with each other.

At first, the government professed neutrality, but after two years, when this position had worn transparently thin, a spokesman on foreign affairs told Parliament: "Our position should not be misunderstood through facile comparison with the neutrality adopted by some other countries. It may well be right for such countries to adhere to a policy of non-involvement, but we are the former colonial power. We have links extending over 100 years. We have 16,000 of our people in Nigeria, great investments and much trade of enormous mutual benefit to Nigerians and ourselves. We could not avoid involvement; we had no other honorable options."

The Commonwealth Office put a good face on a bad thing by making the prime argument for preserving the federation the very nonviability of such artificial constructions. They gave Foreign Secretary Stewart such things to say in Parliament as: "Not many honorable Members have stressed the great importance of secession not only in Nigeria but throughout Africa. It has been a difficulty facing many African states whose boundaries originally were drawn to meet the rivalries of European Powers rather than on any ethnological principle or principles of self-determination."*

Michael Stewart became an ardent believer in and advocate of this argument: "It has been difficult for such states to weld different tribes into one people. But I believe that African statesmanship . . . has been right to maintain the principle that African states should endeavor to weld

---

* Later, another minister, who served briefly as a government spokesman during the Nigerian-Biafran conflict, complained how civil servants of the diplomatic service cleverly take in politicians—transitorily serving as government ministers—by flattery, by deception, and by their system of briefing those "whom it calls, with a nice sense of irony, its political masters."

different tribes into one nation and should regard as a counsel of despair that, whenever it is difficult to bring different tribes into one nation, the remedy should be secession and disintegration. If that were accepted as a general principle, it would be a very dark outlook for the future of Africa as a whole. . . ."

It was a high-sounding position that had a lot of appeal for editorial writers. Of course, it nearly came unstuck when a succession of African states began to recognize Biafra in the spring of 1968—Tanzania, Ivory Coast, Gabon, Zambia. British diplomats in Africa were quite busy during those days making certain that other nations, about to follow their lead, did not.

Odumegwu Ojukwu had been deeply troubled by the massacres of the Ibos. He felt personally responsible for having urged those who fled the Northern Region following the May killings to return. A short time later he expressed his feelings to his fellow military governors: " . . . after the May incident, General Ironsi shouted, 'Go back,' and nobody listened. Then I went on the air and told the Easterners to go back, and they went back. Not so long after that, these people were killed—a lot of them. . . . I am only a human being. It is a thing of my conscience, and it will always remain there."

Those massacres are best described in the words of a journalist who witnessed them and had no reason to give a biased account, as he had only just arrived in Nigeria the week before. He later told a Canadian parliamentary committee that in May 1966 the first of the Ibo massacres of that year occurred in the north of Nigeria, followed, in the fall, by what he characterized as "a far more savage outbreak of violence . . . and by smaller scale Ibo hunts in Lagos and elsewhere." He was present in the Northern Region and said that both events "were beyond doubt outbreaks of savagery which were led by Federal soldiers joined by large numbers of the Northern population."

He told the parliamentary committee, " . . . Many thousands of Ibos were slaughtered in towns and villages across the North, and hundreds of thousands of others were blinded, crippled, or maimed, or in the majority of cases, simply left destitute as they attempted to flee to the Ibo homeland in the Eastern Region."

"Some of the fleeing refugees did not make it home," the journalist reported. "On one train that arrived in the East there was the corpse of a male passenger whose head had been chopped off somewhere along the line. Another group of Ibo refugee men, women and children, whom I happened to see—I would say about 100 or more of them—were waiting in the railway station in the city of Kano, the largest city of Northern Nigeria, for about three days, with no security guard, for the arrival of a refugee train, and a Land Rover full of FMG soldiers came and mowed them down with automatic weapons.

"Killings such as that were repeated elsewhere by soldiers and by civilians," he testified. "At Kano International Airport, shortly after the arrival of a VC-10 flight from London, a detachment of FMG soldiers went after the Ibo customs men in the immigration shed. Those of the customs workers who fled into the airport bar or onto the roadway outside the terminal were pursued and shot down. In another Northern town the Ibo executive assistant of a regional government official was hauled out of the house and hacked to death in front of his boss's family. In still another place a prominent Ibo woman merchant was stripped and impaled with broken glass and then beaten to death."

The journalist did not want to exaggerate the slaughter, he told the Canadian M.P.s, but it was general, as was the destruction of property: "Ibo shops and Ibo hotels were ransacked and looted while blocks of non-Ibo businesses were carefully left untouched. In the city of Kano alone the numbers killed in a weekend exceeded a thousand; most people felt it was possibly double that. Either way, it was a lot of people. No one will ever know how many thousands were slaughtered that fortnight in the North, or how many hundreds of thousands fled home to the East."

He concluded that "whatever the number, these events speak for themselves; and it should be remembered that they seem to have bitterly convinced many Ibos—I was not told this by Biafran officials, but have spoken to hundreds of Ibos myself in the last few years—that the Northerners are bent on wiping them out."

At the time of the first coup in January 1966, the commanding officer of the Fifth Battalion in Kano was a young lieutenant colonel, Odumegwu Ojukwu. Son of one of the wealthiest men in Nigeria, "Emeka" Ojukwu had been sent to private schools in Lagos and (at thirteen) in England. Later, at Oxford, he studied modern history and played rugby. He initially intended to go from Oxford to study at the Inner Temple to become a barrister, but Nigeria was about to become independent and his father and Nnamdi Azikiwi (soon to be the country's first president) persuaded him of the need for young Nigerians to return home to quicken the pace of "Nigerianization."

Choosing to go into the civil service rather than the family business, he was sent to the Eastern Region, where he worked among his own people, getting to know the Ibos in a way he might not have if he had remained driving a sports car around Lagos. Then, partly to escape his family's wealth and name, Ojukwu joined the army. Ironically, he chose the military as the one institution that was organized along the lines of a unified nation, that cut across regions and tribes in what would soon be Nigeria.

After training in England, the new lieutenant was posted first to Kano, then to army headquarters in Lagos. More training in Ghana followed, then Ojukwu served with the United Nations force in the Congo. With Nigeria now independent, Ojukwu became the first indigenous quartermaster general.

Ojukwu had no part in the coup d'état of January 1966; in fact, he joined immediately with the administrator and the emir of Kano to keep the province peaceful and free from bloodshed. When those in the government left alive asked the army chief of staff to run the country, General Ironsi appointed military governors for the regions. He asked Ojukwu, then thirty-three, to become governor of the Eastern Region. Soon after came the anti-Ibo riots in the North; then, in July, a second coup d'état, this one by Northern soldiers.

Ojukwu phoned the next senior officer after Ironsi (it was not yet known what had become of Ironsi—he had in fact been killed in a most brutal way, along with the military governor of the West, with whom he had been dining). He urged Brigadier Ogundipe, a Yoruba, to take over: "Sir, the situation is so confused that I feel that somebody must take control immediately. I would suggest that you go on the air and tell the country what has happened and that you are taking control of the situation." Ogundipe quickly found he was taking control of nothing; when he stepped outside and told a sergeant to do something, the noncommissioned officer—of Northern origin—told him, "I do not take orders from you, until my captain comes."

Ojukwu also talked on the telephone with the chief of staff, Yakubu Gowon, telling him that he thought the army must deal with the problem created by the coup, that any break in the line of seniority would lead to a breakdown of discipline in the army. Ojukwu felt they were "heading for something terrible."

However, Gowon did not command the troops either. The Northern soldiers were bent on killing Ibo officers and men to avenge the deaths of their own officers killed during the earlier coup. Things were out of control, there was chaos for a few days, no one was governing the country. But then, the instigators of the second coup had had no intention of holding Nigeria together: the code name for the coup was the Hausa word for secession, *Araba*. A Hausa lieutenant colonel, Murtala Mohammed, emerged as the leader of this move to break with the South.

Senior civil servants, who had a personal stake in preserving the federal system of government, urged Gowon to hold the country together. The British high commissioner and the U.S. ambassador intervened, pressing Gowon not to allow the North to secede, warning that there would be no further British or American foreign aid if the federation broke up.

The struggle behind the scenes went on for more than three days, during which those not directly involved could not know what was happening; what they witnessed was the hunting down and killing—often in ritualistic, brutal ways—of officers from the Eastern Region. Finally, out of the chaos and confusion, Gowon came forth as the new head of government. His broadcast to the nation is still the subject of controversy, for it seemed that he was about to announce the breakup of Nigeria along North-South lines; "Suffice it to say that putting all considerations to the test—political, economic, as well as social—the basis for unity is not there, or is so badly rocked, not only once but many times. . . ." At that point there was a break, as if the speech had been hastily rewritten, then Gowon went on to say that the Nigerian government should see what could be done to "stop the country from drifting away into utter destruction."

The contradiction in the speech reflected the contradictory forces at work those three days: the Northerners pulling the nation apart, the civil servants and British and American ambassadors trying to hold it together. What emerged was a government titularly headed by the thirty-two-year-old lieutenant colonel, there apparently because he was the most senior officer of Northern origin still alive (not a Hausa, however, but a member of a minority tribe and a Christian).

There were five officers—not from the North—senior to Gowon. For Ojukwu, this was not a legitimate transfer of authority, such as had taken place earlier when the remnant of government left during the first coup asked General Ironsi to take over and reestablish order. As a result, those responsible for the first coup were jailed. (The Ibo officers were dragged out months later and killed by Northern soldiers.) The leaders of the second coup, on the other hand, took over the government. It was not clear at what point Gowon acquiesced in becoming head of government, though it seemed unlikely he had been one of the plotters.

Ojukwu charged Gowon with becoming "Supreme Commander by virtue of the fact that you head—or that you are acceptable to—people who had mutinied against their commander, kidnapped him and taken him away; by virtue of the support of officers and men who had in the dead of night murdered their brother officers. . . ."

"How can you ride above people's heads and sit in Lagos purely because you are at the head of a group who have their fingers poised on the trigger?" Ojukwu later asked Gowon. "If you do it," he warned, "you remain forever a living example of that indiscipline which we want to get rid of, because tomorrow a Corporal will think—because he has his finger on the trigger—he could just take over the company from the Major, commander of the Company, and so on."

It was then that Ojukwu made the mistake he came to regret deeply, urging Ibos who had fled the killings in the north to return—to the worse massacres in September and October. The new slaughter spread from the north to other parts of Nigeria. As Ibos made their way back to their tribal homeland in the east, many maimed, nearly every family having lost one or more members, they brought with them and to the people in the Eastern Region bitterness, fear, and a conviction that they could find no security living among the other peoples of Nigeria.

The civil servants who had fled undertook to prepare a government of a new nation that would be their own. At the same time, the Federal Government—now become the Federal Military Government—began the first in a series of measures that would eventually become a blockade of the Eastern Region. The army and police started to enforce a prohibition against food going to the Eastern Region from the western area of Nigeria. This was October 1966, seven months before the East would secede.

Whether Nigeria could be saved and held together concerned the British more than the Nigerians themselves. At this point, the Easterners were still ready to consider some sort of loose confederation such as the Northerners had long demanded. According to Ojukwu, the British advised Gowon that the interests of the Northerners lay in a strong Federal Nigeria that those who controlled the North could dominate. If they continued to do so, then the British would continue to play a primary role in Nigeria. For Britain, and for the British civil servants who continued to work in the Northern Region, the Ibos had always been a troublesome element in the federation, a people with democratic traditions who were not easily controlled. Many British were as glad to see them out of a central position in the federation as were those who had driven them back to their homeland and those who now held civil service and other jobs they had left.

Ojukwu and other Ibo leaders were not so easily dismissed—they had too long been strong supporters of Nigerian unity. They sought a meeting of the Supreme Military Council. Ibo army officers, particularly, had been hunted and killed during the July coup, so Ojukwu could not travel safely to other parts of Nigeria; the meeting therefore had to be held in Ghana, at Aburi, in early January 1967. It brought Ojukwu and Gowon face to face for the first time since the coups, along with the military governors of the other regions. They had been junior officers together and slipped quickly into the easy camaraderie of the officers' mess, calling one another Bob, Jack, David, Emeka, etc. In this spirit, they were able to reach a surprising amount of agreement.

Unanimously they renounced the use of force as a means of settling the Nigerian crisis and decided on discussion and negotiations as the only way of settling their problems. A major one: the people who had fled from one region or the other back to their homeland. Gowon said, "I think the person with the greatest problem on this today is Emeka. He has got more people than any other Region in this respect. We are all agreed that whatever assistance that can be given, the East should have the major share. . . ." There would be discussions about rehabilitation within two weeks, they agreed, and displaced Federal government employees in the East would continue to be paid their salaries for at least another three months. These measures were, of course, very important to Ojukwu and the people in the East.

None of this was to come about, however. Once back in Lagos, Gowon could not get civil servants of Northern origin to implement the decisions, ". . . largely," Ojukwu later charged, "because they were not in consonance with the avowed Northern Nigeria policy of dominating Nigeria under the supervision of the British government."

What followed, instead, was a series of measures that the people in the Eastern Region felt were designed to expel them from Nigeria, matched by countermeasures of their own which moved the East in the direction of separating from the federation. One gave the Federal Military Government power to declare a state of emergency in any region. Others were economic: the government, which held the revenues of Nigeria (especially those flowing in from oil exports), would not help the Eastern Region with its large burden of refugees; instead, the regular remittances to which the East was entitled were withheld. Government employees in the East were denied their wages. Federal supply of equipment and material to agencies there was cut off. Flights of Nigeria Airways planes were suspended; all airports in the Eastern Region were closed to outside traffic. Eastern assets in Nigeria were frozen, as were those owned jointly with Nigeria abroad; foreign currency exchange was cut off. Eastern seaports were closed to shipping, and export of Eastern produce was banned except through Lagos.

The blockade of Biafra had begun three months before there was a Biafra.

.   .   .

As the legislative body of the Eastern Region (the Consultative Assembly and the Council of Chiefs and Elders) deliberated these developments, Gowon issued a decree dividing Nigeria into twelve states. It was a measure favored by the minority tribes, but by breaking the Eastern Region into three states it removed the major oil deposits and installations from Ibo control. To Ojukwu—and to his people—"it was an act of extreme provocation."

"We were now thoroughly convinced," Ojukwu said later, "that only our separate political existence could guarantee our basic needs of survival and security of life and property." On May 30, 1967, the Eastern legislature proclaimed "the territory and region known as and called Eastern Nigeria, together with her continental shelf and territorial waters, shall henceforth be an independent sovereign state of the name and title of 'the Republic of Biafra.' "

On July 6, the Nigerian Army attacked from the north. As they advanced, Nigerian troops methodically killed men and boys over ten. Now, nearly a year later, war and blockade were taking a heavy toll. The strafing and bombing struck down people indiscriminately. Starvation was more selective, taking its largest toll among children under four. The enclave was compressed to an area only a hundred miles long and some thirty miles wide. Originally there may have been as many as twelve or fourteen million people in the territory proclaimed Biafra, eight million of them Ibos. How many now survived, how many were still within the area under siege, no one knew for certain, but their numbers were estimated variously at nine to eleven million.

To the other Nigerians, the Ibos were not only leaving Nigeria, they were departing with the oil under the lands with which they were seceding. Here lay the explanation for the paradox that the "Nigerians" had driven the "Biafrans" out, yet seemed to be fighting to keep them in the federation. What they actually wanted was the land the Ibos were on and what lay under it—without the Ibos.

Chapter 3

"**P**eople in some camps are still getting one meal a day. *But under-nourishment affects everyone:* the camps, the refugees, the entire population." Heinrich Jaggi was preparing another report to Red Cross headquarters in Geneva. A remarkably steady man from the little village of Adelboden in the Bern Oberland, Jaggi had represented Swiss business firms in Nigeria for years. When the split in the federation came, the ICRC asked him to serve as its part-time delegate; the job had now become chief Red Cross delegate in Biafra, and more than full-time.

Jaggi reported malnutrition and illness not only among the five hundred thousand refugees in the 500 camps; about three million more, who had been absorbed by their extended families and villages, had no means of subsistence. They needed food and medicine as urgently as the people in the camps, Jaggi informed Geneva, and he estimated malnutrition and illness among infants and the elderly at 10 percent a month. Up to five hundred thousand would die in the coming months, he warned, and this number would increase still more unless massive humanitarian relief got under way.

The Red Cross delegate met with Leslie Kirkley, who had just arrived in Biafra. Kirkley, director of the famine relief agency Oxfam, had already begun appeals for funds, with ads showing starving Biafran children. When they appeared in London newspapers, the Nigerian high commissioner complained that this kind of appeal lent support to "the fiction that a state called 'Biafra' exists."

The ICRC had instructed Jaggi to inquire about the possibility of a neutralized airfield in Biafra, set aside exclusively for relief. Nigerian officials had been telling the Red Cross they did not want relief planes using the one airstrip in Biafra, as arms flights were landing there: "It would be different, if you had your own demilitarized airstrip." Of course, there was only one airfield in Biafra, rushed to completion the month before after Nigerian troops captured the airport at Port Harcourt.

The Biafran Foreign Office responded affirmatively to Jaggi's inquiry. He and Kirkley conferred with Ojukwu, who told them a second airstrip was under construction—he would place it at their disposal for day and night flights as soon as it was ready. Jaggi radioed Geneva a plan for use of the relief airstrip.

Kirkley cabled his office in Oxford to charter a cargo plane. Within hours an option was taken on a Hercules owned by a Canadian company. The Hercules, known in the U.S. Air Force as the C-130, can land in a short space, on an unimproved field if necessary, and load and unload cargo rapidly through a rear door with a ramp. Oxfam would be able to carry in twenty tons or more on each flight.

Michael Leapman, a reporter for the *Sun*, had flown to Biafra at the same time as Kirkley and began filing stories back to his newspaper in London. (When they appeared, a press officer at the Commonwealth Office raised grave questions about Leapman's integrity in reporting what, it was suggested, was "Biafran propaganda.") A free-lance American journalist and photographer, David Robison, also began sending out reports. He quoted Jaggi as saying: "The death rate is an upward sloping curve. In a month there will be more than a million dead here; before the end of August, two million are likely to die, and either we sit still and watch six million people go down the drain within six months or we pressure for a cease-fire."

Dr. Herman Middelkoop, the Dutch missionary doctor heading the Protestant relief effort in Biafra, told Robison: "Our present goal, 40 tons a day, will only postpone the death of a few people. It is like giving a drip feed to a person with a stroke. The catastrophe cannot be averted without a complete cease-fire within a month, opening up all transportation into and within Biafra. The figure of several million people likely to be dead by the end of August is quite correct, and that six million people will die in the next six months without a cease-fire and massive help, I have no doubt."

Robison went around the children's wards of one hospital with Dr. Aaron Ifekwunigwe, a young Biafran pediatrician. All the children he saw "had yellowish, almost golden hair, scaling skin, body sores, swollen ankles and legs, diarrhea, lack of appetite and an apathetic, lethargic look." Dr. Ifekwunigwe explained: "When the child's body gets swollen and the child won't eat and has diarrhea, it is an almost irreversible cycle. The only proper help is protein, nothing else."

An Irish nun, of the Holy Rosary Sisters, said, "I fear that between two million and three million people are going to die. Even if the war stopped tomorrow, hundreds of thousands are condemned to death now. I go out to the Odube camps every fortnight to look for severe malnutrition cases among the children. Last week there were 700 to 800 cases." And an Irish priest said to Robison, "All the joy has gone out of life. In the old days, you used to drive with the right hand and wave with your left. Now, the children don't even have the energy to wave."

Kirkley flew back to London. When he landed, he was met at the airport and rushed to a BBC studio to appear on the television program "Panorama." Wherever he went, journalists asked: how many are dying and how many will die if massive relief does not arrive soon? His estimate that two million could be dead before the end of August "unless we pull out all the stops in Britain and other countries" did not go over well with officials at the Commonwealth Office.

"I do not think that the suffering that is going on in Biafra can be met by the stopping of British arms supplies to Nigeria," the Commonwealth secretary, George Thomson, told Commons. "That human suffering can best be met by the kind of constructive influence that Britain has brought to bear on the Federal Government in securing its cooperation in getting supplies there."

Government spokesmen had had to respond to questions in Parliament since the beginning of the year, long before the rest of the world had even heard of Biafra. As early as March, after the ICRC had sought authorization to airlift food and the Nigerians proposed a land corridor instead, a British diplomat said to Red Cross officials in Geneva, "Look, if the Biafrans won't agree, why don't you just withdraw."

British diplomats, even then, began suggesting to ICRC officials: "If you wait for the war to end, then we will help you rush in food." As starvation mounted in April, May, and June, British officials failed to reassess the situation and decide it had taken on a new dimension, necessitating a change of policy. Perhaps it was only the principle of bureaucracy and government at work: a policy once set in motion tends to stay in motion. But as pressures on diplomats and the government increased with the worsening of starvation, they sought to manage the problem as best they could, using the policy line already set in motion, adding only what seemed a pledge by the foreign secretary "to reconsider, and more than reconsider . . ." should the Nigerian Government "proceed without mercy either with the slaughter or the starvation of the Ibo people. . . ."

Within the cabinet there were troubled debates, but the total secrecy surrounding deliberations within the British system conceals precisely what was said. While responsibility for policy rests with the government, policy is also made, day to day, at the working level. Donald Tebbit in the Commonwealth Office had not had experience in Nigeria, but Sir David Hunt, the British high commissioner, had served earlier as deputy high commissioner during the first years of Nigerian independence. ("High commissioner" is the title for an ambassador from one Commonwealth country to another.)

A capable man,* Hunt attributed his appointment as ambassador to Nigeria to his friendly relationship with Prime Minister Harold Wilson, going back to the days when both had been dons at Oxford. He also felt he had a special understanding of the country, as his wife's uncle was a foreign businessman with extensive interests throughout the newly independent nation.

Hunt's role was certainly a key one during those crucial days of British and Nigerian policy formulation, but it would be difficult to say exactly where responsibility resided for the rapidly evolving response to the mounting concern about starvation in Biafra. British involvement with the Nigerian government was an incestuous relationship. It would be impossible to sort out where decisions were made, or by whom—in Lagos or in London, by this Nigerian official or that British diplomat. They were talking all the time. The British were able to present themselves as interested but innocent bystanders, trying to be helpful, using their influence to persuade the Nigerians to accept humanitarian relief. British diplomats, in the spirit of compassion of the Walrus and the Carpenter, told their opposite numbers in the American government that they intended to display "conspicuous zeal" in support of humanitarian relief.

The Nigerians cared little about public opinion. At various times government spokesmen stated publicly that "starvation is a legitimate weapon of war" and they had every intention of using it against their enemy. This presented a problem for British policy makers: public pressure might force them to cut off arms shipments; should this happen, Nigerian officials threatened to turn to the Soviet Union for arms and ammunition. Most Nigerians were not in the least inclined toward communism (in fact the society has a propensity for some of the worst excesses of capitalism), but the Soviets had eagerly entered into the Third World game the Nigerian government had begun playing, responding quickly to the request for bombers and fighter planes when Britain declined to provide them.

---

* When in his thirties, Hunt had been private secretary to both Labour Prime Minister Clement Attlee and Conservative Prime Minister Winston Churchill.

Though the FMG barely mentioned the proposal for a land corridor, the British seized upon it. They began talking of little else: "General Gowon promised his Government's full and ready cooperation in allowing relief supplies to be taken through an agreed corridor in the fighting lines under the control of the International Red Cross, and was ready to put at the disposal of the Red Cross whatever airports or seaports were considered most practicable. . . ."

The Nigerians had first proposed the land corridor when seeking to discourage the Red Cross from flying into Biafra; the ICRC dutifully sought agreement from the Biafrans and found the corridor unacceptable. Now British spokesmen repeatedly told critics in Parliament that an airlift would not do; as one put it, " . . . perhaps my honorable Friend did not hear what I said in my statement when I emphasized that supplies had to go overland if they were to go in in the requisite volume to meet the needs of the Biafran people. The removal of the obstacles to the land route lies not with ourselves or the Government in Lagos, but with the authorities in Biafra."

Later, someone coined the felicitous phrase "a mercy corridor" for the Enugu to Awgu route. The military situation there was not generally known outside Nigeria and Biafra. The road was serving as the supply route as well as invasion route of the Nigerian First Division. It had just captured Awgu, in fact, and continued advancing down the Enugu-Awgu road. The offensive aimed (according to the newsweekly *West Africa*) to "help a 'pincer movement' on Umuahia from Afikpo (in Federal hands for several weeks) and Awgu, if it were decided to attack Umuahia."

The Biafrans did not take any more seriously now the proposal to turn this road into a relief corridor than they had when it was first made to them four months before. They had no intention of removing the land mines, filling in the traps, rebuilding bridges or opening up their combat lines at the point where the First Division was attacking. Nor did the Nigerians have any intention of turning the road into a demilitarized relief route.

If the military situation had not been enough to give the Biafran leaders pause, the logistical situation would have: the bridge across the Niger River at Onitsha had been blown. Trucks from Lagos now had to go north to Lokoja, cross the river by ferry (inadequate to transport present military traffic), then take the long trip south again to reach Enugu, a journey of some seven hundred miles. By rail, relief would have had to go even farther north, then south again, but this was not really possible; any railroad cars not caught in Biafra at the outbreak of the war were urgently required by the Nigerian Army. As a Christian Council of Nigeria relief report put it at the time: "The areas of greatest need are not accessible by road or rail."

This was known in Nigeria, of course. So the government was not really offering a land corridor at all. British spokesmen called for a "land corridor," then a "mercy corridor," for more than a month before anyone in the outside world scrutinized the proposal closely. The *Manchester Guardian* finally did: "In the macabre propaganda war being fought over the plight of the starving Biafrans, Nigeria's Federal Government seems to have won a round. By offering an overland route through Enugu, it puts on Colonel Ojukwu the onus of refusing to take the food. . . . But the Enugu route is an air route, depending on small airplanes using what was a provincial airfield. From there the food would go by lorries (and at present these are not available) through a shifting battle area. This combines the worst of both alternatives. . . ." When asked whether they rejected the Enugu-Awgu proposal because it threatened them militarily, a Biafran negotiator replied, "No. Because it was preposterous."

They had other reasons as well. They did not want to take food from their enemy, had no trust that the Nigerians would allow relief supplies through, were concerned about the issue of sovereignty, needed to establish a more secure route of entry if their new country was to become viable, and feared that food coming through Nigerian lines might be poisoned.

The British seized upon the last as if it were the sole reason Biafran leaders were rejecting the "mercy corridor." It sounded ridiculous to anyone outside Nigeria who did not know that poisoning was a common way of getting rid of one's enemies in parts of that country.* The Biafrans could not take seriously a proposal to fly food in small airplanes to a small airfield from which it would then have to be trucked through combat zones, in which the roads were mined and the bridges blown, when it could be flown directly, in large aircraft, to the larger airfield in Biafra.

This is what Leslie Kirkley proposed to Commonwealth Secretary George Thomson and Lord Shepherd (the government's spokesman in the House of Lords, who had just returned from conferring with Nigerian officials in Lagos). Kirkley sought their help in getting Nigerian permission to fly the Hercules relief plane into Biafra. The Canadian owner would allow it to fly into Biafra only in daylight, with authorization from the government.

In Parliament, a principal argument for continuing arms shipments

---

* Later, outside experts (a team headed by U.S. Senator Charles Goodell and the nutritionist Jean Mayer) would confirm that food brought into Biafra through Nigerian territory had, in fact, been poisoned.

to Nigeria was the "constructive influence" it gave Britain in getting the Nigerians to cooperate in permitting humanitarian relief—via the land corridor. What Thomson and Shepherd told Kirkley in the quiet of the Commonwealth Office, however, was the opposite of what they said when presenting the government's position to the Houses of Parliament. There was no "influence" in Lagos, they said; quite the contrary: the Nigerians were always threatening to turn to the Soviet Union if Britain did not continue its supply of arms. Thomson and Shepherd told Kirkley that the Nigerians would not accept daylight flights into Biafra—they were willing to agree only to the land corridor.

Not willing to give up, Kirkley sent Harold Wilson a telegram, asking him to intervene personally with the Nigerians to get authorization for the Hercules to fly into Biafra. The prime minister's reply, released to the press from Downing Street, ran through the arguments being developed across the street in the Commonwealth Office—Oxfam should impress upon Colonel Ojukwu that he must not hold up a land corridor—then stated: "The Federal authorities have naturally insisted that relief flights through their air space can only take place if there is agreement with them first: clearly there is no threat of the shooting down of relief planes on flights which have been properly cleared and authorized by the Federal authorities." Of course, Oxfam was asking Wilson's help to get just such authorization.

In Lagos, General Gowon denounced Oxfam for "involving itself politically" in the Nigerian conflict. Federal authorities made clear their position on relief flights: "Any such act will constitute a gross violation of Nigerian airspace and an act of hostility against Nigeria. Instructions have, therefore, been issued to the Nigerian Air Force to seek and destroy all aircraft which enter into Nigeria on missions not authorized and cleared by the Federal Military Government with regard to emergency relief food and medical supplies from Britain. . . ."

Wilson suggested that Oxfam's relief efforts should be coordinated through the International Committee of the Red Cross. Leslie Kirkley dropped the option on the Hercules and began waiting for the ICRC to act.

Chapter 4

The Nigerian government "has decided that all non-governmental relief should move through the ICRC." The message from Lagos came into Red Cross headquarters a few days after Prime Minister Wilson counseled Oxfam to coordinate under the International Committee of the Red Cross. A quite different sentiment prevailed in the Nigerian capital that day, as reflected in a Lagos *Daily Times* story headlined "DEAL WITH MEDDLERS": "Recent events have clearly shown that the time has come for Nigeria to be extra cautious about the involvement of some foreign humanitarian organizations in the Nigerian civil war. . . . Isn't it ominous that the World Council of Churches are reported to be flying medical and food supplies to rebel-held areas of the rebel East Central State without the sanction of the Federal Military Government."

The story then turned to the ICRC: "It is also reported that the International Red Cross has been flying medical supplies to rebel-held areas without the prior agreement of the Government. . . . All these provocative acts amount to an inevitable assault on the sovereignty of this country. . . . The Federal Military Government should view with the greatest concern the cynical activities of the World Council of Churches and of the International Red Cross. . . ."

And Chief Enahoro, in a press conference at the United Nations that same day, spoke of starvation as being "a legitimate aspect of war." The following day the FMG circulated a note to UN members, setting forth the proposal for a land corridor, warning that any supplies brought into any part of Nigeria by means not authorized by the FMG would constitute a violation of its airspace, an act of hostility against Nigeria.

Even if the ICRC had not already reached an impasse in its attempts to obtain authorization to feed the Biafrans, the choice of the Red Cross to coordinate all other agencies would have been odd in any event. It is not generally realized that three organizations make up the International

Red Cross: the ICRC, the national Red Cross societies in each country, and the League of Red Cross Societies.

Customarily, the ICRC acts in wartime—protecting prisoners of war, caring for the military wounded, tracing missing persons, promoting observance of the Geneva Conventions. The national societies provide medical and other personnel to the ICRC for these wartime activities but also have a peacetime role, coming to the aid of victims of natural disasters and other catastrophes. In 1919 they set up their own headquarters, also in Geneva, the League of Red Cross Societies. So it was the league that had had experience in organizing large international relief operations; the ICRC had little capacity for coordinating a vast logistical effort of the kind now needed in Biafra and Nigeria.*

A century earlier, a Genevan, Henry Dunant, appalled at the suffering he witnessed on the battlefield of Solferino, formed the committee that got governments to organize Red Cross societies in their countries and to create the Geneva Conventions. The ICRC became the guardian of the conventions—in peacetime, educating governments and the public about these humanitarian rules of warfare and, in wartime, carrying out activities on both sides of a conflict to ensure their observance.

Certain characteristics of the ICRC, arising out of this traditional role, made it peculiarly unsuited for carrying out the vast relief operation now required, especially for acting as coordinator of the numerous other relief agencies. As the direct descendant of Dunant's original committee (perpetuating itself over the century by co-optation—present members choosing new members), the ICRC had taken on in Swiss life something of the importance of the Academy in France. The neutrality of Switzerland provides the base from which to work impartially on both sides of a conflict.

The ICRC remained entirely Swiss, inevitably constrained by this in its activities: though it could call upon Red Cross societies for personnel and support, the committee confined itself to using Swiss in carrying out the tasks of diplomacy and administering its activities in war situations. Furthermore, the ICRC derived its operating style not just from Switzerland but from Geneva, a city that is orderly, formalistic, and given to law and order.

The ICRC took an equally legalistic approach to its diplomatic activities. Its officials believed, with justification, that as guardian of the Geneva Conventions, the committee could hardly do otherwise; they could not go about the world preaching to governments that they must abide by inter-

---

* At that time. The ICRC has since undergone a period of self-appraisal and both geared itself up for and had considerable experience in carrying out logistical operations in a number of large emergency situations.

national law unless the ICRC did so itself. This meant that in a conflict they could not violate the sovereignty of a nation by entering or crossing its territory without authorization. In the case of Biafra, now completely surrounded by Nigeria, they felt they must have the permission of the Nigerian authorities if they were to provide humanitarian relief to Biafra.

(The ICRC is not only the guardian but also the principal interpreter of the Geneva Conventions, and its legal advisers tended to take a cautious and constrictive view of what the Red Cross could do in the situation. Others interpreted the conventions differently, contending that if the Nigerian government had lost control over its airspace, it could not set the terms for entrance of humanitarian relief to a civilian population in need.)

ICRC officials had already bent their own rules a bit. Even after the FMG declared "null and void" the April permission for the Red Cross to fly "at their own risk," they continued to send in an occasional flight anyway, refusing to acknowledge that the original permission was no longer valid. They were even using the planes of Hank Warton, the charter-flight operator who was flying guns and ammunition into Biafra. By loading food onto Warton's planes whenever there was space available, the church relief agencies had opened themselves to a Nigerian charge of being involved in arms-smuggling. The ICRC went to elaborate lengths to avoid this, concealing the fact that they were using Warton's aircraft, painting new registration numbers on, having the planes take a round-about route so they would not be coming from the island of São Tomé (from which the church agencies operated and Warton flew), and always chartering an entire plane so it would be carrying only food and medicine.

An ICRC relief plane had crashed at the beginning of July, killing the crew. The press identified the plane and the pilot as Warton's, to the embarrassment of the Red Cross.

Even when the committee briefly had permission, of sorts, to fly at its own risk, ICRC officials had not pressed the opportunity to begin an airlift sufficient to meet the growing needs about which Jaggi's reports were alerting them. They not only failed to foresee the enormity of what was coming, they lacked the funds and supplies to do anything about it. Immobilized as it was, it might have seemed curious that the ICRC had been given the mandate to coordinate all relief; its officials maintained complete secrecy about diplomatic negotiations, however, so few knew the problems they had already encountered. To those attempting to get some control over the twenty or more agencies now trying to rush relief into Biafra, the very limitations of the ICRC must have appeared virtues.

The British High Commissioner's Office and the Commonwealth Office could count on ICRC officials not violating their own self-imposed secrecy during negotiations. Nor would Red Cross officials ever speak out critically about a government upon whose goodwill they depended to continue their humanitarian work.

Though the Nigerians had no intention of giving any organization permission to move food into Biafra, they had already kept ICRC officials tied up in negotiations for months—learning in the process that the Red Cross would never do anything "illegal." The British persuaded the Nigerian government to invite the ICRC to coordinate all relief. Spokesmen of other governments began saying "the world's mandate" has been given the Red Cross.

ICRC officials contend they must remain "naifs" in a highly political world. They cannot become involved in the politics of a situation or carry on the kind of partisan diplomacy governments do. They depend upon the decency of governments to allow them to carry out their humanitarian work. And then, of course, what was about to happen to them had never occurred before in the previous century of their history.

The Red Cross president went down the hill to the old League of Nations building to ask Secretary General Thant's assistance. There is sad symbolism in the fact that Samuel Gonard had suffered a slight stroke without realizing it; those around him did not recognize right away that he was no longer the vigorous man he had been, just as they did not recognize right away the true purpose of the message they had received that day from Lagos.

It was certainly odd that at the moment Red Cross officials turned to the UN secretary general for help (informing him that "the ICRC is deeply concerned with the difficulties it is meeting . . ."), they should learn that the Nigerian government had decided all relief should be coordinated by the Red Cross. Perhaps it seemed natural enough to be asked to play the leading role in a wartime situation. They can be forgiven their failure to recognize their own lack of capacity or to foresee the way they were about to be used. Possibly the mounting gravity of the situation caused them to hope for a breakthrough.

They told U Thant of the new possibility—the plan Jaggi and Kirkley had worked out with Ojukwu for the use of a neutralized, demilitarized airstrip in Biafra, completely under control of the Red Cross, to be used exclusively for relief flights. This was, after all, precisely what Nigerian officials had been telling the ICRC was needed if relief flights were to be permitted. Perhaps with the help of the secretary general it would at last be possible to begin full-scale relief.

. . .

As it happened, Thant had a reason that day for conferring with the Red Cross officials that related directly to their problem. The United Nations had proclaimed 1968 the International Year for Human Rights. The conference just held in Teheran had requested the secretary general to consult with the ICRC, then draw the attention of all UN members to the rules of international law relating to armed conflicts: "to insure that in all armed conflicts the inhabitants and belligerents are protected in accordance with the principles of the law of nations derived from the usage established among civilized peoples, from the laws of humanity and from the dictates of the public conscience."

This phrase has long standing in international humanitarian law. It means that when all else fails, even when international law has gaps, there are still things combatants must not do to one another or to noncombatants. By including the phrase "in all armed conflicts," the Conference on Human Rights was seeking to cover just such civil wars as the one now taking such a heavy toll in Nigeria.

The ICRC had been struggling with this problem for more than half a century. Only one of the many articles of the Geneva Conventions at that time—Article 3—applied to "conflicts not of an international character." Legal scholars regarded Article 3 as a high-sounding but frail instrument with which to confront belligerents caught up in the passions of civil warfare. The International Red Cross had tried to do something more about the problem as recently as three years before, agreeing upon three basic principles that should guide every government or other authority conducting military operations:

that the right of the parties to a conflict to adopt means of injuring the enemy is not unlimited;
that it is prohibited to launch attacks against the civilian population as such;
that distinction must be made at all times between persons taking part in the hostilities and members of the civilian population to the effect that the latter be spared as much as possible.

High-sounding words, but as any scholar of international law is quick to say, the more high-sounding the words, the less binding they are on governments. And governments have considerable reluctance to create international law that may place restraints upon themselves when they wish to put down some of their own people who have risen up or are seeking to break away. The one principle of international law upon which all governments agree is "non-interference in the internal affairs of a sovereign nation." The Red Cross continued—and continues—to try to strengthen international law in those kinds of conflicts that, since the end of World War II, have made up the bulk of wars and taken so many civilian lives.

So, it might be thought, the purposes of the secretary general and the ICRC officials coincided that day, for the latter had tried for ten months to get authorization to provide relief to Biafra. Now they turned for help to U Thant. In meeting with them, he in turn was acting on the direction of the Conference on Human Rights, which had expressed the conviction "that even during periods of armed conflicts, humanitarian principles must prevail." The conference had commented that "the widespread violence and brutality of our times . . . erode human rights and engender counter-brutality."

However, Thant had already formulated his own position. The report of a UNICEF representative in Lagos to his headquarters in New York bears out a Lagos newspaper account that the Nigerian ambassador to the United Nations, Edwin Ogbu, had briefed the secretary general on the "correct situation in Nigeria," that the FMG "still regarded the crisis as her internal affair. . . ." The UNICEF representative reported being asked by Ogbu how he should advise General Gowon to respond to U Thant's offer to send a special representative: "He confessed that his immediate reaction was to advise General Gowon against this, since he had had discussions with the Secretary General in Geneva and had been assured that the statement he advised U Thant to put out represented the best approach to the problem. Although I was not informed, I understood that this statement was the one referring to suggestions that aid would reach the people in Biafra through a 'mercy corridor' through the fighting lines. . . ." The UN secretary general does not, of course, take instructions from governments, but U Thant's position seems to have been in accord with that of the Nigerian ambassador.

The secretary general held a press conference; the *New York Times* headlined the story:

THANT BIDS BIAFRA YIELD ON RELIEF

**Tells Rebels to Accept Aid through
Territory Held by Federal Forces**

Thant told the reporters he had discussed the situation in Nigeria the previous year with General Gowon and had been in touch with him since. The secretary general said he believed the FMG "is desirous of facilitating all international aid and assistance to the people in distress in the Eastern

Region." He appealed to the leaders of the Eastern Region (Biafra) to take advantage of the Nigerian government's offer and "to cooperate more fully with the international community in its genuine endeavor to ameliorate the miserable plight of the peoples in that Region."

Thant said he had assured the president of the ICRC of his "fullest cooperation" and commented: "In my view, the International Red Cross should be the only channel for the transmission of international aid to those stricken people in the Eastern Region."

The executive director of the United Nations Children's Fund, Henry Labouisse, was in Geneva, and U Thant met with him and with representatives of the World Health Organization, the Food and Agriculture Organization, and the World Food Program. The secretary general warned them that the UN agencies must not provide relief to Biafra unless requested to do so by the Nigerian government. The representatives agreed they would not provide emergency assistance without a specific request from the Federal Military Government. Labouisse told Thant that UNICEF had an arrangement with the FMG, made the previous December, which he regarded as sufficient authorization.

This had come up in New York the week before: a *New York Times* editor telephoned UNICEF to check a story just received from David Robison, its stringer in Biafra, quoting Jaggi and Kirkley as saying that as many as two million might die during the coming months. The agency's director of information told the editor there was nothing in Robison's story UNICEF was in a position to deny.

Then he added "background," thinking he would not be quoted, but the *Times* reported the next day that UNICEF had been trying "desperately" to reach the victims of the Biafran-Nigerian war. Supplies were "in position and available." UNICEF and the International Committee of the Red Cross had been trying repeatedly, without success, to bring the conditions to the attention of the Nigerian government; their representatives had not been able to obtain permission to reach the victims.

The chargé of Nigeria's UN mission complained to UNICEF about this candor. He cited the agreement made the previous December. A deputy director of the Children's Fund pointed out that while the FMG had entered into such an agreement, there had been little fulfillment: UNICEF and the Red Cross had been able to fly in only limited food and medicine, at night.

However, UN agencies must be responsive to member governments of the United Nations. UNICEF agreed to put out a small, clarifying press release, stating: " . . . An understanding with the Government of Nigeria has existed since December to channel UNICEF emergency assistance through the International Committee of the Red Cross to children and their mothers in all areas affected by the war there. There has been some delay in implementing the agreement effectively due to various difficulties. . . ."

Sasha Bacic, the Yugoslav heading UNICEF's Africa programs, analyzed the situation at this point: "The aid that has already been sent and distributed in the Federal-held territory was supplied by UNICEF on the precise understanding that the agreement concerned both sides. By accepting our aid . . . the Government has confirmed again its approval and acceptance of the aid agreement. A contracting party cannot benefit from the stipulations of an agreement that are in its favor and then refuse to carry out the remaining obligations that are incumbent upon it."

Bacic made a suggestion: " . . . If the fiction (we believe it *is* a fiction) of an agreement reached by the ICRC (on behalf of UNICEF, also) and the Federal Government and concerning relief aid for children and mothers of both sides is maintained, why not confront the Federal Government with a request to let UNICEF's supplies destined to children of Biafra go through in a normal way."

It was worth a further try, given the mounting gravity of the situation. E. J. R. (Dick) Heyward, an Australian from Tasmania, who as UNICEF's deputy director had been the intellectual and moral force behind the organization for twenty years, was deeply troubled about the children in Biafra and Nigeria. Reports kept coming to him from UNICEF representatives in Lagos (this one from an African, who, therefore, could not be accused of racism): " . . . It must be stated at once, and quite categorically, that one cannot escape the conclusion that the Government and various tribal groups have indicated, both by word and action, their complete displeasure at providing any assistance for men, women, and children of the Ibo tribe. This statement has been made after deep and careful consideration, and quite objectively. In the first place, there are quite a number of interested voluntary organizations apart from ourselves that are eager and willing to provide relief of one kind or another. Some have already provided material, etc., etc. Paradoxically though, it is a fair commentary to state that the utterances of spokesmen of the FMG are not matched by appropriate deeds. . . ."

The same UNICEF representative went on to convey something of what lay behind this intransigence: "Among the large majority hailing from that tribe (Yorubas) who are most vocal in inciting the complete extermination of the Ibos, I often heard remarks that all Nigeria's ills will be cured once the Ibos have been removed. . . ."

Neither Heyward nor Bacic had any illusions about what they were up against when they met with others the same day the ICRC sought the assistance of U Thant. After discussing various possibilities, they decided to request from the U.S. government, as a first shipment, 5,000 tons of food of the kind needed by children suffering protein malnutrition. One of those present, not as familiar as Heyward and Bacic with the unsuccessful attempts of the past eight months, said in some consternation: "I don't understand. The problem is so enormous that what is needed is nothing less than a United Nations relief force, with a logistics general in command and with contributions of planes and trucks and personnel from United Nations members. Why are we only talking about getting 5,000 tons of food to sea that can't reach the area for two months?"

There was silence for a moment. Then Bacic said somberly: "A million of those people are just going to die—that's all."

Henry Labouisse, informed of the new UNICEF initiative in New York, decided to go to Lagos to see what he could do himself through what he called "personal diplomacy." His own inclination was to play his visit "low key," with a minimum of publicity, not to dramatize his mission or to focus world attention so as to arouse hopeful expectations.

As head of the United Nations Children's Fund, Labouisse certainly would have been the logical person to press for access to the children in need. (A survey done by the pediatrician Dr. Ifekwunigwe three months earlier indicated that 89 percent of those starving at that time were under five years of age.) The UN had proclaimed in the Declaration of the Rights of the Child that "the child shall in all circumstances be among the first to receive protection and relief."

An activist secretary general like Dag Hammarskjöld might have gone to Nigeria himself. Thant had been kept informed about UNICEF's unsuccessful efforts, and now the president of the Red Cross had asked for his help. He did suggest to Labouisse that he go to Lagos as his special representative, but the UNICEF director declined, feeling he stood a better chance of getting food to the children as head of the nonpolitical United Nations Children's Fund than he would if he took on the more political role of representing the secretary general.

When Thant arrived back in New York from Geneva, reporters waited to question him as he entered the United Nations, even though it was a Saturday. What was the UN going to do about relief for Biafra? The international community was ready to send massive relief to Nigeria, he told them, but, of course, all aid from the World Health Organization or the World Food Program would have to be at the request of the Nigerian government.

The secretary general then cabled General Gowon: he was "increasingly concerned by the urgency and magnitude of the needs of civilian victims of the hostilities in Nigeria." Thant mentioned "receiving numerous messages from many quarters, drawing my attention to the seriousness of this problem." He recounted what UNICEF had been trying to do, that the UN agencies were ready to make a contribution "with the concurrence of your Government" and "to channel their supplies directly through the International Committee of the Red Cross."

Speaking of Gowon's offer "to insure access corridors via airports or seaports in Federal-controlled territory," the secretary general expressed the hope "that everything possible will be done by your Government to enable the Red Cross, the United Nations and the voluntary agencies concerned to carry out their humanitarian task." He pointed out that earlier, in Geneva, he had appealed "to those in charge in the Central Eastern Region" to cooperate fully "to relieve the desperate plight of the peoples in that area."

Thant concluded with his one specific proposal: "I would be glad to send a representative to Lagos immediately to discuss the modalities of this humanitarian task if your Excellency agrees."

A United Nations official, well placed to know, later explained that the proposal for "a special representative was really a response to the demand of public opinion that something be done—something like a special representative had been in the works since the Secretary General had been asked about the starvation at a press conference." That Thant had no greater purpose in sending a representative to Lagos eventually became clear from the person he chose—a man a few ranks down in the office of the UN high commissioner for refugees.

When Thant's cable arrived at the Nigerian Ministry of External Affairs, it aroused consternation. The suggestion of a special representative greatly agitated Nigeria's UN ambassador Edwin Ogbu; his immediate reaction was to advise General Gowon against it. He also contemplated returning immediately to the United Nations to try to prevent it. (Gowon's reply to Thant's cable did suggest that the secretary general discuss the matter with Ogbu, "who will be returning to New York shortly.")

The Nigerian ambassador became even more distressed when Thant made his cable public, expressing as it did his concern at "the urgency and magnitude of the needs of civilian victims of the hostilities" and the "concern of the United Nations and the whole world that this tragic situation should not be allowed to deteriorate further." This was viewed as amounting to recognition of Biafra—the United Nations according the relief problem international status rather than keeping it an internal matter, as the Nigerians would have liked.

Ogbu expressed his concern to a UNICEF representative in Lagos and asked what he should advise General Gowon. The UNICEF officer pointed out that it would be discourteous to reject out of hand a suggestion coming from so eminent a person as U Thant and expressed his own opinion that "the head of the military government, if he has nothing to hide and if he has a case to present, would find it in his best interest to receive the representative." He suggested "this might be a good opportunity for the Federal Military Government to acquaint an impartial observer with the true facts as they stand, provided there is nothing to conceal."

When Labouisse got off the plane at Lagos International Airport, he had to make clear—to the relief of Ogbu, who was there to greet him—that he had not come as the secretary general's representative. Neither he nor Thant intended anything like Ogbu's worst fears. They were, after all, seeking the Nigerian government's permission to provide food to the children starving in Biafra.

Chapter 5

Joseph Palmer arrived in Geneva. Palmer, U.S. assistant secretary of state for African affairs, had just spent four days in Lagos, conferring with Nigerian government officials, the British high commissioner and American ambassador Elbert Mathews. (While there, the Lagos *Daily Times* quoted Palmer as calling upon "the rebels" to "renounce secession so that peace and tranquillity may return to the country.")

Palmer had been the first U.S. ambassador to independent Nigeria. In that capacity he had been a booster of the new nation, selling American businessmen on the idea that Nigeria had a great future. During his early days in the Foreign Service, he had served a number of years in London. He was no less committed than his counterparts in the British Commonwealth Office to preserving Nigerian unity, and his successor, Mathews, was almost as active as Sir David Hunt in trying to hold Nigeria together. (The year before, Mathews had flown to Enugu to try to dissuade Colonel Ojukwu from seceding.)

The extent of this involvement is reflected in a letter written the previous fall by another diplomat in Lagos: ". . . I happen to know the American Ambassador here quite well and could hardly believe the report he apparently gave to Congress that the Federal Government could protect the Ibos. He was here when the soldiers broke into a prison and shot the Ibo detainees; he was here when the soldiers who were apprehended for killing Ibos in Ibadan were released and the charges against them dropped; he was here when the Ibos were being hunted down in Lagos. Furthermore, he is aware of the fact that whatever Embassy had Ibo employees had to forfeit its diplomatic immunity whenever the soldiers felt like it. He knows very well that the UN compound was violated—its doors were burst open and its Ibo employees were molested and taken away. He knows too, of Ibos who were collected and taken to Ikeja where they were lined up for shooting, and some of them were rescued at the point of being shot. Others, of course, perished . . . "

Mathews and Palmer were alarmed that the opening gambit that had gained the Soviet Union entrée into the Middle East a decade earlier—arms shipments—would succeed again in Nigeria. By 1968, Soviet communism had lost its revolutionary fervor and much of its political appeal in the world, but Soviet leaders still pursued Great Power expansionism, following the same radical-Socialist-Moslem route into Northern Nigeria that had gained them entrance into the Middle East. The threat of a Soviet foothold in West Africa, with its potential for a Soviet naval presence in the South Atlantic, could not help but arouse a reflexive alarm in Mathews and Palmer: they did not want to be held responsible for "losing West Africa to communism."

Even before the Soviet Union became involved, Mathews had publicly expressed "complete support" for "the political integrity of Nigeria." However, within days of the outbreak of the war, the United States took a policy decision not to sell or otherwise supply arms or ammunition to either the Nigerians or the Biafrans.

Palmer and Mathews were answerable to the undersecretary of state, but Nicholas Katzenbach was reluctant to overrule the professionals—they knew Nigeria and Africa firsthand, he did not. The previous autumn, doubting the accuracy of reports coming from the Lagos embassy, Katzenbach had sent an assistant to check on what was happening. The assistant spent a weekend there and came back with an impression of "just how inflamed the Nigerian Ministers are" and with "a better appreciation of what Mathews is up against."

For the undersecretary, with responsibilities throughout the world, relations with the Nigerian government were not crucial. To the Foreign Service personnel in the Bureau of African Affairs, "relations with the Government of Nigeria were an earth-shaking matter," as another Katzenbach assistant put it, "Nigeria being the most populous country in Africa. For the Ambassador and his staff in the Embassy in Lagos, maintaining good relations with members of the Nigerian Government was even more than earth-shaking—they had to meet Nigerian officials face-to-face every day."

So policy-making remained at the working level—Mathews in Lagos and Palmer in Washington. Even after starvation in Biafra aroused public concern, putting great pressure on the U.S. and other governments, for months Katzenbach did not overrule the experts, though he pressed them to come up with a solution. At one abrasive session, Palmer said, "I'm afraid if we push the Feds too far, they'll turn to the Soviets." Katzenbach countered, in exasperation, "Dammit, Joe, if they would feed these people, they could have the country."

How the Africa bureau set about to manage mounting public concern can be seen in its response to initial reaction to starvation in Biafra. At the time Palmer arrived in Geneva, *Life* magazine appeared with "Starving Children of Biafra War" on the cover and, inside, photos of emaciated infants. For weeks, people in Ireland and England had been aroused, as priests, nuns, and Protestant missionaries in Biafra prompted earlier news coverage in those countries. In Britain a "Save the Biafrans Committee" had already been organized and a rally held in Trafalgar Square. Now Americans began demanding to know what was going to be done, and a Committee to Keep Biafra Alive began forming in the U.S. The White House responded with a statement from President Johnson: " . . . While we have no intention of interfering in Nigerian affairs, we do not believe innocent persons should be made the victims of political maneuvering. Deaths caused by warfare are tragic enough. But mass starvation that can be prevented must be prevented. I urgently appeal to all those bearing responsibility to allow supplies to get to the people who so desperately need them."

Though Palmer was away, other officials in the Africa bureau gave this statement a new direction, picking up the line the British and Nigerians had been fashioning:

• The *Baltimore Sun* reported: "But specialists here believed Mr. Johnson's statement would increase pressure on the Biafran leader, Lieutenant-Colonel Odumegwu Ojukwu, to accept an arrangement whereby food would be moved overland under the control of the International Red Cross but subject to inspection by the Nigerian Federal Government."

• Reuters carried the president's statement, plus: "Officials said the President's appeal was directed chiefly at the Biafran authorities who have refused to permit international relief supplies to reach the Eastern Region through territory held by the Federal Government."

• The *New York Times* added: "Other Administration officials made it clear that the United States was not prepared itself to undertake any relief program that would offend the sensibilities or sovereignty of the Nigerian Government . . . . These sources indicated specifically that the United States did not favor an airlift of food to the landlocked rebel area."

In Geneva, Palmer counseled ICRC officials to concentrate on building up stockpiles of food in the Federal areas of Nigeria, to position trucks at Enugu so as to be prepared if the land corridor should open up.

The Red Cross had nothing like the funds needed to coordinate relief. The Swiss government regularly supports the ICRC, and in emergencies national societies solicit donations from their own governments and raise funds through public appeals. For the massive relief effort now required, the Red Cross needed large contributions of food and money from governments. The response to its May "SOS" totaled only about two million Swiss francs, something less than half a million dollars.

The ICRC estimated that 200 tons of food had to be transported into Biafra each day, and a tremendous relief problem was building up on the Federal side as well. The eighteen relief flights flown into Biafra up to that time had carried only 180 tons of food and medicine.

The Red Cross officials could not begin planning overall relief without assurance of adequate funds and a continuing flow of food. Inevitably, in a relief effort of this magnitude, the United States would have to be a major supplier of both. ICRC officials asked Palmer what had become of the request made to the U.S. government for financial assistance? He replied, "Well, it's being studied."

Death by starvation takes about six weeks. In his medical column in the *New York Times*, Dr. Howard Rusk sought to convey something of this prolonged agony, saying it is "incomprehensible" to anyone who has never experienced the physical cycle of starvation. "The first few days," he stated, "the stomach complains with cramps and bloating while it gradually shrinks in size."

Water helps a little, Rusk wrote, but the starving children cry during these first few days and "eat anything to stop the hunger pains. Rags, straw, clay, chalk and even poisonous weeds, berries and twigs have been reportedly ingested. As weakness increases, cries change to whimpers, then there is the nausea. This comes while nature is burning all of the body's fat from the muscles and all other tissues where it is deposited. . . . Nature becomes kinder to the starving at this juncture, kinder than the politicians arguing about boundaries and power. A great overpowering lethargy develops and a kind and wise nature offers large doses of sleep to ease the pain of slow death." Dr. Rusk wrote that body proteins have been depleted and "the abdomen becomes distended with fluid, the extremities swollen with water and now degeneration of the vital organs such as the liver and kidneys starts in earnest. . . . At this stage, the individual's inability to combat other diseases gradually decreases and he may be mercifully spared further suffering by the terminal effects of any type of infection. At this juncture, if nutrition is restored and the patient recovers, it is often with permanent damage to the vital organs either from the ravages of starvation or the aftereffects of infection. These complications may lead to chronic invalidism and premature death."

For the Catholic and Protestant missionaries in Biafra, it was harrowing as they awakened each day to the wailing of mothers whose babies had died during the night, as they had to bury more and more children they had known. They had become relief workers, a network of feeding stations already in place, lacking only food.

Their appeals to Geneva, Rome, New York became more urgent. Church World Service, Caritas, Catholic Relief Service, and other agencies had been doing what they could since the previous autumn—contributing to a Red Cross flight, paying to ship in food or medicine whenever space became available on a plane carrying in arms or ammunition, occasionally chartering a plane of their own.

In March, Father Anthony Byrne of the Irish Order of the Holy Ghost set up a relief base for Caritas on the island of São Tomé. (He chose that island rather than Fernando Po, from which the Red Cross flew, for "security reasons"—there were no Nigerians on São Tomé.) Byrne chartered Hank Warton's planes for six flights to fly in sixty tons of food, mostly powdered milk.

Using Warton's planes and flying from an island that was still a Portuguese colony both angered Nigerian officials and provided them material with which to denounce the church relief operation. Byrne's comment, in private, was: "I would consort with the Devil himself to get food in to those children." He said with anger and deep emotion: "What is happening is genocide—it is genocide."

The missionaries who had remained with their parishes as the front advanced understood the situation well. In New York for a news conference, Byrne and other priests expressed the opinion there was almost no likelihood of a road corridor being opened. Opening a land corridor would inevitably benefit the attacker, they believed. The road north from Port Harcourt would be best, but the Nigerian commander in the area, Colonel Adekunle, was adamant that no food go into Biafra. Further, Byrne said, Biafrans would not touch food handled in any way by people on the Nigerian side, as they had an "ages-old, deep-rooted and irreversible fear of poisoning."

Before June, the church relief agencies mostly supplied medicines to their missionary doctors at the hospitals in Biafra, with distribution out of Queen Elizabeth Hospital in Umuahia (Biafra's administrative capital since Enugu had fallen to the Nigerian Army). As starvation became widespread, they set up feeding centers in some of the refugee camps but could provide only three meals a week. Much more was needed.

The international church agencies are large; they have ongoing programs of assistance in many developing countries. They could raise funds by organizing appeals through church parishes throughout Europe and North America. But they had never been faced with anything like Biafra before. The World Council of Churches commented: " . . . The dimension of the problem has already reached proportions beyond the capacity of voluntary agencies."

When consciousness of the starvation broke upon the world, church relief officials believed that now, at last, governments and the United Nations would begin to act. As July wore on, however, it became apparent that neither governments nor the UN was doing anything. Those who possessed giant cargo planes and the capacity to organize an airlift were not doing so. Church relief officials knew little or nothing about organizing an airlift; churches do not have air forces.

Those running the church agencies, on the other hand, had better information than governments about what was happening in Biafra. They had reports from their own people on the spot, and top officials of the international agencies began making trips themselves into Biafra to assess conditions. Other governments relied on information from the British who in turn believed only what they learned from Lagos, discounting reports coming out of Biafra.

Three American church agency officials meeting with Secretary of State Dean Rusk listened in quiet astonishment to a briefing by experts from the Bureau of African Affairs. Finally, Bishop Edward Swanstrom of Catholic Relief Services said, "That's the way it was two or three months ago. Now let me tell you what the situation was this morning." He proceeded to give a detailed account of the relief and military situation.

Rusk asked, "How did you get this information?"

The bishop replied, "By telephone, this morning. A plane flies out of Biafra every morning, tells the people at São Tomé what the situation is, then they telephone me by way of Lisbon. I get a report every morning."

Protestant and Catholic agencies in West Germany used funds provided by their government to purchase some secondhand passenger planes—DC-7s. A meeting of the World Council of Churches had just passed a resolution encouraging the church relief organizations to "make a new and vigorous attempt to mount a continuous and effective airlift . . ." Soon two of the planes were on their way to the island of São Tomé.

Pope Paul VI announced the start of Caritas's own flights: "We cannot think of that good and hard-working people now stricken by civil war and dying of hunger without deep sorrow. Through our charitable agencies close to the International Red Cross and other beneficial initiatives, we have sent aid in food and medicine. We have hired planes and we have tried to do what we could with difficulty, risks and much expense. But it seems a little thing in the face of the needs."

The Lagos newspapers ran headlines, "VATICAN SMUGGLES SUPPLIES TO REBELS ," and a picture of the Pope captioned: "Pope Paul—admitted the Vatican was hiring blockade-running planes into rebel areas." The stories made it clear that the "blockade-running planes" were being used "to smuggle food and drugs to the rebels in the shrinking areas under Ojukwu's control . . . ." The Nigerian ambassador to the UN told a news conference it was unfortunate Roman Catholic relief agencies were trying to get food to Biafra despite FMG restrictions: "We have protested to the Pope through the Papal delegate in Lagos that he is taking the attitude that this is a religious war, which it is not. There are many more Christians in the rest of the country than there are in rebel-held areas."

General Gowon warned representatives of the international relief agencies that the Nigerian government would not tolerate interference in the domestic affairs of Nigeria. He got them to pledge that all relief would be channeled through the International Committee of the Red Cross.

Being told to coordinate under the ICRC, waiting to learn something, anything, from the ICRC as the starvation death toll mounted each day, officials of other relief agencies became increasingly enraged. They had begun providing the ICRC with information—the foods and medicines they could supply, what kinds of personnel they had available, their capacities in the field for distribution. They heard nothing in response from ICRC officials. A great silence emanated from "La Maison" on the hill in Geneva.

Forward planning was urgently needed: how much and what kinds of food and medicines, trucks, aircraft, medical personnel should each of the twenty or more relief agencies be sending? Organizing such a vast relief operation would take time, but time was being lost.

During one meeting held at UNICEF headquarters in New York, a Catholic Relief Service official passed around a cable just received from Father Byrne on São Tomé: "FOR GODS SAKE SEND BABY FOOD. I HAVE RUN OUT AND THE BABIES ARE DYING BY THE THOUSANDS."

Father Fintan Kilbride, an Irish priest, would have been in Biafra where he had served for fourteen years had he not been injured in the crash of a plane flying medicines into Port Harcourt six months before. His hands shook as he read to others at the meeting a London newspaper report: "The International Red Cross has set a confidential date—September 15th—for the start of full-scale relief, medical and public health operations, and this postulates another 49 days formal warfare . . . ."

There was an angry outcry around the table. Something of this sort had been suspected and feared among relief officials. They began talking of issuing a statement, then and there, denouncing the International Committee of the Red Cross. Heyward of UNICEF, chairing the meeting, tried to calm the angry men. August Lindt had just been appointed ICRC high commissioner for relief. He knew Lindt, Heyward said. He was an effective and dedicated man. Heyward was certain that Lindt would do everything in his power to find some way to get food flowing in. They should give him time.

Jan van Hoogstraten of Church World Service spoke with controlled wrath: "Yes, I know Mr. Lindt; he had me thrown out of Yugoslavia after the war." And Rabbi Marc Tanenbaum of the American Jewish Committee added, heatedly, "Yes, and I know the International Committee of the Red Cross. I lost a good many of my family in Europe during the war because of them."

Chapter 6

"**B**uild up stockpiles of food around the periphery of the enclave. If people are hungry enough, they will walk out to get the food," British diplomats counseled officials of the International Committee of the Red Cross. "Build up stocks of food and trucks; prepare an overall program to bring relief to all the victims once the war is over. Then we and the American government will help you rush in massive humanitarian relief and save all those people."

The British had been talking to top officials of the Red Cross this way for months. Both knew the Nigerians were blocking the start of relief, though the British tended to say: "If the Biafrans will not agree to a land corridor, then the best you can do is to build up stockpiles around the periphery until they do. Position the food and trucks so they will be available should agreement on a land corridor come or when the collapse comes." It came from the British high commissioner in Lagos, from Lord Shepherd when he was in Geneva, later from Lord Hunt after the British government charged him with looking into the relief problem, most of all from the British consul in Geneva who served as liaison from the Commonwealth Office to the Red Cross.

Now, in July 1968, a new element was added—the British telling ICRC officials that the collapse of Biafra would come by September 15. "A few thousand might die now, it's true," they conceded, "but then it will become possible to save millions." Red Cross officials had no idea why they were so convinced the war would end by mid-September. The Nigerian Army had shown no capacity up to this time for bringing off complete victory, on schedule.

The ICRC began acting on British advice, building up stockpiles of food at Enugu, Asaba, and Calabar. The Red Cross did not inform anyone that this was in response to British and U.S. suggestions. Top ICRC officials kept their own counsel, talking worriedly only with each other, not letting others know about the plan being urged upon them. They found themselves in an impossible position as a result of Nigerian intransigence toward relief and the British attempt to cover this up so as to continue their arms supply and get the war over as quickly as possible.

The British had muddled their way into using the ICRC as their instrument for this purpose, seeking to get control over the relief agencies. At one point the Commonwealth secretary cited to Commons as an authority the ICRC's director general, Roger Gallopin, misnaming him and mistitling him: "Mr. Richard Gallopin, Executive Director of the International Red Cross, said yesterday that a land route through Nigeria was the only way by which medical supplies could be brought to Biafra." And, later: "The important thing to bear in mind about air transport is that the International Red Cross is convinced that the only way in which the volume of relief supplies now needed for Biafra can be got into Biafra is by land route, because the present airstrips in Biafra are inadequate to meet the volume of supplies required . . . . "

Playing upon the ICRC's vulnerability as a cautious, legalistic, secretive organization whose officials could be counted upon never to speak out in a way that would antagonize governments, the British gradually built up the ploy by which they were now managing the relief problem—keeping the other agencies under control. Even if top ICRC officials did not know how or why they had come to be given the mandate to coordinate relief, they soon became aware of how they were being used.

Through July and early August, governments pressured the humanitarian agencies to coordinate their relief under the ICRC. Other foreign ministries adopted the British line, finding it useful, pressed as they were by rising public opinion in each of their countries to do something about the starving children in Biafra. Immobilization set in. Officials of other relief agencies and national Red Cross societies were fast losing patience with the ICRC. They sought to coordinate information about personnel they had available and shipments of food and medical supplies, but the Red Cross did not communicate information in return. There was no overall assessment of needs, no coordination of shipments. It was infuriating to officials being told they must coordinate under the Red Cross.

For ICRC executives it was a dilemma. The ICRC could either lose the support of governments if they spoke out or took action, or lose the goodwill and cooperation of other international relief agencies if they did not. The bind they had been put in threatened the very future of their organization.

The director general of the Dutch Red Cross was quoted in *de Tijd* a few months later, commenting on this period of inaction: "As I said before, we must exhaust all possibilities of negotiating by the rules before putting a relief action into effect. We are not simply a relief organization, we also have political duties. For people in Biafra the delay was obviously appalling. I can assure you that from various quarters the heaviest political pressure was applied to prevent us doing anything at all for Biafra, on the grounds that this was an internal affair."

Using the ICRC was only part of British diplomats' efforts to conceal Nigerian obstruction of relief and to display their own "conspicuous zeal" in support of humanitarian action. Government spokesmen suggested to Parliament they were ready to use the Royal Air Force to fly in food, if the Federal Government gave permission for the planes to enter Nigerian airspace.

The Nigerian government's announcement that instructions had been given its air force "to seek and destroy" any aircraft such as the one Leslie Kirkley had chartered to fly in Oxfam food undercut everything British spokesmen had been saying. So Okoi Arikpo, the Nigerian external affairs minister, called a press conference. Though the British government had reiterated in London nearly every day that the Nigerians were ready to open a "mercy corridor" from Enugu to Awgu, this had barely been mentioned in Lagos. Correspondents in the Nigerian capital reported Arikpo's statement that the FMG was prepared to open a land corridor as if it were news—a breakthrough.

This produced the intended effect. Newspapers reported, under headlines such as "BIAFRA REJECTS MERCY ROUTE ": "Hopes of urgent relief for Biafra's war victims faded cruelly yesterday as Biafran spokesmen denounced the offer of the Nigerian Federal Government to open a 'mercy corridor' under International Red Cross auspices . . . . "

The British government sent Lord Hunt to Nigeria to look into relief needs. Hunt was Britain's national hero: he had led the expedition that conquered Mount Everest. A retired Army brigadier, handsome, modest, a thoroughly decent human being, he was a perfect choice for the mission. As he had no particular qualifications to inquire into relief, two officials accompanied him: the director general of Save the Children Fund, Sir Colin Thornley, and the deputy director general of the British Red Cross, Brian Hodgson. (Both, until six years before, had made their careers in the British Colonial Service.)

Hunt's mission made it possible for government spokesmen in London to say such things as " . . . these discussions are, as I am sure the House will appreciate, extremely delicate, and I do not want to say anything today which can be an obstacle to their success. Lord Hunt arrived in Lagos on Saturday morning and has already made certain preliminary recommendations," etc. Later, Prime Minister Wilson reported to Commons: "We have kept in close touch with the work done by Lord Hunt and his colleagues . . . in the last two weeks in Nigeria. I understand that Lord Hunt is returning to report in the next day or two. I hope to have then a full report on the situation in relation to both surface and air routes. . . . "

It was difficult for the Biafrans not to play into the hands of the British. In sending Lord Hunt to Nigeria, the British announced they were granting £250,000 for relief to both sides. Hunt was to work out the arrangements; this had been discussed with the Nigerians earlier when Lord Shepherd was in Lagos. (At that time, General Gowon, a Christian, said to Lord Shepherd, with no ambiguity or pun intended, "I have given the Lord charge of my heart." Colonel Ojukwu, also a Christian, speaking publicly about this same mission of Lord Shepherd, remarked, "It is quite clear that, as far as Biafra is concerned, this particular Lord cannot be our Shepherd.")

So, a few days later, when another Lord arrived, bearing gifts from the British government, Ojukwu and the Biafrans did not welcome him: "Whilst the Government of the Republic of Biafra is grateful for all genuine offers of assistance, it cannot understand how the British Government can offer assistance in one hand and, on the other, furnish the Lagos Government with the arms for increasing the misery, suffering and destruction of these same people. The Government and people of Biafra see neither sense nor logic therefore in such an assistance to the people of Biafra if they are only being fattened at the expense of the British public, just to be killed by arms supplied by the British Government. . . . "

Amid all the talk of land corridors, someone finally sought to do something realistic about the Enugu-Awgu proposal. General Ankrah of Ghana, who the year before at Aburi had attempted to reconcile the Nigerian antagonists, now was one of six heads of state making up the consultative committee appointed the previous September by the Organizaton of African Unity (OAU). Nigeria, the largest country in Africa, dominated the OAU on this issue; many African nations also had problems of secession along tribal lines. The OAU instructed the committee to go to Nigeria's head of state "to assure him of the Assembly's desire for the territorial integrity, unity and peace of Nigeria." The committee had done that and little more.

Now, with the Nigerian conflict being spoken of as "Africa's shame," some members sought a more active role for the OAU consultative committee, rather than its merely continuing as a creature of the Federal Military Government. The British also very much wanted the war ended.

The talks they had started through the Commonwealth Secretariat at Kampala having failed, they eagerly sought a new forum for bringing Nigerian and Biafran negotiators together.

So the consultative committee met at Niamey, the capital of Niger, just north of Nigeria, seeking to set in motion new peace negotiations. In addition, General Ankrah, who was in regular contact with Ojukwu, brought with him a resolution aimed at finding a way to make the land corridor acceptable to the Biafrans.

Pressures were mounting on the Biafrans not to reject relief as they seemed to be doing by refusing the land corridor. Before leaving for Niamey, Ojukwu told correspondents about the defenses protecting Biafra and said a land corridor "would remove those obstacles and create routes through which Gowon's war-machine can roll easily into our homeland." He went on: "Anyone genuinely interested in sending relief to us, should do so direct to Biafra by air. To this end, we have set aside an airport for that purpose."

Having said this, Ojukwu—under pressure to appear reasonable—then proposed two upriver and overland corridors of his own: one up the Niger River to Oguta, the other from Port Harcourt up the road to Igrita. Both would have to pass through territory controlled by or being fought over by troops under Nigerian Colonel Benjamin Adekunle. Adekunle had just embarrassed the British by terming all relief plans for Biafra "misguided humanitarian rubbish," saying that any food sent in would "only go to soldiers' stomachs and help prolong the fighting." As for use of Port Harcourt, Adekunle said its port facilities were needed exclusively for military supplies. He was, as always, blunt: "If children must die first, then that is too bad, just too bad. Ojukwu could stop the war."

The Nigerian delegation, headed by Gowon, arrived at Niamey first. Ankrah proposed demilitarizing the Enugu-Awgu corridor, five miles on either side of the road, and—to assure the Biafrans it would not be turned into an invasion route—patrolling it with neutral troops from other African nations. The Nigerians argued vehemently against this for four and a half hours. Members of the consultative committee saw that there was no possibility of getting the land corridor. When the closed session broke up, one Nigerian delegate said to a correspondent waiting outside: "Ankrah was completely isolated."

Gowon left before Ojukwu arrived the next day. The Biafran delegation found itself confronted with a *fait accompli*. Though Ojukwu felt, after he talked with the committee for two hours, that there was a softening on the part of some members, the final communiqué had already been agreed upon before he arrived. Even as he spoke, officials of the OAU Secretariat were preparing it. The resolution called upon the Nigerian Government "to implement without delay its decision to establish a 'mercy corridor' with appropriate collecting points" and for "the secessionists" to cooperate by accepting relief supplies through this corridor. As the meeting was in secret, the public could not know that the Nigerian government had vigorously resisted demilitarizing the Enugu-Awgu corridor and patrolling it with neutral African troops.

A few days later, Lord Hunt returned to London. The Commonwealth secretary could at last report his recommendations to Commons for relief on the Federal side, and added: "Lord Hunt also expressed firmly the view that the land route is the most effective way by which adequate relief supplies can quickly be brought to those who are suffering inside the Ibo area. General Gowon confirmed to him the willingness of the Federal Government to open a relief corridor from Enugu to Awgu and then to an agreed point on the Okigwe road, where Colonel Ojukwu's authorities could take over. The suitability of this road was checked by members of Lord Hunt's team. Sir Colin Thornley himself drove down the road without difficulty or obstruction in a relatively short time. . . . "

The way the British were talking with news correspondents at the time is summed up well in a paragraph from *Newsweek*: "Indeed, the British contend that the Biafrans have grossly exaggerated the extent of the starvation among their own people—and stalled relief operations—in a blatant attempt to arouse world opinion and force Lagos to make political concessions. 'There's a sizeable problem,' says one Whitehall official, 'but not necessarily as large as has been quoted. Those starving people are being used by Biafra as political pawns. The callousness of it beggars description.' "

Chapter 7

A strange mood had built up in Lagos. People there believed things believed nowhere else in the world. It was felt that starvation in Biafra was little worse than in many parts of Africa, that stories in the world press showing starving Biafran children were the result of a clever propaganda campaign on the part of the Ibos. Efforts of relief agencies were resented; even the Red Cross was not regarded as impartial. Government officials thought its actions tended to strengthen the "Ibo propaganda line."

A top United Nations official in Lagos advised Henry Labouisse soon after his arrival that there was great suspicion and hesitation in the FMG on the whole issue of humanitarian relief. U Thant's message to General Gowon, a few days before, amounted in their eyes to turning the relief situation into an international matter and, in effect, UN recognition of Biafra.

Labouisse had not been as deeply involved as his colleagues in UNICEF, Heyward and Bacic, in trying to find some way to get relief into Biafra; he was now receiving on-the-job training. A former U.S. ambassador himself, he lunched the day after his arrival with Ambassador Mathews; then he conferred with the British high commissioner, Sir David Hunt. He had just spent an evening in Geneva with Assistant Secretary Joseph Palmer; they dined together with U Thant at the villa of Prince Sadruddin Aga Khan, the high commissioner for refugees. These influences were countered by his own staff in Lagos and by the encounter he soon had with Nigerian officials. Before meeting with the chief medical adviser to the Nigerian government, Labouisse was told by one of the UNICEF staff that this doctor had the attitude that "babies are also rebels and they should be treated as such." So Labouisse was not surprised when the chief medical adviser informed him that there was no great immediate need for relief in areas that had come under Federal control.

Labouisse told him he understood there *was* great need and that if the chief medical adviser assured him there was none, he would be glad to announce this to the world and use UNICEF's funds in other countries where they were needed. This changed the tone of the discussion, and they took up the medical needs of children affected by the war.

On another occasion, Labouisse was summoned by Chief Enahoro, who was angry about a cable just received from New York. A full-page advertisement had appeared in the *New York Times*; the cable described it as "tendentious." (Large letters above a photo read: "We are the children of Biafra. By August we will be dead." Part of the text read: "To say that they brought this situation on themselves—that they chose to rebel against the Federal Government of Nigeria—is to engage in irrelevant politics. The children, after all, declared war on nobody.") Enahoro complained that the ad sought contributions for UNICEF. Labouisse said he knew nothing about it, but would look into it as UNICEF felt responsibility for the use of its name.

In New York, Dick Heyward was concerned that the United States government had begun holding up food for Nigeria and Biafra. While the State Department had announced that the U.S. was providing 5,000 tons of food only four days after UNICEF made its request, this was a response to the photos of Biafran children in *Life* and the public outcry they evoked. When UNICEF officials requested a second 5,000 tons of high-protein food, the Bureau of African Affairs responded: The embassy in Lagos is advising Washington to defer the decision—"there is plenty of food in the area."

There was not the kind of food in the area needed to retrieve children from kwashiorkor, that could be transported easily to the children in need. This high-protein supplement could be manufactured only in the United States from a formula using corn, soya, and powdered milk (CSM); it would require two months to process it and ship it by sea to Nigeria. Heyward was worried about a dock strike threatened in September; unless production of the CSM mixture began soon, it might not be possible to ship it. (The World Food Program, following U Thant's instructions and its own inclinations, was taking an unbending position that it could not make any food available without an official detailed letter-of-request from the Nigerian government.)

Between the first UNICEF request for food and the second, the FMG had set about to get control over the relief situation. Though it had just, ostensibly, given the "mandate" to the ICRC to coordinate relief, it had also set up a National Rehabilitation Commission, put a retired police official in charge, and announced it would buy food and other supplies in

Nigeria "at reasonable prices" for distribution in war-affected areas. (This could hardly include Biafra.) The FMG informed relief agencies and embassies that instead of importing food, they should purchase all of it locally. When the U.S. Agency for International Development routinely requested its Lagos representative to clear the second UNICEF request, the embassy advised Washington to hold up on it. The embassy's principal concern was to do nothing that would offend the Nigerian government.

Heyward was also troubled about a request that may have been made to the U.S. for cargo helicopters. UNICEF's idea was to get helicopters operating, first distributing food on the Nigerian side of the lines, then, when the Nigerians began to accept them, to press for authorization to start moving food into Biafra—overleaping the combat lines and, it was hoped, the political difficulties as well. It was, it would appear in retrospect, a quixotic idea, but anything seemed worth trying in those early desperate days of starvation.

Officials in New York did not know whether Labouisse had requested cargo helicopters through the U.S. mission in Geneva before leaving for Lagos. If he had, it was like a message in a bottle cast into the ocean, for no response came from the State Department and it was difficult to know where to plunge in to find it. Labouisse could not be cabled about anything that might antagonize the Nigerians, as he had not taken along an encoding machine and operator as the UN Secretariat had suggested—messages in code would, he felt, arouse even more suspicions on the part of the Nigerians about his visit.

In Lagos, Labouisse went from one government ministry to another, conferring with officials, trying to persuade them of the urgency for relief, the need for an overall assessment, the necessity for long-term planning. The officials he talked with were all "hawks," he wrote U Thant; some were simply more hawkish than others. He felt a difference between those—including Gowon—who showed a sincere interest in relief and those who did not.

He assured the officials that UNICEF assistance was being coordinated through the ICRC and emphasized this when he conferred with General Gowon, as well as the fact that his UN agency works only with governments—in this case, the Nigerian government. Gowon reiterated his government's wish that all relief agencies coordinate under the ICRC.

Was Gowon ready to authorize passage of relief convoys through the combat lines, Labouisse asked, as the Nigerian chargé at the UN had assured UNICEF a few weeks before? He was ready to open a corridor immediately from Enugu to Okigwe, a town still in "rebel hands," Gowon replied, adding that, when it became possible, there could be other corridors from Calabar in the southeast. He "gave his word" that this was a genuine offer and did not conceal any intention of benefiting militarily from the opening of such corridors.

Labouisse knew that the delegation headed by Gowon at Niamey had just rejected the securing of a relief corridor with neutral troops from other African countries, but he attributed this to the "Congo complex" of the Nigerians. While Gowon took pride in his own service in the UN force in the Congo, Labouisse wrote U Thant, the Nigerians feared any similar "occupation" of their country; they did not want foreign troops on Nigerian soil.

On a map, Gowon pointed out the corridors proposed, charging Ojukwu's alternatives were "unrealistic." He also showed Labouisse the areas held by Ojukwu's forces and those in Federal "liberated territory," stating that great need existed east and south of the "rebel-held territory." Gowon stressed his concern about the suffering of the people in these areas, whether of Ibos or other tribes.

His forces would be instructed to let relief vehicles with red cross markings, driven by international personnel, move, after inspection, through the lines and into rebel territory. Supplies would then be unloaded at some central point—Okigwe, for example—where they could be picked up by relief teams. Heavy trucks might have trouble because bridges had been blown or weakened by the retreating "rebels." Trucks of three to five tons would be best. He guaranteed absolute security from his troops and that no military advantage would be taken of this corridor. If he wished to invade, Gowon said, he had other routes.

Like others who would come to Lagos seeking to get relief started, Labouisse was impressed with the sincerity and goodwill of Gowon. He wondered, however, whether Gowon would be able to implement his approach all the way down to the field level. He reported to U Thant: "I have met others in the Government who do not seem to share his appreciation of the situation, who appear to be more hawkish and less openly sympathetic to humanitarian needs."

Labouisse asked the Nigerian position on flying in food and medicine, until land corridors could be opened. Gowon declared he could not allow such planes to go through as long as he was not satisfied they were flying relief supplies only. He had evidence, he said, that Ojukwu's agents reserved cargo space for arms in planes carrying uninspected relief supplies shipped by relief organizations. Planes were landing in an area, he told Labouisse, where he strongly suspected food would go first to feed rebel soldiers. While it was not possible to police the entire airspace of Nigeria, he could not allow this airspace to be violated. He had ordered military action against such violations. He admitted that the capability of the Nigerian Air Force for intercepting flights at night was limited and remarked to Labouisse: "I blink my eyes at the night flights."

Gowon told Labouisse he was himself a member of a large family and loved children. He said that, as a result of Ojukwu's actions, the weak and the children were those who suffered. He pointed to a picture in a magazine of an emaciated child, then showed Labouisse a newspaper picture of Colonel Ojukwu. "Look at him!" he exclaimed. "He's still as fat as ever."

August Lindt flew into Lagos the day after Labouisse. Lindt was a man of action who, for the moment, became an excuse for inaction.

When word had reached the ICRC that it had been named by the Nigerian government to coordinate all relief, headquarters had been briefly immobilized since Roger Gallopin, the director general, was away and no one would make any decision of importance until he returned a week later. Then its executives awaited the arrival of Lindt, the new high commissioner who was to be relief coordinator. After he departed for Lagos, they began waiting for him to negotiate agreement between the Nigerians and Biafrans.

Days slipped by, weeks, a month. To those in other relief agencies anxious to act and being pressed by governments to act only under the ICRC, the weeks seemed like years. The impression arose that the ICRC was incompetent. Labouisse wrote U Thant: "I think that the ICRC now does fully recognize the urgency and importance of the situation and is doing its best to meet it." Under Secretary of State Nicholas Katzenbach, questioned later whether there was a deliberate effort to get the ICRC to hold up on relief, said, "Trying to get the ICRC to delay is like taking coals to Newcastle."

Inside the ICRC, there were activist and legalistic factions. While Gallopin insisted on abiding by the legalities so as not to jeopardize the long-term mission of the Red Cross, vice-president Jacques Freymond urged maximum humanitarian action. Freymond, it would appear, was often a faction of one.

He had begun counseling Gallopin to bring in a second person to handle the Nigerian situation exclusively. He pointed out that the previous year, when both the Arab-Israeli and the Nigerian war had broken out at the same time, it had proved too much for one man to handle; the infrastructure of the ICRC was inadequate. A good man for Nigeria-Biafra, he suggested, would be the Swiss ambassador to Moscow, August Lindt. Freymond and Lindt had been friends since their service with the Red Cross during World War II. Freymond apparently sought to bring in someone as aggressive as himself to counterbalance the caution of Gallopin and others on the committee.

Lindt was a man of considerable experience, first as a journalist, then as a Red Cross official, then as United Nations high commissioner for refugees and chairman of UNICEF's Executive Board. Now, at sixty-two, he had no hesitation about his own abilities for taking on such an assignment. Indeed, all his experience until now had prepared him as well as anyone to find a way to get humanitarian relief moving—if that had been the mission given him.

On his way from Moscow to Lagos he stopped long enough in Geneva to be briefed. The blockade around Biafra was absolutely tight; the Nigerian government intended to keep it that way. The impression among ICRC officials was that Nigerian authorities would propose only those means of access not acceptable to the Biafrans. Some ministers in the Nigerian government felt the best policy to follow was "Let's finish this, once and for all."

ICRC officials had no thought of beginning relief without authorization from the Federal Military Government. All they could do was make the best possible use of the tolerated night flights from Fernando Po. But at this point there was only one plane, which could carry less than ten tons, and the estimated need in Biafra was 200 tons of food each day.

The ICRC had started building up stockpiles of nonperishable foods in Federal Nigeria as close to Biafra as possible: 1,500 tons at Enugu, 700 tons at Asaba/Agbor, and 1,000 tons at Calabar. These would serve as centers for distributing food to people coming under Federal control as Nigerian troops advanced, and when the collapse came, food and trucks would be in position to expand relief to those in areas now under Biafran control. Red Cross officials were developing twenty-two relief teams—ten as standby for the Biafran area when access became possible after mid-September.

If the ICRC officials did not entirely accept the counsel of the British and the State Department to stockpile relief supplies on the Biafran periphery, they were proceeding as if they did. Lord Hunt, just back from Lagos, was in Geneva when Lindt arrived. He and Lindt and Roger Gallopin had dinner at the Beau Rivage, one of the hotels along the edge of Lake Geneva in the center of the city. Lindt wanted to telephone General Gowon, but was told that you can't call a head of state at ten in the evening. Eager to get on with his task, Lindt called Dodan Barracks in Lagos anyway but could not get through to Gowon. He flew to Nigeria the following day.

Lindt had two objectives in Lagos: to press for a break, somehow, to gain access to Biafra and, meanwhile, to begin relief in areas already under Federal control. He did not have much time. By estimate of the Red Cross delegate in Biafra, deaths from starvation had risen from three thousand a day to six thousand, then eight thousand, then ten thousand. Other relief agencies would not wait much longer for the ICRC, however intense upon them the pressures from governments. The planes that German church relief agencies had acquired were beginning to arrive at São Tomé.

One excuse governments were making for not providing assistance was the lack of an on-the-spot survey of needs, of statistics on the numbers who needed to be fed, of estimates of quantities of food or kinds of medicine required. It was obvious the need was greater than all relief agencies combined could meet, yet foreign offices were insisting on a quantified assessment of the exact situation.

In New York, Heyward worked up a paper he called "Guestimates," and Labouisse gave Lindt a copy when they conferred in Lagos. Lindt provided the Red Cross estimates in return: the total population in Biafran territories, five to six million; in territories that had come under Federal control, four to five million. The ICRC assumed less than two million of these did not require emergency relief but only rehabilitation, so those in need of urgent relief assistance were estimated at seven to nine million. This was close to Heyward's estimate of nine million who could be reached and aided.

There was no way to carry out either a census or an accurate survey, of course. Battle lines kept shifting, leaving people on one side or the other; some were caught in combat zones, others hiding in the bush where they could not be reached; some were walking out of the enclave to their former farms, then walking back with food on their heads. Where they were, how many there were, what condition they were in, how or when they were to be reached could only be an educated guess, based on the experience of relief workers.

Lindt told Labouisse that the ICRC was assuming there would be no access to Biafra before September 15 but that on or around that time there would be access, one way or another.

When Gowon met with Lindt that day, he repeated the same proposals for a land corridor he had made to Labouisse, but agreed to one other—from Asaba. Asaba was across the Niger River from Onitsha, and the bridge had been blown; even if food could have been moved from there, it would then have been in an area heavily contested by Biafran and Nigerian forces.

It had been more than three weeks since Ojukwu had promised Jaggi and Kirkley a relief airstrip. The Red Cross had attempted negotiating about this in Lagos, but at the time the Nigerian government ordered its air force to "seek and destroy" all unauthorized aircraft. Lindt asked whether the FMG still insisted it did not want relief planes going into Uli, where arms shipments were landing, but would accept ICRC flights to a demilitarized, neutralized airfield, entirely under Red Cross control. Gowon stated that this was correct; such an airfield was still acceptable. Lindt got Gowon to agree that the April note tolerating night relief flights remained valid.

Gowon did not like the ICRC using Hank Warton's planes. When Lindt sought permission for one flight each night to service Red Cross medical personnel in Biafra, Gowon questioned how Lindt could be sure arms were not being put aboard the planes. Critical himself of the use of Warton's planes, Lindt said he would charter another aircraft, exclusively for Red Cross relief. Gowon agreed to this, but for only one flight each night.

Lindt informed Geneva of this renewed permission, and the ICRC immediately chartered a DC-6. Lindt sent Gowon a letter of understanding to firm up the permission. He intended, after the plane began flying once a night into Biafra, to try to get the authorization increased to two flights. Each would carry ten tons of food, something short of the 200 tons or more estimated as needed, but then Lindt had been on the job only one day.

Chapter 8

What were the British doing? Hugh Fraser and Michael Barnes, the government's severest critics on Biafra in Parliament, were getting clues. Fraser spoke of information that had reached him about tracked Saracen armored personnel carriers being shipped by the British to Nigeria and a big consignment of Saladin armored cars now waiting to go. He said, "In the name of humanity, it would be foolish to ship instruments of war which would convert corridors of mercy into avenues of massacre. . . . "

"I can assure the Right Honorable Gentleman," Commonwealth Secretary George Thomson responded for the government, " . . . it is not the case that there are large numbers of Saladins awaiting shipment to Nigeria, as he seemed to fear. . . . "

Michael Barnes got closer to it: " . . . It is quite clear, as it has been for some time, that there is a big buildup of arms and military equipment going on in the Federal side. It is justified by the Federal Government in the following terms, and I have also heard it justified by some honorable Members in the same way. The argument is that the quickest way to save starving Biafrans is for the remaining Biafran towns to be taken as quickly as possible by Federal troops so that the war can be won. Then, the argument goes, Oxfam, the International Red Cross and other relief can go in. A more sophisticated version of the argument is that the best way to get a land corridor from Enugu working is for it to be opened up by force so that relief can go through."

"Such an argument," Barnes went on, "totally underestimates the determination, rightly or wrongly, of the people remaining in the Biafran-held area to fight to the last man and the last bullet—and the death-toll if such a military solution were added to the colossal starvation figures. . . . "

But Fraser and Barnes and other M.P.s could not be sure. Military secrecy kept them from knowing about British arms shipments and the buildup of the Nigerian Army. Government officials in Britain had much tighter control over information than their counterparts in the U.S. and some other countries through the system of D-notices (Defense Notices) that warned editors against publishing news stories that would violate the Official Secrets Acts.

Also the men of the Foreign and Commonwealth offices were adroit at getting their favorite correspondents and editors to print what they wanted. As one London newspaper editor put it in his testimony at the Official Secrets Act trial after the war: "All we got was the old boy unofficial network all the time. Half of our time we live with a Government trying to persuade us not to publish something which we think we ought to. The other half of our time we spend resisting attempts by the Government to get us to print things we are not interested in."

So what the British were doing could not be known, by Parliament or the rest of the world. ICRC officials did not speak out about what the British, Americans, and Nigerians were saying to them. The director of relief of the ICRC, Charles Ammann, interviewed on the BBC some months later, remarked, "The British Government did not give us advice. They expressed the opinion that it was better to wait and put forward an overall program for all the victims, who were estimated at about six to eight million." He said that the British and American governments had some sort of guarantee from Lagos that a military victory was very close. The interviewer asked, "Did they in fact say that by letting a few thousand die now we will save millions?" Ammann replied, "Yes, millions . . . but even if they thought that would finish the war quicker, it was an opinion. . . . One can never predict the future. . . ."

Like other relief agency officials, Dick Heyward was distressed to the point of anguish by the delay. He communicated a number of times each day with Charles Egger, the other UNICEF deputy director, who had gone to Geneva to maintain close liaison with the Red Cross. One day, he cabled: "It seems to me that while the unblocking of the surface routes remains stalled, the airlift should be expanded, and quickly. Lagos refusal to give permission for more than one flight per day while so many children are starving, is intolerable. I think that ICRC, after informing Lagos, should send more flights, not neglecting Federally-held territories such as Calabar. . . . If ICRC has not the strength to act directly, could they not act through the churches, lending them planes, giving them supplies, so that only the operating expenses had to be paid. . . ."

The State Department was still refusing UNICEF the second shipment of children's food, and there was no response to the request for cargo helicopters that, it turned out, Labouisse had made before leaving Geneva. UNICEF began exploring the possibility of hiring helicopters commercially.

At a congressional hearing, Joseph Palmer responded to a question about roads in Nigeria not being usable during the rainy season: "No, the road coming down from the north—there are difficulties in moving it—but it can be moved. This has not been the problem. So far as land movement is concerned, it has been the position taken by the Biafran government in refusing to facilitate the reception of the food and movement of it through the lines, the Federal Government has made clear its willingness to move in this direction. The Red Cross, I believe, accepts this as being a genuine offer and has been trying to persuade the Biafrans to cooperate from their side to receive it. There are great limitations in movement by air."

In private, however, Palmer was deeply troubled. Though committed to Nigerian unity, he had many Ibo friends from his ambassadorial days and heard from them regularly by letter. One U.S. official, working closely with Palmer, quoted him as saying: "If I could think of some way of saving Nigeria and saving the Ibos, I would do it."

To try to get around the stranglehold Palmer and the Africa bureau held on relief within the U.S. government, UNICEF enlisted the aid of Vice-President Hubert Humphrey's office. Humphrey was only a few weeks away from the Democratic National Convention and running hard to assure his nomination for the presidency, but the involvement of his staff opened the possibility of getting Hercules cargo planes from the United States without the Africa bureau being able to block the request.

Heyward proposed this possibility to the ICRC. The idea was to get assurance, first through the White House, for provision of government cargo planes, then to inform both sides of the plan to proceed with an airlift. Heyward reasoned that once major governments had provided aircraft capacity, the Nigerians and Biafrans would have to allow the plan to proceed. He told Egger to warn the ICRC that public frustration and anger were mounting rapidly in the United States—as in Europe—and in the case of other relief agencies it was directed at the ICRC and UNICEF for their inaction. He advised Egger to inform Red Cross officials that the voluntary relief agencies were awaiting Lindt's return from Nigeria; if this did not bring action, they were ready to bypass the ICRC.

Roger Gallopin expressed interest but wanted to take no action until Lindt returned. He pointed out that the ICRC, given the principles upon which it operated, would have to make such a request simultaneously to a number of governments, not just to the U.S., and would have to consider very carefully the timing of its approach to the "Host Government"—the

Nigerian government. Gallopin was reluctant to make such a request to the United States without informing the Nigerians at the same time.

A day or two later, Gallopin decided that the ICRC had excellent relations with government missions in Geneva and would therefore naturally follow normal diplomatic channels in submitting such a request, rather than the route Heyward had now opened. In fact, the Red Cross had already made several informal approaches for cargo aircraft to various governments through their missions in Geneva—including the American mission—with no positive results.

It was now early August 1968. More than three months had gone by since the Red Cross's "SOS Biafra." Heyward had begun getting confirmation of the report which had angered church relief officials when Father Fintan Kilbride had read it to them from a London newspaper at the meeting a few days before—the report that the ICRC had set a confidential date in September for the start of full-scale relief. Heyward cabled Egger: "Why not have carriers with food positioned in international waters? We conclude collapse will bring much larger problem relief protection population. [A UNICEF official] reports Lagos plan send out teams to investigate and report back mid-August and Lagos ICRC plan to have relief working by mid-September. Trust Lindt's return will produce quite different approach, but if not wonder if UNICEF should act separately for the sake of the problem, its reputation and Labouisse?"

Labouisse decided to go out to South-East Nigeria and survey conditions himself. Nigerian officials had not traveled into the countryside to find out what was happening, so in Lagos there was little or no firsthand information about the actual situation in areas in the East that had come under Federal control.

Labouisse flew to Calabar and encountered Edward Marks of the Agency for International Development. It was, of course, AID staff in the Lagos embassy that had been reporting back to Washington that there was "plenty of food in the area," holding up UNICEF's second request for children's food. Marks, assigned to the U.S. Embassy in London, had been summoned back from vacation and sent to make an independent assessment of relief needs in Nigeria. Having been told reassuring things in Lagos, like Labouisse he had now come to see for himself conditions in the reconquered areas.

Together they conferred with Red Cross officials. The doctor in charge of that area expressed concern that too much attention was being given to the opening of relief corridors into Biafra while not enough was being done to organize effective relief for those who could be helped without difficulty. Refugees in the area, estimated at more than two hundred thousand, were mostly of the Ibibio and Annang tribes who lived north of there. Caught between the combat lines that seesawed back and forth in the area, villages and crops destroyed, most were left without anything—even clothes. Others had retreated into the bush to get away from the troops, probably starving in areas difficult to reach.

The Red Cross doctor estimated those who could be aided, in all areas that had come under Federal control, at some seven hundred fifty thousand. Food that could be purchased locally could not exceed 20,000 tons, he estimated, while the need for such foods as rice, garri, or beans was 200 tons each week. The worst cases of starving children required special formula food and medicines, as well as medical care.

Most supplies sent from Lagos had lacked proper documentation, so the Nigerian Army had claimed the supplies as their own. Getting supplies to this area from Calabar would be difficult, as the Cross River, before flowing into the sea, empties into a large lagoon at Calabar. (Labouisse had just come across the lagoon by ferry, and the trip had taken two-and-a-half hours.) There were only two ferries, of different sizes, but they could not be used exclusively for relief as they were needed by the people in the area. Also, there were only three trucks, and the fuel supply was poor.

Labouisse and Marks traveled about the area separately, but they saw many of the same sights. Labouisse came upon one makeshift village (made of palm leaves) of five thousand refugees, mostly children and elderly, with few males. Louis Gendron, a UNICEF official accompanying Labouisse, kept notes on what they encountered. "All were in the very last stages of starvation. Children and elders were prostrated and crouched on the earth—ready to die." A mother called upon a Catholic missionary to baptize her child, who was dying, "and in one hut which had only a roof but no walls there was the desiccated body of a child possibly two years old. Next to him, but not protected by the roof while the rain started falling, was another boy of the same age, also crouched on the ground entirely naked—probably alive, but not for long, who did not even stir when the rain started."

Gendron wrote: "Between the huts, in fact in the middle of the path, were numerous graves—just a little mound of earth which had not even been hardened by the rain and which was a good indication of the number of deaths during the preceding night or early part of the morning. We were told that there were ten or fifteen deaths every day, and we have sufficient evidence to believe that this figure is probably not exaggerated."

From there they went to Ikot Ekpene, a major town, where the prison was being used to house a thousand people "mostly children, out of whom four hundred receive—*in principle*—every day, one bowl of rice, plus a little fish which comes partly from the army, partly from the Red Cross and which they started receiving about two weeks before our visit."

Labouisse and Gendron arrived at the prison housing the refugees at the time of food distribution: "There was a long line of children and mothers, most of them stark naked and all of them in a terrible condition of starvation. Although there were not so many apparent cases of kwashiorkor, and there was a lot of activity among them, kicking and fighting for the food—which showed they were not at the desperate point which we had seen in the others in other places. However, the best comparison which could be given to this line of walking skeletons comes from the photographs of the concentration camps of the last war. The pittance they received was the usual cup of food which most of them ate while walking back to their barracks. . . ."

They were experienced relief officials but these were the worst conditions they had ever seen. They asked about the apathetic attitude of the parents toward the death of their children and were told that ordinarily people in that area would be extremely affected by the death of a child (unlike those in places where child mortality customarily runs high), but the present apathy of the refugees was caused by their own physical condition.

They saw a reassuring sight, however—the effects of three weeks' proper care on sixty-two orphans, " . . . now again nice and cute little youngsters with big smiles who were, although not yet chubby, in definitely good condition. Comparing these with the ghastly state of the children remaining in Ikot Ekpene prison, it was evident that with proper food many lives could be saved."

Back in Lagos, Labouisse described to various government ministers what he had seen, not in Biafra but in their own Nigerian-controlled areas. The ministers expressed disbelief and said they did not have information about such conditions. "Well, I've just come from there," he told the chairman of the National Rehabilitation Commission, who responded: "Maybe I should go out there and see for myself." Labouisse said, acerbically, "Yes. Why don't you do that."

When Marks returned to Lagos, he cabled his report to Washington, the first survey of conditions the State Department would receive from the field. State was just then putting out its weekly Disaster Memo to relief agencies, estimating the rate of deaths at two hundred to four hundred a day. "Reports of 6,000 deaths a day greatly exaggerated," it said.

. . .

The State Department, or rather its Bureau of African Affairs, minimized the numbers dying as it was coming under mounting pressure to act. Like foreign offices in other countries, it was being pressed by citizens, organizations, newspapers, congressmen, and other government officials to do something. Mail about starvation in Biafra was coming into State at twice the volume of that being received about the war in Vietnam.

Nicholas Katzenbach pressed Palmer and his bureau repeatedly for some solution to the problem. The response was always the same: We hate to see all those people die, but there's nothing we can do without approval of the government in Lagos. First, it would be unthinkable to violate the territorial sovereignty of Nigeria. Second, to push too hard or too far will result in less aid getting in rather than more; Gowon calls the tune, therefore wooing Gowon and not offending Gowon is the only way to get aid to Biafra.

The undersecretary and his staff argued in return that since it was Britain's position that was at stake in Nigeria, this gave the U.S. freedom to disregard the feelings of Lagos. It would not really matter if the United States was unwanted and rejected in Nigeria for ten years after the war.

Confronted with these pressures, the Africa bureau finally responded to the question ICRC officials had raised with Palmer the week before in Geneva, granting the Red Cross "drawing rights" against a reserve fund of $1 million. This was nothing like the financing needed if the ICRC were actually to fulfill "the world's mandate," but there was no reason to expect the ICRC really to undertake the kind of relief operation people were now calling for and awaiting.

One candidate for the presidency, for example, warned of "the makings of one of the most tragic events in human history." Richard Nixon stated: ". . . The great humanitarian traditions of the American people dictate that its government speak out against this senseless tragedy—and act to prevent the destruction of a whole people by starvation." He went on to urge: "President Johnson should leave no diplomatic or economic tool unused in his efforts to break the log-jam—and to help rescue this people from the agony of death by starvation. . . ."

By the end of July, television camera crews had gotten into Biafra and news programs began showing films of children starving; the next day, relief agencies were overwhelmed with telephone calls from people wanting to know what could be done. All through Europe and North America the sight of innocent children dying in a cruel and senseless way was causing a mounting wave of emotion and indignation. Groups organized; the most political called itself the American Committee to Keep Biafra Alive. Fund-raising began across America and Western Europe, through churches, on street corners, in supermarkets.

In the Netherlands, an extraordinary fund appeal revealed the depths of feeling in a country which had suffered through a grave famine during the "hunger winter" at the end of World War II. Dutch television showed a one-hour program on conditions in Biafra; Dr. Herman Middelkoop and his wife flew home from Queen Elizabeth Hospital in Biafra to tell their countrymen what was happening. Then the television went off the air for an hour while postal and telegraph offices remained open (this was at ten o'clock at night); people all over Holland went out to mail or telegraph in their contributions for food for Biafra.

Outside the United Nations in New York, thousands walked in a twenty-four-hour procession, carrying candles at night, to protest the starvation. New York City policemen were busier than usual that year with marches and riots, and one remarked about their duty at the vigil: "This is the first demonstration we've ever been in sympathy with."

Numerous correspondents flew into Biafra. One of them, Lloyd Garrison of the *New York Times* (who had been expelled from Nigeria the year before), reported tragic conversations with priests: "I don't know, I don't know. I'm fast losing faith in humanity. I don't know how the Lord can permit this." Those who traveled into the enclave were struck by the fact that Biafrans laughed as always; they soon learned that beneath this seeming gaiety, each Biafran had already accepted his own death. Garrison quoted one: "For every Nigerian our soldiers kill, they will kill ten of us. But then we know what happens, even if we don't fight back. So why not fight, if you are going to die anyway?"

George McGovern, joined by fifteen other senators, sent a letter to Lyndon Johnson urging him to support a United Nations or private airlift for supplies. Senator Eugene McCarthy called upon the president to ask for "a mandatory relief airlift of mercy to Biafra." Vice-President Humphrey issued a statement saying it was "morally intolerable to have innocent children starving," and another a few days later: "It is up to the International Committee of the Red Cross to take prompt, active, risk-taking initiatives. It can tell governments what should be done in Biafra to end the suffering and starvation. *This should be done now.* Every day of further delay means the death of thousands of innocent persons, especially children."

Chapter 9

August Lindt flew to the island of Fernando Po, on his way to Biafra. Heinrich Jaggi, returning from a brief trip to Geneva, joined him there, and they planned to fly into Biafra on the newly chartered DC-6. To land at Uli airfield in Biafra they needed the radio-transmitting frequencies and a secret code word. For Hank Warton and his pilots, flying was a business; they were not eager for competition. So the first flight of the new Red Cross plane had to be delayed a few days until a Biafran official came out with the code word.

It was the last day of July when Jaggi and Lindt arrived in Biafra, and they met with Ojukwu the following day. Ojukwu understood the relief situation all too well. He had just commented to a group of foreign correspondents: "It is to be hoped that the International Red Cross will not lend itself to the Anglo-Nigerian political maneuvers. Up till now, and before the British Government's intervention, the Red Cross have been dealing with us without having to seek the approval of Lagos. In this way, they have brought us a lot of relief supplies. They have a representative here in Biafra who is in a position to advise them best. We sincerely believe that the universally respected and trusted international humanitarian organization will live up to its tradition in spite of the pressures of international politics."

Lindt asked Ojukwu whether he could give the ICRC an "exclusive" airfield for relief planes only, and when. Yes, Ojukwu told him, in two or three weeks. The Biafrans were widening a stretch of highway near Uturu and Obilagu, constructing another airstrip in the same way they had built the one between the villages of Uli and Ihiala. Lindt began thinking he had the possibility for a breakthrough. The Nigerians had been refusing the ICRC permission to fly into the only airfield in Biafra, as arms planes were landing there; it would be different, they said, if the Red Cross had its own airport, exclusively for relief. He had asked Gowon whether this was still the case and been assured it was. He then double-checked this with the Nigerian Ministry of External Affairs.

Back on Fernando Po, Lindt encountered a Canadian pilot, originally Danish, named Axel Duch. The head of the Norwegian church relief agency, Pastor Elias Berge, had managed to get a donation of 3,000 tons of stockfish, a food customarily imported and eaten by the Biafrans in peacetime. Berge had traveled to Fernando Po, then returned to Scandinavia, recommending that the church relief agencies start flying the stockfish in from that offshore island. Pastor Viggo Mollerup, head of the Danish church relief agency, had now sent Duch to try to start an airlift. He had arrived in a plane called the "Angel of Mercy."

The ICRC did not approve of the church agencies starting their own airlift, Lindt told Duch, nor did it want to join with them in doing so. He could not reveal to Duch the code signals needed to fly into Uli, he felt, without jeopardizing his relations with the Biafrans. However, Lindt did give Duch a Red Cross passport and permission to go into Biafra in the ICRC plane so that the pilot might seek authorization himself from the Biafrans.

Then came an incident that was to sour relations further between the church relief agencies and the Red Cross. The Biafrans were anxious not to do anything that would interfere with the start of the Red Cross airlift into the new airfield, and Jaggi told them the ICRC did not favor a church agency airlift. Godwin Onyegbula, the Biafran foreign minister, told Duch the Biafrans did not want anything to do with the Angel of Mercy, as they believed the operator from whom it was chartered had hijacked one of their planes.

Onyegbula told Jaggi, "You got the man in here, you get him out," but Jaggi said Duch did not want to go. A short time later, as Duch was talking with some relief agency representatives, he was arrested. The Biafrans explained that Jaggi did not think his Red Cross passport could be legitimate since Duch was not an ICRC employee. Twenty-four hours later, he was deported. It was the beginning of a total break between the church relief agencies and the ICRC.

"If I understand correctly, Mr. Ambassador, the assistance of the International Committee of the Red Cross depends then on Nigeria! You tell us the agreement of the two sides is indispensable. . . ." Lindt was back in Geneva and facing for the first time the full wrath of the church and other relief agencies. "You tell us, the assistance of other voluntary agencies endangers the diplomatic negotiations of the ICRC. What does that mean?" one churchman went on. "Indeed, I have a sense of frustration. Where do we go from here on humanitarian problems? Indeed, will the nations of the world stand passively by and witness the killing of millions of human beings? What becomes of international morality? What is the responsibility of the churches? Are we not all descendants of the human community? How long are you going to continue this assistance that doesn't arrive and will never arrive? What are you going to do, Mr. Ambassador? Are you satisfied with this 'relief'? In our world of today, what are we doing? What are you doing? You? . . . "

The anger had been mounting in Europe for weeks, with the ICRC coming to be seen as the principal obstacle to getting food moving to the children starving in Biafra. The writers Günter Grass and Max Frisch, for example, traveled to Geneva with the editor of the German literary and political weekly *Die Zeit* and concluded that "at present the ICRC is more active in the diplomatic than the humanitarian field." The leaders of the main West German political parties and others joined them in an appeal: " . . . The latest initiative of Ambassador Lindt has failed. So far, church organizations, such as Caritas, have rendered more effective assistance. The ICRC finds its hands tied by Conventions which render assistance in case of war only if it is a case of war between sovereign states. . . . "

The appeal in *Die Zeit*, which was widely reprinted in other European newspapers, went on: "We call upon the world to support the following appeal: the ICRC should uncompromisingly interpret Article 3 of the Fourth Geneva Convention in the spirit of Henry Dunant and his humanitarian idea, which implies that such humanitarian aid shall be enforced in the face of resistance."

The future existence of the ICRC was threatened. During a highly emotional meeting held the day after he got back from Nigeria and Biafra, a representative of Oxfam warned Lindt: "Mr. Ambassador, do you know that the patience of the world is exhausted? I fear that Mr. Lindt has a bad time ahead of him. We are told this is not the moment to rush, not to compromise especially on this or that, or again on this thing or that thing. I tell you, Mr. Ambassador, your mission and that of the ICRC have been defeated by political maneuvers, you have been beaten on your own ground. One of these days it's going to be necessary to take an account and balance up what you have accomplished. Then it will be necessary to go to the United Nations. How much longer must we wait, Mr. Ambassador?"

Lindt responded, "It is necessary to wait a week. If the results are good, we will move ahead quickly. If the results are negative, then it will be necessary to consider realistic alternatives."

Another relief agency official, from Germany, said to Lindt, "Our planes have been refused authorization to fly. What is it necessary to do? To wait? Don't forget, German public opinion is waiting also. Considering that, we would like to know if we have here, and for the first time, *a total defeat of the International Red Cross.* . . . I ask you, what should we tell the public about this failure?"

"We are doing all that we can," Lindt told him. He did not feel he could reveal his negotiations thus far and only mentioned the possibility of a neutralized airfield for relief. He was challenged by one of the Swedish relief officials: "What have we prepared for the future? It is necessary for us to have plans right now. Are you considering public opinion? For us, we must take it into account. Accordingly, what position does the ICRC take? Are we prepared from now on to make a declaration: we have all the time in the world? For I am very much afraid that we are going to be forced to do something under the pressure of public opinion. Has the ICRC decided—yes or no—to undertake a massive campaign from now on?"

Lindt replied, "An airfield is being constructed, somewhere in Biafra, I cannot tell you where. Action is also paralyzed by logistics problems which are very complicated. I am very much aware there is propaganda being carried on."

A quiet drama was taking place that would change the whole equation and increase the pressures on Lindt and the ICRC even more. A small, tired-looking, fifty-nine-year-old commercial pilot of the Swedish air cargo company Transair, returning from a long trip with a group of Swedish and Norwegian businessmen, found he was scheduled to fly out the next day to pick up a shipment of food and medicine from German Catholic Caritas and take it as far as an island off the coast of Africa. From there, pilots flying for Caritas would transport it the last leg into Biafra.

Count Carl Gustaf von Rosen had vowed, after two years of flying for the United Nations in the Congo, never again to get mixed up in the troubles of the new African nations. When he was a young man, he had flown medicine and food to the guerrillas still holding out against Italian troops in western Ethiopia. In appreciation of that, Emperor Haile Selassie later gave him a coffee plantation; he also asked von Rosen to organize the Ethiopian Air Force. When the Russians invaded Finland, von Rosen— a Swede—flew with the Finns. He was in Holland, attempting to bring out his first wife who was Dutch, when the Nazis invaded; he managed to elude German antiaircraft fire and fly his plane across the Channel, only to have to avoid British antiaircraft fire before landing in England. He flew medicines into Warsaw in May 1945. But now he was approaching retirement age, and no longer inclined to go looking for adventure.

Leaving Malmö in a DC-7, von Rosen picked up the Caritas shipment in Frankfurt, then flew across the Sahara, landing at São Tomé early Sunday morning, August 11, 1968. Father Anthony Byrne and the Portuguese governor and others immediately surrounded von Rosen and his crew, beseeching them not to unload their cargo but to fly it straight into Biafra. Nigeria had acquired radar-controlled antiaircraft, and Warton's pilots declared the situation had become too dangerous. Some had returned home and others refused to fly, demanding higher pay.

Von Rosen explained that he and his crew could not take such an action on their own; the plane did not belong to them. Besides, the insurance would not cover either the plane or the crew if they were to fly into a war zone. What if they were shot down, as seemed entirely possible? They could not be so irresponsible to their wives and children.

Von Rosen agreed to go with Father Byrne to the governor's house. There, as they talked, the full dimensions of the situation began to come home to him. He then went up in a Caritas plane with the chief pilot who, at Byrne's insistence, tested out the air defenses. The pilot was very nervous. He tried to make radio contact with the Red Cross plane he thought should be flying from Fernando Po but got no reply; he concluded that the ICRC fliers were equally unwilling to risk the antiaircraft fire. (In fact, Lindt had suspended the daily ICRC flight so as not to jeopardize his negotiations for the neutralized Red Cross airstrip.)

Von Rosen could not sleep that night. If pilots were called upon to bomb villages and kill children, he thought, they would take even greater risks and be decorated for doing so. He began to feel that if he and his crew turned back, they would never again be able to face their wives and children. Thinking about the way pilots evaded radar in wartime by flying at treetop level, he awakened his navigator. They talked of the possibilities of breaking the blockade. He soon found that his crew members were with him, ready to take the chance.

A problem arose, the same one Lindt and Jaggi had encountered two weeks before: the chief pilot flying for Hank Warton would not turn over the code word needed for landing at Uli Airport—he regarded it as a trade secret. This meant that von Rosen and his crew would have to fly in daylight. There was practically no chance of landing at night, unexpected, without being shot down by Biafran antiaircraft fire.

They made their preparations, taking off at 4:18 in the afternoon, in time to arrive at Uli a half-hour before nightfall. (Near the equator the sun sets close to 6:00 P.M. and rises at about 6:00 A.M.) Flying just above the ocean, they approached the coastline within an hour. Their apprehensions grew. They swept in low over the Niger Delta, staying as close to the ground as possible, passing over villages, with Port Harcourt visible in the distance on their right. As von Rosen described the scene, except for some Nigerian military posts the whole area appeared dead. They could make out corpses between the houses. The only living things were vultures.

Nigerian defenses did not spot them but, at that speed and altitude, could not have hit them anyway. On schedule, right where they expected to find it, they came upon the airstrip, between the palm trees. Von Rosen climbed abruptly, so Biafran gunners could see it was not an enemy plane but the kind Caritas used for transporting relief supplies.

Upon landing, the Swedish crew members were surrounded by cheering, crying people. At their head was Father Desmond McGlade, in charge of relief at the field. He told von Rosen they had not seen a plane for a week and had become convinced they had been abandoned by the world. As von Rosen recounts the story, the plane's arrival signified more to those waiting than the nine tons of food and medicine he and his crew had flown in.

It was decided to send the plane back to São Tomé for another load, with the second pilot flying it one way, the third pilot back, so all three would get the experience necessary for an airlift.

Von Rosen was driven through the darkness to meet Ojukwu. They talked at length, von Rosen coming to understand what was happening in and to Biafra, what was needed to help the civilian population survive. Greatly impressed by Ojukwu, he left at two o'clock in the morning; to fly back to São Tomé it was necessary to be clear of the coast before daybreak. At the airfield he gave a lift out of Biafra to a journalist and three church relief representatives who had been stranded. The journalist was Lloyd Garrison of the *New York Times* and one of the churchmen was the Reverend Edward Johnson of the Presbyterian Church of Canada.

While officials on São Tomé sought to persuade them to stay on, von Rosen and his crew felt they had to return to Sweden, make a detailed report, then organize an airlift as quickly as possible. Taking Garrison and Johnson with them, they arrived at Malmö, weary and dirty, after midnight on August 13. Garrison telephoned the *Times* about how the Swedish pilot had broken the blockade, opening a new route into stricken Biafra.

That evening Colonel Ojukwu signed an agreement with Harry Jaggi, turning the airfield at Obilagu over to the ICRC exclusively for relief flights. The understanding even permitted Nigerian inspection at the neutralized airstrip, as well as on the island of Fernando Po. Next morning, from Geneva, Lindt cabled Gowon requesting authorization for flights into the Red Cross airstrip. Then Lindt went to meet with representatives of national Red Cross societies.

They were as angry with the ICRC as private relief agency officials had been the day before. Now, however, Lindt told them more about the possibility of an airlift: "The best solution would consist of internationalizing this airlift under the exclusive control of the ICRC. There is in Biafra an airfield, but it is not yet in operational condition; one of the parties has given its agreement. The other has not yet replied. If the airlift is established, we would be able to achieve sixteen flights daily, which should be the equivalent of two hundred to three hundred tons a day. But even this amount would be largely insufficient. . . ."

More promises of negotiations by the ICRC were not good enough, however. Even though the representatives of the national societies appreciated the ICRC's concern to act "legally," they were feeling great pressure in their own countries from people who did not understand that their national Red Cross was not the same as the International Committee. In the minds of most there is only one Red Cross; officials of the national societies knew their organizations were being gravely damaged in the public's mind by inaction; confidence in them might be undermined for years to come. According to one report, the Swedes made very clear what would happen if the ICRC did not act, and act soon: "We will break with you! This will be the end of the Red Cross."

With words such as these echoing in his ears, Lindt met that afternoon with the international press corps in Geneva. The correspondents were no less hostile, though professionally more restrained: "One has the impression that the Red Cross has not moved very far. What you have said here is not very different from what Mr. Gallopin said here two weeks ago. You have arrived much too late in Biafra!"

Lindt could only reply that he thought for the first time there was a possibility of achieving concrete results.

Another correspondent exclaimed: "Your mission to Nigeria and Biafra is blocked, as far as any concrete measure is concerned. You have not brought anything back with you to Geneva. You have nothing new to report since your trip there." It was a difficult time to face the press on behalf of the Red Cross.

Lindt gave the correspondents an evaluation of the situation and told them of some of the scenes he had witnessed: "In this camp the young children were in very bad shape—it's one of the worst camps I saw in my life, and it might be, I do not exclude it's the worst one. Three children were dying a day. And from what I saw and from what I heard, this figure might have already increased by now—it might have doubled, it might have been tripled."

He told them of the condition of the people of Biafra: " . . . They still have cassava and yams. A yam crop will start, I think, this week, and it looks good. For the people in the best years, they have reserves and they can stand it for a certain time. But the children, especially the young ones just weaned from the breast of the mother, should have protein. . . ."

Lindt described the effects of protein deprivation: "Almost all the young children between one and a half and four years develop kwashiorkor and that . . . is true in the areas under control of the Federal troops. But kwashiorkor is now slowly gaining ground also in the older age groups. It's very difficult to say how many are the needy in Biafra, because it depends on the estimate of the total figures, but one thing is certain, that amongst the children kwashiorkor is increasing in a geometrical progression. I have no doubt that . . . there are millions of children and women and old people who are desperately in need of aid. Priority: protein!"

Lindt estimated the numbers in need in Biafra and the Federal areas at somewhere between four and seven million, commenting: "It's one of the greatest relief tasks which is facing our generation."

Lindt had been a journalist before becoming a diplomat; he knew how to hold a good press conference. But he was leading from a position of weakness, and, at the points where the ICRC was most vulnerable, he stated a shaky case with added vigor. He told the correspondents the ICRC had plans under way to build up stockpiles of food at Enugu and Calabar and to position trucks at Enugu. He described four ways of doing this: by chartered plane (only one was in use); by rail, "but the rail doesn't reach anymore Enugu . . . and at the moment is transported into Enugu by lorries"; from Lagos "by lorries—it's a terrible detour through the North—700 miles"; and to "buy local food in the North—surplus food." Though none of these was yet working in an effective way, he spoke forcefully, making it all sound quite impressive. He mentioned nothing, of course, about this being the plan the British had been urging the ICRC to prepare for September 15.

Finally, Lindt spoke of the "one thing I would describe as a bit more advanced than the others—that is, the question of an air corridor." He filled in the reporters on the background of the new development: "The Federal Government of Nigeria has said several times that the question of an air corridor would be more easily solved if there existed on Biafran territory an airport, even improvised, but completely and entirely under the control of the International Committee. That is to say, neutralized— in the absolute sense of the word: the direction of the airport, the air tower, all the controls in the hands of people directly responsible to the International Committee of the Red Cross. . . . "

This was now a reality: "Not long ago, Biafran authorities decided to place at the disposal of the International Committee of the Red Cross an airstrip. Red Cross personnel already in Biafra have taken possession of this airstrip. It is not yet operational; it is necessary to equip it. It is necessary for the Federal Government of Nigeria to affirm this under- standing immediately, as it is obvious that this collaboration must be as- sured in order for daylight flights to take place regularly. Many questions of details must be considered. At this time, the Federal Government of Nigeria is examining the question. . . ."

Someone in the rear of the room began to ask a question. The tele- vision cameras swung around to catch a dramatic confrontation. It was not a journalist but the Reverend Edward Johnson, who said in his flat, Canadian voice: "Mr. Commissioner, I have been in Biafra until two o'clock yesterday morning; left there by Swedish aircraft, which was the first one to break the blockade for four days. No other planes came in since Friday night. But this Transair Sweden plane under Count von Rosen, as cap- tain, made two flights, in and out, one in daylight and one at night, and these people feel that they can continue to make these flights and hope that they may be able to do so. They took in that night twenty tons of supplies. I would like to ask, sir, if you would encourage responsible groups, such as this, during this time, before negotiations can be worked out, to try to take in what supplies they can take in—and which they have the courage to take in at this time."

Earlier that day, to the national Red Cross societies, Lindt had char- acterized news of the "breaking of the blockade" as a "romantic adven- ture" that could carry in only "symbolic relief." Now, to the press, he spoke more moderately: "I would like to say this, that at this moment where for the first time the possibility of relevant imports into Biafra has become actual, I think that the other things, however courageous the people are, are not very meaningful."

A reporter asked: if "the ICRC is incapable of undertaking any action in Biafra or Nigeria" because of legal considerations, would it "envisage withdrawing in favor of some organization that is not itself limited by these legal considerations?"

Lindt responded, "We have no intention of withdrawing. You have said something that is not true, of not being able to act in Nigeria."

But he was questioned further: "I just wanted to know, has the Red

Cross prepared for any action if the answer from Lagos happens to be no?"

"We are ready at short notice," Lindt replied.

After the press conference, he talked with the Nigerian ambassador in Geneva, Sule Kolo, and the Nigerian minister of transport, who had been present during the press conference. They gave Lindt the impression that their government would agree to the ICRC flying into the new airstrip. But next morning the formal response came from Lagos. The answer: No.

Pastor Viggo Mollerup had also been at Lindt's press conference and the next day flew to Sweden in search of Count von Rosen. Despite Axel Duch's bad experience in Biafra, Pastor Mollerup had not given up on the idea of an airlift. He and von Rosen agreed to organize a humanitarian airlift—an operation they called "Nordchurchaid." It would be based on the church relief agencies of Sweden, Denmark, Norway, and Finland, in collaboration with the planes of the German church agencies already on São Tomé.

They planned fourteen flights every twenty-four hours and set about chartering cargo planes in Norway and Denmark, in addition to von Rosen's Transair in Sweden. Within days, the first Swedish plane was on its way to São Tomé, flown by a pilot who had broken the blockade with von Rosen. They assumed they would only have to carry on for a few months: the United Nations would surely take over once the General Assembly convened in September.

Von Rosen was encouraged by Swedish prime minister Tage Erlander. It happened that representatives of the Scandinavian Red Cross societies were meeting in Stockholm; they urged von Rosen to go to Geneva, to confer with August Lindt.

Von Rosen and Mollerup arrived in Geneva, skeptical of the ICRC and not predisposed to get along with Lindt. Lindt insisted on meeting only with von Rosen; they had a bad session. Von Rosen and Mollerup decided, however, that they were going to have to get along with Lindt, so the Swedish pilot met with him again that evening. Lindt spelled out his plan for a Red Cross airlift. He did not much like the idea of the church relief agencies organizing one of their own, but finally came around to expressing the opinion that it might be wisest "not to put all the eggs in one basket"—a statement that would prove prophetic the following year.

Returning white-faced from the meeting with Lindt, von Rosen said his lips were sealed: "I have given my word," he told Mollerup. What Lindt had confided to him were the details of Operation INALWA, his plan to start flying a Red Cross airlift into the demilitarized airstrip at Obilagu—even without the authorization of the Nigerian government. He would have five aircraft, he said, and on the first day he would be in the lead plane as all five flew in daylight into Biafra.

Von Rosen exclaimed: "Why, you're a madman! You do that, and they'll shoot you down!"

Chapter 10

The decision to fly food into Biafra without Nigerian authorization was the most difficult ICRC officials had ever had to take. They feared jeopardizing the long-term mission of the Red Cross if they violated the territory of a sovereign nation. British suggestions that they hold up relief until after the collapse of Biafra in mid-September offered a way out. At the same time they were moved by the reports of people dying, as the toll rose from eight thousand to ten thousand a day. Also, the pressures mounting in Europe became overwhelming: the ICRC would be equally damaged if it failed to begin humanitarian relief.

They could no longer acquiesce in inaction. When the Nigerians said no to the neutralized airstrip, the ICRC gave Lindt approval for his plan to start an airlift without FMG authorization. But the ICRC made its announcement with characteristic caution and secretiveness.

Shocked perhaps by its own unthinkable decision, the committee released a statement obscured in elliptical phrases. There in the third paragraph was the key sentence: "Considering the increasing urgency, the ICRC, in close cooperation with national Red Cross societies and other relief organizations, will nevertheless assume responsibility for taking every possible step to deliver the most urgently required relief supplies to the famished population."

Governments knew what this diplomatic language meant; they had their own lines into the ICRC deliberations. For example, Joseph Palmer's deputy, C. Robert Moore, was in Geneva that week in the company of the vice-president of the American Red Cross, participating in meetings with the ICRC, national Red Cross societies, and other relief agencies. Other governments were equally informed, either directly or indirectly, of the ICRC's decision and plans. Only the public remained unaware that the Red Cross had decided to fly food into Biafra without FMG permission.

Certainly the meaning of the diplomatic phrase, buried in the obscure statement, was not lost on the Nigerians. The next day a major newspaper in Lagos reported, under the headline "RED CROSS TO DEFY GOVERNMENT ": "The ICRC said yesterday it would 'assume responsibility' for taking every possible step to deliver the most urgently required relief supplies to the rebels. . . . " The Red Cross had alerted those who were out to block its humanitarian efforts while keeping its intentions concealed from the public, who would have mounted pressures upon their government to support its neutral airlift.

The day the ICRC made its muffled pronouncement, Harry Jaggi journeyed to Obilagu and found the airfield completed, ahead of schedule. Advisers to the ICRC from the Swiss Air Force rushed to completion their report on how the airlift should be organized.

During those busy days, Lindt received a personal letter from General Gowon, making clear that the airstrip proposal was unacceptable but expressing his government's thanks for the ICRC's assistance to date. Lindt took this as Gowon's way of suggesting that the negative decision had not been his own.

Lindt still regarded the April letter allowing the Red Cross to fly at its own risk—which he had gotten Gowon to reaffirm during their conversation a few weeks before—as a legal basis for relief flights. He began again, in fact, the one flight from Fernando Po into Biafra each night that he had suspended the week before. Governments, however, clearly did not regard the April 10 note as legal authorization; Lindt renewed the request for cargo planes that the Red Cross had been making to governments without getting a favorable response.

The plan was this: the Red Cross would have five planes and hoped to make four daylight flights with each, carrying about ten tons apiece. This would supply 200 tons of food daily—though, of course, under operating conditions in the rainy season, such a maximum could not be sustained.

A Swiss colonel would be in charge of operations. On August 19, the date for beginning flights would be decided. This would be designated "X-Day." On X-Day minus 3, Lindt would inform the FMG that five Red Cross planes would begin daylight relief into the neutralized airfield on X-Day. There was no question of negotiating about this. The three days' notice would be given only to allow the FMG time for it to warn field commanders, so—it was hoped—they would not fire upon the aircraft.

Full flight details, registration numbers of the aircraft, flight plans, etc., would be given to the Nigerian government. On X-Day minus 1, Roger Gallopin would call a press conference in Geneva and announce that the ICRC was starting the long-awaited airlift into Biafra the next day. The expectation was that world opinion would rally in support of the Red Cross and make difficult any Nigerian interference with the airlift. Lindt would fly in the first plane.

The morning after Count von Rosen had concluded that Lindt was either a genius or a madman, Lindt met with representatives of the national Red Cross societies to enlist their support and, through them, the assistance of their governments. He handed them a confidential report, titled Operation INALWA (derived from "International Airlift West Africa"). The plan envisaged INALWA developing in two stages: starting with the five planes from Fernando Po, then, the second stage beginning in mid-October, flying from Douala in the Cameroons with eight to ten aircraft, gradually building up to fifteen or twenty.

The latest reports from Jaggi told of a worsening situation in Biafra, Lindt informed the representatives. He said everything must be tried to bring substantial aid to the victims. He warned that the idea of the Red Cross would suffer in the eyes of the people of the world if they failed in their efforts. If the first flights could be carried out without incident, then the ICRC would continue them.

Lindt made clear, however, presumably with von Rosen's words still echoing in his mind, that the flights would take place in uncertain circumstances. First, it was doubtful that the FMG would agree to permit them. Second, there was only a slight possibility that the Nigerian government might tolerate them. Finally, even if the FMG instructed the military not to shoot down Red Cross planes, military commanders in some areas might not obey such instructions.

Lindt hoped that Lagos might finally respect the relief flights. But, he added, Nigerian antiaircraft now seemed well equipped and effective: "At any rate," he said, "we must be ready to continue even if we lose planes."

He thought that the operation could begin on August 26, just six days away. He asked everyone present to keep this date completely confidential, so as not to prejudice the overall operation. A Scandinavian Red Cross official spoke of the tremendous pressures from the press and the public; he asked whether it would not be possible to make the plan known to the media. Lindt insisted that the details of the plan and the meeting be kept confidential for the time being.

Warning the Red Cross representatives that he did not know how the Nigerian government would react, Lindt asked whether they could agree with his plan. The societies of Finland, Norway, Sweden, Switzerland, and the Netherlands gave their support. The Canadian Red Cross delegate said he would have to consult his government. The American delegate asked that he not be required to express an opinion.

He did not say so at the meeting, but Lindt was worried how the British government would react. He had sought a meeting with the prime minister, but Wilson had proved unapproachable.

Leaving Lagos two days before, Chief Anthony Enahoro explained to newsmen that he did not know whether he would be returning to negotiations then under way at Addis Ababa and described his sudden trip to London as a "special mission." He had been summoned to confer with Lord Shepherd and other officials at the Commonwealth Office. Nigerian rejection of the Red Cross neutralized airstrip presented the British government with new problems.

The British and Nigerians now embarked upon an intensive effort to involve the ICRC in new negotiations that would delay the start of the airlift. Presumably they sought to play upon the reluctance of the majority of the committee to do anything "illegal." They went through a series of proposals, seeking to tie Lindt up negotiating a plan unacceptable to the Biafrans.

One suggested that Nigeria would accept an airlift provided the planes first touched down in Federal territory. (This had been found unacceptable to the Biafrans the previous November). The *New York Times,* reporting this, mentioned that it "is understood to have been discussed today by Chief Anthony Enahoro, Nigeria's Information Minister, and British officials." Another proposal: the Nigerian government would agree to make available an airstrip for relief purposes, but not the one chosen by the ICRC, which, the FMG explained, was too close to the front line. Yet another (elaborated in the *Financial Times* of London) contained at least four elements unacceptable to the Biafrans: "Nigeria has proposed mercy flights from Lagos to Biafra's main airstrip which would have to be neutralized. The relief aircraft, according to this proposal, would be escorted into Biafra by Federal aircraft and the Nigerian authorities would reserve the right to suspend the flights without notice or prior consultation."

Chief Enahoro flew from London to Geneva, conferred with Lindt and urged him to come to London; but Lindt—not to be diverted from organizing what he called "my air fleet"—declined. He informed Enahoro about the plan to fly to Obilagu. Enahoro then returned for a long discussion with Commonwealth Secretary George Thomson. A four-man delegation was dispatched from Lagos to the negotiations going on between the Biafrans and Nigerians in Addis Ababa. They brought with them a "compromise package deal" that came to be spoken of as a proposal of Emperor Haile Selassie. Selassie was, in fact, deeply committed to finding some solution to the humanitarian problem, but he had few illusions about the possibilities; since the Niamey meeting he had concluded that there was no possibility of a land corridor.

As part of the "compromise package" flights would have to land at Uli rather than Obilagu which the Nigerians stated "is not acceptable as it is now in the direct line of immediate advance of Federal troops." It seemed, though, as if an air corridor as well as a land corridor might be possible, for the Biafran delegation accepted the proposal—in principle. At the very time he had planned to begin Operation INALWA, Lindt had to fly to Addis Ababa to learn whether there would be, after all, a "legal" way of beginning humanitarian relief into Biafra.

For a blunt message of another sort had been coming through to the ICRC for a number of days. The morning Lindt had met with national Red Cross society representatives, Geneva headquarters received a radio message from its delegate in Biafra: at 11:30 that morning, the neutralized airstrip, now under Red Cross control, had been bombed and rocketed by Nigerian Air Force planes. A few days later, the Nigerian planes bombed the airstrip a second time, injuring workers on the field. The large red crosses painted against white backgrounds along the runway made perfect targets.

The British government perhaps thought it had the situation well under control. Then, suddenly, Prime Minister Harold Wilson, Foreign Secretary Michael Stewart, and Commonwealth Secretary George Thomson found themselves surrounded by M.P.s shaking fists in their faces and shouting angrily: "Shame, shame."

Parliament had adjourned at the end of July, not due back till October 14. By then the Nigerian "final offensive" would be over, Nigerian troops would have overrun the Biafran enclave, and humanitarian relief would have begun. The government would not have to make good on the foreign secretary's pledge to reconsider policy, for when the invasion of the Ibo heartland came, parliamentary critics would be far from Whitehall and Westminster.

The unanticipated happened: the Soviet Union and four Warsaw Pact allies invaded Czechoslovakia "at the request of the party and Government leaders of the Czechoslovak Socialist Republic." For days, the world was caught up by the drama. Czechoslovakia did not seem so far away as it had to Neville Chamberlain thirty years before, and Parliament was called back into session to discuss the crisis. Many members wanted to debate Nigeria as well, so the government was compelled to schedule a second day for that.

George Thomson set about to take the heat out of the Commons debate: "Perhaps I might begin a report that will have many grave, somber and disturbing features, with one encouraging development. The House will have been happy to hear that Emperor Haile Selassie's formula for relief operations was this week-end accepted in principle by both the Nigerian and Biafran delegations. A great deal of credit is due to the persistence and patience shown by the Emperor. The formula is basically about simultaneous use of land and air mercy corridors into Biafra. . . ."

The debate on Nigeria somehow had to be concluded without a "division" in Commons—a vote on a motion to terminate the supply of British arms. The evening before, fifty-one of the government's party had signed a motion "to stop all arms supplies for Nigeria immediately" and "to approach the Governments of those countries still permitting the supply of arms to either side for a joint ban." What angered M.P.s now was the interview many had heard that previous evening on the BBC program "24 Hours": General Gowon stating the "final push" is on, the Nigerians have taken the major fight into the heart of Ibo territory and the war will be over in about four weeks.

This was exactly what government spokesmen had been assuring Parliament would not happen, even as the British had been secretly building up the Nigerian Army for weeks. So they had to lie to Commons for what they perhaps thought would be one last time: "While this debate has been proceeding we have been in touch with Lagos, and General Gowon has told us personally that when he said that the final push is now in progress he was referring to the continuous preparatory operations in both the northern and southern sectors for a final Federal push." Derisory hoots greeted this in the House.

Fears in Parliament of what Nigerian troops would do during their "final push" into the Ibo heartland were intensified by an interview widely reprinted from the Amsterdam newspaper *De Telegraaf*, quoting the Nigerian commander on the southern front, Colonel Adekunle: "I want to see no Red Cross, no Caritas, no World Council of Churches, no Pope, no missionary and no UN delegation. I want to prevent even one Ibo having one piece to eat before their capitulation. We shoot at everything that moves." Asked what his forces would do when they overran the center of Ibo territory, Adekunle replied, "Then we shoot at everything. Even things that don't move."

Reginald Maudling spoke of this to Commons: "It would be utterly intolerable to provide British arms to anyone who intends to work on the basis of Colonel Adekunle's recent statement. It must be repudiated."

Thomson sought to reassure the members: "One must not take too much notice of the flamboyant language of a colonel in the field. . . . The way to judge a military man is not by the flamboyancy of his language to the press but by his professional qualities as a soldier and, in this context, by the degree of discipline that he is able to enforce amongst his troops. My information—into which I have looked most anxiously—is that in his professional capacity, as distinct from his public relations capacity, Colonel Adekunle leads troops who have shown self-discipline."

Hugh Fraser spoke of "the line adopted by some Ministers . . . that because we supply arms there would be no all-out assault which could lead to the genocide of the Ibo people in Biafra. Yet only last night it was announced that Colonel Gowon is to launch his major offensive. We have also had a statement from the Commander of the Third Division that he will shoot everything that moves. No doubt according to the Commonwealth Office that is a totally irresponsible statement. They would claim that it has no validity. But in fact he is the local commander of the troops. I have seen African troops, and I know that they pay attention to the local commander rather than to people sitting back in Lagos."

Fraser warned: "I believe that the conditions previously laid down by the Foreign Secretary are about to arise and that there is grave danger of the destruction of the Ibo people. The Ibo people have shown their right to self-determination more clearly, perhaps, than any other people in the world. In spite of deprivation, war and starvation, for twelve months these people have shown that they believe, rightly or wrongly, that they are faced with the destruction of their race, and they are prepared to defend themselves against that."

Another critic, of the government's own party, Frank Allaun, commented on Gowon's television statement that Federal troops would win within four weeks: "My contacts with Biafrans lead me to believe that they are prepared to die to the last man and woman before this happens. People may say that they are wrong, but that is what will happen. It would take months, but it need not take place at all." He went on to say: "I find intolerable the complicity of the British Commonwealth Office with the Federal Government it is backing. Commonwealth Ministry officials are misleading the British people. Whether this is deliberate or not, I will not say; they may be misleading themselves."

Allaun suggested that while British diplomatic officials in Lagos and Whitehall had "a lot to answer for," the Commonwealth secretary, the foreign secretary, and the whole cabinet were ultimately responsible for what was happening. Thomson interrupted to say the responsibility should be put where it belongs: "It is on my shoulders. He should not attack my advisers, who have no opportunity to answer back and whose advice I accept or reject."

Allaun agreed it was a cabinet responsibility, but went on to quote what the Commonwealth Office had said: "Sunday's *Observer* reported that Chief Enahoro and the Commonwealth Office doubted the reports of widespread starvation in Biafra. My goodness, we have seen the reports of scores of British reporters and foreign reporters, and these reporters are not making these things up. I think that that was an astounding statement for the Commonwealth Office to make."

The government made a considerable point in both Commons and Lords that "In the propaganda field the Ibos have often seemed to be winning the war of words while losing the battle of arms." The Biafrans had hired a public relations firm in Geneva, Markpress, to put out their press releases; the British government convinced many M.P.s and others that the Biafrans were carrying on a fantastically successful propaganda campaign, while the Nigerians were inept and not getting their message across. A government spokesman, citing examples, stated, "I could go on at great length giving examples of Ibo propaganda which are not only untrue but grossly defamatory in their allegations about British policy and intentions." He went on to say: "One can scoff at some of these wilder inventions, but the fact remains that Ibo propaganda, perhaps more credible, but none the less untrue, may well have colored the judgment of some that it has reached, although the press here has scrupulously quoted the source of its reports. Particularly tragic is the way in which the Ibos seem to become the victims of their own propaganda. The belief which has been instilled in them that any concessions would lead to a planned genocide by the Federal authorities is certainly a stumbling block to achieving a ceasefire. We do not accept that the Federal Government have any such intention against the Ibos. . . ."

As the British government spokesman remarked at one point: "Obviously if a lie is repeated often enough, there are some people, who should know better, but who believe it."

This was said by William Whitlock, the undersecretary of state for Commonwealth affairs, in the course of remarks that led to what newspapers variously described the next day as "scenes of fantastic disorder," "extraordinary scenes of turmoil," and "extraordinary scenes of anger." The previous day, the government, before the debate on Czechoslovakia, had slipped a motion past its critics on Nigeria. The critics became aware of how they had been outmaneuvered only when Whitlock rose at 3:28 in the afternoon, with Commons due to adjourn at 4:00 P.M., and began reading from a lengthy disquisition about the Nigerian conflict. As the *Guardian* commented the next day: "To conclude a shoddy day's work the wretched Mr. Whitlock was evidently under instructions to prevent a vote being taken by the procedural device of 'talking out' the last minutes of the time allotted for the debate."

Whitlock said, among other things, "It is patently untrue that the

Federal Government are proceeding without mercy to the starvation of the Ibo people and we believe it to be equally untrue that they have any intention of seeking a merciless slaughter." He then went on at some length about "the Ibo propaganda machine." As he discussed the subject of minority tribes that did not favor Biafran secession, Frank Allaun arose: "On a point of order, Mr. Speaker. In view of the need to take a vote, I beg to move that the Question be now put, as I am assured that nothing recorded in the Chamber yesterday prohibits a decision before four o'clock if it is the will of the House."

The Speaker said: "The honorable Member is right. There is nothing in yesterday's Motion which prevents a decision of the House being recorded by a vote but only provided the debate ends before four o'clock. I am not prepared to accept Closure."

Whitlock rose again, but before he could speak, Hugh Fraser asked, "Further to that point of order, Mr. Speaker. Could the Minister give an assurance that he will sit down one minute before four o'clock?"

Whitlock began: "I was saying that we believe that most of the—" and Members shouted at him: "Answer!" Philip Noel-Baker rose, but the noise from the gallery, where visitors were shouting, was so great that he could not begin to speak. "Order!" the Speaker called out. "Noise does not help at all. A point of order, Mr. Noel-Baker."

"Further to the point of order, Mr. Speaker," said the recipient of the Nobel Peace Prize. "I am sure that my honorable Friend would desire to give an assurance to the House that he will sit down before four o'clock." The Speaker declared, "That is a point for the Minister, not a point of order for me. Mr. Whitlock."

Whitlock began again: "I was saying—" numerous Members interrupted, shouting "Answer!"—Whitlock: "—that we believe that most of the five million non-Ibos—"

"On a point of order," James Davidson said. "It must be obvious to the Government Front Bench, Mr. Speaker, that it is the will of the House to vote. May we, please, have an answer from the Minister that he will sit down before four o'clock and give the House an opportunity to vote?"

Whitlock: "I am attempting to reply to the debate, and I shall be better able to do so if honorable Members allow me to continue. We believe—" The Speaker asked Stanley Henig, who had arisen, "Does the honorable Member seek to raise a point of order?"

"Yes, Mr. Speaker. May I ask whether you have ruled that it is never in order for the closure to be moved while an honorable Member is still speaking? I believe that on past occasions honorable Members have successfully sought to move the closure."

The Speaker responded: "The honorable Gentleman must not

broaden the ruling that Mr. Speaker made. It is in order for Mr. Speaker to accept a closure when he thinks that he will accept a closure, even if an honorable Member is speaking. Mr. Speaker is not however prepared to accept the closure. He is bound by the Motion of yesterday."

Jeremy Thorpe of the Liberal party waxed sarcastic: "Further to the point of order. Since the Minister has indicated that he wishes to reply to the debate and, therefore, presumably wishes to assist the House in its deliberations, in case it did not register in his mind on previous occasions, may we repeat the question and ask him to indicate whether the Government are frightened that he should sit down at a minute before four o'clock?"

To this the unfortunate Whitlock began to reply, "This debate has been arranged by the Government in response to requests by honorable Members—," but was unable to finish because of the outbursts.

Peter Bessell, another Liberal, questioned: "May I ask your guidance, Mr. Speaker? Is it the custom in this House for the Government flagrantly to deny the wish of the House in the matter of a vote? In the circumstances, cannot you persuade the Government to act in an honorable and decent manner?"

The Speaker replied, "If Mr. Speaker were to attempt to persuade the Government, this would be the first time in history and it would also be a failure."

Whitlock: "We believe that most of the five million non-Ibos—"

Michael Barnes rose to ask: "Is it not the case, Mr. Speaker, that on two earlier occasions this year all honorable Members loyally heeded the advice of both Front Benches that it would be best not to divide the House on the question of Nigeria? Is it not equally the case that today there is overwhelming feeling in this Chamber that the matter should be put to the vote? Can you explain, Mr. Speaker, why it is not possible for you to accept the closure before four o'clock, or would you accept a closure a little nearer to four o'clock?"

The Speaker responded: "The position is quite simple. The House decided yesterday that today's business should be taken on the Adjournment and that at four o'clock Mr. Speaker should adjourn the House without the Question put. Those are the instructions of the House to Mr. Speaker. I cannot vary them. I am not without sympathy with the desire of many honorable Members to register their opinions by voting. I am powerless to do so unless the debate ends before four o'clock."

Whitlock: "If Colonel Ojukwu were to succeed . . . " He continued until Winifred Ewing intervened: "On a point of order. Could I, as a fairly new Member, ask for your guidance, Mr. Speaker? Is not one of the functions of the House of Commons to arrive at the democratic will of the House at the end of the debate?"

Mr. Speaker: "That is a delightful philosophic question which I would love to discuss with the honorable Lady."

Harold Wilson had now entered the chamber and taken his seat on the front bench. Sir Knox Cunningham asked, "Could I put this philosophic question to you, Mr. Speaker? If the Minister feels unable to sit down at one minute to four o'clock, would he ask the Prime Minister, who is sitting beside him, and who is in charge, to ask him to sit down so that the will of the House may be shown by a vote?"

Whitlock: "Throughout this tragic dispute we have persistently worked for peace, first by trying to help—" Sir Stephen McAdden asked, on a point of order: "As it is manifestly out of order for honorable Members to read their speeches, would it not be just as well if we took a vote now?"

But the Speaker said, "It is in order for honorable Members to make use of copious notes."

Michael Barnes moved that the question be put; the Speaker said he had already explained that he was not prepared to accept that motion. Gilbert Longdon suggested: "It would appear likely that the proceedings of this House this afternoon will bring Parliament into contempt. Naturally, I do not presume to ask you, Mr. Speaker, to bring pressure on the Government, but I ask you to uphold the rights of Private Members, most of whom here wish to vote."

The Speaker responded: "I must defend Parliament against the honorable Member. A Motion was carried yesterday, and it defines the proceedings of the day. The honorable Member and his colleagues should have taken exception to that Motion yesterday." To which Sir Douglas Glover rejoined: "When the House reached that decision yesterday it had no idea of the sort of arguments the Government would make. It is quite obvious that nearly every Member in the Chamber wishes to have a Division."

The Speaker: "I am not responsible for what was in the minds of honorable Members when they came to their decision yesterday. But they came to that decision."

Whitlock rose once again; once again the Members shouted, "Sit down, sit down!"

Philip Noel-Baker: "On a point of order. May I suggest to the Leader of the House that, for the good name of the House, he should ask the Undersecretary of State to sit down and allow a vote to be taken?"

Whitlock: "May I remind the House that it was the Government who recalled this House in order that Members on either side of the House might have an opportunity to put their points of view on this terrible tragedy of the war in Nigeria. My right honorable Friend the Foreign Secretary has said that he would end the arms supply if the Federal Government were conducting irresponsible military activity which would prevent talks from taking place, if those talks had any chance of success, military activity which would cause wanton and unavoidable slaughter going on in Nigeria. That is the situation—"

It being four o'clock, the Speaker adjourned the House, without the question being put, until October 14. Members from both benches swarmed down around the prime minister, foreign secretary, and Commonwealth secretary. It was some minutes before Wilson, Stewart, and Thomson could finally leave the chamber, white-faced and shaken.

That evening, General Gowon appeared again on British television, repeating that the final push had begun; the order had gone to front line commanders three days before. He promised that the offensive would be finished quickly.

Chapter 11

The planes began arriving at São Tomé and Fernando Po. The church airlift got under way quickly: six flights went in each night on August 28, 29, and 30, putting the Red Cross under real pressure to move.

The trip Lindt had to make to Addis Ababa held up the start of Operation INALWA. Once there, he found that the Nigerians had linked the air corridor to the land corridor, proposing that heavy supplies of food go overland from Enugu while medicines could be flown to the demilitarized airstrip—after agreement on details. Haile Selassie told him there was no possibility of a land corridor, and Lindt concluded that the Biafran delegation had made a tactical mistake in accepting the latest proposal "in principle."

The Nigerians continued casting about for a proposal to keep the ICRC from starting its airlift. Gowon had earlier said, "Why doesn't Ojukwu make available to the Red Cross the airfield he is already using to bring in arms. We could consider an agreement over that. . . . " Now, on television, he elaborated on this; Uli airstrip would be acceptable "under strict conditions of control which will insure that it is used only for handling relief supplies."

Before being compelled to go to Addis Ababa, Lindt had notified the Nigerian government that the next morning he would personally lead five ICRC planes, starting a daylight airlift from 9:00 A.M. to 5:00 P.M. each day from Fernando Po to the Red Cross airstrip at Obilagu.

External Affairs Minister Arikpo summoned the Swedish, Danish, and Norwegian representatives in Lagos and informed them that his government was disturbed that planes supplied by their governments were going to begin flying the next morning. This was especially unfortunate, he told them, in view of the compromise solution that seemed possible at Addis Ababa. Then Arikpo stated: "General Gowon has instructed the

Foreign Ministry to say that the FMG would not be able to take responsibility for what might happen to unauthorized flights."

This was tough diplomatic talk, but the Scandinavian governments stood firm. Responding to the note the FMG sent them through their ambassadors, Denmark, Finland, Norway, and Sweden stated: ". . . the airplanes . . . are being operated by the International Committee of the Red Cross, are duly marked with the Red Cross colors and signs, and are not under the control of the Governments." The FMG had, in effect, threatened to shoot down their planes if they flew the next day. They went on to "urgently appeal to the Federal Government of Nigeria not to undertake any action to prevent the supplies from being brought to the people in need, but to grant the airplanes under the control of the International Red Cross free and unhindered passage."

The FMG had succeeded in delaying Lindt a few days, but finally X-Day minus 1 arrived. More than four months had passed since the urgent appeals to Red Cross societies for assistance in meeting the rising starvation; more than a hundred days had gone by since the ICRC had made its appeal at Kampala for a lifting of the blockade. Count von Rosen, in a press conference in New York at this time, estimated that for every plane that did not go in, three thousand babies died.* Now, in September, the death toll in Biafra was rising to twelve thousand a day.

In Geneva, Roger Gallopin announced the start of the Red Cross airlift into Biafra. He said the five planes now on Fernando Po would "also fly regularly by daylight" (the ICRC having been flying one flight a night during part of August). Their combined load would be fifty tons, and the number of flights "will progressively increase." The ICRC informed the Nigerian government of the registration numbers of the aircraft and the radio wavelengths they would use to identify themselves to ground forces. The Red Cross would supervise distribution of relief supplies, and the Nigerian government could control the cargo being loaded on the planes.

Nigeria's response was immediate: "The Federal Government states categorically that it absolves itself from any responsibility arising out of the consequences of any unauthorized and illegal flights intended to land at Obilagu airstrip. The Federal Government appeals to all countries which have influence on the ICRC to urge them not to carry through the action, unprecedented in the history of the Red Cross, of overflying Ni-

*Von Rosen had come to New York with a letter from Emperor Haile Selassie to the UN secretary general, but U Thant declined to receive him, on the ground that von Rosen was not an accredited diplomat representing a government.

gerian territory and the positions of Federal troops without agreement of the Government. Such internationally illegal action could lead to grave incidents for which the Nigerian Government cannot be held responsible."

A dramatic confrontation: the Red Cross about to begin the airlift; the Nigerian government, in scarcely veiled language, implying that relief planes would be shot down.

It was becoming a bit hairy for the British. The shooting down of Red Cross relief planes, especially the one carrying Ambassador Lindt, would be worse than an embarrassment for the Wilson government. In Lagos, Sir David Hunt and American ambassador Mathews sought desperately to find a way to keep this from happening. Hunt phoned Swiss ambassador Fritz Real at one o'clock in the morning, saying it was imperative that Lindt come to Lagos to meet with General Gowon. Hunt and Mathews both warned there would be a break between the FMG and the ICRC if he did not.

Reluctant though he was to be diverted further, Lindt finally flew from Fernando Po, expecting to meet with Gowon at five o'clock that afternoon. He was told Gowon was busy. He wanted to return to Fernando Po, but there was trouble with his plane and he had to remain overnight in Lagos.

The next morning, Nigerian Air Force planes again bombed the airstrip at Obilagu.

Gowon was under great pressure from governments not to interfere with the Red Cross airlift. Swedish prime minister Tage Erlander, for example, cabled that day "not to take any negative action against the relief supplies for the suffering civilian population," pointing out that "flights carried out by the International Red Cross could not give rise to suspicions that they were being used for anything but humanitarian purposes."

The British had come up with a proposal that Gowon agreed to put forward. When he finally met with Lindt, he offered to allow the Red Cross to fly, as an emergency measure, in daylight for ten days, beginning two days later. (That would be until September 15, when the British, the U.S. State Department, and the Nigerians expected Biafra to collapse.) But not, Gowon added, to Obilagu—into Uli instead.

Gowon and Lindt discussed the proposal for five hours, and Lindt thought he had a deal. Earlier, in Addis Ababa, he had talked with the Biafran home secretary, Christopher Mojekwu, who happened to be Ojukwu's cousin. Mojekwu expressed the opinion that daylight flights into either Obilagu or Uli would be acceptable to the Biafrans. Lindt notified

ICRC headquarters in Geneva of the Nigerian offer, then flew to Fernando Po and into Biafra that evening.

When Lindt stepped from the plane all smiles, Jaggi told him that the Biafran foreign minister, Godwin Onyegbula, was "hopping mad." Onyegbula had just heard on the BBC that the Nigerians had announced that Lindt had agreed to the FMG proposal. "What are you doing?" Onyegbula shouted. "We've constructed an airport for you and turned it over to you. Now you say you're going to fly into Uli!"

Lindt was flabbergasted to learn that daylight flights into Uli might not be acceptable to the Biafrans. He rode through the blacked-out countryside to Umuahia to discuss the situation with Ojukwu. During dinner, he thought that Ojukwu was more willing to consider the possibility than Onyegbula.

If the Biafrans agreed to the ten days of flights into Uli, Lindt felt that "the Nigerians would not have a leg to stand on," Gowon having already publicly accepted the agreement. As Lindt was leaving, Ojukwu said, "Well, it might work," and they agreed to talk again the next morning.

In thinking that Ojukwu might be more willing than his foreign minister to accept daylight flights into Uli, Lindt was mistaken. Ojukwu opposed any plan that could endanger the airfield at Uli. The Nigerian announcement before Lindt had even arrived in Biafra aroused his suspicions further. Lindt, of course, could only try to negotiate between the Nigerians and Biafrans, not enter unilaterally into an agreement. When he denied he had agreed in Lagos to the proposal, Ojukwu was provoked into using the same tactic the FMG had employed. He directed that a communiqué be broadcast that night over Biafran radio.

The next morning, Onyegbula told Lindt, "It's all settled. The flights cannot go into Uli. This is the communiqué we issued last night." Radio Biafra had announced that Biafra was pleased to learn that " . . . the Nigerian Government has accepted the principle of direct relief daylight flights into Biafra." The communiqué told how Biafra had placed Obilagu airstrip at the disposal of the ICRC for this purpose and that the Biafrans now looked forward to "the commencement of massive daylight flights."

What was Lindt to do? The Nigerians said the Red Cross could fly in daylight into Uli but not to Obilagu. The Biafrans said they could fly day or night into Obilagu but not to Uli during the day. To make matters worse, Lindt received a cable from the FMG, flown in during the night by the Red Cross plane. In Lagos, he had requested written authorization for the ten days of ICRC flights. The cable, from the Nigerian Air Force commander, set forth operational guidelines—at what altitude the Red Cross could fly and where, etc. But that was not all. The final paragraph stated that the Nigerian Air Force reserved the right to fly over Uli while relief planes were landing and to carry on military activities. This was unacceptable. In talking with Gowon about ICRC willingness to cooperate with the FMG, Lindt had stressed it would be against Red Cross principles to bring supplies into the country under armed escort. Gowon, for his part, had assured him that no conditions were attached to the ten days of flights.

Heinrich Jaggi expressed the opinion they could not *not* fly now. The ICRC announcement had been made. The airfield was set. The planes were ready, and at least one pilot was prepared to fly in daylight—no matter what. "As a humanitarian matter," Jaggi said, "we *must* fly." Lindt agreed. He had already sounded out the pilots at Santa Isabel on Fernando Po. One, the Finn, was willing to fly in daylight without authorization. Lindt decided to fly, at night, into both Obilagu and Uli.

No one except Lindt and Jaggi, and later Gallopin and a few others, knew what had happened. Lindt had not started flying in daylight in defiance of the Nigerian government. The Nigerians had succeeded in preventing daylight flights but not in blocking the airlift. For the first time in its history, the ICRC acted "illegally." (Though Lindt insisted the April letter provided a legal basis for flying, no government acted as though this were the case.)

The airlift had begun. How this had come about was concealed by the secrecy the ICRC maintained about its negotiations. As a result, the world did not know what would be a central fact during the remaining sixteen months of the war: the Nigerians had learned that the Biafrans felt they could not, without endangering themselves militarily, agree to daylight relief flights into Uli.

September 1968–June 1969

Chapter 12

The day the airlift began, Roger Gallopin invited other relief agencies to ICRC headquarters to discuss their mutual problems. By this time, enormous damage had been done the Red Cross. Other agencies and some national Red Cross societies had become estranged from the ICRC. They only knew they had been held up from starting meaningful relief for nearly two months while governments pressured them to coordinate under the Red Cross. They did not know how the mandate had been given or how the Red Cross was being used to manage the situation.

Top ICRC officials told no one of British and American pressures upon them to hold up starting relief until mid-September. To officials of the other agencies it appeared that August Lindt and the ICRC were in some kind of collusion with the governments blocking relief. They did not know he had persuaded the ICRC committee members to take a momentous decision: to defy the Nigerian government and, for the first time in Red Cross history, to violate the territory of a sovereign nation.

Just how the British and Nigerians were using the Red Cross was not clear to ICRC officials themselves. They were trapped within their own conviction that they could not jeopardize their long-term relations with governments. Their secretiveness made them the perfect instrument for British diplomats whose overriding priority was to cover up the fact that the Nigerian government wanted no food going to "the rebels."

Envenomed as the atmosphere was by the unexplained performance of the ICRC, officials of the other agencies were nonetheless glad for an opportunity to work out some kind of operating relationship. It was the coordinating meeting they had been seeking all through July and August.

Roger Gallopin gave them no explanation of the fact that he had announced two days before that the Red Cross would begin flying in daylight the next day and then had not done so. He could not explain what he did not fully understand himself. Communication with Lindt in

Biafra was difficult; not everything could be said over radio. Gallopin only knew that flights were going into Obilagu at night instead of in daylight after the Nigerian government had announced agreement for ten days of daylight flights to Uli.

Later, when Gallopin and others at ICRC headquarters learned more, they were annoyed that Lindt, after persuading the committee to stand up to the FMG and to be ready to defy Nigerian refusal to allow Operation INALWA to begin, seemed to them to have knuckled under to Biafran refusal to allow daylight flights to Uli.

The two situations, of course, were not comparable. While it was possible to fly at night into Biafra as the Nigerians had no night fighter capability, there was no way to land at Uli against the wishes of the Biafrans, as they would have to remove the obstacles that obstructed the airstrip during daylight hours as a defense against the Nigerians. That some officials in Geneva equated the two revealed an emerging attitude toward the Biafrans that would lead the ICRC seriously astray at the climax of a crescendo of events the following summer.

By this time, also, an enormous toll had been taken since the Red Cross had sent its "SOS Biafra" and appealed for a lifting of the blockade three months before. More people had already starved than were estimated to have died up to that time in the Vietnam War over the previous ten years. More were starving each week than had died under the first atomic bomb at Hiroshima or were killed in all four Arab-Israeli wars up to that time. With the death rate continuing at ten thousand to twelve thousand a day during September and October, more would die of starvation those next two months than were killed during the entire Spanish Civil War.

Those carrying on the diplomatic-propaganda cover-up of the fact that the Nigerians were deliberately blocking relief downplayed these death estimates, speaking of them as "the numbers game." Relief workers from all parts of Biafra met every Wednesday morning at Queen Elizabeth Hospital in Umuahia. They reported on the numbers who had died in their areas that past week. Dr. Clyne Shepherd, who chaired the meetings, told a Canadian parliamentary committee when he was out of Biafra briefly: "People wonder about the statistics of dying people in Biafra. For some months now I have personally been involved with the chief delegate of the Red Cross in Biafra in working out these statistics. It is not an easy job. Nobody can have all the information with the country in the kind of turmoil it is. We have been working with an uncertain size of population because of the moving about of large numbers of refugees. We have to take into consideration the basic death rates in the country. We arrived at the figures we have published by taking everything into account. As regards population size, we have tended to err on the side of being conservative. Where we were not sure of death rates and the mortality, we were conservative.

"The figures we have produced are obtained from random samples of death rates in villages, refugee camps, and hospitals from every province in Biafra. By the end of July, six thousand deaths a day from malnutrition or starvation only was the figure we arrived at. Recently, last month, the Red Cross published a figure of eight thousand to ten thousand deaths. Knowing how this figure was reached, I would agree with it as being reasonably accurate. But all our figures, I would remind you, are likely to be on the conservative side."

"I talked with two fathers about their children," one relief official who visited Biafra reported. "The first said the best thing to be done would be to take the worst cases in the village as they were close to death, while the second father said he would not take the worst cases as they were condemned to death anyway."

The airlifts of early September could not begin to slow the mounting rate of starvation. The ICRC estimated the need for protein-rich foods at 14,000 tons a month (assuming 125 grams a day for each of the 3,600,000 people requiring supplementary feeding). In fact, during the first month, the two airlifts together—each getting in six, eight, or ten flights a night—managed to transport only 3,081 tons, including medical supplies as well as food. So conditions could not get better, but would get worse, unless either the war ended or the capacity of the airlifts increased greatly.

The Swedish Red Cross was sending in twenty-five "kwashiorkor combat teams," each composed of five or six medical and nutritional personnel. The relief effort was beginning to build up, but no one knew how long it would be needed. The ICRC had chartered its aircraft for only a short time—continuing to believe, as British diplomats were telling Red Cross officials in Geneva, that the war would end by mid-September.

The military offensive was intense, and relief agency officials began worrying about the situation that would develop if Nigerian troops broke through and overran the enclave. They believed that the Biafrans would not give up, but turn instead to guerrilla warfare. The people would take to the bush, and it would become more difficult than ever to bring relief to those in need.

What this would be like was already foreshadowed by conditions in an area to the north of the Biafran enclave, about which relief officials were helpless to do anything. An estimated four hundred thousand to five hundred thousand were reported hiding in an area that had come under Federal control, extending from Afikpo Road, between Ake Eze and Afikpo, northward as far as Nomeh. A UN representative spoke with some who had come out after hiding from Federal troops for as long as ten months.

The British, Nigerian, and State Department conviction that Biafra would soon be conquered affected the thinking of relief agency officials. They experimented with methods of getting food to people no longer accessible by regular airlift. They became very aware of the inadequacy of the DC-6s and the DC-7s for air-dropping, with or without parachutes, should this become necessary. They began a desperate search for rear-loading cargo planes more suited to such work.

Without the kind of assistance only governments could provide, the airlifts inevitably had a jerry-built quality about them. "Obilagu is unbelievable," one relief official reported after flying into the new airstrip. "It isn't very wide and it goes uphill and downhill. It's lighted by flares which are simply oil cans with rags stuck in them for wicks." (The Red Cross worker who had improvised these runway lights was, in fact, rather proud of them. It took considerable ingenuity to have all the young boys he had recruited from a nearby village light them at precisely the right moment— less than a minute before a relief plane was about to land—then extinguish them a moment after the aircraft was safely down. In ordinary times he was a dance-band leader in Geneva.)

"There is no place for aircraft to turn around," the relief official reported, "so, believe it or not, they turn around by backing and filling like a truck on the airstrip, using their propellers in reverse, or reverse pitch."

"What they do is put one airplane at the head end of the strip, the second in there too, and the third at the other end of the strip. So you have two and one off-loading simultaneously. And then, whichever one takes off first, the one at the far end, or the first at the other end, flies *over* the other airplanes on takeoff, which requires a helluva lot of skill and courage because you have to gain altitude of at least fifty feet to be sure of clearing the aircraft at the other end of the field, which means you have to take off approximately a thousand feet before the end of the runway."

Monseigneur Carlo Bayer of Caritas praised the courage of the airlift plane crews. He stressed to other relief agency officials that the captain of the first flight each night must be courageous so the others would follow him. If the intensity of the antiaircraft fire caused the lead pilot to lose heart and turn back, others would decline to fly. At times the planes had to go up to 20,000 feet to avoid the antiaircraft. Flights had to be timed so that the first aircraft would cross the Nigerian coast no earlier than dusk, then—if each was to make two flights that night—the latest that church relief planes could leave São Tomé was one o'clock in the morning, so they could unload and make it back across the coast before the sun came up again.

During these early days it often took an hour or longer to unload a plane, tying up not only the aircraft but the field, which did not yet have adequate parking areas. Other planes would be stacked up in a holding pattern, waiting to land. Once the food had been lugged off the planes, however, it was quickly distributed to the feeding stations organized by Caritas, the World Council of Churches, and the Red Cross.

The DC-6s and DC-7s, former passenger planes, were ill suited for an airlift. Bags of food and cartons of medicine had to be carried up through the passenger side door and unloaded the same way. UNICEF had sent George Orick to look into the logistical situation, to see what could be done about improving the tonnages of the new airlifts. Remembering from his earlier days in Biafra a roller-conveyor system at the brewery in Umuahia that in better times made Golden Guinea beer, Orick arranged to have the rollers used to speed up the unloading of relief planes at Uli.

Cargo planes with aft-loading doors could have been turned around much more quickly, thereby increasing the tonnage of food flown in. The Hercules was obviously the plane needed, and relief officials began a search for C-130s.

Only Sweden had provided a Hercules to the ICRC; whether other governments would do the same once the airlift had begun was, as the foreign minister of Canada put it, "at the moment hypothetical." The ICRC's earlier request having been largely in vain, UNICEF took up the search, methodically approaching Australia, Canada, the Netherlands, and the United States.

These countries were not willing to help. Governments would not provide aircraft unless the FMG and the Biafrans reached a formal agreement. A few C-130s were available commercially, but a huge deposit of oil had just been discovered at Prudhoe Bay, on the North Slope of Alaska, and the oil companies were leasing and purchasing every available commercial aircraft for operations in that remote arctic place.

McGeorge Bundy, by then president of the Ford Foundation, was enlisted in the search and soon found that the State Department would not allow U.S. military aircraft to be used even in the Red Cross airlift. Bundy learned from the president of the Lockheed Corporation about the availability of one prototype C-130B. By the time the church relief agencies managed to scrape together the $1.2 million needed to hire the aircraft for the first six weeks, it too had become unavailable.

Without the help of governments and their air forces, the Red Cross and church agencies had difficulty organizing an airlift in the midst of war. Significantly, the air advisers to the ICRC were a Swiss and a Swede, who might not be the most knowledgeable about combat operations. Churchmen were getting on-the-job training, learning about such things as aluminum planking needed to expand airfield parking stands and side-band radios for air control.

UNICEF arranged for more expert advice, sending General William Tunner and another retired U.S. Air Force officer to recommend how Nordchurchaid might improve its airlift. "Tonnage Bill" Tunner had had more experience organizing and operating airlifts than anyone in the world. He had run the airlift "over the hump," from India and Burma over the Himalayas into China during World War II; he had led the UN airlift during the Korean War; and, as commander of the Berlin airlift, he had used 900 planes to fly 8,000 tons of supplies every day to that city of 2.25 million people. Now, summoned from retirement in Virginia, he was appalled at what he found: a dozen or so old side-door passenger planes being used to supply some eight million people besieged in an area of 3,000 square miles.

Tunner had been called upon many times to airlift relief supplies to victims of natural disasters far less grave than he now witnessed. He could not understand why the American government was not making available the best cargo planes possible. He returned deeply disturbed and committed to getting the U.S. to provide Hercules aircraft.

Sights and sounds in Biafra would haunt George Orick long after he had left: carpenters and cabinetmakers working full-time on the making of coffins; a father riding along on a bicycle with the body of his dead daughter strapped on the rear carrier; the sound of wailing heard each morning as parents awakened to find a child dead.

At the same time, Orick, like other travelers into Biafra, was impressed with the effectiveness of the Biafrans in keeping a state functioning and the ingenuity with which they conducted a war under impossible circumstances. Those arriving and departing at Uli airport were struck by the thoroughness with which immigration and customs officials checked passports and went through all the formalities of a modern international airport arrivals center. The landing at Uli, which soon became a hair-raising experience when night bombing commenced and landing lights could be kept on less than a minute, was itself a display of Biafran effectiveness. Over the coming weeks the number of flights landing and taking off each night rose to thirty and forty or more, making Uli the busiest international airport in Africa. The "air traffic control chaps" had carried out the same function at Lagos International Airport before the war. They somehow managed to keep all these planes coming and going, in the dark, stacked and in holding patterns as much as possible away from Nigerian antiaircraft fire, with planes arriving from at least four different airfields, and did so with a minimum of accidents and confusion.

After six years in Nigeria as a businessman, Orick had had to leave the year before when police questioned him about his efforts to save Ibos being slaughtered on the street in front of his home in Lagos. A magazine article he had written at the beginning of the year had been quoted by Ojukwu at length to foreign correspondents, but, when Orick asked to meet with him upon arriving in Biafra, Ojukwu said, "I would meet with George Orick, the man, but I cannot meet with Orick as a representative of the United Nations that does not recognize Biafra." Orick was nonetheless allowed to come and go in Biafra, making seven trips back and forth from São Tomé while he, Father Byrne, and Count von Rosen (now chief of operations of the church airlift) sought to make improvements in the airlift, working with whatever means came to hand.

On São Tomé, Orick tried to do something about unloading the first shipment of UNICEF food, the 5,000 tons the U.S. government had donated before the State Department held up for forty-five days when the Nigerian government began saying, "There is plenty of food in the area." (As the ship carrying the food approached Nigerian waters, a decision had to be made at UNICEF, New York, where to unload it: the U.S. obviously intended it for Nigeria, as "Biafra" did not exist. Dick Heyward went to Sasha Bacic of the Africa Desk and asked him what he thought. Bacic wrote on a sheet of yellow legal-sized paper: "2,000 tons to São Tomé, 3,000 tons to Lagos." Thus began the back-door supplying of U.S. donated foods to the church airlift through UNICEF. ICRC officials complained to Labouisse in Geneva about this; upon his return to New York, Labouisse bawled out Heyward and Bacic. But an important step had been taken toward sustaining the airlift.)

Now the ship, the *Orient Exporter*, stood off São Tomé, waiting to unload. The island had no good harbor, and oceangoing vessels had to stand offshore, with their cargo lightered in by barges, the ship's own gear lifting the slings of food and swinging them onto the small wooden barges that pitched and rolled in the sea, smashing against the side of the larger ship. Finding this going slowly, Orick enlisted the help of the Portuguese governor of São Tomé who was sympathetic to Biafran relief and involved in helping the church agencies get their airlift working effectively.

George Orick had more time to assess the need and estimate food prospects during the coming months than relief personnel caught up in the desperate day-to-day activity of trying to feed and care for the starving and ill. He made an assessment that would influence the thinking of relief agencies and ultimately lead to breakthroughs with the U.S. government. Carbohydrate foods (yams, cassava) within the besieged enclave would soon be exhausted, he concluded, perhaps by the end of the year. Until now lack of protein affected mainly the smallest children, but when supplies of starchy foods ran out, the whole population would be starving.

Orick reported: "Reflexive paralysis now grips nearly all of the relief agencies involved in the disaster. This paralysis permits day-to-day operations to continue at their present inadequate levels and blocks thinking about meeting the stupefying disaster that will commence in less than ten weeks."

He observed that while the airlifts from Fernando Po and São Tomé were dramatic, the tonnage they could carry into the enclave was only 10 percent of what would be needed when the population lacked starch staples as well as protein. "No serious plans are being made to move food to the disaster area in anything even remotely approaching the quantities necessary to avert the enormous starvation which will surely occur as this year ends."

Orick commented: "While the Biafrans show every indication of fighting to the end, whatever that may be, the United Nations and most of the potentially effective governments of the world wish—and therefore believe—that the Biafrans will be beaten or will come to terms momentarily. This world wish is mistaken for logic and stands as the biggest obstacle to realistic planning to alleviate starvation."

Chapter 13

The war had not ended on schedule. Something had gone wrong with British and State Department calculations. Hank Warton stopped flying ammunition at the crucial moment, when the Nigerian "final offensive" was under way. Biafran troops were down to five bullets or less per soldier—a second soldier would go into battle behind the one with the rifle, prepared to pick up the gun if the first fell. The Nigerians had counted on defeating the Biafrans before the annual OAU meeting in Algiers. But policy-makers in Lagos and Whitehall had not foreseen the intervention of a major power in support of Biafra.

There had been an intimation of this in July when an oracular pronouncement issued forth from a meeting of the French Council of Ministers: "Le Biafra est un peuple, il a droit à disposer de lui-même." The statement had the unmistakable tone of Charles de Gaulle himself. Biafra anticipated French recognition, followed soon after by recognition from African nations of the French Community, but it did not come. Nigerians were angered; they thought French business interests were eager to get at the oil. Quite to the contrary, businessmen with interests in Nigeria, as well as the French Foreign Ministry, were alarmed that support for Biafra would jeopardize French commercial interests and the safety of French citizens in Nigeria.

A split developed within the French government, the Quai d'Orsay seeking to maintain good relations with Lagos while the Elysée Palace (President de Gaulle) moved in the direction of supporting self-determination for Biafra.

"The human tragedy of Biafra preoccupies and moves the French Government," the July statement continued. But quite apart from the French wish to assist in the humanitarian effort, the communiqué went on to reflect de Gaulle's preoccupation with nationhood: "The bloodshed and suffering of the Biafran people for more than a year shows their will to affirm themselves as a people."

France began channeling military assistance to Biafra—covertly—a bare minimum of arms and ammunition to help meet the Nigerian "final push." DC-3s flew at night from the airfield at Libreville in Gabon. This French Community nation would receive its regular supply of arms and ammunition from France, use it up within a week or so, then France would replenish it the following week—and so on. The operation was concealed in the secrecy surrounding the man who carried on de Gaulle's relations with the French Community: Jacques Foccart, secretary general for African affairs, who was widely assumed to run France's clandestine services.

Before mid-September, the British and Nigerians became fully aware that France had intervened. De Gaulle made a pronouncement: "France has assisted—is assisting—Biafra within the limits of the possible." He commented that though France had not taken the decisive step of recognizing Biafra, this was not excluded in the future. He suggested the possibility of confederation as a way of reconciling Biafra's right to self-determination with the rest of Nigeria.

General Gowon reacted angrily, rejecting any idea of confederation. Lagos newspapers attacked France. Demonstrators denounced French intervention in Nigeria's internal affairs. French companies operating in Nigeria, especially the oil company, felt threatened. State Department officials urged French diplomats to reverse the arms policy. French businessmen and the Foreign Ministry finally prevailed for a time, and the ammunition supply halted. The Nigerian offensive forged ahead: Aba fell, Owerri, Uli was threatened, Obilagu airstrip overrun and being fought over. But then the policy of self-determination for Biafra reasserted itself, and Foccart began the shipments of ammunition through Gabon again.

Angry British and American diplomats began charging that France was prolonging the war. They felt French intervention flowed, as much as anything, out of de Gaulle's dislike of "les Anglo-Saxons," going back to his humiliations—real and imagined—in London during the war. There was always the likelihood that support for Biafran secession aimed at splitting up the largest British Commonwealth country in the midst of a number of smaller French Community nations. But French actions that followed never seemed calculating or consistent enough for such a policy.

The Biafrans always felt that had French support only gone all out, even for a month, they could have inflicted defeats on the Nigerians that would have led to a negotiated settlement. Instead, the split within the French government caused the supply of arms to falter at crucial times and, during the September Nigerian offensive, the Biafrans nearly lost the war.

The Nigerian "final push" aimed at dividing Biafra. The First and Third Divisions were supposed to link up on the Owerri-Okigwe road, cutting off Umuahia, the capital, from Uli airfield. The Third Marine Commando Division, under Colonel Adekunle, justified its name by attacking in boats up the river to Oguta, only eight miles south of Uli airstrip. For a time it was threatened and out of action. This forced the Biafrans to cancel their agreement neutralizing Obilagu, and French arms flights began arriving at this second airstrip. Lindt objected strenuously on behalf of the Red Cross.

It made little difference, for soon no flights—of either relief or arms—could land. The Nigerian First Division attacked through the demilitarized zone established for the Red Cross. Nigerians and Biafrans fought over Obilagu, and the airstrip became a no-man's-land for months to come.

Meanwhile Ojukwu, marshaling his forces in the south to repel the advance of the Third Marine Commando Division, drove the Nigerian troops back from Oguta, securing Uli airstrip so that both arms and relief flights began landing there once again. To do so, however, Ojukwu was forced to pull Biafran soldiers out of the southern line. Nigerian forces were then able to rush around the western end of the weakened southern defense and capture Owerri, a major city.

The interruption of ammunition supplies nearly finished the Biafrans, but de Gaulle's support had not been in the scenario. Once French arms shipments began again, the Biafran forces counterattacked. Of course, British and American diplomats could not believe that Biafra would not collapse on schedule. The way this influenced events is suggested by a personal experience of the author, when I was with UNICEF and serving as the person at the United Nations dealing with the press on Nigeria-Biafra humanitarian relief.

A group of international law scholars met in New York in September to consider what might be done, either through the United Nations or in other ways. They gathered in the law office of Arthur Goldberg, who had retired a few months before from the post of U.S. delegate to the UN. I was asked to brief them on the current situation and the political and military difficulties being encountered in providing humanitarian relief. After I had done so, one professor spoke briefly about the possibilities of the Geneva Conventions, another said a few words about the Convention on the Prevention and Punishment of Genocide.

Ambassador Goldberg intervened: "Well, now, actually it won't be necessary for us to do anything about this, as Biafra is going to collapse in three or four days and then it will be possible to rush in all the food that will be needed."

"Well, that's not exactly the case, Mr. Goldberg," I said. "In the last few days the Biafrans have begun driving the Nigerians back on the southern front. They are getting supplies of arms from the French and have begun to show a good deal of strength. Everyone coming out of Biafra says that the people have a tremendous will to resist, as they expect to be killed anyway if they are overrun, so it's not necessarily true that Biafra will collapse in a few days."

Goldberg turned to me and said, "Now, now, I think I detect in what you say a certain note of partisanship. You must be careful in these matters not to become partisan. If you want to get humanitarian relief in, you must remain objective."

I replied, "I think I *am* being objective. It's just that I have better information than most people. I'm talking with people every other day or so who come out of there. Only yesterday the man running our helicopter operation flew back. Three days ago he was flying over the combat area around Uyo and Ikot Ekpene. He has to maintain close liaison with the Nigerian military because he's sending his pilots out each day flying in close to the combat lines, so he has to know where they are. He just told me that the Biafrans are driving ahead all through that area and the Nigerians are falling back."

"No, no. I think you'll find that Biafra is going to collapse in a few days," Goldberg rejoined, "and you must be careful to remain objective in these matters."

The meeting broke up after that, the professors of international law being more inclined to believe Ambassador Goldberg than me. Biafra did not collapse for another sixteen months.

I returned from the meeting to the United Nations, angry, and telephoned a State Department official, saying: "You're getting terrible intelligence about the Nigerian war. I wouldn't ordinarily bother you about it, but it's interfering with us getting humanitarian relief in to the people who are starving there."

He responded, "Well, you know, this isn't all that important around here. In all the top-level policy conferences I've ever been in, it has only come up in a peripheral way. But I'll have my Nigeria man call you and talk with you about it."

Only a few days after he began serving as chief of operations of the church airlift, Count von Rosen flew to Addis Ababa to see for himself whether the negotiations that had briefly diverted August Lindt the week before could possibly succeed. He quickly concluded that the Nigerian delegation, with British advice, was making proposals known in advance to be unacceptable to the other side as they would imperil Biafra.

When he returned to São Tomé, von Rosen found Uli airport threatened and closed, the Nigerian offensive pushing ahead, Warton's planes not flying in ammunition. A ship with French arms was waiting off Gabon to be unloaded for the Libreville airlift but there was a delay and Biafran soldiers were running out of ammunition. Von Rosen and George Orick attempted to convince Warton he should begin flights again. Warton was willing to make relief flights but adamantly refused to transport ammunition.

He insisted that the Biafrans owed him $1.5 million, but looking at Warton's books Orick could see only $600,000 outstanding, which he regarded as a normal operating balance. Orick questioned Warton further, whereupon Warton pulled out his United States passport and said: "This is why!" It was brand-new, just issued in Lisbon the month before. More than a year earlier, the State Department had lifted Warton's passport and his airman's certificate as well. Orick understood him to mean that the passport was essential—without it Warton would not be able to continue in business as an international air charter operator.

Eighteen tons of ammunition stood at the airport waiting to be lifted in. Von Rosen and Orick sought to find a way to do this. The secretary in the church relief office refused to sign the necessary papers, feeling it would be immoral to use church planes to carry ammunition. Finally von Rosen persuaded the crew of a C-46 to fly without payment, by promising premiums for later relief flights. Workers began throwing bags of milk powder off the plane and loading on the ammunition. The C-46 made two flights that night.

By this time, there were many journalists on São Tomé, awaiting visas or a flight into Biafra. They vied with the pilots, crews, and relief workers for accommodations at the Hotel Geronimo—people slept in shifts, the beds being used around the clock. Von Rosen began holding press briefings each day at noon. All along, he had taken the position that it did not make sense to feed the Biafrans to save them from starvation if they would only be killed by other means later. At one news conference he stated that food and arms were inseparable.

News stories appeared charging that church relief planes were being used to transport arms and ammunition. Pastor Viggo Mollerup flew in from Copenhagen. He and von Rosen had a heated exchange, Mollerup making it emphatically clear that Nordchurchaid planes could not carry ammunition. Von Rosen resigned. Axel Duch took over as chief of operations.

Count von Rosen returned to Malmö, more committed than ever to saving the Biafrans. His quest would lead to his dramatic reappearance eight months later in an entirely new role that would not only change the war but, ironically, be used as a pretext for interfering with the airlift.

In Biafra a few days later, George Orick was meeting with Heinrich Jaggi when a Dutch nutritionist, Alida de Jager, arrived at Jaggi's house. The Nigerian offensive was nearing Okigwe, she told Jaggi, the town had been evacuated and, she said, "there's nobody there but the village idiot, a corpse and the Red Cross."

"Shall we go?" Jaggi said to Orick, and they drove north from Umuahia. It was Jaggi's duty, as ICRC delegate, to inform medical personnel running the station at Okigwe that while Red Cross tradition would be for them to stick by their posts through the midst of battle—to care for the wounded and continue on the other side as the battle passed over and beyond them—this, of course, was a matter of individual decision, not required of them.

Jaggi and Orick found the Red Cross compound at Okigwe in a no-man's-land between the two forces. Elements of the Nigerian First Division had driven down the Enugu-Awgu road from the north and already overrun Obilagu airstrip on the road to the east. Company C of the Twenty-first Nigerian Battalion was on the hill above the command; the noise of the troops came across to them in the clear night air. The buildings of the medical station were beside the main road along which the Nigerian troops might be expected to drive. A Red Cross flag flew over the compound, and members of the medical team wore the Red Cross badge on the left side of their shirts.

They were Yugoslav and Swedish doctors and other medical personnel sent to Biafra by their national Red Cross societies, plus an elderly English missionary couple, Albert and Marjorie Savory, who had been working in Nigeria since 1947 at the Oji River Leprosy Settlement. The Savorys were now running a World Council of Churches (WCC) feeding station. Jaggi explained that the Nigerian Army had been given the location of Red Cross medical installations and its troops had been issued a Code of Conduct, but it was up to them whether they chose to stay at their post while the battle flowed around them.

One of the Yugoslav surgeons asked Orick, who had been introduced as a UNICEF consultant: "I would be interested in hearing what the consultant has to say."

Orick replied, "I would be less concerned whether the Nigerian Government in Lagos knew of your presence than whether the Nigerian commander of these troops we can hear clanking up the hill knows who you are."

The Red Cross team decided to stay and care for the wounded. Jaggi and Orick made it back across the bridge south of the compound in time, before Biafran soldiers blew it up to block the advance.

As the sound of Nigerian gunfire drew closer, the doctors took shelter inside the Red Cross buildings. The ICRC later described what happened: "As the fighting approached Okigwe, the Yugoslav surgical team running the Okigwe State Hospital ordered the removal of some 200 patients from the hospital. The hospital area, about a hundred yards away from the Federal forces' main line of attack, was immediately declared a neutral zone. Red Cross notices were placed along the roads leading to the hospital, which clearly displayed the red cross on the roof and doors. The Yugoslav doctors and Swedish relief workers, who had withdrawn to the hospital as the fighting drew near, improvised two shelters and decided to stay put. They were joined by Mr. and Mrs. Savory of the World Council of Churches.

"In the afternoon of the 30th September, the ICRC delegates, hearing no further fighting, waved a small red cross flag outside their shelter. A Nigerian officer ordered: 'Come all out International Red Cross.' The delegates left their shelter with raised arms. They were surrounded by soldiers. One of them being drunken punched Yugoslav doctor Vucinic and Swedish delegate Renstroehm. The other soldiers searched everyone, confiscating everything in their pockets. A Nigerian officer tried to intervene, striking his soldiers with a stick. It was then that Dr. Vucinic, head of the Yugoslav surgical team, saw that the soldier who had struck him was loading his weapon. He threw himself to the ground, and all the delegates did the same. There was a volley of shots. A few minutes later, Dr. Vucinic stood up and saw that two of the ICRC delegates and Mr. and Mrs. Savory were dead. The officer commanding the Nigerian battalion in the Okigwe region was immediately informed and sent his Land Rover to convey the bodies and survivors to the command field headquarters. The ICRC base at Lagos was informed. The ICRC delegates spent the night in camp, exposed to the whim of threatening Nigerians who called them 'mercenaries' and 'Biafran rebels.' "

Secretary General Thant's representative investigated: "Federal soldiers deliberately and without provocation by the persons concerned shot and killed two Red Cross officials and two WCC representatives: they wounded three other Red Cross officials. Several rounds were fired at a distance of 3–5 meters. The officer-in-command, who has not been identified, was present at the site of the shooting but was either unwilling or unable to prevent it. . . ."

The ICRC and a number of governments protested strongly to the Nigerians about this wanton killing. Biafrans were bitter: there was no comparable protest, they charged, about the numerous civilians killed by Federal troops when they entered Biafran towns or by the daily air raids on civilian centers in Biafra. Of course, the humanitarian role of the Red Cross was at stake when Red Cross workers were killed.

Chapter 14

Genocide is an ugly word—scarcely anyone in high position uttered it except to say it was not taking place. For example, Arnold Smith, the Canadian serving as secretary general of the British Commonwealth: ". . . The charges that genocide is a policy of the Federal Government, in my judgment, are entirely unfounded. It is not the policy of General Gowon and his colleagues. According to my information, which coincides with that of the International Observers in the territory now occupied by the Federal authorities—a territory in which there are now some millions of Ibos—there has not been genocide. Certainly there have been some deplorable excesses and atrocities on both sides. These things are apt to happen in a war and I do not try to minimize their horror in any way, but I think that impartial observers would agree that in territory controlled by the Federal Government there has not been the implementation of a policy of genocide. . . ."

A statement as carefully worded as a lawyer's brief—finding no genocide "in the territory now occupied by the Federal authorities," no implementation of a policy of genocide "in territory controlled by the Federal Government." People were dying in vast numbers in the territory *not* controlled by the Federal government. Finding no policy of genocide toward them by observing what was happening elsewhere now became a highly successful component of British and Nigerian diplomacy.

Very likely it started innocently enough, perhaps even with good intention, but the "International Observers" mentioned by Arnold Smith soon became something else—an important part of the cover-up. The confrontation in the House of Commons that left Prime Minister Wilson and his ministers shaken put them on notice how awkward it might be for them in a few weeks. They could hardly be certain that, when the war ended, the hastily recruited and barely trained Nigerian troops would behave with exemplary restraint or could be kept under tight discipline by their officers.

There had been numerous reports of atrocities that the British were at pains to minimize in public. For example, the International Committee on Investigation of Crimes of Genocide brought forth some dramatic depositions at the time. They are the sort of accounts British and Nigerian officials would have called "Biafran propaganda" but also what the British feared would happen if the Nigerian Army finally overran the crowded Ibo homeland.

One report described the conduct of Federal troops upon entering Asaba in October 1967. They demanded food, according to A. Onya-Onianwah, and his village first sent four men off with money to the soldiers, while the women collected yams, palm oil, and vegetables for preparing soup. When the men did not return, they sent four more. Then: ". . . some Federal soldiers came to us at our meeting place and asked us to shout 'One Nigeria.' We all shouted as required." The troops then took them to a nearby village where they met groups from other villages. On the way, they saw a number of corpses: "These ugly sights filled us with dread but we could not run away in the presence of these armed soldiers." After they had danced for a time for the soldiers ". . . we were ordered to stop. The women were asked to move over to one side leaving only men on the other. We, the men, were then escorted to Ogbe Osowe where we saw horrible sights—many people who were already killed and some who were being tortured before they would be killed. Among the corpses I could from a distance distinguish some of the four men we sent on a mission. Then we knew to our sorrow what had happened to them and what fate awaited us."

Twenty of the men were selected, lined up, and told: "Today, I be your God, me, first; God second. God give you life, me I go takam. Two minute time you go die." After the twenty men were shot, another twenty were picked and the same ritual followed. Onya-Onianwah continued: "When the men were separated from the women and led away, some mothers followed behind to watch the fate of their children and as they were executed before them there was wailing and yelling. One woman gripped one of the soldiers and provoked him by biting him in order that she be killed and follow her son just dead. She was, of course, shot."

Onya-Onianwah and about fifty other men were taken away to what turned out to be another "killing ground" where there were already other victims: "A lot of them were yet to be buried whilst there were already a few mass graves around." He later told the international commission: "Just as we were lined up to be shot, one major came out from a Land Rover which had just then pulled in and announced that the killings should stop in obedience to the latest orders. The major then addressed us telling us to be grateful to God for being spared the fate of our unfortunate brothers." Onya-Onianwah and some other survivors later fled.

Such reports alarmed Parliament. General Gowon issued a Code of Conduct in an attempt to halt the carnage. Calculated killing seemed to have subsided, but British officials could not be sure that in the anticipated moment of victory, young Nigerian soldiers might not go on an extended rampage.

A single incident had more impact on popular consciousness than these reports of earlier massacres. Seen widely on television throughout Europe and America, one killing brought home to viewers in their living rooms the brutality about which they had heard only vaguely until then. The journalist John Barnes was present and tried to intervene to prevent it; later he described the incident in *Newsweek*.

As they reached the northern end of town, Barnes reported, a triumphant cry rang across the football field and a Nigerian soldier emerged from the bush prodding a nineteen-year-old Ibo ahead of him. The youth, trembling, said he had come back to look for his parents. Lieutenant Macauley Lamurde screamed at him, "You are a rebel soldier," slashing the boy across the chest with his swagger stick.

"My God, my God," the boy moaned, as if he knew what was in store for him. Barnes asked him his name. He said it was Mathias and repeated that he was only looking for his parents.

Hoping to save his life, Barnes said to the lieutenant, "You cannot kill this man. Your code of conduct prohibits it. You will not kill him, will you, Lieutenant?"

Lamurde replied, "No." But then he bellowed at the boy, "Stand to attention!" When the young Ibo did so, Lamurde shrieked, "Look, he is obviously a rebel soldier!" Another officer tied Mathias's hands to his leg and kicked him over. The boy pleaded: "I'm not a soldier. Sweet Jesus, save me!"

Barnes wrote: "Leaning casually on his swagger stick, Lamurde pumped three bullets into the boy's body, then another into his neck. Then one of Lamurde's men dragged the corpse across the road and heaved it into the bushes."

The Nigerian government had to take some action; it did not reassure the public to see on their television screens a few nights later the execution of the lieutenant who had shot the boy. Rather, this witness of a single barbarous act made vivid to them what Barnes wrote: "Whatever promises are made by the Federal government, every male between 15 and 50 knows that he has little chance of surviving if he falls into the hands of Nigerian troops."

The British suggested to the Nigerians that they create an international observer force to accompany Federal troops. The FMG asked four nations to provide observers: Canada, Poland, Sweden, and the United Kingdom, expressing the hope that "all will arrive in Lagos within the week ending September 14th." This would get them on the scene the day before the start of the Organization of African Unity meeting in Algiers.

The letter to the four governments stated: "The Federal Government's reason for establishing this Observer Team is in pursuance of its desire to satisfy the world opinion, contrary to the malicious propaganda of the rebels, that there is no intentional or planned systematic and wanton destruction of civilian lives or their property in the war zone."

In addition, the FMG invited observers from the OAU and suggested U Thant send "not a UN observer as such" but a person he could personally trust to report to him on his findings. Thant gave his representative in Lagos this new role of observer. The Nigerians wanted the UN reports provided to them so they could be published along with those of the international observers. However, the UN required that they be released in New York. This was a fine distinction; during the ensuing months the public became bemused into thinking that reports of the observers assembled by the Nigerian government represented some official international authority—even the United Nations.

That the observers team was not entirely impartial was clear from the inclusion of a British observer—during the first month a retired major general, Henry Alexander. British critics of their government's policy pointed out that Alexander was managing director of an oil shipping company deriving three-quarters of its profits from Shell, the major holder of oil concessions in Nigeria. Soon after his brief tour at the front, General Alexander would return to London to become one of the most outspoken partisans of the British-Nigerian position.*

The agreed terms under which the international observers operated restricted their activities and shaped the impact they had upon public opinion. They reported only what they observed in each place they visited, at the time they were there. They did not investigate what may have happened in the past, such as charges of the massacre at Asaba. Their mission was to witness the conduct of Federal troops on the Federal side of the combat lines, which meant they did not go into Biafra. Transportation and housing were provided by the Nigerian government; they were

* Eventually even, allegedly, precipitating the Official Secrets Act trial over the release of the "Scott report," the analysis made by the defense adviser in the British Embassy in Lagos, Colonel Robert Scott. Jonathan Aitken, the journalist put on trial, gave his version of how he obtained the copy of the report that soon found its way into the press: during a discussion at dinner, "General Alexander said rather curtly words to the effect of 'You're talking rubbish. I've just had a report in from Lagos which proves the Nigerians are going to finish this war off very soon. I'll let you see it.'" A version that, not surprisingly, General Alexander disputed in court.

escorted by Federal army officers; they spent all their time in Lagos or with the Nigerian Army when in the field, subjecting them to day-to-day influence of the attitudes and beliefs that had grown up on that side of the war. From time to time their public utterances suggested they were not overly sophisticated politically and, as military officers, they seemed to have slipped into an easy camaraderie with officers in the Nigerian Army.

The observers were assured that they could take the initiative as to what area they would visit and when, but at times they were interfered with by a local army commander. They submitted their reports to the FMG and agreed to hold up release to the public for twenty-four hours, thus permitting the government to manage the news about them. (While the UN sought to keep its observer separate from his military counter-parts, a Nigerian news release lumped them together as "The International Observer Team," listing first the representative of "The United Nations Secretary General.")

For their first tour, the British, Canadian, and Swedish observers spent five days in the field, visiting two areas on the northern front. They found the Federal troops ". . . alert, cheerful and well disciplined." They neither saw nor heard any evidence that the troops had committed acts "with intent to destroy—wholly or in part—the Ibo people or their property." The observers said they did see considerable evidence that the troops in the area were "assisting the local population, in particular by feeding them until the Civil Administration and the Red Cross could take over the responsibility."

Their first report was, on the whole, reassuring: "Discussions with village leaders and refugees confirm that the Ibo people feared the Federal troops until they actually met them. This fear is the result of the actual fighting and the propaganda put out by the rebels which leads the Ibos to believe the Federal troops will kill them. . . ."

Similarly the secretary general's representative found Federal troops "alert and well disciplined" and abiding by the "code of conduct." He reported that Ibos who had either remained behind or returned to their villages seemed to have "confidence in the conduct of the Federal troops." Some spoke of having been in the bush as long as ten months, he said: "Fear of warfare and a natural timidity towards armed soldiers, together with the belief spread among the Ibo people that the federal forces were bent on exterminating them, had driven most civilian villagers into hiding during periods of conflict."

The most newsworthy conclusion of the military observers: "*Genocide.* There is no evidence of any intent by the Federal troops to destroy the Ibo people or their property, and the use of the term genocide is in no way justified." This and subsequent reports with similar conclusions ("We did not see or hear any evidence of genocide") were confined to areas the observers had actually visited on the Nigerian side of the combat lines, not inside Biafra; newspapers nevertheless headlined their stories: "International Panel in Biafra Finds No Proof of Genocide" and "No Genocide Proof Is Found in Biafra."

It was not understood that the observers confined their observations to the conduct of Nigerian troops in specific areas already under Federal control. A member of the Canadian Parliament remarked, while questioning the diplomat in charge of the Africa section of the Canadian External Affairs Ministry: "We are interested in whether or not people . . . are dying of starvation . . . and yet our observer team has given us a report which is based only on one side of the line, which has nothing to do with what is going on in Biafra, but only what is going on in the Nigerian portion. Is this correct?"

A British M.P. asked the foreign secretary whether observers could not be sent into Biafra: "Would it not help to have observers on both sides? How can ten men observe the activities of a Nigerian army of eighty thousand soldiers, particularly when their itinerary is provided by Lagos and it may be that their visits are stage-managed?"

"We cannot accept the accusation of stage-managed visits against a team of distinguished, experienced, and competent men who have given a report on this matter," Michael Stewart responded. "If we are examining the allegation of genocide, clearly their business is to be where the Federal troops are. Their presence in areas entirely held by the Ibos where there are no Federal troops would have no relevance to allegations of genocide against the Federal troops. . . ."

The secret report of the defense adviser of the British Embassy in Lagos, which found its way into the press in the final days of the war, spelled out the eventual effect of the international observers: "The only propaganda success the Federal Military Government has had is their recruitment of an Observer Team to tour the battle areas to dispel rebel accusations of genocide. In this they have been highly successful and world opinion is now convinced that the Federals are not bent on destroying Ibos as a race."

Confining the question of genocide to the conduct of Federal troops neatly excluded the question of who was responsible for starvation in Biafra. A team of military observers operating on the scene could not have reached any conclusion about that, as responsibility for it lay concealed somewhere in the abstract world of politics and diplomacy, shrouded in the secrecy of Red Cross negotiations between Nigeria and Biafra, wrapped inside the cocoon of confidential deliberations of governments. U Thant stated on a number of occasions that no individual could determine whether genocide was being committed or not; only a competent organ of the United Nations could do so. In saying this, he certainly did not intend to encourage any nation to bring the question before such a competent organ.

The United Nations had declared in 1946 that "genocide is a crime under international law which the civilized world condemns—and for the commission of which principals and accomplices, whether private individuals, public officials or statesmen, and whether the crime is committed on religious, racial, political or any other grounds—are punishable. . . ."

To implement this declaration, the UN created the Convention on the Prevention and Punishment of Genocide. By the fall of 1968, seventy-two nations had become parties to it, agreeing to undertake "to prevent and to punish" genocide. This included such acts as "killing members of the group," "causing serious bodily or mental harm to members of the group," or "deliberately inflicting on the group conditions of life calculated to bring about its physical destruction," when "committed with intent to destroy, in whole or in part, a national, ethnical, racial or religious group . . ."

The Nuremberg and Tokyo war crimes trials had already established the principle that government leaders can be held responsible for crimes against humanity. The Genocide Convention stated: "Persons committing genocide . . . shall be punished, whether they are constitutionally responsible rulers, public officials or private individuals." Not only should the act of genocide be punished but also complicity and conspiracy to commit genocide.

Was genocide being committed in the Biafran situation? Were any individuals deliberately inflicting on the Biafrans conditions of life calculated to bring about their physical destruction in whole or in part? Were any officials conspiring to commit genocide or entering into complicity in genocide?

Any of the seventy-two nations that had acceded to the convention could have called "upon the competent organs of the United Nations to take such action under the charter of the United Nations as they consider appropriate for the prevention and suppression of acts of genocide." In fact, the convention obligates them to undertake "to prevent" as much as to punish such acts. None did so.

U Thant did not want the United Nations involved in Nigeria-Biafra. The day the Red Cross airlift began, the foreign ministers of the Scandinavian countries—Denmark, Finland, Iceland, Norway, Sweden—sent him a message assuring him of their full support. They requested "in view of the central position which the Secretary General holds in the humanitarian assistance work" that he suggest what measures might be taken.

Thant replied that he fully shared their concern but took exception to the suggestion that he had a central position: ". . . The Secretary General feels obliged to point out that from the beginning of international humanitarian efforts in Nigeria, the central role relating both to initiation and coordination has been exercised by the International Committee of the Red Cross." He said he would pass on the offer of further Nordic assistance to the ICRC.

The Scandinavian foreign ministers were not alone in turning to the United Nations. Expectations rose, as time for the General Assembly neared, that now the UN would finally act. The churchmen who began the airlift did so thinking they would have to continue it for only a short time. Pastor Viggo Mollerup later told an interviewer he had been sure that "the UN could not ignore the matter—that it would start some kind of relief effort along the lines of the Congo aid."

This was exactly what U Thant wanted to avoid. The Congo had been a trauma from which the UN had not yet recovered. Thant was, in a way, a product of the Congo crisis. The public remembers Nikita Khrushchev taking off his shoe and pounding with it on his desk at the 1960 General Assembly, but this traditional Communist tactic of demeaning Western-style parliamentary institutions was only a more visible manifestation of what the Soviet leader set about to do to the United Nations.

Two months earlier, the entire UN had been mobilized to provide an administration until orderly government could be organized in the Congo (now Zaire), abruptly given its independence without sufficient preparation. Secretary General Dag Hammarskjöld rushed in personnel from the United Nations, as well as a peacekeeping force.

During the ensuing strife, as the Soviet Union backed one faction, Belgian mining interests supported the breakaway Katanga regime, and other nations sought to establish a stable Western-oriented government, UN staff became directly involved in a conflict in a way they had never been before and certainly would never want to be again. Some came away bearing real as well as psychic scars, such as the broken nose of Undersecretary General Brian Urquhart, who was nearly killed one night in Katanga when he was seized, carrried off, and had his face bashed with a rifle butt.

Hammarskjöld's leadership and the United Nations action frustrated Soviet attempts to take advantage of the chaos in the Congo, and Premier Khrushchev decided to come to the General Assembly himself. But he made the mistake of taking a slow boat from Kaliningrad to a pier on the East River south of the United Nations. (The 7,500-ton *Baltika* took ten days to make the voyage, bearing not only the Soviet prime minister but the Communist heads of state of Hungary, Rumania, and Bulgaria as well.)

By the time Khrushchev arrived in New York, Hammarskjöld had succeeded, at an emergency session of the General Assembly, in rallying the support of the smaller nations to gain 70–0 approval (with Soviet-bloc abstention) of a resolution instructing the secretary general to continue "vigorous action" in the Congo situation.

Affronted, Khrushchev not only expressed his displeasure by pounding his shoe on the desk but made a speech calling for the ouster of Hammarskjöld and replacement of the post of secretary general with a "troika" of secretaries general—one for the Western world, one for the Communist world, and one for what the Soviet Union was coming to call "the Third World."

The Soviet premier did not succeed in this, but later, after Hammarskjöld was killed in a plane crash while flying out of Katanga Province, Khrushchev did manage to get a secretary general from the Third World, by temperament as much as by ideology disinclined to act, thereby immobilizing the Secretariat quite as much as Khrushchev had intended with his plan for a troika of secretaries general, each pulling in a different direction.

The Soviet Union had long been pressuring the secretary general to try to limit his powers, but Hammarskjöld was not one to be restrained. Now, in a Burmese diplomat, disinclined to act in any way that might reflect adversely upon himself, Khrushchev found a man more to his liking. The coming of Thant to the UN coincided with the arrival in the General Assembly hall of representatives from many new African nations, plus a finanacial crisis brought on in part by Soviet refusal to pay its share of costs for the Congo operation.

All these factors and events, still vivid and compelling in the minds of officials on the thirty-eighth floor of the Secretariat, served to immobilize Thant. He was under constant pressure from Soviet representatives aimed at inhibiting any initiatives whenever a situation arose in which they had an interest—and they had an interest in most situations. Now the large bloc of new African nations was coming to play an important role in the United Nations, in league with either newly independent Asian or Arab nations, often coached and encouraged by Soviet diplomats. They were turning the UN into a "Third World" instrument rather than the instrument of Western nations it had been during its first decades of existence. Khrushchev was gone, but his plan to immobilize the secretary general and the UN had succeeded in an unforeseen way.

In the Nigerian situation, Thant was under direct pressure not to act—or, as we have seen, to allow any part of the United Nations to act. His instructions to the UN specialized agencies had fallen on receptive ears; with the exception of UNICEF, they were not inclined to get involved in Biafra. Throughout the summer, while the State Department held back on responding to its second request, UNICEF tried to get its sister UN agency, the World Food Program, to provide food. WFP officials responded that they could not act until they received a request from the Nigerian government. UNICEF officials sought to show them how they might stimulate such a request—it was unthinkable to them that they should. Finally, more than four months later, UNICEF succeeded in having the secretary general's special representative get General Gowon to make a request to the World Food Program.

Occasionally Thant responded to the humanitarian pressures upon him. His speech to the OAU meeting in Algiers expressed his "distress and dismay at the mounting toll of destruction, starvation and loss of life resulting from the tragic fratricidal strife in Nigeria." He went so far as to say: "In the name of humanity, it is essential that everything be done to help relieve the impact of this tragic conflict."

Thant reiterated, however, the position he always took in his public utterances, citing the OAU's resolution of the previous year that recognized the "sovereign and territorial integrity of Nigeria" and pledged "faith in the Federal Government."* It further recognized the Nigerian crisis as "an internal affair. . . ." Thant went on: ". . . This resolution is a basis for my attitude and approach to this problem, and I believe that the OAU should be the most appropriate instrument for the promotion of peace in Nigeria."

Senator Edward Kennedy urged that the humanitarian problem in Nigeria be placed on the agenda of the General Assembly. He proposed that the General Assembly pass a resolution directing the secretary general to expedite conclusion of a "mercy agreement" that would recognize the humanitarian obligation of governments to back a UN effort with food, funds, personnel, and equipment, including logistical support for an airlift.

The secretary general showed at a press conference that he could take an initiative if he wanted to. He drew from his pocket a piece of paper, stating: "Just to put this to the test—of course, this is not a very realistic proposal—I was wondering whether, at a session of the General

* According to one UN official, Thant's attitude in private was the same as that which he expressed in public.

Assembly, if a resolution on such lines were to be tabled and put to the vote, it would not receive a majority endorsement. The resolution would be phrased somewhat on these lines. . . ."

He then read from his proposed resolution, concluding: "I was wondering whether, if such a resolution were tabled, it would not receive the majority vote. Of course, it is, as I have said, not a very practical proposition, since the item is not before the Assembly and not on the agenda. But what I am trying to explain is that I have been all along trying to reflect the conscience of humanity from this vantage point of the international organization.

"What I am much more concerned about is the unprecedented tragedy in this little country. . . ." Thant told the correspondents. "I think it is unthinkable, incredible, when you think of the sufferings of these people." He was not talking about Biafra or the Biafrans, however. The wording for the General Assembly resolution he suggested called for the cessation of bombing of North Vietnam.

On the subject of Nigeria and Biafra he told the journalists: "My attitude towards the question of the Nigerian internecine strife is well known. My approach to the problem and my policy towards it are guided primarily, if not exclusively, by the decision of the Organization of African Unity, which was arrived at last year in Kinshasa. I shall continue to be guided by the decisions of the OAU which, in my view, should be the main machinery for the settlement of this dispute. As you all know, the OAU has repeatedly—last year as well as this year—adopted resolutions recognizing the sovereignty and territorial integrity of Nigeria."

Thant acknowledged that the OAU had expressed deep concern "at the disastrous and calamitous fate of these unfortunate people in the Eastern Central Region of Nigeria." He spoke of the UN specialized agencies, particularly UNICEF, giving food, milk, and medicine to the victims, and added, "I want to take this opportunity of expressing my thanks to the International Committee of the Red Cross for the splendid job it has been doing." He concluded: "I believe the problem will be settled very soon."

The compartmentalization of vast bureaucracies being what it is, U Thant apparently saw no inconsistency in carrying out the earlier instructions of the International Conference on Human Rights, sending a letter to all United Nations members (as well as to the UN specialized agencies), drawing their attention to the existing rules of international law on the subject of human rights in armed conflicts; urging them, until new international laws could be adopted, to ensure that in all armed conflicts "the inhabitants and belligerents are protected in accordance with 'the principles of the law of nations derived from the usages established among civilized peoples, from the laws of humanity and from the dictates of the public conscience.' "

As the time for convening the General Assembly drew near, numerous scholars of international law prepared papers setting forth how and why the United Nations could and should act. They put aside the argument that the OAU's resolution preempted UN action and spelled out various ways that the UN could be seized of this problem, citing principles of humanitarian intervention based upon historical experience that had been incorporated into the United Nations charter, the specific provisions of the charter, and the various human rights declarations approved by the General Assembly.

One expert, for example, commenting on the concept of human rights incorporated into the charter, stated: "What is crucial to notice in this connection is that the human rights provisions are not merely declaratory but carry with them legal obligation. This obligation is emphatically reinforced by the Universal Declaration of Human Rights and the two Covenants of Human Rights recently adopted by the General Assembly."

The third article of the declaration provides that "everyone has the right to life, liberty and security of person." A question arose, when the declaration was being framed, about the need for guaranteeing "the right to life." A Nobel Peace Prize recipient for his work on human rights, René Cassin, explained his draft provision: "The problem is not as elementary as it appears to be. In 1933, when Germany began to violate these very principles, all the nations of the world asked themselves whether they have the right to intervene in order to assure respect for these principles and to save humanity and they did not intervene. It is for this reason that I believe it to be of fundamental importance to affirm the right of human beings to exist."

However, only governments could act; individuals had no standing before the United Nations, nor did the UN contain any machinery or procedure through which the victims of suffering could petition. "Millions of lives are in hourly jeopardy and, therefore, immediate action is respectfully urged," Odumegwu Ojukwu wrote the president of the General Assembly. The letter, sent to all members, pleaded that they call upon the assembly "to take such action under the Charter as they consider appropriate for the prevention and suppression of acts of genocide being perpetrated by the Nigerian Federal Government and its armed forces, supported by the Governments of the United Kingdom, the Soviet Union and Egypt. . . ." But only four nations recognized Biafra; neither it nor its head of state had any legal or diplomatic existence as far as the United Nations was concerned.

By now the Canadian government was under intense pressure to increase the supply of food reaching Biafra. Mitchell Sharp, its minister of external affairs, came to the United Nations prepared to introduce a resolution.* He contacted Thant and conferred with Nigerian foreign minister Okoi Arikpo and others about bringing the matter of humanitarian relief before the General Assembly. Thant urged him not to introduce a resolution, warning that to raise the Nigerian question would be divisive.

Arikpo spoke harshly to Henry Labouisse, complaining about the initiatives UNICEF had been taking. As one State Department official put it: "He read the riot act to Labouisse—not once, but a number of times." Arikpo complained bitterly to Thant about the efforts of UNICEF. The secretary general warned Labouisse to "stop meddling in the Nigerian situation."

Until then Labouisse had been trying to find ways to increase relief, concentrating that past month on attempting to get governments to provide C-130s to the Red Cross airlift. That ended when Arikpo and Thant spoke to him. A few days later, when it was suggested that he present to the UN a report setting forth the facts of starvation and inadequacy of relief, Labouisse became agitated, his hands shook, and he exclaimed nervously, excitedly: "I'm not going to get into 'the numbers game'! I'm not going to get into 'the numbers game'!"

From that time forward Labouisse became reluctant to do anything that would offend the Nigerians or bring down upon him Thant's wrath. UNICEF continued providing the bulk of medicines and serving as a main channel for U.S. donated foods to the airlifts. But there was no more aggressiveness, no more imaginative initiatives. Thus the Nigerian government not only blocked attempts to bring the problem before the United Nations but succeeded in inhibiting one of the two official international relief agencies—the one whose mission is the children of the world.

---

* While his critics in the Canadian Parliament thought Sharp completely cynical and unyielding about the problem of humanitarian relief, he was personally deeply distressed about the starvation. On one occasion, while talking with a journalist, he broke down and wept.

Chapter 15

The Red Cross airlift had barely begun when the Nigerian government set about to bring it to an end. Within days Chief Anthony Enahoro was in Bern trying to get the president of the Swiss Federation to intervene to stop the Red Cross from violating the sovereign territory of Nigeria. Though the FMG had agreed to daylight flights, he complained, the ICRC had gone ahead without authorization and flown at night. Nigeria had agreed there would be no air activity while relief flights were coming in, Enahoro said. But, already briefed by the ICRC, the Swiss president knew about the condition that had been added, reserving the right of the Nigerian Air Force to fly surveillance over Uli airstrip while Red Cross planes were landing during the day.

The Nigerians mounted a campaign to the public as well, stating that they had reached agreement with the Red Cross to fly to "the bigger of the two airstrips, at Uli" the 3,500 tons of supplies on Fernando Po. "Unfortunately," the FMG reported, "this helpful arrangement has again been blocked by Mr. Ojukwu and his secessionist associates who have declared that they would not agree to Red Cross flights to the airstrip."

Prime ministers, foreign ministers, and government spokesmen in Europe and North America soon began asking: "Why won't the Biafrans accept the proposal for daylight flights offered by the Nigerians?" Pressures upon them within their countries had become intense, and they gladly took up the line that Biafran authorities refused to agree to the airlift after agreement had been reached with the Nigerian government.

The Nigerians also unleashed a campaign of sustained invective against Red Cross personnel in Nigeria. Middle-level Swiss functionaries gave some cause for this: they had little idea how to behave in an African country, newly independent, still sensitive to colonialism, resentful of "white faces." Whatever the real basis for antagonism toward the Swiss Red Cross officials, however, the attacks went beyond natural hostility.

The government still anticipated victory momentarily and wanted the foreigners out of the country. It had been a British idea to bring the Red Cross in to get control over the other relief agencies. Now that Lindt had gone ahead and started the airlift, the Nigerians were no longer willing to tolerate the ICRC presence.

At the weekly meeting of relief agencies working in Nigeria, Yewande Oyediran, the chairwoman, raised the question of the ICRC's handing the relief operation over to the Nigerian Red Cross. To some relief officials this seemed unrealistic not only because the Nigerian Red Cross society, formed a few years before, was not experienced but also because the expected collapse of Biafra would bring vast numbers of people in grave need under Federal control. There was serious question whether the relief organizations would send volunteers or whether governments would continue contributing funds in a country notorious for corruption, if the ICRC were no longer in charge.

At the beginning of October, the Nigerians gave the ICRC a memorandum titled "Transitional Period," which stated: "The reorganization should aim at a conclusion of the takeover by the end of 1968, if not earlier."

Given the rapidly deteriorating relations between the FMG and the ICRC, Henrik Beer, secretary general of the League of Red Cross Societies, attempted to make the transition more realistic. The government did not intend, however, that the Nigerian Red Cross would actually control relief. A harbinger of the controversy that would arise after Biafra finally did collapse appeared in the memo: "The Red Cross relief programmes must be fitted into the Government overall relief and rehabilitation plans. . . ."

Allison Ayida of the Ministry of Economic Development made clear to a relief official visiting Lagos what this would mean for the stricken Biafran population once it came under Federal control. (After the conquest of Biafra, he came to play the key role in postwar relief and rehabilitation.) Though considerable attention would be paid war-ravaged areas in the East after cessation of hostilities, Ayida said, it must not be overlooked that many parts of Nigeria remained very underdeveloped and had a rightful claim on resources. He pointed out that the areas of the East (Biafra) were among the most highly developed in Nigeria. It would be reasonable to bring them back only to their prewar level while concentrating investments on other parts of the country.

August Lindt could do little about the sudden crisis: in Nigerian eyes, he was the prime culprit. He had begun Operation INALWA without authorization, knowing full well that the Nigerians opposed an airlift even if Gowon had made the gesture of offering ten days of daylight flights into Uli. As he came and went between Nigeria and Fernando Po and

Biafra, trying to get relief operations organized on both sides of the lines, Lindt found that he could not get to meet again with Gowon or others of importance. He was, in effect, persona non grata in Lagos.

So Roger Gallopin had to try to negotiate some continuation of the ICRC's role. Red Cross officials could not accept ouster from Nigeria. They had evolved a working principle that the Red Cross must act equally on both sides of a conflict if it is to remain impartial and acceptable to both belligerents. Nigerian officials understood this; their sudden determination to get the ICRC out of their country not only manifested anger but would end Red Cross activities on the Biafran side as well, thus halting the airlift.

When he arrived in Lagos, Gallopin did not have a strong position. The unwillingness of governments to support the ICRC in the face of Nigerian anger created a financial crisis. Without funds, the Red Cross could not long sustain the increasingly costly relief action. Gallopin had to prevent the ouster of the ICRC; he had to gain from Gowon seeming acceptance of a continuation of the Red Cross. He met with Gowon without Lindt, which angered Lindt.

Gowon was annoyed with the ICRC about a number of matters. He had just told Ambassador Mathews and Joseph Palmer that the ICRC's current difficulties came from his relations with Lindt; he was offended that after their September 3 meeting Lindt had never told him what had happened: "World opinion was left in the dark that Ojukwu had turned down daylight flights to Uli, while the world was not left in the dark when the FMG turned down the airstrip at Obilagu." Also, the Nigerians resented news accounts that a DC-4 had been taken over by the Federal army—keeping the Red Cross from operating it—when actually it was a charter plane both the Army and the Red Cross were using in Nigeria. Gowon complained that Lindt had put out information about the neutralization of Obilagu but had remained silent when Biafrans rescinded the neutrality at the time Uli was out of action. He would have expected the ICRC to let him know, Gowon said, but the first he learned of it was when Federal troops got to Obilagu airstrip and did not find Red Cross personnel.

Meeting with Gallopin, Gowon said the Eastern Region must not be recognized as sovereign: "You are a correct institution, but composed of Swiss people and your newspapers keep talking of 'Biafra' as if it actually existed." He expressed his concern that the ICRC, in negotiating with Biafra, was treating it as equal with Nigeria, thereby according it a recognition of sovereignty.

In this hostile atmosphere, Gallopin negotiated compromises, agreeing to "Nigerianization" of the relief operation, with Saidu Z. Mohammed of the Nigerian Red Cross as relief coordinator, more Nigerians in higher posts, relief teams composed of one-third international relief workers and two-thirds Nigerians, no foreign replacements for present personnel until the Nigerian Red Cross certified that no qualified Nigerian was available to fill the post.

There was perhaps misunderstanding, perhaps calculated ambiguity. Later, as the war dragged on, the Nigerians insisted that Gallopin had agreed to hand over relief once the Nigerian Red Cross was prepared to assume its new duties. But the Red Cross hung on, not willing to give up its mandate, interpreting differently the transition period needed to complete "Nigerianization."

At this point, however, ICRC executives were playing for time; they still expected the conflict to end at any moment, as the British had been promising. In any event they did not have funds for more than a few weeks, so they could not think beyond the present crisis. Their immediate concern was to avoid the disgrace of being thrown out of the largest relief operation they had been charged with conducting up to that time, in the ignominious circumstances of being slandered in Lagos for arrogance and luxurious living by Red Cross personnel.

The U.S.—necessarily a major relief donor—and other governments remained hung up on the conviction that access to Biafra would come with its collapse. Their planning assumptions originated in their embassies in Lagos and suffered, consequently, from the "Lagos mentality," at the opposite pole from relief agencies operating in Biafra.

As the war continued through October, governments had to adopt new assumptions for future relief. At first the date for the anticipated collapse was merely pushed forward another two months. Then Agency for International Development representatives in the American Embassy in Lagos prepared a paper stating that "D-day, or the day on which open access to Biafra is possible, will occur on or about March 1, 1969." Presumably it would take at least that long for the British to get the Nigerian Army resupplied and ready for the next "final offensive."

"Nos caisses sont vides—absolument vides," Red Cross President Samuel Gonard told government representatives invited to a meeting in Geneva. In September the ICRC had not been able to pay all the salaries of relief workers in Nigeria. By the end of October, Red Cross expenditure exceeded income by three million Swiss francs. Now, in early November, officials in Geneva did not know how they were going to continue relief on both sides of the fighting. Stressing that the emergency had now gone beyond what any relief organization could do, Gonard demanded the participation of the international community.

August Lindt told the ambassadors there had been remarkable improvement among those it had been possible to help thus far. He recalled one of his first visits to Biafra three months earlier: approaching a refugee camp he had heard strange sounds and could not tell whether they were from birds or cats. When he got closer he realized these were the sounds of whimpering children. On a recent visit, approaching this same camp again, he heard much louder sounds—this time they could be recognized as laughing children.

What was being done, however, was not enough. Lindt warned of the increasing shortage of carbohydrate foods. For the next four months, the ICRC required another thirty million Swiss francs for minimum operating costs, supplies, and purchase of foods locally.

Even as governments allowed the Red Cross to flounder along this way—literally from hand to mouth—they kept pressure on the church agencies to coordinate with the ICRC. For example, when the American agencies sought financial assistance to charter the C-130 McGeorge Bundy had located, the State Department offered them $500,000, on condition they place their relief operation under the International Committee of the Red Cross.

The search for C-130s set in motion a new diplomatic-propaganda ploy that would dominate relief efforts for the remainder of the war. Though each government behaved somewhat differently, what Canada did at this point serves as an example of how prime ministers, foreign ministers, and their diplomatic advisers attempted to cope with what was, for them, "the Biafran problem."

When the ICRC made the decision to begin its airlift, governments had to decide whether to support it. National Red Cross representatives passed on to their governments the request for cargo planes. The head of the Canadian Red Cross, Major General A. E. Wrinch, kept his government fully informed, requesting C-130s and urging Canadian participation. So Canada knew of the plan about which the public remained unaware, but like other governments declined to make C-130s available unless the Nigerians agreed.

Only Sweden took the position that a C-130 turned over to the ICRC became a Red Cross plane on a humanitarian mission. Had others insisted, as the Nordic governments did, that the Red Cross should be allowed to fly to the neutralized airstrip, it might have been possible to build up an airlift sufficient to meet the protein needs of the children. But most gave priority to political rather than humanitarian considerations.

Canadian prime minister Pierre-Elliott Trudeau felt this was a "just war" on the part of Nigeria. A professor of international law, his approach was highly legalistic, not on the side of the Geneva Conventions but against violating the sovereignty or interfering in the internal affairs of another nation. He had his own secession problem—though, as one parliamentary critic pointed out, anyone who would compare Quebec and Biafra understood neither Canada nor Nigeria. Then, of course, there was the close working relationship between Canada and Britain in the conduct of international affairs, not to mention relations with that other large Commonwealth country, Nigeria. As Canadian external affairs minister Mitchell Sharp put it: "I would venture to say that Canada had closer relations with Nigeria than any other country in the world except Britain and, as far as Nigeria is concerned, we are in a sense the second most important country to the United Kingdom itself."

When two Canadian M.P.s returned from a visit to Biafra, their account of the situation distressed and agitated their countrymen. Axel Duch, chief of operations on São Tomé, had impressed upon them the inadequacy of the planes being used and the limited amount of food that could be flown in. He urged them to get their government to provide C-130s. They met with Trudeau, who suggested they confer with Sharp, then attending the General Assembly in New York. Sharp approached the Nigerian foreign minister about giving one Hercules to the Red Cross for relief within Nigeria and two for delivering food to Biafra. Arikpo hesitated.

Confusion reigned, for weeks. What had Arikpo actually said to the Canadian M.P.s? Would the Nigerian government permit daylight flights? Sharp understood that the FMG was prepared to allow the planes to fly for the Red Cross in daylight. The Canadian government checked this through its embassy in Lagos; it was confirmed that Canada could turn the aircraft over to the ICRC. Three Air Force Hercules headed toward Nigeria and Fernando Po.

For a time the Canadian government gratified its citizens, taking action, it seemed, to help the Biafrans. Apparently, however, Arikpo had spoken to Sharp only about allowing Red Cross flights in daylight from Lagos or Fernando Po to Uli. One Hercules arrived in Lagos, another at Fernando Po, the third got as far as Brazil. The Canadian government awaited authorization for them to fly in daylight. Lindt sought permission from the Nigerian Foreign Office. Chief Enahoro's younger brother (whom Lindt regarded as less of a hard-liner on relief) stated that the conditions of the April letter to the Red Cross continued to apply. This meant that the ICRC could fly, but "at its own risk and peril."

For the Canadian government, the "agreement" was no agreement at all.

Now a significant development took place. Trudeau sent his top assistant, Ivan Head, to Lagos to clarify the situation. He met with Gowon, who guaranteed the safety of Red Cross flights in daylight into Uli airstrip from either Lagos or Fernando Po (the same position that had prompted Head's trip in the first place). Gowon made one condition: that Ojukwu undertake not to use Uli during daylight hours for arms flights.

The Nigerian government had been gradually formulating this new negotiating position since early September, when rejection of the ten-day offer revealed that the Biafrans could not agree to flights into Uli during the day when the field was obstructed to prevent its seizure. Until then, Lagos adamantly opposed relief flights in daylight, charging that they would interfere with its air force's military operations. From September on, the Nigerians would speak of nothing else—this became the preferred proposal, almost supplanting a "land corridor."

Trudeau, informing the Parliament about the "agreement" his assistant had obtained, praised the Nigerians: "This statement by General Gowon is, I suggest, both significant and laudatory. It illustrates clearly the sincerity of the Federal Military Government in its declarations of good faith toward the Ibo peoples." He went on to say: "I therefore now address a public and urgent appeal to Colonel Ojukwu to seize this opportunity to open up his airport to daylight relief flights and so permit the Red Cross to increase substantially food shipments to those civilians in the rebel held areas needing help."

The Canadians received no response from the Biafrans. The Hercules at Lagos Airport stood idle, the ICRC not able to get permission for it to begin flights between there and Port Harcourt. However, the Hercules on Fernando Po clandestinely made eleven night flights for the Red Cross into Biafra. The Canadians could not admit this, not having authorization from the FMG. Finally, with no word from the Biafrans and no agreement of both parties, the planes were called back to Canada. The government had at first mollified its critics then angered them.

More important, its maladroit handling of the Red Cross request for C-130s prompted the FMG to formalize the response that was to serve the British and Nigerians well during the remaining fourteen months of the war. Having succeeded in managing the Canadian initiative, Lagos sent a formal note to the ICRC, withdrawing the "agreement" under which it had been flying "at its own risk." Giving as its reason "the difficulty of identifying ICRC flights at night," the FMG informed the Red Cross "it has now been decided that all ICRC flights should take place in daylight hours" and invited the ICRC to enter into discussions with Federal Military authorities about making such arrangements.

Before leaving for Biafra, August Lindt confided to representatives of other relief agencies that he felt the Canadian announcement about daylight flights before he had had a chance to consult with Ojukwu would make his negotiations with the Biafrans very difficult.

Canada's attempt to manage public opinion while not angering the Nigerians provoked new difficulties for the church airlift as well. A query from the Canadian UN representative prompted the Nigerian ambassador there to state: "I am to inform you that the churches are operating at their own risk. For example, Caritas has been operating independently and the World Council of Churches operates under the ICRC only when it suits them." (In Lagos it was suggested that the initials WCC stood for "War Can Continue.")

This had never been said before, and churchmen operating the airlift felt it added to their difficulties that the FMG had now spelled out that they were operating at their own risk. "The Federal Military Government," the statement went on, "has expressed its preference that all voluntary agencies operate under the aegis of the International Committee of the Red Cross. This preference remains unchanged."

Thus governments muddled along through the summer and fall of 1968 with one eye on mounting public concern in their own country, the other on Lagos, losing sight of the humanitarian problem. They stepped up their pressure on church agencies to bring their airlift under the ICRC. And Nigeria embarked on a new campaign to bring the Red Cross airlift to an end.

Chapter 16

Nigerian aircraft began appearing at night over Uli, circling and dropping bombs on the field where arms planes and relief planes alike were landing and being unloaded. Relief workers on the ground called the bomber "The Intruder." The pilot (thought to be a Belgian mercenary) had the macabre fancy of identifying himself by radio as "Genocide."

The bombing was not accurate, the explosives apparently being rolled out of the side door of an old DC-3. They would come crashing down in the darkness at odd intervals, sometimes falling miles off target, other times hitting on or close to the airstrip. Occasionally an incident occurred such as that on a night in early November, when a church plane, laden with ten tons of stockfish, was at first told to hold for security reasons, then—upon landing and taxiing toward a parking place—was suddenly encircled by what a pilot nearby took to be bomb or rocket explosions.

The Swedish pilot and Norwegian copilot were wounded, five Biafrans unloading the plane were killed, and another thirty-five Biafrans and five Europeans wounded, including the Irish priest supervising the unloading. Anticipating that Nigerian bombers would come with daylight to destroy the damaged plane on the ground, the pilot, though wounded in the arm and leg and weak from loss of blood, decided to fly it back to São Tomé. The trip was hazardous—pressurization failed, and it was necessary to fly at very low altitude; there was little oil, so the pilot had to fly with two engines switched off.

Later, church airlift officials conjectured that the explosion may have been caused by an antipersonnel rocket or hand grenade dropped during unloading of an arms flight, rather than an attack from the air, but this did not reassure the pilots. They continued to fear bombing by "The Intruder." His erratic attacks occasionally interrupted the airlift, causing planes to hold, circling in the darkness over the airfield. If their fuel became low before his did, they had to turn back to São Tomé or Fernando

Po, unable to deliver their cargo. On nights when bombing reduced the number of flights, the impact on the children was immediate, as there was no reserve stockpile of protein—food was distributed to feeding stations within a day or two.

The possibility of carbohydrate starvation within a few months had relief officials deeply worried. Dr. Herman Middelkoop sent his cable to U Thant in October 1968 stating: "Carbohydrates likely to be exhausted in next seven weeks," warning that, by December, as many as twenty-five thousand people could be dying each day.

Having brought this assessment back from Biafra, George Orick met with Africa bureau officials. He told them that Biafra was not about to collapse and warned them about the numbers who would soon be dying as remaining stocks of yams and cassava were eaten.

Orick was still shaken by all he had seen in Biafra. He had encountered the doctor who had delivered his first son when he and his wife lived in Lagos. The doctor now ran a kwashiorkor clinic and told Orick he feared as many as 70 percent of the children in Biafra might already be affected. Other physicians said that an entire generation of children already might have been wiped out. Most under four were either dead, well along into kwashiorkor, or liable to sustain permanent brain damage even if they could be saved right then.

Orick informed the State Department officials that in smaller villages the hair of about half the children under ten years of age had turned either medium brown or totally yellow-brown. In urban areas and densely populated rural areas he saw fewer children with obvious signs of kwashiorkor. In some villages he had observed groups of children none of whose hair remained black. Assuming that as many were entering the earlier stages of the protein-deficiency disease as were in the terminal stage, he concluded that 40 to 50 percent of the children were suffering from kwashiorkor.

He sought to have the government pay the cost of transporting U.S. donated foods all the way to their destination. This was customarily done (under Public Law 480), but Biafra was not a customary situation. Moving food by ship from an American port to "Nigerian waters" cost about $45 a ton; the cost of flying it in the last 105 or 350 miles from the offshore islands was far greater—about $300 a ton. The voluntary relief agencies could not continue meeting this expense for long.

Within the Africa bureau some officials were totally committed to Nigerian unity, others more anguished by the starvation. Orick talked with one whose humanitarian concern outweighed established policy, who explained that if they suggested reimbursing relief agencies for flying food into Biafra, Assistant Secretary Palmer would say no. But there were certain regulations to be followed: if UNICEF and the church relief agencies made a request in the right way, then it could be done. The machinery is there, he said, all you have to do is push the right button.

There had, in fact, been a memo since mid-August, setting forth the opinion of the Office of the General Counsel in the Agency for International Development. The government could pay the cost of shipping U.S. foods into Nigeria or Biafra "by whatever route is most expeditious." The memo stated: "This will make possible shipment of supplies originating in the U.S. through Fernando Po . . . or São Tomé. . . ." The memo concluded that large quantities of supplies could be sent to the offshore islands from where "they will be broken into smaller consignments to be transhipped by plane or surface into Nigeria/Biafra."

This represented considerable divergence from established government policy. During a stormy session of U.S. voluntary agencies with State Department and AID officials in midsummer, Jan van Hoogstraten of Church World Service had raised this very question. Would the government reimburse agencies for transporting American food into Biafra from the offshore islands? The official in charge of United States disaster relief responded: such shipments could not be reimbursed, as U.S. operating agreements were with the Nigerian government. Van Hoogstraten repeated the request and was told that the food should be routed to Nigeria.

Another relief official questioned why the U.S. was supporting the International Committee of the Red Cross but could not assist the other agencies. The disaster relief official explained: the ICRC was entirely neutral and looking at this situation objectively. If the other relief agencies had food and supplies, they should turn them over to the ICRC, which would try to get them through.

Van Hoogstraten rose in great wrath, denouncing the Red Cross and the delay then taking place. But State Department officials held firm. There would be no assistance of the kind the voluntary relief agencies were seeking. An assistant to the secretary of state told the agency representatives this was a political question: the ICRC is acceptable to the Federal Military Government, he said; other agencies should offer personnel and relief under the aegis of the ICRC.

That was midsummer. Now, in midautumn, pressure from Congress and the public had been eroding the firm stand of the State Department. Orick "pushed the button," informing Church World Service and Catholic Relief Service of the AID counsel's opinion. They renewed their request. From that time forward, the U.S. government began reimbursing them not only for shipping food to Nigeria and "Nigerian waters" but for the last leg of the journey, by air into Biafra. Quietly, by the back door, the United States suddenly became the principal funder of the "illegal" airlift, putting the airlifts for the first time on an assured financial basis.

The U.S. was, in fact, going both ways simultaneously: it made $2.5 million available in response to the Red Cross's plea for funds. This ambivalence reflected the division within the government between nearly everyone who felt starving children should be fed and the few officials concerned about not losing influence with Nigeria.

This latter attitude came out when Orick was urged by some Americans to help in enlarging the airlift. If both the Red Cross and church airlifts were supported largely by the small Scandinavian countries, plus Holland and West Germany, surely the peoples of the United States, Canada, Great Britain, France, and other nations could organize and sustain a similar—even larger—airlift.

Still in shock from all he had witnessed in Biafra, Orick did not act for a few days. Finally, pressed by the others, he phoned the head of the Nigeria desk at State: "Maybe we have a way to solve some of your problems for you," he said. "What would you say if a group of American citizens were to organize a Nordchurchaid-type airlift?" There was a pause, then Orick quietly hung up the phone and stared into space for a moment, stunned. Those watching finally asked, "What did he say?" Orick replied, "He said, 'If they do that, the United States government will do everything in its power to block them.'"

The mood in the country and the nation's capital became one of mounting dismay at the prospect that the entire population of Biafra would soon be starving. "A stupefying tragedy is ripening in Nigeria," the *Washington Post* commented. "So far the starvation caused by the war costs only 5,000 or 10,000 lives a day. Shortly the toll is expected to rise to 25,000 lives a day—*a day*. As it happens, not so many of these casualties will be children, for the reason that rebellious Biafra is nearing the point where it will have run out of children to die. Six or seven or eight million people could die in Biafra in the months just ahead. . . ."

Hubert Humphrey's defeat by Richard Nixon made Edward Kennedy the most likely Democratic candidate for president in the next election. As chairman of the Senate Subcommittee on Refugees, Kennedy took a continuing role in pressing for greater relief. He warned about the threat of carbohydrate starvation: "Without emergency measures now, the number will climb to 25,000 per day within a month—and some 2,000,000 deaths by the end of this year."

He called upon the government to "energize its diplomatic initiatives to end immediately the flow of arms to either side." The senator urged that the United States "substantially escalate its contributions to the relief efforts" and asked President Johnson and President-elect Nixon to agree together on the appointment of a special presidential representative "to galvanize this nation's active commitment to do what must be done in Nigeria-Biafra."

According to news reports, "a deluge of mail, telegrams and phone calls from across the country" was pouring into the White House, State Department, and congressional offices. Senators were demanding to know what State was going to do about Biafra. However, as one administration appointee serving at the policy level in the department later commented, of all officials in government departments, those at State care least what the public or Congress may think or want; they ignore criticism from Capitol Hill, feeling that their own wisdom about international matters is greater than that of most congressmen. Their determination to resist these pressures stiffened when the Nigerian government signed its first economic and technical assistance agreement with the Soviet Union. (A high-ranking British diplomat in Lagos was quoted as saying: "The Russians have yet to plumb the depths of Nigerian ingratitude.")

Neither Lyndon Johnson nor Secretary of State Dean Rusk took great interest in the Biafran situation, obsessed as both were with the war in Vietnam and growing protests against it—and them. In any event, they were lame ducks. Nicholas Katzenbach had no directive from the White House, but pressures from Congress and his own concern finally became too great. Up till this point, during his numerous abrasive sessions with Joseph Palmer, he had been reluctant to overrule the assistant secretary and the Africa specialists or those dealing with Nigeria firsthand in the Lagos embassy. But now he decided to act. Katzenbach instructed Palmer to come up with proposals: What could be done to augment humanitarian relief? What would be the long-term cost to American-Nigerian relations? A task force, under Palmer's deputy, C. Robert Moore, began working "around the clock."

Katzenbach had been invited to speak at Brown University. Concern about Biafra had been rising on college campuses.* Katzenbach delivered what

---

* A three-day conference at Columbia University included as participants Count von Rosen and Peter Enahoro—the latter, in exile from Nigeria, took the opposite position on the war from his brother, Chief Enahoro.

he intended as an "even-handed speech." (His closing remarks, quoting the Prince of Verona in *Romeo and Juliet* saying "All are punish'd," reflected Katzenbach's own view expressed in private about Nigeria and Biafra: "A plague on both their houses.")

Katzenbach warned: "Millions, literally millions, of people face starvation in the next several months unless the war is ended very quickly." The decision of life or death for millions "rests with the leaders on both sides." He went on: "If both parties remain recalcitrant, if both parties continue to put political advantage ahead of people's lives, then one of the most terrible famines in modern times is certain and inevitable."

This "even-handed" approach was, in fact, a lapse into the neutrality that the State Department always professed as its policy on Nigeria-Biafra. It proved too neutral for the Africa bureau, however; fearing Nigerian reaction, the bureau gave the official State Department spokesman statements to read to correspondents on two successive days correcting any wrong impression the undersecretary may have made.

The first: "Under Secretary Katzenbach, in his speech Tuesday night, said that several million people face starvation if the Nigerian conflict continues. I'd like to elaborate on that." The spokesman told how the Red Cross and the Nigerian government were increasing relief efforts in Federally controlled areas but that relief flights were going into Biafra only at night. "Arms flights also have been going into Biafra at night. Those flights complicate and reduce the number of relief missions." He stated that the foreseeable need of as much as 10,000 tons of food each week in Biafra was beyond the capacity of the present nighttime airlift and commented: "About a month ago, the Nigerian Government told the ICRC that it could agree to daylight relief flights into the major airstrip now being used by Biafra if the ICRC could give assurance that the strip would only handle relief supplies in daylight hours. We welcomed this as a reasonable and constructive step by the Federal Government which could increase the flow of relief very substantially. The ICRC, of course, cannot begin such flights unless the Biafran authorities agree." The spokesman then elaborated: "Thus far, the Biafrans have not done so. We find this incomprehensible. It is a source of intense regret and puzzlement to us that despite the millions of Biafran lives at stake, Colonel Ojukwu, who heads the Biafran regime, has not yet given his agreement. . . ."

To make certain the under secretary's balanced view would not be mistaken for U.S. policy, the Africa bureau had the official spokesman state again the following day: "There was the import, suggestion in a story or two that we had in effect somewhat dramatically changed policy in this connection—that is, with our statement yesterday. We don't consider that statement a change in United States policy in connection with the problem of relief. We've made clear on many occasions our overriding concern, which is to get relief supplies to the civilian victims of the war on either side where they are needed. But at this point in time we feel that the Biafran failure to agree to the proposal for the use of Uli airstrip for daylight flights is, as I said yesterday, incomprehensible. . . ."

But the State Department now had its marching orders. After laboring nine days and nights, the special task force finally brought forth its proposal. It would take time to implement. State was glad an excuse came up to delay an announcement that would surely anger the Nigerians.

Chapter 17

The British, for their own reasons, set in motion what seemed a new, intensive effort to start peace negotiations. Faced with a debate on foreign affairs, the government and Foreign Office gave their leaders something affirmative and hopeful to talk about in Parliament.

They sent Lord Shepherd to Lagos and Maurice Foley to Addis Ababa. Foley was the new man on Nigeria. When the Commonwealth Office became part of the Foreign Office that autumn, George Thomson handed over his duties to Foley. In choosing him as undersecretary to handle the tricky and disagreeable Nigerian issue, there were those in the government as attracted to Foley's Irish Catholic connections as by his experience in Africa. In the Foreign Office, and State Department as well, some viewed the intense pressures upon them as a sort of papist plot—a feeling strengthened perhaps by the fact that among their principal critics, Hugh Fraser, in Parliament, and Edward Kennedy, in the Senate, were Catholics. Whatever the reason for the choice, Maurice Foley soon proved himself the man for the job, displaying more conspicuous zeal than George Thomson ever had.

He carried with him a letter from Prime Minister Wilson for Emperor Haile Selassie, while Lord Shepherd bore a similar message for General Gowon. Thus the government could say to Commons: "The whole purpose of the mission on which my two honorable friends are now engaged is to see whether there is any possibility of getting the cease-fire and the truce before or after Christmas, as soon as we can."

The British government would indeed have been delighted with any possibility of a cease-fire or truce; by this time a sense of stalemate—and despair—had set in. Nigeria's "short, sharp police action" and "swift surgical operation" had dragged on through a number of announced "final offensives." The most recent had by now petered out, and British officials continued to speak bitterly of the French having "prolonged the war." Biafran forces, far from collapsing, reentered the city of Owerri, which had fallen to the Nigerians during the September offensive.

The war was costing Nigeria in a number of ways. There were tax riots in the West among the Yorubas. Troops opened fire on the crowds, people were killed, buildings burned. *West Africa* commented about Nigeria's financial difficulties: "But the thought still nags: what happens to the Federation economically if, as now seems possible, the war drags on for months?" Shell-BP (British Petroleum) resumed oil production in some of the devastated areas, but production—before the war at a level of 500,000 barrels a day—was now back up to only 200,000 barrels a day. Gulf was beginning production offshore, and Mobil was planning to do so. Experts from Europe were repairing the oil refinery at Port Harcourt, and new facilities being constructed in the Midwest of Nigeria would get around the obstacles to production and shipment caused by the war. Oil production was rising, but there was an appetite for the greater wealth anticipated if only the war could be brought to an end.

In Parliament, Foreign Secretary Michael Stewart had to fend off one more effort to halt Britain's supply of arms to the Nigerians. He believed ". . . it would be wrong to advocate the single-handed stopping of the supply of arms by this country." As for "an attempt to get universal stopping of the supply of arms," he did not think this could be done effectively; while "it would be quite easy for me, as a diplomatic gesture, to say that Great Britain calls for this action without any consideration of the kind of response I should be likely to get," he added, "I should risk very greatly that not only Nigeria, but all Africa, would regard this as a hostile move, and a move helpful to the idea of tribal secession. . . ."

On the other matter—what one M.P. characterized as "possibly the greatest preventable human tragedy the modern world has known"—the foreign secretary commented, "Unhappily, I have to tell the House that Colonel Ojukwu still maintains his objection to daylight flights." Stewart said he had heard it argued that some of the figures given for deaths from starvation had been exaggerated: "I hope and believe that that is true. But, even when allowance has been made for that, already there is a great tragedy occurring and an even greater one looming up in the months ahead unless food can be got in by a land corridor.

"Here again, I have to tell the House," the foreign secretary went on, "that the Federal Government agreed some time ago to what were called mercy corridors to get food in by land. I believe that the concern of Colonel Ojukwu is that, if there were such corridors, they might be used for sudden military incursion into the territory which he now holds. Whether or not we think that it is reasonable to maintain that objection in the face of starving people—and I am not sure that it is—we must see if we can try to overcome it."

He suggested that Lord Shepherd was trying to do this on his present mission to Lagos, to arrange "some kind of international safeguard," then added, "The House will understand that much still depends on the attitude of Colonel Ojukwu. We have asked, and shall continue to ask, all those who are in contact with him to get him to modify his attitude on these matters and not—I am afraid that I must put it this way—to hold his people to ransom."

Lord Shepherd and Maurice Foley did not succeed in getting a cease-fire. Haile Selassie did propose a one-week Christmas truce. Ojukwu ordered Biafran troops to observe an eight-day cease-fire, but the Nigerian government declared a truce only for the Moslem feast day of Eid-al-Fitr and for Christmas Day. General Gowon responded to the emperor's proposal that "the rebel leadership are not genuinely interested in any cease-fire arrangements and in seeking lasting peace." He wrote Selassie: "Until there is a change of attitude by the secessionist hierarchy, the one-week truce proposed will only create an illusion to the whole world and raise false hopes."

Ojukwu, in his Christmas broadcast, charged that Nigeria had violated the truce it had proclaimed for the Moslem feast day with intensified activities on every front and "the longest and heaviest air raids of the war over civilian populations." He at last broke the silence on daylight flights. Biafra had come under growing pres ire to agree to this Nigerian proposal. Once the Federal government told the ICRC it no longer "authorized" relief flights at night and said that the Red Cross must obtain Biafran agreement for daylight flights into Uli, August Lindt began seeking to negotiate this with Biafra. Governments pressed Biafra to agree. Toward the end of November, Lindt suspended relief flights for a time to put pressure on the Biafrans. Ojukwu became so angered by this pressure that he warned the ICRC and the Swiss government that if Lindt did not stop pressing for daylight flights he would throw the Red Cross out of Biafra.

A more reasoned Biafran response had to be made to this constant campaign for daylight flights into Uli. Its origin in the events of early September remained shrouded in Red Cross secrecy. Without knowing that the Nigerians had formulated "daylight flights into Uli" as their preferred relief route once they learned the Biafrans felt this would endanger their only airfield, the public could think this was a plausible proposal.

As Michael Stewart said to Commons: "One of the difficulties is that

Colonel Ojukwu feels that if food came in by day it could then be presumed that all night flights were bringing in arms, and the Federal Government could legitimately try to shoot down night flights. That would not be welcome to Colonel Ojukwu, and for that reason he is not prepared at present to give his consent to daylight flights."

Ojukwu spoke bitterly of this in his Christmas message: "For weeks now, the Nigerian junta and Mr. Harold Wilson have been conducting vile propaganda against us on the subject of daylight flights of relief into Biafra. Their aim, of course, is to assuage their practice of genocidal aggression. Fortunately, they have not been able to deceive the world which cannot forget their persistent claims that starvation is a legitimate instrument of warfare. The truth is that Mr. Harold Wilson and Nigeria want to use daylight flights of relief as a cover for fulfilling their cherished and passionate ambition of destroying our main airfield."

In a separate statement, the Biafrans set forth why opening up Uli during the day would endanger their security: Nigerian aircraft with false markings might mingle with relief planes landing at Uli in an attempt to destroy the airfield upon which Biafra depended for its survival, and antiaircraft defenses would be immobilized and the alertness of civilians diminished, thereby making air raids more destructive.

Ojukwu made his affirmative response: ". . . We are prepared to make available to any relief organization, which does not find existing night facilities adequate, an area in Biafra where they can build an airport for daylight flights. With the blockade we have neither sufficient money nor materials to do this. But we have the skilled manpower and expertise—engineers and other technicians—which we are prepared to place at the disposal of any organization wishing to take up this offer. . . ." He added: ". . . Construction of the airfield for daylight flights can be completed within a very short time—and I speak from proven experience."

A separate airfield for relief flights during the day would be no more acceptable to Nigeria than the neutralized Red Cross airstrip had been four months before. The FMG wanted no flights at all, as soon became evident.

Having delayed while awaiting British efforts to achieve a truce, the State Department finally announced that the United States would sell eight large cargo planes to the two airlifts—four to the Red Cross and four to the church relief agencies—at a token price of $3,670 each. The C-97Gs (used until a short time before by Air National Guard units) had a rear-loading capability and could transport at least fourteen tons of food. Though not as good as the Hercules, the old cargo planes were larger and better for hauling cargo than the former passenger planes being used until now. With them, the two airlifts could more than double their tonnage.

Support for the airlifts went beyond anything State had ever contemplated before Nicholas Katzenbach finally intervened. Quietly, pilots and crews for the C-97s were recruited from Air National Guard units in California, Florida, Louisiana, and Mississippi—"Sunday pilots," civilians who kept up their flying on weekends.

Even though the United States turned the planes over to the Red Cross and Joint Church Aid* on condition they carry only relief supplies and that cargoes be inspected, Nigerian officials reacted with rage. General Gowon summoned Ambassador Mathews to warn that American provision of the cargo planes could have "serious repercussions." The government-owned newspaper termed the sale of the aircraft "a hostile act."

A Nigerian statement said the C-97s would "directly and indirectly increase the arms-carrying capacity of the rebels." It further charged that the U.S. action would "encourage the rebels to continue to resist and prolong the war thinking that the United States Government was now prepared to intervene in their favor to Balkanize Nigeria" and would strengthen their rejection of a land corridor.

Mathews sought to placate the Nigerian leaders. The U.S. Embassy released a statement saying that this relief move did not reflect "either directly or indirectly, United States Government political support of the rebellion, nor does it portend such support."

Pro-Communist factions in Lagos and Ibadan made the most of the opportunity, sending demonstrators into the streets protesting the U.S. action. Six professors at the universities of Ibadan and Lagos expressed this anti-Western sentiment in a letter to the Lagos *Sunday Times*: ". . . The measure only underlines a long policy of secret aggression against Nigeria. The supply of these planes for keeping the rebels alive represents a diplomatic assault whose significance such hallowed terms as 'imperialism' and 'neo-colonialism' are inadequate to convey. . . ."

Until two months earlier, the island of Fernando Po had been a colony of Spain. Now, along with the mainland territory of Rio Muni, it had become the independent nation of Equatorial Guinea. The ICRC had arranged with Spain to fly from Fernando Po, but had no such agreement with the

* By this time, Nordchurchaid had evolved into Joint Church Aid (JCA), an umbrella organization for the thirty-three church relief agencies operating the airlift into Biafra.

new nation. The Nigerians seized the opportunity to bring the Red Cross airlift to a halt.

Not that they had given ICRC officials any reason for complacency. One December evening, the Nigerian Air Force bombed and strafed the ICRC hospital, clearly marked with red crosses, near Awo-Omamma in Biafra. The ICRC immediately protested this violation of the Geneva Conventions that had killed and wounded a number of people, including Red Cross personnel. A day after the protest, Nigerian MiG-17s and Ilyushin bombers attacked Queen Elizabeth Hospital in Umuahia and the house nearby of the chief Red Cross delegate in Biafra. Twenty-two ICRC senior staff attending a briefing narrowly escaped death, though many other people were killed and wounded. Jaggi queried Red Cross headquarters in Geneva: "Could it be that severe attacks of Friday and Saturday on Umuahia are response to your protest last Wednesday in respect of bombing of Awo-Omamma hospital?"

Nigerian planes bombed the Awo-Omamma hospital again a few weeks later. Blunt warnings, once again, but the real attack on the ICRC was more subtle. The new government of Equatorial Guinea halted the airlift, ostensibly because relief planes carried fuel as well as food. The ICRC said it needed the fuel for its trucks distributing food to relief points and for generators producing electricity for its hospitals.

The Red Cross commented: "This means that for every night the ICRC is prevented from flying, the 850,000 persons who rely on the ICRC for their 70-gram-a-day subsistence ration will have to go without even this meagre allowance." At this time, the FMG interrupted Red Cross flights within Nigeria as well.

When Foreign Minister Okoi Arikpo paid a goodwill visit to Equatorial Guinea, the new nation's president, Francisco Macias Nguema, expressed support for efforts to keep Nigeria unified and announced that his government would soon open an embassy in Lagos. Some ICRC officials thought Diallo Telli, secretary general of the Organization of African Unity, had also intervened on behalf of Nigeria, while Joint Church Aid executives believed the Soviet ambassador to Lagos had played a role. In any event, humanitarian concerns presumably did not loom large in the thinking of President Macias, who soon set about eliminating his political rivals with a will nearly unmatched even in our own times.

August Lindt flew to Fernando Po, managed to get a fortnight's delay in interruption of the airlift, but two weeks later the situation remained unchanged. Red Cross relief flights were halted again—this time, it seemed for good. The ICRC sought to have Joint Church Aid fly in the needed diesel fuel. That the fuel was merely a pretext for halting the airlift soon became clear—Macias announced he would allow only daylight flights.

Half the airlift had been halted, but Joint Church Aid continued and the C-97s soon arrived. To avoid publicity that would further antagonize the Nigerians, the planes flew straight from California. So American church agency officials on the East Coast did not have a chance to brief the pilots about the situation they were flying into. Officials on São Tomé urged them to begin as soon as possible. The pilots expected a little flak, knowing there was a war on. They also learned about "The Intruder" who called himself "Genocide." The night before, he had bombed two planes.

The first flights, finding their way through the dark night, got caught in a thunderstorm. They were finally in the holding pattern for Uli. The Dutch plane ahead of them was picking up ground fire. The Nigerians began using fake radio beacons to lure the C-97s off course into heavier concentrations of flak. But they had been warned about this.

Fifteen miles southeast of Uli, expecting an approach beacon in four minutes, the pilots heard from airport control that "The Intruder" was dumping bombs on the airstrip. So they were stacked up in the dark, circling in the holding pattern, becoming more nervous. Suddenly, crackling in on their headsets, a heavily French-accented voice identifying himself as "Genocide," said, "I've been waiting for you Yanks." He told the Americans he was letting the Dutch plane and other flights go in and waiting for the new relief planes. He would follow them in when landing, he said, and drop his bombs on them.

The mercenary pilot and the Americans continued in radio communication for some time—a lengthy exchange of obscenities. The C-97s circled for two hours, waiting for "Genocide" to tire of waiting for them to land. Finally, their fuel running low, they had to return to São Tomé, not having delivered the fourteen tons of food aboard each plane. Half the relief planes that night had to turn back, about average on the nights "The Intruder" was bombing.

This was more than the Sunday pilots had counted on. Some returned to their wives, families, and regular jobs in the States. It took Joint Church Aid another two weeks to find new crews with which to make the C-97s fully operational.

Secretary General Thant had just received a report from his special representative in Lagos. Among other things, it stated, "During the period under review the Observer had found no evidence of genocide according to the accepted definition." The report quoted the Genocide Convention, making clear the "accepted definition" included "deliberately inflicting on the group conditions of life calculated to bring about its physical destruction in whole or in part."

Asked at a UN press conference for his assessment of the humanitarian situation, U Thant set forth his usual answer about being guided by the Organization of African Unity, then commented, "To the best of my knowledge, the Federal Military Government in Lagos has not impeded the flow of relief goods to the civilian victims of the war. To the best of my knowledge, the Federal Military Government in Lagos is willing to cooperate with the international community and relief agencies in order to tranship the necessary supplies and foodstuffs to the afflicted people in the area."

Thant concluded: "Thus, my assessment of the problem is that impediments have not come from Lagos. That is my conclusion, based on the conclusion of my Special Representative . . . who has been there for some time as you all know."

Chapter 18

Within hours of being sworn in as secretary of state, William Rogers urged the foreign minister of Equatorial Guinea to allow the Red Cross to fly again from Fernando Po. Two days later, President Nixon ordered an urgent, full-scale review by the National Security Council, stressing that he wanted a vigorous, energetic policy. The United States was to do everything possible to augment relief, without getting politically or militarily involved. The strong position he had taken during his presidential campaign now committed the government at its highest level to a more active role in support of humanitarian relief.

The day after his meeting with Rogers, the Equatorial Guinean foreign minister saw Secretary General Thant, who expressed "his earnest hope" that relief flights "may be resumed without delay." A number of governments also pressed the small new nation to permit the Red Cross to recommence its airlift from Fernando Po.

The ICRC proceeded on another tack. August Lindt obtained permission to fly from the airport at Cotonou, the capital of Nigeria's neighbor to the west, Dahomey (now Benin). Lindt found its president, Emile Zinsou, a medical doctor, a genuinely humanitarian man. Humanitarian or not, the Swiss and French governments encouraged the arrangement with financial benefits for Dahomey. Whatever advantages accrued to the impoverished nation, it soon proved costly for Dr. Zinsou himself. Dahomey's brief history had been marked by revolving-door governments, and Zinsou no sooner reached agreement with the Red Cross than new political difficulties began. Yorubas lived on both sides of the Nigerian-Dahomeyan border—those in Zinsou's country began attacking him as pro-Biafran. His regular opposition seized upon the airlift to create a political issue.

The Red Cross began flying again at the beginning of February, but relief planes from Cotonou had to make a longer journey over the ocean, around the length of Nigeria, instead of the short hop from Fernando Po. Each plane was lucky to get in even two trips a night rather than the three or occasionally four possible from the offshore island. U.S. and other pressures finally outweighed those from Nigeria, and Equatorial Guinea compromised, allowing Red Cross flights to begin again but limiting the ICRC to three aircraft authorized to fly from Santa Isabel airport.

Interruption of the airlift had taken its human toll. (During the first days of January 1969, Red Cross planes flew in only 304 tons, compared with 2,050 tons the previous month.) It had, however, forced governments and even Thant to take a firm stand in support of the Red Cross airlift.

With the C-97s and SuperConstellations provided by Canairelief, a Canadian church group, both airlifts built up. But food tonnages remained inadequate, and there was renewed determination to do something about it. A majority of U.S. senators and a large number of congressmen introduced a Concurrent Resolution reflecting the concern of Congress: ". . . The President should act to increase significantly the amount of surplus food stocks, relief moneys, non-combat aircraft, and . . . other vehicles. . . ."

Innocuous enough, but, after the furious reaction to the C-97s, the Bureau of African Affairs wanted to avoid angering the Nigerians further. Officials at State set about to keep the resolution bottled up in the House and Senate committees. It clearly had majority support, and senators and congressmen urged that it be reported out, but they never got a chance to vote on it.

However, Nixon's review produced a National Security Council (NSC) policy giving high priority to humanitarian relief. It created a special coordinator for relief who would travel into Biafra as well as negotiate in Lagos, an unusual step skirting close to diplomatic recognition. Appointment of C. Clyde Ferguson, former dean of Howard Law School, seemed to reflect the subtle racism sometimes guiding U.S. appointments at that time, which assumed an American black could negotiate better with Africans than a white.

To allay any alarm about Ferguson's role as a negotiator with both sides, Nixon wrote Gowon assuring him that the United States had no intention of interfering in the civil war. We're not sending arms aid to you, he said. We're not sending arms aid to the other side. We have no territorial ambitions or political preferences how this war comes out. You must understand that the American people are appalled by human suffering. Because of this, Nixon went on, I am appointing a relief coordinator. He is not a peace mediator; he is not there to negotiate an end to the conflict on Biafran terms or on your terms. He is there to speed the flow of relief, because people on both sides have been malnourished. We are sure that you have an interest in feeding your people, those held by the rebels and people on your side.

Although the president appointed Ferguson as special coordinator, the Africa bureau moved quickly to bring him under the State Department. He was provided offices there and staff from the Foreign Service. Instead of being responsible to the president, he was placed under the new under secretary of state, Elliot Richardson. Ferguson proved an able man, but once sworn in, Nixon did not seek his advice or meet with him again while the Nigerian war was on. A number of times when Nixon asked advocates of Biafran relief what more he might do, they suggested he should have Ferguson report directly to him. Each time he expressed surprise that this was not already the case.

Within the White House, Roger Morris, the National Security Council staff man responsible for Nigeria-Biafra, became an activist in support of humanitarian relief with the full backing of the national security adviser, Henry Kissinger. But Joseph Palmer and the Africa bureau found a staunch ally in Richardson. Unlike his predecessor Nicholas Katzenbach, who had begun to assert policy direction over Palmer and the bureau during his last two months in office, Richardson went in the other direction. In spite of the President's NSC directive, Richardson deferred to the professionals in the bureau who gave top priority to maintaining good relations with Nigeria.

They especially felt threatened by a new advocacy in the country. Groups organized originally to support humanitarian efforts, after months of trying, concluded that relief would become sufficient to overcome starvation only if the United States recognized Biafra. The U.S., they argued, could then provide aid directly. This, of course, was anathema to the Africa bureau. Richardson's own resistance became visible when he testified before Senator Edward Kennedy's subcommittee a few months later. He made his prepared testimony available to the committee only twenty minutes before the start of the hearing rather than the customary twenty-four hours, as he wished to beef up the section opposing recognition of Biafra: "This brings me to the ultimate political question which has been raised so often in criticism of our official posture toward the Nigerian civil war. Is our relief policy hostage to some deeper political commitment to the unity of Nigeria? And in the same vein, is United States recognition of an independent Biafra the answer to our dilemma?"

Paradoxically, Richardson seemed to respond yes to the first question, which he obviously meant to deny, by answering the second: "Recognition of an independent Biafra is not a panacea, either for relief, an end to the war, or for the future stability of West Africa. . . . Furthermore, recognition would have no tangible effect on the hostilities. To the contrary, it would only harden the positions of both sides, at the risk of rising Soviet influence in Federal Nigeria. . . . This Administration, therefore, does not contemplate either support for or recognition of the secessionist authorities. We regard a peaceful and just reconciliation of Nigeria as in the best interests of Africa and all those, like the United States, who wish her well."

The fact that the under secretary subscribed to the hard political line of the Africa bureau rather than the new humanitarian policy of the White House, and that the president took only a desultory interest once he had set the policy in motion, meant that initiatives to enlarge relief would be defeated or contained over the coming months. One of these arose out of a mission undertaken by Senator Charles Goodell. He asked the nutritionist Jean Mayer to organize a team, which the two then led into Biafra.

The medical, nutritional, agricultural, and logistics experts, summoned together very quickly, were in Biafra within days. Tuesday morning, as they lay in a ditch by the side of a road being strafed by MiGs, Dr. Roy Brown of Tufts University turned to Mayer and said, "Listen, when we get out of here—*if* we get out of here—I would like you to go over with me, very carefully, just what it was you said to me on the telephone last Friday morning."

Goodell stopped off first in Lagos to meet with Gowon and others in the FMG. He felt most of the Nigerian leaders present strongly opposed relief to Biafra. They insisted that flights must originate and shipments be inspected in Lagos. In Biafra, Ojukwu told Goodell he felt it was not possible to get agreement on relief: the Nigerians were not going to allow food to go in, as they were using starvation as a weapon of war. Goodell sought to get Ojukwu to agree to daylight flights but found that the Biafran leader regarded them as a military danger. Daylight flights into Uli would leave the airfield unprotected; a bomber could hit Uli during the day, putting it out of commission, then arms flights would not be able to land at night. As for the relief route up the Niger River, Ojukwu said he did not want to be in the position of accepting relief from the Nigerians.

The team of experts traveled around Biafra, collecting information. Going back to the United States, they wrote in hotel rooms, in airports, on typewriters on their laps in planes, all the way to Kennedy Airport. Their report covered demographic factors, the food situation, agricultural production, the nutritional status of the population, health and medical facilities, educational needs, the transport and airlift situation, the Biafran economy, the government and morale of the people; they made recommendations in all these areas. It was the first report with a semiofficial gloss, as Goodell had taken the team into Biafra with the blessing of Secretary of State Rogers. In releasing it, Goodell warned: "'Unless something dramatic is changed almost immediately, a minimum of 1 million and probably 2 to 2-½ million Biafrans will die in the next 12 months."

On Saturday Goodell conferred in Washington with Rogers and Secretary of Defense Melvin Laird. The following Monday morning they took up his recommendations at the National Security Council meeting. Goodell was assured that the recommendations had been cleared with the president: the U.S. would make available to relief agencies "on a feasible and emergency basis such cargo planes, ships, maintenance personnel and parts as are found necessary to perform the humanitarian mission of getting food and medical supplies to the starving."

A short time later, Goodell encountered the president at a White House reception and Nixon told him, "I appreciate what you're doing on Biafra and your report. Keep in touch—I'd appreciate your advice on this." But the senator soon found that in spite of the assurances he had been given by Rogers and Laird, in spite of the president's National Security Council directive, policy had not changed. Joseph Palmer and the Bureau of African Affairs still made the decisions, and Under Secretary Richardson went along with them. When the U.S. church relief agencies requested two more C-97s, they did not get them.

"Daylight flights into Uli" became a campaign building to a crescendo. The fate of two attempts to provide an alternative to Uli so that daylight flights might become possible suggests the cynicism by now prevailing in the diplomatic community after months of managing public opinion. Each proposal was a variation on the previous summer's plan to begin daylight flights to the neutralized airstrip at Obilagu. One, by Congressman Allard Lowenstein, set about to reactivate the Obilagu airstrip, now outside the enclave, not entirely under either Federal or Biafran control. The other, undertaken by Reverend Edward Johnson of Canairelief, sought to create a second airstrip inside Biafra, as had been done for the Red Cross six months earlier.

Lowenstein, a new congressman but no novice to politics, was taken very seriously at the State Department and, it would seem, at the British Foreign Office. As one U.S. official put it: "This wasn't just some rinky-dink politician from the backwoods—this was the fellow who had brought down Lyndon Johnson."

Shortly before the start of the congressional session, Lowenstein flew to Lagos and then into Biafra, seeking to learn from the highest officials on both sides what they would agree to. He figured that 90 percent of Nigerian proposals were unacceptable to the Biafrans and 90 percent of Biafran proposals were unacceptable to the Nigerians. He was seeking the 10 percent on which there might be agreement, and he excluded daylight flights into Uli.

Lowenstein shuttled between the two sides until he thought he had worked out something acceptable to each—the use of Obilagu airstrip (which by Christmas had come to be in a no-man's-land, being fought over by both sides). Then he made what he later came to regard as a "serious blunder." Thinking the plan should be negotiated by an African, he flew to Addis Ababa and turned it over to Haile Selassie.

Lowenstein met in London with Maurice Foley and felt the British undersecretary was really trying to get a relief agreement and was passionately concerned about getting food in. He was also impressed with the high-powered conference Foley set up for him at the Foreign Office. He came away from these meetings with a genuine sense of agreement. This was in early January 1969.

In February, Foley wanted Lowenstein to return to Biafra. Officials at State also expressed concern to him. The proposal had in some way been changed, and they wanted him to get the agreement of the Biafrans. Lowenstein had been careful when first there to check with the Biafran military commanders; he felt certain he had gained their acceptance of the plan. In Addis Ababa he had stressed there must be no changes in the proposal: there would be problems if anything was altered. He did not know who had actually negotiated for Haile Selassie, whether it had been the emperor's Foreign Office or whether it had been turned over to the OAU Secretariat.

But changes unacceptable to the Biafrans had been made. At this point Lowenstein was not even sure what they were. In Biafra he was told the width of the corridor had been altered, as well as certain protections of the corridor that the Biafran military had earlier accepted. Lowenstein felt he needed to have Biafran agreement so he could then put pressure on the Nigerians. With this as leverage, he believed he could build support in the Congress and other countries. Whoever blocked the use of Obilagu would be seen as using starvation as a weapon. The Biafrans appeared to him now to be blocking the proposal.

Lowenstein thought that Ojukwu felt the plan met their requirements, but he had yet to confer with his Council of Ministers. In fact, the Biafrans felt this was the land corridor of the previous summer all over again. The altered corridor did not, in their opinion, give them protection against a thrust southward by the Nigerian First Division (even though the international observers and the ICRC had been added as protectors). This was no imagined threat: the Biafrans knew Nigerian forces were building up for an offensive. When it came, little more than a month later, it would sweep south of Obilagu airstrip to capture the Biafran capital, Umuahia.

Lowenstein returned to Washington disappointed with the Biafrans, and this had a chilling effect on their supporters in Congress. A politically diverse group, they had been passionately committed to relief. Congressmen Lowenstein and Donald Lukens and Senators Goodell and Kennedy cabled Ojukwu, urging him to reconsider the use of Obilagu airstrip, at least for a limited period.

The British and Nigerians made the most of this. The *New York Times* urged Clyde Ferguson to "press Biafra's leaders for one thing above all when he visits Umuahia this week . . . acceptance of a plan to use the Obilagu airstrip for a massive daytime food airlift." The editorial commented: "A flat Biafran refusal will persuade many that Colonel Ojukwu prefers to exploit the misery of his people for political ends rather than relieve it."

". . . As you are well aware," Ojukwu replied to the American congressmen and senators, "I developed the Obilagu airstrip last year and physically handed it over to the International Committee of the Red Cross, to be used exclusively for relief." He recounted how Nigeria proceeded to bomb, rocket, and strafe the airstrip and that an infantry attack had then overrun it. "At the moment, our troops are engaged in serious fighting at the airstrip," he continued. The Biafrans were prepared to discuss various alternative routes and had made many proposals themselves, but "it must not be forgotten that we have so far held back the enemy because of the obstacles we have put on movement of their motorized columns into Biafra. It will, therefore, be self-defeating for the Biafran Government and people to adopt any policy that would undermine our capacity to prosecute a war which involves the security of all Biafrans. . . ."

Ojukwu suggested that another airfield Biafra was constructing be used for daylight and night relief flights. This new airport was "well away from the perimeter of battle," not, like Obilagu, in an "area being contested by the forces of both sides." The fate of this second airstrip provides a revealing counterpoint to the campaign being orchestrated to use Obilagu, now that it no longer lay inside Biafra as it had the previous summer when the Red Cross sought to use it for daylight flights.

Reverend Johnson of Canairelief thought it would be better if Joint Church Aid planes had their own airfield so they could not be accused of providing cover for arms flights. He received an enthusiastic response—go ahead, Ojukwu said, as he had the previous June to Leslie Kirkley of Oxfam and Harry Jaggi of the Red Cross. In Biafra, Johnson met with officials who spread out a large map. What was sought was a field not close to the border that could be used by JCA flights twenty-four hours a day, exclusively for relief. Ojukwu suggested three or four possible sites. Johnson pointed to one on the map, saying, "This one would be best." It was about fifteen miles along the road from Umuahia toward Uli. They drove out to look at it. It was a smooth open field that would not require much grading. The Biafrans had grading equipment, but asphalt and other materials would have to be brought in from the outside. They were enthusiastic about the plan and provided Johnson with a formal letter inviting Joint Church Aid to proceed with it.

A day-and-night relief airfield interested JCA officials, but they had two major concerns. First, they had a reasonably good operation going; the new plan might provoke the Nigerians to interfere with it. Second, it would take forty planeloads to move asphalt and other equipment needed; that would mean forty fewer planeloads of food flown in during that period.

Back in Canada, Johnson began feeling the heat. A churchman visiting him from Lagos said that the FMG had instructed him to inform the Presbyterian minister that his support for a second airstrip in Biafra would be considered an act of hostility. The Nigerian High Commission in Ottawa criticized Canairelief and Johnson in strong terms.

The FMG likewise told the Canadian government that it would regard support for an airfield a "hostile act." Ojukwu would take over the airfield and use it for military purposes. (The Canadian government was not providing support to Canairelief even for humanitarian relief and had no intention of assisting construction of a second airfield. External Affairs Minister Sharp took the position that Canada dealt only with governments, so there was no way that Ottawa could support anything in Biafra.)

This hostile Nigerian reaction was felt throughout the international community. When JCA executives met again, they decided not to move ahead with the airfield. The cost would be great, and they could expect no help from governments in the face of angry Nigerian opposition. Diverting food planes to fly in construction materials would have a devastating effect on large numbers of children. And they feared greater Nigerian harassment of Uli, harming the existing airlift.

Clyde Ferguson flew to Lagos, then into Biafra, then back to Lagos—a president's representative would not customarily enter a secessionist territory to confer with rebel authorities. He proposed full daylight flights into both Uli and Obilagu for a sixty-day period. The Biafran negotiator for humanitarian relief regarded this with indulgence, remarking later that Ferguson was at this time "only a tyro." Ferguson quickly concluded that there was "little likelihood of resolving the airlift problem along the lines suggested. . . ."

He and Lindt agreed to divide up the negotiating, Lindt taking the airlift and Ferguson trying for a surface route. Given negotiations over the previous year, Lindt had the better of that understanding. But a new man on the job, lacking a grasp of the situation in depth, was doomed to repeat the mistakes of the past. Ferguson began casting about for another proposal.

One came his way. A West Point lieutenant colonel spending that year as a White House scholar, Arthur Eugene Dewey, had taken the problem of Biafran relief as his project. A helicopter logistics expert, he at first explored that possibility but then decided an upriver corridor would be better than cargo helicopters. This idea had many fathers, but most advocates of a river route thought of sending vessels up the Niger to Oguta (once a port for Iboland but now a heavily fought over area). Gene Dewey developed a plan instead for using the Cross River, up the lagoon from Calabar in the southeast, along the river skirting the eastern edge of the Biafran enclave, running between territories of both combatants, therefore perhaps acceptable to both—or to neither.

Ferguson took Dewey as his deputy and the Cross River route as his negotiating proposal. He knew of Nigerian intransigence toward all relief and was aware that the British had taken what he spoke of as "the hard position." He encountered a hardened position on the Biafran side as well, for by this time Ojukwu had become very wary of the American attitude toward relief. Ojukwu's immediate reaction was to regard the Cross River proposal as another red herring. However, he told the Biafran relief negotiator, Sylvanus Cookey, to receive Ferguson.

In the State House, they worked out a complex route—the more complex it became, the more Ojukwu believed it a tactic to block relief. This was a mistake, for Ferguson was not the State Department and sincerely wanted to achieve a breakthrough on relief. Ojukwu had been through a lot of negotiations, however, and almost immediately mistrusted the proposal.

At about this time, the Netherlands suggested regular meetings of the European nations to discuss Biafran relief, leading to creation of "The Hague Group." The Dutch diplomat who became its chairman knew little about the problem at first, but his thinking soon paralleled that of his opposite number in the British Foreign Office.

To outsiders, the Hague Group appeared a monthly gathering of diplomats intended to improve relief, but it quickly took on another role. At its first meeting, Clyde Ferguson asked the other government representatives for ninety days "during which nobody would float any proposals other than the Cross River route and daylight flights into Uli." They agreed.

Thus the Hague Group came to coordinate the diplomacy of governments in Europe and North America so as to control future negotiations about new ways for augmenting relief into Biafra. Specifically, they wanted no new initiatives of the kind Lowenstein and Johnson had made. From now on the group set about to concentrate international efforts on two—and only two—negotiating proposals: the Cross River route and daylight flights into Uli.

Chapter 19

The bombing of civilians in Biafra had been going on for a long time but intensified during the first months of 1969; by early March it became a serious problem for the British government.

Such independent observers as Jean Mayer reported: "'Every major hospital has been bombed and strafed, even though all had large crosses on the roof, and even though many were far from towns, crossroads or any other legitimate target. At present, red crosses are being camouflaged (even on the roof of the headquarters of the International Red Cross) as they only attract Nigerian Ilyushins and MiG-17s without giving protection. All schools had to be closed because the children were strafed and bombed. . . ."

The British Foreign Office as well as the Nigerian government tended to discount all such reports as "exaggerations" or "Biafran propaganda," but finally one account appeared that was too vivid and from too illustrious a source to be successfully discredited. Winston Churchill III traveled to Nigeria and then into Biafra as a journalist for the *Times* of London. In Lagos, General Gowon and the air force commander assured him that Nigerian planes bombed only military installations.

However, writing in the *Times* a short time later, Churchill commented on his own experience: " Arriving from Lagos convinced that reports of the bombing of civilians were mere Biafran propaganda, and that reports of famine and starvation had similarly been invented or exaggerated by the churches and the Red Cross, only a few days in Biafra were enough to shatter these two fundamental misconceptions. A walk among the ruins of a clinic or a marketplace in which dead, dying or horribly wounded civilians are lying on every side destroys the first, a journey into the countryside demolishes the second."

At one point, Churchill and Lloyd Garrison of the *New York Times*, returning from the front at Owerri where they had witnessed an impressive performance by Biafran troops, came upon a hospital that had just been bombed, with eighteen patients killed. Then they heard MiGs flying over and bombing in the distance. As they traveled on in their Land Rover, they came upon a sight as bad as either had ever seen. The fighters had bombed an open market; the bodies of some two hundred people lay everywhere. Later that day, a priest passing them with a truck filled with wounded told them that another open-air market had just been bombed. They drove to this town and again found more than two hundred killed.

Churchill was profoundly shaken by these sights. When he wrote about them in the *Times,* his celebrated name caused difficulties for the British government. Sir David Hunt was sent around "to express the British Government's anxiety" and reported that "General Gowon said that the Federal Military Government had issued strict instructions to its Air Force to avoid civilian targets and to attack only military installations."

The Foreign Office and government officials also set about to discredit Churchill. Garrison came to the defense of his fellow journalist, writing in a letter to the *Times* that he had been present and witnessed the same bombing raids against civilians, which, he added, were commonplace in Biafra.

Another journalist wrote to say that he had been subjected to the same kind of vilification when he was among the first to report starvation in Biafra: "The day [my article] appeared, my friend was telephoned by an official of the News Department of the Commonwealth Office . . . and told that he should not place reliance on my reporting since I was known to have been hopelessly swayed by Biafran propaganda. Other colleagues tell me that a different spokesman even hinted to them that I might be in the pay of the Biafrans."

The Foreign Office had succeeded in managing the news until now in subtle ways, but these obvious efforts created rancor. The *Spectator,* for example, commented: "The point is that the British Government, which at no time has had a single representative or observer inside Biafra, has consistently maintained that the official pronouncements of the Nigerian military government represented the truth, while reports from missionaries, charity workers and journalists from all countries actually on the spot were Biafran-inspired lies. That the Government is now pretending that the latest bombing reports come as a shock and surprise, and put an entirely new complexion on the war, is merely contemptible. The plain fact is that, throughout the past year, the Government has at worst knowingly based its policy on lies and defended it by calumnies, and at best simply not wanted to know the truth. Neither case is the hallmark of an honest Government pursuing an honorable policy."

The uproar over the bombing once again threatened continuation of the arms supply to Nigeria. The government had to agree to holding a debate in Parliament at the very time a flotilla of Soviet warships sailed into Lagos harbor for a goodwill visit.

The venerable James Griffiths, who had been responsible for Nigerian affairs while serving as secretary of state for the colonies during the last Attlee government, told the Commons of his own experience with bombing when visiting Biafra: "There are Russian Ilyushin and MiG planes, and Egyptian pilots . . . most of the bombing in market places, roads and town is by awful antipersonnel bombs. Biafra is an ever-shrinking territory, crowded with eight to ten million people." He went on: "Millions of them are homeless and many are starving. Those who have been to Biafra know the scenes. The roads, the markets and the villages are crowded. I have seen the bombing there and, inevitably, there has been heavy loss of life. There is a pattern to it. It is quite clear from what I saw, or the evidence of bombing where people have been killed, that bombs fall near big buildings . . . one sees evidence of bombing of villages close to a church, a hospital, or a convent."

Griffiths recounted a scene that would make the bombing vivid to people in Britain: "I went to a convent in Nuguru. There, a bomb had fallen on the edge of the building and the sick bay had been hit. Children were killed. I saw a church on the road to Umuahia, and the little villages round the church, almost like countryside villages in this country. Bombs had fallen there, too."

Griffiths warned: "We talk about discrimination in bombing. There can be no discriminatory bombing in a place like Biafra, in which there are so many people roaming about. Stop it altogether; that is the only thing to do."

Clearly the government had to do something out of the ordinary to divert this rising tide of indignation. It had sent the Foreign Office's senior civil servant to confer in Lagos, but that was the usual thing it did just before a debate. It needed something in reserve. So when Edward Heath coyly slipped in a question to the prime minister during question time—whether Wilson would be paying a visit to Nigeria—the P.M. flushed angrily and told Heath his "curiosity could best be satisfied during that debate."

The government held its announcement—that Wilson would himself undertake a peace mission to Lagos—till the closing minutes of the six-hour debate. Anticipating this, Sir Alec Douglas-Home commented, "I am not sure I see in the Prime Minister a sort of supercharged dove, if he intends to go to Nigeria to try to work a miracle. I hope that this will not be trotted out at the end of the debate as the kind of gimmick which we come to expect from the Government on these occasions."

Of course it was, and cartoonists began having fun depicting Harold

Wilson as a "supercharged dove." Another portrayed the prime minister being dropped onto the country, pipe in mouth, as one of a stick of bombs bearing the Union Jack. In fact, he arrived in Nigeria by more conventional aircraft but with Her Majesty's Ship *Fearless* standing by in the harbor as a place for peacemaking—or to provide a riposte to those Soviet warships.

Not a great deal came of the visit. Before he left London, Wilson stated that it was not his intention to mediate between Nigeria and Biafra, and General Gowon made clear at the welcoming ceremony that Nigeria would brook no interference in its internal affairs. He expected "no dramatic peace initiative," Gowon said, though Michael Stewart had suggested to Parliament that this would be the purpose of Wilson's trip to Nigeria.

Wilson attempted to meet with Ojukwu as well as Gowon. His critics at home charged that he had deliberately waited till the last minute so that communication—by way of London—would come too late for the Biafran leader to arrange to see Wilson, but it would appear that Wilson made a serious effort to meet with Ojukwu. Nigerian objections to the prime minister's flying into the secessionist area delayed this, until Wilson's suggestion for a meeting elsewhere in Africa came too late. By that time a new Nigerian "final offensive" had begun, and Ojukwu could not leave his army and his country.

At a press conference the day Wilson left Nigeria, Gowon said that air strikes against Biafra would continue as long as they were militarily useful, accusing Ojukwu of "stage-managing" many of the scenes of destruction against civilians, which correspondents had witnessed, by having Biafran demolition teams fake bomb craters with dynamite.

The Nigerian offensive had begun the day before Wilson arrived in Lagos and, while there, he visited the headquarters of the First and Third divisions. He certainly knew the latest final push would be under way, for the British had been building up the army for months. After Wilson departed, troops of the First Division fought their way down the dirt roads from the north, encountering stiff resistance, but the Nigerians finally broke through to capture Umuahia. The Biafran government had to withdraw and set up in another town; the Protestant missionary doctors evacuated Queen Elizabeth Hospital, and the Red Cross delegation moved its headquarters to a new location.

The fall of their capital would have been a greater psychological blow to the Biafrans had their troops not closed the ring on a garrison of twenty-five hundred Federal troops in the southwest city of Owerri, destroying the Nigerian force and recapturing the city which had been lost seven months before. For the Nigerians, capturing Umuahia would have been the triumph it seemed to the outside world, but the real objectives of the offensive eluded them. The army chief of staff, meeting earlier in the field with division commanders, had stressed that taking the Biafran capital would be less important than cutting Umuahia off from Uli. Splitting Biafra and capturing the airfield would end the war. Having achieved neither, the government replaced the three divisional commanders not long afterward, thus asserting greater control over military forces in the field. But the Biafran capture of Owerri put a buffer between the Third Division and Uli airfield, making ultimate victory more problematical. The Nigerians began to despair of winning militarily.

The Biafrans also faced an uncertain future, for their supply of arms and ammunition faltered twice—in March an interruption resulting from a French flirtation with the Nigerians over future oil concessions; later, after President de Gaulle lost the referendum he had called and went home to Colombey. Jacques Foccart was out for a time and the Quai d'Orsay reasserted itself, temporarily cutting off arms flights from Libreville.

Biafra still survived—but precariously, at the end of a tenuous pipeline that could be turned off at any moment.

Some pilots made the landing at Uli three or even four times a night. The obsolete cargo planes converged from the four airfields at Fernando Po, Cotonou, São Tomé, or Libreville, homing in on the radio beacon in Biafra, avoiding Nigerian antiaircraft fire, stacking up with a dozen or more other aircraft circling in the night, waiting for the traffic controller to call them in. The landing itself was harrowing, for the plane descended in darkness, the pilot watching for the runway lights to flash on to show him where to set down on the eighty-foot-wide airstrip or whether he had overshot and must pull up or whether another plane might be taxiing on the runway. "The Intruder" had begun dropping nine-minute flares, lighting up the airfield and surrounding area, making bombing more accurate, delaying landings, using up time so pilots had to turn back, as fuel got low, without delivering their cargo.

Not all of them made it. One night in early May, a Red Cross DC-6 crashed in the forest near Uli and burned, killing the crew of three Swedes and a West German. The next night a Joint Church Aid plane, its wheels locked up, had to belly-land on the airstrip, putting the runway out of commission for the rest of the night. The crew survived, but the next day Nigerian MiGs came and destroyed the disabled C-97 on the ground.

Fatigue played a part in the crashes. Pilots were supposed to fly only two nights, then take a night off, but some were more dedicated and some liked the extra money. They had begun flying into Uli earlier—starting before dusk so as to get in more flights each night, trying to time their departures so they would cross the Nigerian coast just at nightfall or get there even a bit earlier, taking their chances that no Nigerian jets would be in the area or, if they were, would be piloted by mercenaries who might leave them alone.

The Red Cross had ten planes—six at Cotonou and four at Fernando Po (though the Equatorial Guinean government allowed only three to fly from that island). Joint Church Aid had eleven planes at São Tomé, but two had to be cannibalized to keep the others flying. JCA scrounged for its spare parts; one Catholic Relief Service official in New York would locate them in the United States, then airfreight them to the island off the African coast.

Reading between the lines of an evaluation of the C-97 operation written laconically by Colonel Dewey for Ambassador Ferguson, one gets the impression of an airlift being run by the Marx Brothers, with Chico and Harpo in charge of maintenance. One crew member put it: "Spare parts is everything to this operation. We are absolutely outside civilization here." Or Colonel Dewey, in more West Pointian prose: "In exploring the significance of lack of experience in the C-97 . . . it is much more important to have had experience with unscheduled charter operations in an unsophisticated environment than to have the sole qualification of being a C-97 pilot."

Nonetheless, they flew. With the addition of the C-97s, the tonnages of food and medicine flown in each night became respectable if not adequate. Uli could ordinarily handle between thirty and thirty-five flights; on a night when the weather was clear and "The Intruder" stayed away, as many as forty-four flights might land and take off between dusk and dawn.

The combined airlifts reached a peak at this time with an average of 289.3 tons a night during April and 257.3 tons a night in May.* Conditions improved in the besieged enclave. Ojukwu (now a general, to match the rank given Gowon) exhorted his people to create a "Land Army," and

* In February the two airlifts, together, had gotten in a total tonnage of 3,987. During March, the tonnage was up to 7,330, and in April (when "The Intruder" was away) it reached 8,681. The crashes of the Red Cross and JCA planes in early May, the spare parts shortages, changes of crews, and return of "The Intruder" to renew intensive bombing of Uli caused the combined tonnage of both airlifts to drop slightly during that month, to 7,977. This was not counting smaller amounts flown in from Libreville by the French Red Cross and by an Irish group called Africa Concern.

they began planting every cultivable spot of ground. The apathy of kwashiorkor began to disappear as the airlift got in more protein supplement; relief workers reported that "The children have begun laughing again."

Red Cross officials and the churchmen who ran Joint Church Aid concentrated on building up the airlifts, being cautious not to do anything to antagonize the Nigerians. For example, when UNICEF worked out with the French Red Cross a way of bringing its airlift out of Libreville under the ICRC so it could qualify for United States food and reimbursement, the ICRC felt compelled to turn the arrangement down—arms flights also originated out of Libreville, and the French supplied the arms. The letter to the French Red Cross explained: "The ICRC is already encountering numerous difficulties due to the fact it is working on both sides of the fighting, and we must not, at this moment when our operations are at last developing normally, risk offending the Federal Military Government."

Epidemics of such diseases as measles and tuberculosis posed a danger to people weakened by malnutrition. Relief agencies had begun mass vaccination and immunization campaigns at the end of 1968; Clyde Ferguson spoke after his first visit of his deep concern about the need to step up this effort. He estimated that three-quarters of the population might have tuberculosis by early May. "Roughly," he estimated, "about three million people need some supplement to their diet." At the present level of the airlifts not this many could be helped.

August Lindt also warned at this time: ". . . There are still large groups of the population which cannot be reached and there is great hardship. The food situation in Biafra is becoming more and more critical and will deteriorate even further in the months preceding the harvest in September. There are signs of general malnutrition and a disturbing increase in tuberculosis."

Ferguson estimated that 480 tons of food a day would be required to provide a subsistence level for all the people in need in Biafra. This much food could be flown in if governments made available C-130s or even if the U.S. replaced all the old passenger planes on both airlifts with old C-97s, but governments were no more prepared to do this now than they had been the previous autumn.

The tonnage added by the eight C-97s made the difference in the spring of 1969. Ferguson pointed out a short time later: ". . . We do know that a figure slightly in excess of 300 tons dramatically changed the whole health picture and food picture in the enclave over a period of about sixty days. . . ." This reassured people, creating a sense that the situation had improved. The public had a limited attention span and the twists and turns of negotiations had gone on many months. The line the British had set in motion finally had a brainwashing effect. In making an appeal for funds, Jacques Freymond, acting ICRC president at this time, spoke of "the weariness of public opinion." August Lindt found that public pressure had turned off and he no longer could get governments to do anything.

When, a short time later, starvation became the only weapon that might yet defeat the Biafrans, people were not ready to become caught up a second time in the plight of starving children. The editor of *Life* magazine, whose business it was to know such things, would tell his staff: if there is one thing the American people do not want to read about or look at, it is starving Biafran babies.

An incident occurred that caused Europeans to lose sympathy for the Biafrans. Guerrillas fighting against Nigerian forces in the Mid-West Region captured eighteen workers of a prospecting team from the Italian oil consortium ENI. Most were Italians, three were Germans. Others, missing, turned out later to have been killed during the battle. Tension mounted as people in Europe became caught up in the fate of the "Italian oilmen."

This intense concern embittered Biafrans. Ojukwu gave vent to their resentment: "Today, because a handful of white men collaborating with the enemy, fighting side by side with the enemy, were caught by our gallant troops, the entire world threatens to stop. For eighteen white men, Europe is aroused. What have they said about our millions? Eighteen white men assisting the crime of genocide: what does Europe say about our murdered innocents? Have we not died enough? How many black dead men make a missing white? . . ."

In this angry mood a Biafran special tribunal sentenced the "Italian oilmen" to death for assisting Nigeria in the war. Everyone intervened, asking mercy for the oil workers: the Pope, the president of the ICRC, presidents of countries recognizing Biafra, other governments. The following day Ojukwu reprieved the men, and they returned home. The damage had been done, however; people in Europe were in no mood to be outraged again on behalf of the Biafrans.

British officials had begun to despair of the Nigerians ever defeating the Biafrans. A report received from their defense adviser in Lagos before Wilson's trip contrasted unfavorably the capacities of the Nigerian Army with those of the Biafrans, and the failure of Nigerian troops to achieve their objectives a short time later bore this out.

Major General Henry Alexander, after serving as the first British representative on the international observers team, had since been an outspoken supporter of the Nigerian cause. As such, he had access to information from the Foreign Office and High Commissioner's Office, and an article he wrote for the *Sunday Telegraph* reflected the gloomy assessment of diplomats and British government officials of Nigerian chances for victory. Alexander criticized Nigerian forces for violating fundamental military principles and emphasized, as he had before, that the Federal Air Force could not knock out Uli airstrip.

Nigerian leaders had equally come to have doubts. They did not see how they could win. The Nigerians and the British differed, however, on a crucial matter. In Lagos there was a lack of belief about starvation in Biafra. Their own propaganda had convinced Nigerians that relief agency reports of horrendous starvation were a product of Biafran propaganda. The British, on the other hand, understood the extent and gravity of the starvation. According to U.S. officials, the British thought that starvation could weaken the Biafrans to the point where they could not go on fighting.

At this time small planes suddenly appeared in Nigerian skies. Flying too low for antiaircraft fire, too slowly for supersonic jets to intercept them, the little, propeller-driven planes attacked in swift succession the airports at Port Harcourt, Enugu, and Benin, rocketing the control towers and destroying eleven of the MiG fighters and Ilyushin bombers that had been bombing and strafing civilians in Biafra.

Count Carl Gustaf von Rosen had returned to Biafra in a new role. Having decided the previous September that the Biafrans could not be saved with food alone, and following his angry exchange with Pastor Mollerup, he had given up his post as chief of operations of the church airlift. Years before he had flown for the Finns against the Soviet invasion and later, at the request of Haile Selassie, had organized an air force for Ethiopia. From his son who worked for an aircraft manufacturer in Malmö he learned about a small one-seater the Swedish Air Force had developed for reconnaissance and guerrilla warfare training. Von Rosen spoke with Ojukwu about his plan, then managed to raise in Europe the modest funds needed to build a tiny air force for Biafra, using the miniplanes intended for countering guerrilla warfare. Biafra arranged a covert by-pass of Swedish neutrality to purchase five of the planes and shipped them to France for outfitting with rockets.

With four Swedish pilots and two Biafrans formerly in the Nigerian Air Force, von Rosen soon had the squadron flying out of bush airfields that could not be found by the Nigerians. After the first forays against the planes that had been bombing and strafing civilians, they next attacked a power station and an oil refinery. Soon more Biafrans were trained, and the Swedes turned the air force over to them. It went on to do considerable damage, aimed at affecting the Nigerian economy, so as to persuade the FMG to negotiate an end to the war.

The British defense adviser later reported: "The Nigerian Air Force cannot survey rebel airfields continuously by day and therefore the rebels will always be able to carry out hit-and-run raids from well-camouflaged bases. This pattern is clearly established, aimed at limiting or stopping oil production, discouraging expatriate participations in other vital sectors of the economy such as shipping. Whilst the weapon used by the rebels is simple, its effect on the national economy, particularly the loss of oil revenues, and therefore the outcome of the war, could be critical."

The miniplanes angered Lagos both because of the serious damage they were causing and because they were making the Nigerians look ridiculous. Apart from the Egyptians seconded from the U.A.R. Air Force, there were a number of mercenary pilots—British and of other nationalities—on the Nigerian payroll. They were told to start shooting down planes or face being fired.

In the midst of all this, August Lindt was detained after flying into Lagos airport one evening in late May. He was held prisoner for sixteen hours along with his assistant and the pilot of the small Red Cross plane. The Swiss ambassador finally learned of this the next morning and got Nigerian officials to release the three.

At about this same time, State Department officials warned Bishop Swanstrom and Edward Kinney of Catholic Relief Services to make clear to the Biafrans that the air raids might provoke the Lagos government into reprisals which could have a devastating effect on the airlift. Lindt received similar warnings that same day. Ojukwu heard the warnings but tended to discount them as one more of the threats regularly reaching him.

The same story was put about to journalists, preparing the way for blaming Count von Rosen and the Biafran miniplane raids for any interference with the airlift. *Newsweek* concluded a story about the effectiveness of the small Swedish planes: "The prospects for Biafra, however, are not all rosy. If the federal government retaliates for the Biafran raids by blocking the relief flights coming into Uli airport—something it has refrained from doing—Biafra's lifeline to the outside world will be severed."

June–September 1969

Chapter 20

Relief workers at the hospital at Ikot Okoro, on the Federal side, saw a Nigerian MiG fighter plane circling the area. It was about 6:30 on a Thursday evening, June 5. The sky was clear, except for one cloud. Visibility was excellent. The MiG kept circling, circling, for fifteen minutes. The relief workers heard in the distance the sound of the first Red Cross relief plane of the evening approaching from Fernando Po.

Thorsteinn Jonsson, an Icelandic pilot, also in the air, was flying one of the first JCA flights of that night, heading in from São Tomé. It was still daylight, but dusk was coming on in the east. He had just crossed the coast, flying at 11,000 feet, and was within the coastline of Nigeria when, over the radio, he heard a shout: "We're being shot at by MiGs." Then: "We're on fire." Then: silence. Jonsson kept trying to raise the other pilot on the radio as he sought cloud cover for his own plane.

On the ground, the relief workers at the hospital heard three shots in rapid succession. They could not see the attack: it happened behind the only cloud in the sky at the time. Almost immediately, the relief plane emerged in flames "and dropped like a stone."

The plane was white, with large red crosses painted on it. Its flight plan had been made available to the Nigerian government in advance, as the ICRC always did with all its relief flights. It was carrying eleven tons of rice. The plane, made available by the Swedish Red Cross, had an American pilot, Swedish copilot, a Swedish loadmaster, and a Norwegian flight engineer. All were killed, their bodies so badly burned that the Nigerians reported finding only two of them.

The FMG immediately released a statement: "This disaster had long been prophesied by the Federal Military Government to the ICRC, which has repeatedly been approached to discontinue night mercy flights in favor of daylight flights so that their identity could at no time be mistaken for Ojukwu's arms planes, many of which are of the same type."

Red Cross officials knew their plane had been shot down in daylight. To get more flights in each night, the pilots had been starting out earlier; Lindt, hearing that the Nigerian government might interfere with the airlift, warned them against crossing the coastline before nightfall. Three days before, a JCA plane had been attacked, the Joint Church Aid pilot reporting: "JCA followed by enemy MiG in downwind leg of approach to Uli. . . ." The Red Cross airbase at Cotonou reported to headquarters: "MiGs active Uli GMT 1845 last night rocket and cannon fire hit JCA plane." The rocket fire damaged the plane and, after being flown out, it had to be scrapped.

The next day, ICRC staff operating at Lagos Airport received orders to withdraw within seventy-two hours. The Red Cross regularly flew supplies from there to the relief operation on the Nigerian side of the lines. A senior security officer at the airport told a Lagos newspaper that the presence of the ICRC was no longer required. "Moreover," he said, "since they are no longer using here as their base, there is no need for them to remain here. In fact, we no longer want to see them. They are spying on our activities here."

The ICRC curtailed its airlift for a few days. Jacques Freymond felt that governments were not backing the Red Cross—the ICRC found itself very much alone. However he decided to start flying again. He also sent Georg Hoffmann to Lagos. (Hoffmann had been withdrawn from Lagos earlier because ICRC headquarters regarded him as too pro-Gowon.) Freymond told him he intended to restart the airlift; Hoffmann reported back from Lagos that if the ICRC began flying again, he would not be able to negotiate with the FMG. As it was, he could not get to meet with Gowon. Freymond decided to go ahead anyway.

Two Red Cross planes with twenty-five tons of food flew into Biafra from Cotonou the night of June 10–11. More were scheduled for the next night. That evening the U.S. Mission in Geneva telephoned Freymond at his home, passing on information from its embassy in Lagos: if the Red Cross flies again, the Nigerians will shoot down the planes. American diplomats had learned from British intelligence, so the story went, that the Nigerians had "acquired a night fighter capability" and had "the will to use it" against relief planes.

Freymond phoned Red Cross officials at the airport in Cotonou and found they had already been directly notified of the situation by the State Department in Washington. He had intended to tell them to fly, but after being informed about the danger of night fighters, they had already held up for that night. Now it was too late to start.

That same evening top executives of Joint Church Aid, gathered in Lucerne for one of their regular meetings, learned from a Catholic Relief Services representative that he had been called by the U.S. Mission with the same warning telephoned to Freymond. This alarmed the churchmen running JCA. They were not military men, not prepared to order their pilots to fly unarmed relief planes against night fighters with orders to shoot them down. The first flights were already in the air, but Viggo Mollerup contacted São Tomé: "Don't fly the second shuttle tonight."

As it happened, a few days earlier Mollerup had arrived at São Tomé when word came that the Red Cross plane had been shot down. He and the Danish Air Force colonel who had just taken over as chief of operations conferred with five of the chief pilots about what they should do during the next ten days, before the Nigerians had had a chance to gauge the reaction of world opinion. They agreed to try flying. Now, however, the pilots began hearing all sorts of reports. The Nigerians had gotten MiG-21s. Five MiG aircraft with night fighter capability had been unloaded from an East German ship in the port of Lagos.

Reports of the dangers from night fighters grew. What might be regarded as a codification was reported some weeks later by a correspondent who covered the Foreign Office for the London *Observer:* "The most significant factor in the rapidly escalated crisis of confidence between the ICRC and the FMG is the apparent growing ability of the Federal MiG fighters to operate competently after dark. Evidence has reached Whitehall that they are now piloted by more skilled men. The pilot who repeatedly ordered the Red Cross plane to land on July [*sic*] 5 and shot it down after it persistently ignored the order is said to have been very 'Eton and Oxford.' Other reports speak of East German pilots." The correspondent explained the significance of night fighter capability: "It is entirely because of this development that General Gowon, the Federal Nigerian Head of State, has at last felt able to insist, as every other Government does, on exercising 24-hour control over his country's airspace. This development could, in the British Government's view, turn out to be the most decisive of the war because it would mean that Colonel Ojukwu could not longer count on a regular flow of arms by night via the small fleet of two DC-3s, two DC-4s and two SuperConstellations that have operated regularly from Libreville. The flights have been greatly reduced in the past four weeks. In the light of Britain's support of the Federal case, this is a welcome development, because it could mean a shortening of the war. . . ."

The reports did not intimidate the JCA pilots. One pilot flew into Uli at night to check whether the Nigerians actually had acquired MiGs with radar. He made it safely. Others started flying cautiously. They flew near sea level, then went up to 1,500 feet over land. The new chief of operations ordered them to obey orders if they were intercepted by Nigerian fighters and given a "follow me" order to land.

Nevertheless, Joint Church Aid's airlift was severely curtailed, down to only a "communications flight" or two each night during the coming weeks. Freymond held up restarting the Red Cross airlift. When Lindt returned from Moscow and learned what had happened, he was critical; he thought Freymond had been weak and should have begun flying again.

The commander of the Nigerian Air Force said, "We are hitting at anything that flies into Biafra. If they are Red Cross planes, they have been warned repeatedly that night relief flights are illegal."

"The hawks are in the ascendance in Lagos" was the sentiment in the diplomatic community. Gowon had lost control; the hard-liners had taken over. Until now Gowon had kept them in line with warnings from their British and American friends: any interference with the airlift would bring the world crashing down upon them. Now they had destroyed a Red Cross plane and there was no great public outcry.

Official statements were low-key. The UN secretary general and the State Department mixed regrets with renewed calls for daylight flights, obscuring the fact that the Nigerian fighter had shot down the Red Cross plane in daylight. U Thant, saying he shared the anxiety of Sweden about the disappearance of the plane and expressing hope that the crew might still be found alive, commented, "This regrettable incident bears out in a tragic way the warnings made in the past by the secretary general about the risks involved in the insistence on relief flights by night only."

"While recognizing the problem created by the intermingling of arms flights and relief flights," the State Department said, "the United States Government deplores this attack. This incident underlines the urgency of alternative relief arrangements for daylight flights and surface corridors." Even this mildest of rebukes made the Nigerians bitter, deepening the ill feeling that began with the selling of the C-97s to the two airlifts.

The feeble reaction to the shooting down of the Red Cross plane emboldened Nigerian hard-liners to mount a new campaign against the ICRC. The press and radio became filled with accusations: the Red Cross had instructed its pilots to become blockade runners; the members of the committee were "hirelings of imperialism"; Lindt had played a "dubious role"; the Red Cross had acted as spies for Biafra and helped it to acquire arms; it should be asked to leave Nigeria and be told that the Federal air force would shoot down "all aircraft which violate Nigeria's airspace"; the

ICRC seemed to be aiming at a collision which would be a "disaster for all concerned."

Even the president of the Nigerian Red Cross, until now a moderating influence between the FMG and the ICRC, declared that the air force was right to have acted against planes that violated Nigerian airspace, adding: "The Federal Government is right to order that aircraft carrying relief materials at night should be shot down. . . . The Government made it clear that genuine relief aids should be carried in the daytime and not at night."

Georg Hoffmann could not negotiate for the ICRC. The climate was so bad he asked Geneva to recall him. For days the Nigerians demanded that the Red Cross remove August Lindt as high commissioner for relief; finally they declared him persona non grata. In his letter of resignation to the ICRC, Lindt remarked, "My determination to remain objective was not always appreciated in this conflict where propaganda and psychological warfare play an important part."

The ICRC felt compelled to respond to some of the more serious Nigerian charges, noting that it had always remained faithful to Red Cross principles: "It has never transported troops, arms and munitions, or supplied military information."

In this superheated atmosphere, the church relief agencies also began feeling stepped-up pressure to get agreement from the Biafrans for daylight flights. Joint Church Aid sent Dr. Middelkoop and Reverend Johnson to Biafra to impress upon Ojukwu the seriousness of the situation and the need to consider daylight flights.

Biafran leaders knew the origin of the campaign for daylight flights. The secrecy surrounding Red Cross negotiations kept concealed Nigerian efforts the previous August to prevent the ICRC from starting daylight flights into the neutralized airstrip at Obilagu. From this experience the Nigerians had learned that daylight flights into Uli were wholly unacceptable to the Biafrans. Lindt later commented that until September 3 the FMG "was dead against daylight flights and the Biafrans dead for them"; then, after September 3, they reversed. The difference: Obilagu was not Uli.

Biafrans, as much as Nigerians and the British, were constantly aware that Uli airfield was the prime strategic target and objective of the Nigerian Army and Air Force. The central importance of Uli was a refrain throughout the secret report of the British military adviser:

• ". . . The rebels remain dependent upon the nocturnal use of Uli. Denied the use of this airstrip, the rebel capacity to resist will falter and end. The seizure or denial of this airstrip is therefore the main strategic objective of the Federals. This can be achieved by (a) physically occupying it, or (b) moving to within medium gun range and then harassing the general area, or (c) effectively hindering the movement of aircraft to and from the field."

and again:

• "Denied this airstrip, the rebels would be unable to continue the struggle."

and again:

• They remain completely dependent upon the Uli airstrip. To reduce their capacity to resist, the Federals must sever this supply line."

and again:

• "They [the Federals] could gain a decisive victory, particularly if they move in concert on the only strategic objective, namely, the rebel terminal airstrip at Uli."

Not surprisingly, Biafrans were wary of any Nigerian scheme involving Uli airfield. They also had just had new cause to redouble their apprehension. Before the shooting down of the relief plane, Christopher Mojekwu, the Biafran home secretary, learned (from "highly placed British sources") of a British plot to deprive the Biafrans of Uli airport. The plan, as he heard it: first, harass relief flights until they could no longer operate; then, on the pretext that it was essential that relief go through, seize the airstrip.

This information could have been the scenario the British were actually following. Or the British may have planted the story deliberately with M.P.s friendly to Biafra so it would get back to the Biafrans and make them all the more apprehensive about agreeing to daylight flights into Uli. Either would work: Uli might be captured or Biafran leaders would continue refusing daylight flights, making them seem to blame for halting or diminishing the airlift and causing mounting starvation of their own people.

With the arrival of Middelkoop and Johnson as JCA emissaries, the Biafrans had to make some sort of affirmative response. The British and Nigerians had built up a line that was now widely accepted. Government leaders kept repeating and the public hearing that daylight flights would separate relief from military aircraft, the Nigerian Air Force would not have the problem of distinguishing arms flights from food planes at night, the humanitarian airlift would no longer provide cover for the gunrunners if the Biafrans would only agree to daylight flights into Uli.

Despite the stories that Nigeria had acquired night fighters, arms planes continued going into Uli from Libreville without being shot down. As JCA pilots tentatively made a few flights, relief officials began to suspect that the Nigerians did not possess night fighters. Now we have the secret report of the British defense adviser, written six months later: "The Nigerian Air Force does not have the capability of interdicting the rebel airfield at Uli by night."

No one could be certain of this in mid-June amid the rumors about MiG-21s and pilots with German accents. Red Cross and JCA pilots were not intimidated, but pressures upon relief agency officials became intense: governmental support—food and funds—for the airlifts could be cut off if they resisted what by now had become accepted, at least in the diplomatic world, as a reasonable proposal.

Middelkoop and Johnson represented those friendliest to the Biafrans. General Ojukwu felt that Biafra had lost the propaganda war over relief. He instructed his negotiators that at no point should they say no to relief proposals. So they gave Joint Church Aid the affirmative response its executives felt they must have. The Biafrans renewed their offer of cooperation to governments or relief agencies ready to assist in completing construction of a second airfield exclusively for relief, then said, "In the light of Nigeria's repeatedly stated determination to destroy or at least neutralize Uli airport, the Government is willing to consider the use of Uli airport for combined day and night relief operations for a limited period, subject to effective international or other third-party guarantees."

Hedged though this was with conditions, JCA and the ICRC both grasped at it as a breakthrough. Governments were equally ready to see in this qualified Biafran response a readiness to enter into an arrangement proposed by the Nigerians.

The Biafrans went further in making a positive response, saying they had "reached agreement with the United States Government on a surface route through the Cross River." Clyde Ferguson had chartered two World War II landing ships capable of carrying 900 tons each; one, the *Doña Mercedes*, had now arrived in Lagos and the other, the *Doña María*, was due shortly. Ferguson decided to try a "one shot"—announce agreement to the Cross River route and send the barges up the river, "Although," he stated, "some technical details remain to be worked out. . . ."

All this talk of agreement on daylight flights and agreement on the Cross River route created an unwarranted sense of assurance about relief for Biafra. In reality, the Nigerians had already made their decision and were determined to go ahead with it. Occasionally one of the more talkative Nigerian officials lifted the curtain to show how the stage was being set. The commissioner for rehabilitation for Calabar called upon the government to oust the Red Cross: "The evil ICRC operations had done in the country were far greater than the good credited to it," he said. "The removal of Dr. Lindt alone will not solve the problem of relief organizations. The only sure way of stopping the interference of these organizations in our affairs is to withdraw their invitation."

The situation was deteriorating rapidly, both politically and nutritionally. The Nigerians arrested a Red Cross medical team leader and held him a few days. The Swedish doctor serving as medical chief of the Red Cross in Biafra cabled: "Relief program rapidly breaking down. After extreme cutdown to three per cent, supply will last another ten days more but cannot take care of increasing number of kwashiorkor all over the country. Resistance in children greatly diminished due to previous period of starvation and seasonal lack of food. Without protein supply during next three weeks rapid process of deterioration to severe kwashiorkor in children, comparable to situation in August 1968. Two daily flights milkpowder absolutely immediate minimum to prevent disastrous setback. . . ."

Similarly, UNICEF heard from the Dutch nutritionist it had sent into Biafra, who had responsibility for sixty-five refugee camps: "Situation rapidly deteriorating. Alarming increase of kwashiorkor all over the country. Unless regular food supplies taken up within three weeks, situation will be the same as July 1968. All efforts and funds spent having served only to give hundred thousands of children one year lease of life before starvation."

The ICRC made a formal proposal to Lagos for agreement on daylight flights. No reply. August Lindt, briefing a meeting of representatives of other relief agencies in Geneva two days later, told them: The FMG does not want any more night flights. Negotiations are now under way regarding daylight flights, but the FMG does not give a clear response. A note has also been sent to the ICRC delegate in Biafra requesting that permission be obtained for daylight flights, but the outcome of that is not yet known. What happens next, as far as the relief operation is concerned, is essentially in the hands of the Nigerians. In Nigeria, Lindt concluded, there is a constant clamor for removal of the Red Cross.

Clyde Ferguson, also at the meeting, expressed the opinion that the situation seemed much worse than it had ever been. He told the relief agency representatives that, while there were still a few moderates in the Nigerian government, most officials were tending toward "an antirelief position, definitely antihumanitarian, showing the beginning of xenophobia."

. . .

Chief Enahoro declared that in spite of what Ferguson may have announced in Washington, the technical conditions necessary for opening the Cross River route had not been resolved: "The Federal Government cannot be committed to any action by an announcement made by any person outside this country."

Tension was building. JCA executives felt compelled to issue a statement saying they were ready to move from night flights to daylight flights "at the earliest possible moment," but to meet the "immediate desperate need" would continue to try to extend their present occasional night flights to the utmost possible "to bridge the period until daylight flights become possible."

Chief Awolowo, vice-chairman of the Nigerian government, stated: "All is fair in war, and starvation is one of the weapons of war. I don't see why we should feed our enemies fat in order for them to fight us harder."

The chief of staff of the Nigerian Army said, "Personally, I would not feed somebody I am fighting."

The FMG summoned representatives of all relief agencies providing humanitarian assistance in Nigeria and Biafra to a meeting in Lagos on June 30, with Chief Enahoro presiding. Red Cross officials anticipated that the government intended to oust the ICRC and would try to intimidate the other relief agencies.

That morning Chief Enahoro told the representatives, "The Federal Government has decided that the coordinating role of the ICRC should cease forthwith." He informed them that their relief agencies from that time forward must deal with the National Rehabilitation Commission the government had set up. The Nigerian Red Cross would also be under the control of the government's commission.

Turning to relief for "rebel-held areas," Enahoro ran through the charges against the relief agencies: arms had been carried in some relief aircraft; local food purchases by relief agencies provided the Biafrans with foreign currency, which they used for arms purchases abroad "and the financing of vicious propaganda and other rebel activities in prosecution of their rebellion"; by indirectly prolonging the war, the relief agencies were causing the loss of more lives. "I am sure you will wish to prevent your charity from being used in the furtherance of secession," he remarked.

He came to the point: "Henceforth, only authorized relief operators who satisfy the Federal Government on the necessary details will be permitted to take relief supplies to rebel-held territory." The FMG was ready to allow any agency to fly every day into Biafra, provided the flights take place between 9:00 A.M. and 6:00 P.M. and provided they take off from Lagos.

Thus the Nigerians added a second condition known to be unacceptable to the Biafrans. Perhaps they were not so sure the Biafrans still feared daylight flights into Uli, now that they had just announced they would agree to them. So, as the Red Cross representative attending the meeting cabled ICRC headquarters: "Enahoro definitely stated that condition for resuming urgent service or full scale flights—which could be done any time from now—is that the plane takes off from Lagos." The Nigerians had learned as far back as November 1967 that Biafrans would not accept a relief plane flying in from Lagos. Contrarily, the FMG was stipulating that flights must originate from Lagos Airport just a few weeks after having thrown the Red Cross out of there.

Enahoro succeeded in getting all relief agency representatives except one to acquiesce in the new policy. The Red Cross delegate stated that he must refer the matter to Geneva. Jacques Freymond was angry to learn that Lindt and the incoming president, Marcel Naville, had countermanded his order that other relief agencies instruct their representatives at the meeting not to agree if the FMG sought to oust the ICRC.

Significantly, though they had made the decision a couple of weeks before, the Nigerians waited to announce it till Freymond's last day as acting president of the ICRC. He was known as the "revolutionary humanitarian" of the Red Cross. It seems likely that Diallo Telli, secretary general of the OAU and a staunch supporter of the Nigerian government, had come to Geneva the week before to size up what sort of fellow Naville might be.

Late that afternoon, after word reached Geneva of Enahoro's meeting with the relief agencies, the ICRC asked representatives of these organizations to come to the Red Cross "Maison" overlooking, in the distance, the Lake of Geneva; one who attended the meeting reported to his headquarters "the Hill is shaking terribly and they are seeking comfort everywhere."

Freymond asked the position of the various organizations toward what was happening. The reaction was cautious; those present preferred to wait and see.

Freymond said that the way the decision had been taken was a serious matter. It came after a number of other unpleasant measures against the Red Cross. He suggested that the FMG was hitting the ICRC only because it had no way of getting at the church relief agencies. There was first the arrest of Lindt, followed by the shooting down of the Red Cross plane. And not one word of excuse, he exclaimed, not one word of sympathy for the pilots who had lost their lives. Instead, the FMG sought to justify its action by saying that the plane carried ammunition and to prove it by saying the plane exploded in the air.

The ICRC had not been given any opportunity for negotiations with Lagos, Freymond told the other relief officials. Any contact was avoided. The Nigerians' actions were not only serious but humiliating, a negation of the humanitarian work the Red Cross tries to carry out. It was impossible to accept this. As a personal thought, Freymond expressed the opinion that "everybody should immediately sever all relations with and stop all help to Nigeria till a satisfactory explanation has been given. It is important that we make it clear that no government can wage a war the way it sees fit."

Naville added, "They have to justify their reason for our expulsion." It was Freymond's opinion that the future of humanitarian work was at stake.

During the meeting, relief officials present were surprised and indignant when word came from Lagos that the UN secretary general's representative had accepted the Nigerian government's change of policy, expressing hope that a smooth transition from the Red Cross to the Nigerian Rehabilitation Commission would be assured.

Chapter 21

While Freymond and Naville were meeting with other relief agency officials in Geneva, Michael Stewart was telling Parliament that the new Nigerian policy "reaffirms that the Federal Government is prepared to allow relief supplies to rebel-held areas subject to proper inspection and control." He remarked: "Everything now turns on working out satisfactory arrangements between the Federal Government and the relief agencies . . . and, indeed, on the Biafran response."

The foreign secretary went on: ". . . If accusations are to be made against either the Nigerian Federal Government or against Her Majesty's Government of attempting to starve the Ibos, it is important to bring evidence. It is difficult to know what are the exact facts. That is the real difficulty, I do not deny; that it is often exaggerated for propaganda purposes, I'm afraid is also true. But I can see no reasonable objections to daylight flights. We would be glad to help in that, the Federal Government is prepared to do that. At present, Uli Airport, where the planes would have to land, is made unusable by Colonel Ojukwu during daylight hours. It is important that the obstacle should be removed. . . ."

"As I understand it," Stewart continued, "the Biafran leaders have said that they will only accept daylight flights in addition to night flights and not as a substitute for them. It is at night that arms and military materials are flown into the secessionists. The Federal Government have said that anyone engaged in night flights must do so at their own risk. The only right answer, therefore, is a cessation of night flights and the introduction of daylight flights and, far more important, as all the aircraft we can muster will not deal with what is required, the opening of land routes. This is what matters. . . ."

Stewart advised Parliament: ". . . I know some M.P.s take a different view from the Government and, while I try not to criticize anyone's good intentions, I do say that anyone with any contact with Colonel Ojukwu should shout loudly in his ear that he should allow relief to get in either by daylight flights or land. . . ."

The daylight flights proposal had evolved to a logical coherence that was quite persuasive to any who did not know its origin the previous fall or did not scrutinize it carefully. The argument that Biafran leaders insisted on night flights as a cover for arms shipments was transparently thin at this moment when the relief airlifts had all but halted, yet arms planes continued to land at Uli without being shot down.

British officials could not help but be uneasy that the true purpose of the daylight flights campaign might also become transparent, for they had just lost a pillar of support for their Nigeria policy. The *Times* of London broke with the government's position in an editorial titled "A Policy of Famine" (one of the subheadings also declared "A Deliberate Weapon"), which concluded, "All the evidence now shows that starvation as an act of war is the effective policy of the Nigerian Government."

The *Times* leader was devastating. Though it did not expose the complicity of British officials, it must have sent a chill through them, for in a number of passages it suggested the culpability they shared: "It is the principle of dissociation of sensibility—out of sight out of mind—which permits the most evil things to be done by quite ordinary men. In the last eighteen months well over a million people have died in Biafra of starvation and the diseases associated with starvation. During the whole of that period the British Government, with the connivance of the Opposition, has supported the besieging forces with very substantial sales of arms. . . ." Recounting the details of the shooting down of the Red Cross plane and the resultant suspension of the airlift, the *Times* went on: "Because the famine has already been so prolonged the food stocks are long since exhausted, and so is the stamina of most of the people. It is a people half-starved already who face starvation now. The effect of the cessation of the airlift is likely therefore to be almost immediate. The death rate was already high enough but it is likely to mount rapidly. Many of the aged already died and the casualties among mothers and children may be particularly severe. . . .

"The difficulty is to bring this home to people," the editorial continued. "Perhaps one can start by thinking not about the mass who are in danger, a population comparable in size to the European Jewish population in 1940, but about the individual responsibility for individual lives. British policy is still to give full support to a government which by a process which has involved much confusion is now using starvation as a conscious and deliberate weapon against very large numbers of what it claims to be its own people. As individuals, acting on individuals, we share the responsibility of our Government."

Puncturing the propaganda line the British government had been propagating successfully for more than twelve months, the *Times* stated: "All the evidence now shows that starvation as an act of war is the effective policy of the Nigerian Government. In the past British Government spokesmen have argued, not very plausibly, that the Nigerian Government was only too keen to feed the people of Biafra but that it was the fault of the Biafran Government who chose to starve their own people. General Ojukwu must share a part of the blame, but this was never a very convincing view of the situation and now we have from spokesmen of the Federal Government itself an open admission that starvation is not an accident but is regarded as a necessary and legitimate means of waging war."

The *Times* reminded its readers that a million and a half were already dead and recounted the facts of the shooting down of the relief aircraft, of the earlier indiscriminate bombing of civilians and hospitals in Biafra, of the successful campaign to cut off night flights to the airstrip, then concluded: "When one puts together these pieces of evidence one can be left in no doubt that the Government of Nigeria, whatever intentions it may have had at the beginning of the war, is now prepared to use blockade and starvation, even at the cost of a further million deaths, rather than agree to secession. Leaving aside the massacre of the Ibos, this has the effect of a policy of genocide."

Then, in a passage aimed at those who bore personal responsibility: "Yet one should get away from the big words and the big abstract concepts. Which one of us could actually bear to see a single child die of starvation? Which member of the Cabinet, who must take this responsibility in a personal sense, could bear this weekend, to have a child starving on a blanket between the deck chairs on the lawn and continue to join calmly in the process of tormenting it? Only the capacity of the human mind to steel itself against large figures and abstract terms makes it possible for this policy to be pursued. Men of personal sensitivity and personal kindness, who would not willingly harm a single infant, find it tolerable to support a policy of starvation by the million partly because it is millions that are involved."

Speculating that the death rate might soon be at fifty thousand a month—or some sixty an hour—the *Times* came up with an inspired conceit, drawn from cricket, intended presumably to make this fact understandable to even the most morally obtuse member of the government: "Perhaps the Test match could provide as good a way of keeping track of the urgency of this matter as any other. If the batsmen of either side could manage at last to dominate the bowling then they should be scoring at the rate of a run a minute. If they did, the runs going up on the board would be keeping pace with the death rate that may soon be expected in Biafra, as a result of the admitted policy of a government which has the full moral and material support of our own Government."

Noting that the government had, from the beginning, argued that British influence should be used "to moderate and mitigate the evils of this war" and "that we should not cut off the arms supply because that might destroy our influence," the *Times* commented: "It is the argument that we should retain our influence on events which seems now the most discredited of all. . . . Mass starvation unites a nation only in death. It is quite simply morally wrong to be the accessory to the slaughter of a million people in order to protect oil supplies and anyone who does not see that it is wrong is a moral imbecile. . . .

"If one could only see this matter for what it is, the greatest tragedy or crime for which Britain has shared responsibility in this century, the worst since the Irish famine, we should now devote all our diplomatic power, all the influence that remains, all the efforts of the Government to securing effective relief in terms of food for Biafra, at all costs and at once."

If Nigerian and British policy-makers had concluded Marcel Naville would be docile and more easily managed than Jacques Freymond, they were in for an alarming surprise. Naville had a Swiss father but an Italian mother; like a character in a Thomas Mann novel torn between the order and rationality of Northern Europe and the passion and excitability of the South, Naville would sometimes switch from a calm mood of reason to one of intense emotion. That morning, as he met with journalists, he had been provoked to high emotion.

The words came tumbling out. He told the correspondents: "I want to place before your eyes an image that has haunted me for two or three days. In Biafra we had opened numerous distribution centers. Every morning, in front of these centers . . . an immense queue forms of infants and women who come to have their bowls filled with milk or a bit of fish. We are closing them—we close some of them every day—and every morning this same queue of infants and women is back in front of the centers and the long silent lines wait that—perhaps by some miracle—these doors will reopen."

Naville went on to say, with a note of bitterness creeping in that the day before, they had learned "indirectly, perhaps because it was thought we would not be interested in being informed directly" of the meetings being held in Lagos by Enahoro: "What was said, you know, I do not have to repeat. I would like to remark it was in a manner at least unusual, I will keep to myself what I think, of treating, not humanitarian organizations, but of treating humanitarian action. The measure which was taken, of this measure, which disappoints us I admit, this was not important. I do not trouble myself for long with any wounded *amour-propre* we might have; that is of no great importance. What matters, in reality, it is surprising that a state—which represents a respected people—would consider that one could discharge a whole humanitarian organization the way one would show a faithless servant the door. . . ."

Acknowledging that the Nigerian government was sovereign and free to act as it chose in its own territory, to put an end to coordination by the ICRC of relief on its territory, Naville went on: "Only, you should tell me, there is a way, finally, after the attack upon the Red Cross plane, an attack which killed four, an attack consciously perpetrated, because the plane, we know, flew just before nightfall, at a moment when it was perfectly recognizable and the Red Cross insignia were recognizable, an attack perpetrated without forewarning, on a plane which flew on a route about which information had been provided long in advance. After this attack, to put an end to our activity abruptly is truly to intend to insult all humanitarian action rather than to have any intention of negotiating."

The new Red Cross president commented: "The Nigerian Government also put an end to an organization which has bases in Cotonou and Santa Isabel, putting an end unilaterally to an agreement by which night flights were authorized and now asks us to have eventual relief flights leave from Lagos, coupling that with a certain number of conditions, about which the least one could say is, I don't very well see who the negotiator is who could be able to bring the other party around to accepting these conditions."

Naville said that the ICRC would pass on the new proposals, but "we do not have any illusions." They would pass them on in all good faith, he said, "wanting still to believe in miracles," but "to keep our feet on the ground" they would persevere with the proposals they had already made to the Nigerian government a week before, "and about which we have not yet had the honor of a reply."

Naville's angry outburst included a pointed allusion: speaking of some "non-African powers," he said they are making a tragic mistake in their estimate of the Nigerian situation. To "some arms merchants" ("*certains marchands de canons*") he remarked that "the ICRC is not there to give them an easy conscience" and went on: "And I would also like to remind some others that all the oil in Nigeria would not produce enough detergent to wash their hands clean."

The allusion was not lost on London newspapers the next day. With the headline " 'Cannon Merchants' in Nigeria condemned—Red Cross turns to attack," the *Times* reported Naville's remarks about arms supplies, commenting: "Although he did not specifically mention Britain. . . ."

Officials in the Foreign Office and the British government, edgy already at the pointed references in the *Times* editorial, now had to fear that they might have a wild man on their hands in the new ICRC president. He could reveal just what role British policy-makers had been playing and how. (At the meeting of relief agencies in Geneva a week before, when the Oxfam man remarked that he personally considered the U.K.'s action deplorable, August Lindt had facetiously rejoined that he was no judge of matters in the United Kingdom—bringing a chuckle from those present.) If Marcel Naville began talking, the whole deception could come undone. Worse, they themselves could be exposed for the part they played in it.

Maurice Foley and Donald Tebbit flew to Geneva that day. Foley assured Naville that the Nigerians were not nearly so adamant as they seemed. Gowon was a reasonable fellow and could be talked with. The British would use all their influence and were sure it would be possible to get negotiations on daylight flights. The one person who could do this was Naville. If he would go himself to Lagos, Foley was certain something could be worked out.

Naville was prepared to listen, as he was already beginning to regret his outburst of the day before. Members of the committee were dismayed that he had spoken out in such an undiplomatic fashion, so unlike a president of the ICRC. Some felt he may have been influenced by Freymond (which was not the case).

New pressures on the British came at the end of that week when *The Economist* appeared with an article headed: "Nigeria's new restrictions on food for Biafra are an attempt to starve it out. The time to use that British influence has come." Mentioning the pledge made a year before by Foreign Secretary Stewart that "if the Federal Government was to proceed to the starvation of the Ibo people . . . then the arguments which have justified our policy would fall," *The Economist* commented: "This paper has supported the continuation of British assistance to Nigeria since then on the ground that the Nigerians were helping to get enough food through and that Mr. Stewart's escape clause therefore need not be invoked."

Stating that Britain still had influence in Nigeria, *The Economist* went on: "The time has come to use this influence and to be glad that it has not been lost by a premature cutting-off of arms. . . . Mr. Maurice Foley's flight to Geneva for consultations with the Red Cross can and should be followed up by another mission. A senior official or minister should be sent to Lagos, publicly to warn General Gowon that Britain will not continue to supply him with arms unless he allows relief flights into Biafra on acceptable terms."

The Economist concluded: ". . . The condition that Mr. Stewart set on Britain's support for Nigeria a year ago has now reached its testing point. The influence that has been accumulated should be most specifically exerted."

Three top relief agency officials met that evening with the Shadow Cabinet foreign minister, Sir Alec Douglas-Home, and later with Foreign Secretary Stewart. Both were preparing for a major debate on Nigeria in Parliament that Monday, two days away. Pastor Viggo Mollerup, who ran the Joint Church Aid airlift, had a heated exchange with Stewart when the latter urged him to stop flying in order to bring the Biafrans to negotiate an end to the fighting. Mollerup responded: "Although your suggestion is disgusting, I will not totally exclude that we might consider it, but that could only come into question once you have established a real plan, once you have revealed to us that it has real substance to it—not that it is a superficial plan, intended to be used for stalling operations. JCA executives will consider it on twenty-four-hour notice once you have told us. But any proposal would be regarded as superficial, as long as Britain and France are not involved."

The next day, Stewart met in London with Nigerian External Affairs Minister Arikpo. They asked Naville to come from Geneva to confer with Arikpo. Naville asked Freymond to go in his place. Upon his arrival, Freymond learned that the press had already been informed that a Red Cross official was coming; he remarked he believed in discreet diplomacy and there should be no announcement about their deliberations. That evening Freymond conferred with Arikpo and Edward Enahoro of the Nigerian Foreign Office, Maurice Foley, and Donald Tebbit. Enahoro, while the brother of Chief Anthony Enahoro, was less of a hawk on relief. So Freymond had a reasonable conversation with Arikpo and Enahoro, both moderates.

The following day, however, they were joined by Sule Kolo, the Nigerian ambassador in Geneva and a hard-liner, and the tone of the meeting changed. At the conclusion of the talks, Foley and Tebbit wanted to release a communiqué, but Freymond reiterated that he thought such consultations should be carried on in private. So what happened next came as a surprise: London newspapers reported that the Red Cross and the Nigerian government had reached agreement.

Under the headline "RED CROSS AND LAGOS AGREE IN LONDON," the *Times* said: "Complete agreement was reached in London yesterday between Nigeria, British and Red Cross representatives on relief measures for Biafra. Details will be given in Parliament today by Mr. Stewart. . . . Dr. Arikpo's negotiations with the ICRC were in two sessions lasting one-and-a-half and two-and-a-half hours. The Foreign Office expressed satisfaction at the results yesterday. . . ."

Michael Stewart, later that day, to Commons: "We were able to arrange a meeting in London at the weekend between Dr. Arikpo and Professor Freymond, Vice-President of the International Committee of the Red Cross. Professor Freymond confirmed that the Red Cross would be willing to operate daylight flights as now proposed by the Federal Government subject to detailed agreement on guarantees of safety for Red Cross crews, aircraft and personnel. . . ."

A question put to the Foreign Secretary by a Labour M.P.: "Why did a Foreign Office spokesman say last night that agreement had been reached when today that was denied by the Red Cross in Geneva?"

Mr. Stewart: "I covered the first question quite accurately in my statement. I said that Professor Freymond confirmed that the Red Cross would be willing to operate daylight flights as now proposed by the Federal Government. That is the measure of agreement and it is a very important measure. But, of course, there was no written agreement. I went on to say 'subject to detailed agreement on guarantees of safety for Red Cross crews, aircraft and personnel.' "

In Geneva, the reaction around ICRC headquarters was one of furious anger. Later, Foreign Office officials excused themselves to Freymond about the news reports. Freymond had an additional concern. As soon as he had come out of the meeting with Foley and Arikpo, he telephoned Marcel Naville, warning him not to go to Lagos. The week before, after Foley and Tebbit had urged Naville to confer with Gowon in Lagos, Sule Kolo told Naville he would not be able to visit Nigeria unless he issued a statement clarifying "inaccuracies in the reporting of his press conference." The Red Cross dutifully did this.

Freymond had forebodings about Naville going to Lagos, and he told him that if it were necessary, he, Freymond, would go instead. But by the time he got back to Geneva, Sule Kolo had informed Naville he must go personally—Freymond would not be acceptable. So Naville left a day later for Nigeria.

In the House of Commons, Michael Stewart said, "We are all agreed in wanting to see established between the Federal Government, the relief agencies and the secessionist authorities such arrangements as would make relief possible. The House knows that arrangements of that kind have not yet been achieved. But since I made a statement to the House on Monday, there is an additional fact that there are now conversations going on between the International Committee of the Red Cross and the Federal Nigerian Government in Lagos. When I say 'now going on,' it might be even at this minute or it might be in the very near future.

"The House will remember," Stewart continued, "that there has been an unhappy estrangement between the Red Cross and the Nigerian Government. It is right to tell the House that the conversations last weekend between my honorable Friend and I and representatives both of the Red Cross and the Nigerian Government played a substantial part in the fortunate result that the Red Cross and the Nigerian Government are now again in discussion. In view of some of the criticisms which have been made of Her Majesty's Government, it is right to point this out to the House and to give the credit that is due to my honorable Friend for the part he played in bringing this about. . . ."

In Lagos, Marcel Naville was allowed to meet with General Gowon for only a few minutes—a "courtesy call"—then Chief Enahoro took over. The first thing he did was to say that Olof Stroh, head of the Swedish Red Cross, could not be a member of the delegation. Naville acquiesced, so that one of the most forceful Red Cross officials had to leave. From that time on, Enahoro was very tough.

He insisted that Naville sign an agreement that the ICRC accepted Article 23 of the Fourth Geneva Convention, which sets forth the terms for allowing free passage of humanitarian relief, even to an enemy. Naville and his advisers saw no alternative to his signing: The Red Cross always tells others they must abide by the Conventions; clearly it could not refuse to agree to abide by them itself.

Enahoro then got Naville to issue a communiqué reflecting this agreement. After saying that the ICRC undertook to examine ways to implement the Federal government's policy, the communiqué stated: "In this connection, the President of the ICRC reaffirmed that the ICRC would not enter Nigerian air space without the authority and consent of the Federal Government."

Back in Geneva, Naville and other ICRC officials realized, now that he had agreed to abide by Article 23, that the Red Cross could never again fly into Biafra without the full authorization of the Nigerian government.

A representative of another relief agency wrote his headquarters: "M. Naville is just the victim of a shrewd policy; he has just fallen into the trap and if he would have acted differently he would have fallen into another trap."

Chapter 22

As soon as they had analyzed reports of Chief Enahoro's meeting with the relief agencies, Clyde Ferguson and his staff concluded that there was no further possibility for negotiation. The Nigerians were adamant and intended to starve the Biafrans out. Others in Washington were also troubled by the clear intent of the new move. Jean Mayer was organizing the White House Conference on Nutrition, and met that day with editors of the *Washington Post* on the subject of nutrition in America. In passing, he made some emotional comments about the situation developing in Biafra, not realizing this would be regarded as the better news story.

The next morning the *Post* carried a headline on its front page: BIAFRA MILLIONS SEEN DYING IN FOOD CUTOFF. The article quoted Mayer: "There are three million people in refugee camps completely dependent on outside food supplies. So unless they get the food, they'll die." Mayer read the *Post* story with some uneasiness; he felt his new role did not include making comments on foreign affairs. So it was with trepidation that he received a phone call from President Nixon a short time later. But Nixon expressed his concern to Mayer about the situation and asked him what he thought he, the president, should do. Mayer suggested, as a starter, having Clyde Ferguson report directly to the president. Nixon acted surprised that this was not already the case.

The *Post* commented editorially that day: "One word now describes the policy of the Nigerian military government toward secessionist Biafra: genocide. It is ugly and extreme but it is the only word which fits Nigeria's decision to stop the International Committee of the Red Cross, and other relief agencies, from flying food to Biafra. . . ."

The newspaper made its own recommendation: "For the Nixon Administration there should be no confusion or delay in deciding how to respond. The United States must immediately and unequivocally join in what we trust will be a worldwide demand that Nigeria not interrupt the flow of food and drugs to the civilian victims of the Nigerian civil war. . . . There are no diplomatic or political considerations so overwhelming that the United States must stand quietly by while another government murders a million or more souls."

Later that day, Secretary of State William Rogers was asked in a press conference about Jean Mayer's remarks. He said: " . . . The prospect of mass starvation is so abhorrent and so almost incomprehensible in this day and age that we are going to do everything we can to attempt to get further food and supplies to people who are faced with starvation. . . . We consider it extremely serious. We deplore the thought that mass destruction should be used as an instrument of warfare and we are going to do everything we can to help prevent this mass starvation."

The Bureau of African Affairs set about immediately to correct any wrong impression this may have made, putting out a statement in Rogers's name within hours. Ferguson's staff had already had one in preparation that said, "There is no reason of a theoretical or practical nature why the humanitarian aspects of this problem cannot be separated from the political and military aspects. . . . The United States deplores the severe curtailment of the role of the International Committee of the Red Cross by the Federal Nigerian Government." The Africa bureau amended this draft, to add: " . . . The United States knows that the Federal Military Government is concerned that night relief flights provide cover for arms flights. . . . We are urging the Biafran authorities to accept daylight relief flights with assurance of neutral air corridors and with reasonable inspection on Nigerian territory, over which all relief flights must pass."

About this time, Norman Cousins, the American editor and publisher, was in Biafra on a peace mission, undertaken with the encouragement of the Nixon administration. He later recounted in his magazine *Saturday Review*: "At one of the refugee camps that afternoon there was a question about the latest exploit in space.

" 'Is it true,' a hungry old man asked, 'that Americans will soon be walking on the moon?'

"I nodded.

" 'It is a wonderful thing that America is able to send men to the moon,' he said.

"I nodded again.

" 'Tell me,' he said, 'will they also be able to send us some food? For more than a month, there has been no food. Can you explain why they have stopped flying in the food?' "

Red Cross pilots at Cotonou were becoming restless. They knew that Joint Church Aid had begun flying at full capacity from São Tomé once again and its pilots were encountering no night fighters, in spite of stories Chief Enahoro and others were giving to the press. At least five aircraft making night flights to Biafra had been shot down within the last fortnight, Enahoro told the London *Observer*: " . . . Our air interception operations are now so much more effective that already no plane can be sure of getting through to Uli. Within a matter of months we will be able to insure that only flights approved by the Federal authorities will be able to get through at all."

It had been more than forty days since the Red Cross had flown; the pilots, frustrated by inaction, decided to fly anyway. They cabled headquarters their intention to fly that night unless specific orders to the contrary were received. By midafternoon, four planes were fully loaded and fueled up, ready to go if no countermanding order arrived in time. It did. Had it not, there would have been eight "illegal" flights into Uli that night, with all the repercussions.

The Red Cross pilots sent Naville a telegram, calling upon the ICRC to relinquish control of the airlift to another organization willing to fly with or without permission of the FMG. They could see no end to the impasse; unless flights were resumed within two weeks, they warned, they would go home.

A few days later, more pressure from within their organization put ICRC officials on notice that they could not long lie passively in the elaborate trap fashioned for them by the Nigerians and British. A message came to Geneva from the entire Red Cross staff in Biafra. Provoked by a remark Naville was reported to have made, they radioed: " . . . Much alarmed by statement broadcast over news media and attributed to President of ICRC that nutritional situation in Biafra serious but not yet catastrophic. Field staff eyewitness that situation, seriously deteriorated since mid-June following interruption of relief flights, has now become catastrophic."

The field staff was not only Swiss, though Heinrich Jaggi's name led the signers. They were doctors, nutritionists, and medical personnel recruited by Red Cross societies in the Scandinavian countries, the Netherlands, and other countries of Europe. Their radio message continued: "Alarming daily increase of kwashiorkor and malnutrition. First evidence of steeply rising death rate among children. Due to previous period of starvation and lack of local food, deterioration now far more rapid than a year ago."

The Red Cross team concluded with an urgent appeal that full-scale relief flights be resumed without delay to save hundreds of thousands of children from certain death: "Unless immediate action is taken all efforts during the past year to save civilian population will have been in vain."

Officials in Geneva considered this appeal a lack of discipline on Jaggi's part, and they had him issue a clarification: "The general food situation has not yet reached the low level of this time last year, when thousands of people were dying every day...."

However, the ICRC received lengthier, more detailed reports from its advisers in Biafra: "Today only hospitals and sickbays continue to receive ICRC supplies. The Red Cross feeding centers are run on local vegetables—cassava leaves—and local meat—lizards, snails, grasshoppers and other insects. Each feeding center caters for 100 children only, selected among the worst cases of kwashiorkor and malnutrition. Thus it is that less than five percent of those who benefited from the original programs are still being cared for." And the effects of this: "The child population of the villages which in mid-June was still healthy and happy, in early July showed the first evidence of kwashiorkor: swollen legs, puffy faces and apathy...."

There was tension within the ICRC over the way Naville had handled things in Lagos. The public criticism in some newspapers bordered on ridicule; in private, diplomats were speaking of his having "gone on his knees to Canossa." Within the committee there was concern that the new president had already proved incompetent. The article of the Geneva Convention he had been trapped into signing provides that the government permitting relief shipments "shall have the right to prescribe the technical arrangements under which such passage is allowed." Some questioned whether Nigeria was in fact the "government" of airspace it could not control, but Red Cross legal experts interpreted the article strictly and believed the ICRC must negotiate agreement.

Clyde Ferguson invited Sylvanus Cookey, the young Biafran relief negotiator, to come to Geneva, ostensibly to discuss further the Cross River route (though Ferguson had concluded four weeks before there was no longer a possibility of negotiating agreement with the Nigerians about anything). This allowed a back-door approach to the Biafrans, agreed to by Naville but not involving the Red Cross directly. Freymond invited Cookey and another young Biafran diplomat to lunch at a restaurant in the park on the shore of Lake Geneva. From there it was only a short walk to his office at the Institute for Advanced International Studies, where he presented them with an ICRC proposal for daylight flights.

The new proposal provided for a Red Cross corridor through Nigerian airspace to Biafra. It required both sides to acknowledge and formally certify the security and protection the Red Cross insignia was meant to provide. Both Nigerians and Biafrans had to pledge to facilitate relief flights and refrain from intervention in the air as well as on the ground within the boundaries of the air corridor. There were two other provisions, about flight schedules being given both sides and for a commission to control relief shipments at Cotonou and Santa Isabel bases.

Cookey agreed in principle to this proposal. The "in principle" depended upon conclusion of the negotiations and stipulation that the ICRC must find an international sponsor to "guarantee" there would be no Nigerian interference with the air corridor or Uli airfield. Freymond thought he would be able to bypass Biafran insistence on a "guarantee" by setting up the control commission at Red Cross airbases.

The Nigerians reacted differently. They expressed astonishment, in General Gowon's name, over what seemed to be an ICRC proposal. Why, they wanted to know from Marcel Naville, was he now going contrary to Nigerian government policy when he had agreed in Lagos it was in accordance with the highest humanitarian principles of the Geneva Conventions? It could only be wrong if it violated the conventions; any other reason would be political, not the proper role for the Red Cross. They chided Naville for having said he would collaborate in putting Nigerian policy into effect by informing Ojukwu about it, but he had not yet reported any response. They wanted an explanation: why had Naville sent his new proposal? Had some new factors come up causing a change in attitude toward the Nigerian government's policy?

Even as the letter setting forth this negative reaction was on its way to Naville, however, the ICRC spelled out the details of its new plan. Time of flights would be 9:00 A.M. to 6:00 P.M. only, so they would be in daylight as the Nigerians insisted. Relief planes would land at Uli, which Biafrans had been resisting (though, ostensibly, they now accepted daylight flights to Uli). ICRC bases would be Cotonou and Santa Isabel, not Lagos. Inspection and control of cargoes would be at these bases rather than on Nigerian territory, as the government required. However, Nigerian authorities could order any aircraft flying into or out of Uli to land in Lagos "for supplementary control"—surely unacceptable to the Biafrans. There was something in it for everyone—or, for everyone, something not acceptable.

Cookey accepted the proposal for the Biafrans, again subject to the arrangement of guarantees. In Lagos, however, the Nigerians summoned the ambassadors of "donor governments"—those supporting the Red Cross with funds—to a meeting. After going over the points made in the letter to Naville, Foreign Minister Arikpo called their attention to the wording of Article 23 in the Geneva Conventions: the power permitting free passage has the right to prescribe the technical arrangements under which such passage is allowed. Nothing, he protested, authorizes anyone other than that power to make the technical arrangements. Yet the Red Cross had sent his government a proposal in place of the Nigerian one already agreed to as acceptable.

This is the latest example, Arikpo charged, of some ICRC members ignoring decent behavior. On a number of occasions the FMG had endangered its security by responding to Red Cross appeals that it must abide by its obligations under the Geneva Conventions. If the ICRC thinks some aspects of our policy are contrary to the Geneva Conventions, he told the ambassadors, then it should call my government's attention to these points and help work out improvements.

He called upon the ambassadors to get their governments to help establish relief by using their influence so the ICRC would function in strict accordance with the Geneva Conventions, not at the whim and caprice of some few individuals. My government's relief policy, he told them, offers the possibility of flights on a realistic basis to guarantee a sufficient volume of relief into the enclave while not prolonging the war and extreme suffering for innocent civilians.

Thus it came about that the Geneva Conventions were being used to block humanitarian relief to a civilian population in need. Of course the ICRC as the traditional guardian of the Conventions could not acquiesce in this but put out a brief statement, pointing out that Article 23 gives children and pregnant women "the right to receive medicine, medical material and the necessary food to insure their survival." This right obliges governments "not only to provide free passage for the forwarding of relief but also to effect this rapidly.

"Consequently," the Red Cross concluded, "the clause at the end of Article 23 cannot be used to prevent such relief from arriving at its destination or to delay it. In which case it would run counter to the humanitarian purpose of this article."

Aware they were defying the Nigerian government, Joint Church Aid executives, as they built up their airlift again, took the precaution of observing the rules Chief Enahoro had laid down to the relief agencies. They established strict regulations about the kinds of commodities and passengers their planes could transport into Biafra. The number of flights steadily increased: only 122 church relief flights had gone into Uli during June—the month the Nigerians had shot down the Red Cross plane—but in July there were 321 and in August 337.

Nonetheless, church relief officials were getting reports as troubling as those reaching the Red Cross and UNICEF. Father Dermot Doran, one of the most activist of the Irish priests, reported, "When I went into Biafra in mid-May of this year, there were smiles once again on the faces of the children and the dull and listless looks of both children and adults—the effect of protracted malnutrition—were missing. Yet, last week when I visited Biafra, I saw them once again. The appearance of the children and the aged particularly, has already worsened and, while not yet as critical as last summer, there is every reason to believe that the saddening spectacle of mass starvation will confront us once again unless food availabilities are increased."

He also quoted Father Desmond McGlade, at that time heading Caritas distribution in Biafra: "My parish is in Oguta only eight miles from Uli, in the center of things. It is regarded as comparatively well off, yet our twelve feeding centers served eighteen thousand people. Eight of them try to help fifteen hundred people each and, at one time, were able to distribute a small ration each day. Now we can give only one meal twice weekly and that of about five ounces of whatever we may have. How long can anyone exist on five or ten ounces of food a week? The only other food available is bush leaves or snails the children dig up."

Dr. Herman Middelkoop made a similar report to the Protestant relief agencies. By early August, JCA was estimating child mortality in Biafra "once again above one thousand per day." The church relief agencies began feeling mounting British-Nigerian pressures to curtail the other half of the airlift, though JCA executives at this point may not have fully recognized the purpose of the campaign. One of the arguments the British Foreign Office had already gone to considerable effort to develop was that church contributions for relief, placed in a Swiss bank account, provided Biafra with funds needed for arms purchases.

The pressures at first were subtle. Middelkoop, for example, had a meeting at London airport with Maurice Foley during which Foley sought to suggest that the JCA airlift could not continue because funds for it would dry up in Europe. Public support was waning, Foley said. He told Middelkoop he had been informed by others in JCA that they would not be able to continue the airlift. Though the conversation was guarded, Middelkoop came away with the impression that Foley had been trying to get from him some sort of agreement.

At a later time, Father Doran happened to be at the Vatican when Catholic churchmen from Africa arrived, sent by the Nigerian government, and sought to persuade Vatican officials to halt the airlift. Doran, present but not identified, remained silent, so that it might be assumed he was an Italian priest. Only at the end was he introduced—the rather notorious priest whom the Nigerians often accused of being a gunrunner.

JCA executives felt that the military situation was "not unfavorable for Biafra." The UNICEF representative serving as liaison to the relief agencies in Geneva reported to his headquarters in mid-August: "This is the reason why—mind you, I am reproducing the opinion expressed in the circles of JCA—the Federal Military Government at the instigation of the United Kingdom has decided to put an end to all relief activity on both sides of the fighting line. The FMG has started by interrupting the work of the Red Cross. Stopping the role of the ICRC in the Federal territory is only intended to stop the relief entirely. . . ."

Chapter 23

Three months had gone by since the shooting down of the Red Cross plane. Suddenly the Nigerian government was going to allow the Red Cross to fly into Biafra. There had been vague reports all summer of "daylight flight negotiations." But only governments and the ICRC knew the Nigerians were not negotiating but attacking the Red Cross initiative.

The first definite news came September 4: the FMG no longer insisted relief flights must be inspected in Lagos or elsewhere within the country. Much was made of this concession. "Now, however, Nigeria has magnanimously abandoned its earlier inspection demand," the *Washington Post* commented. "General Gowon, its leader, says Nigeria will allow food planes to fly to Biafra direct from Dahomey; he claims only a right to call the planes down for inspection."

The editorial followed the consensus that had been building up: "Biafra, however, is still balking. The Biafran chief, Colonel Ojukwu, evidently is willing to accede to even more suffering and death, rather than accept the new Nigerian stand. The world's humanitarians, if they are fair, ought immediately to turn their appeals from General Gowon to Colonel Ojukwu. . . ."

On September 13 the public learned that the Nigerian government had signed an agreement with the Red Cross. The following day, the Biafrans rejected it, charging that this agreement was different in important technical details from the one presented to them by the ICRC, which, they said, they had accepted.

To officials of Joint Church Aid and others still concerned with humanitarian relief it seemed as though the ICRC had wittingly colluded with the British and Nigerians to make it seem that the Nigerians agreed to daylight flights (which would never come about and would be meaningless in amount of food flown in if they did), while the Biafrans got blamed for obstructing a reasonable plan. One JCA executive spoke bitterly of "the International Committee of the Double Cross." What had happened or how was not altogether clear, but it seemed as though the ICRC had willingly lent itself to a propaganda charade that had had the ultimate impact on the public.

Here is what actually took place.

About the time the Red Cross made its proposal for daylight flights to the Biafrans and Nigerians, President Zinsou of Dahomey visited Lagos. His troubles had increased since the time he had let the ICRC begin flying relief from his capital, Cotonou. Zinsou was invited to Lagos, then Gowon went to Cotonou. Zinsou agreed not to let Cotonou be used for future relief flights without authorization from the FMG. Earlier, of course, the Nigerian government had reached a similar understanding with Equatorial Guinea, so it had now gained control over both bases.

News stories about a pending Red Cross flight gave the impression the airlift would shortly resume. A single "emergency flight," agreed to when Marcel Naville was in Lagos, was intended to carry medical supplies and doctors to the Red Cross staff in Biafra. But the FMG delayed even this limited operation a number of times.

To overcome this Nigerian reluctance, the ICRC dispatched August Lindt (who had not yet taken up his new duties as Swiss ambassador to India) to persuade U Thant to support its effort. For once the UN secretary general supported humanitarian relief. Following his ritual language of obeisance to the Nigerian government and the OAU Kinshasa resolution, Thant went on: " . . . Until the flow of supplies by land and river corridors is established and operative, some arrangement must be urgently made for the resumption of emergency flights even if concessions are required from both sides. The first question is to move immediately the stocks which have accumulated in various locations from which aircraft of the International Committee of the Red Cross can transport them by day to their destination. I appeal to both sides, based on the most fundamental humanitarian principles, to grant the necessary facilities for the movement of these supplies without delay."

What came of this was limited. One emergency flight of two planes took place at night into Uli. The Nigerians insisted that they land at Lagos on their way back to Cotonou, ostensibly so they could check on personnel being transported out. The Biafrans acquiesced in this. The planes took off while it was still dark at Uli, then landed at Lagos in daylight, at about 7:00 A.M. Any hopes ICRC officials may have had that this might lead to some compromise agreement on daylight flights into Uli, with touchdown at Lagos, were immediately dashed, however, for it was that day that the

Nigerians responded with vituperation to the new Red Cross proposal. Chief Enahoro was adamant that relief aircraft must be cleared by inspection at Lagos "or other approved points in Federal areas" before daylight flights into Uli.

While governments had begun warning anyone who sought to find new ways to get food into Biafra not to do anything that "would jeopardize daylight flight negotiations," in fact throughout that summer Lagos was not negotiating with the Red Cross but rather refusing to negotiate. The ICRC had a subsidiary reason for attempting to negotiate, even if it was encountering angry rejection of its efforts by Chief Enahoro and the FMG. Since the June 30 meeting, when Enahoro had taken the coordinating role from the ICRC and placed the Nigerian Rehabilitation Commission in charge, the question arose, how would the transition be made?

The question became an occasion for stalling: neither the ICRC nor its donor governments were ready to turn relief—even on the Federal side—over to the National Rehabilitation Commission.* Not only did it not exist as an organization with any capacity for carrying on relief activities, but in a country endemic with corruption donor governments were not prepared to provide food, trucks, and other supplies and equipment to a governmental commission with the almost certain expectation that much of it would never reach those for whom it was intended.

So negotiations about the transition from the ICRC to the National Rehabilitation Commission dragged on through the summer. For Red Cross officials it was a necessary exercise if they were to be true to their own principle of neutrality, of working impartially on both sides of a conflict; they could not negotiate about daylight flights into Biafra unless they were still working in Nigeria, and they could not negotiate about the transition on the Federal side unless they were still negotiating and maintaining staff in Biafra.

As the Nigerian government had declared August Lindt persona non grata, the ICRC appointed a new negotiator, Enrico Bignami, a retired executive of the Swiss firm Nestlé rather than an experienced diplomat. Bignami dealt only with the FMG in Lagos while Freymond handled negotiations with the Biafrans in Geneva. This overcame the problem encountered by both Lindt and Ferguson in trying to negotiate with the two sides. Traveling back and forth between Biafrans and Nigerians, Lindt and Ferguson had each soon found himself suspected by both sides

---

*The FMG had prescribed that the Nigerian Red Cross, as well as other voluntary relief agencies, would have to operate "under the direction and control of the Commission."

of being sympathetic to the other, of playing the game of their enemy, an inevitable result in the superheated atmosphere of wartime capitals. The larger problem remained: Chief Enahoro and the FMG made it forcefully clear that the Red Cross should not be offering proposals of its own but only trying to get Ojukwu to agree to the Nigerian position.

Bignami returned to Geneva at the end of August, having accomplished nothing in Lagos. Daylight flight negotiations were getting nowhere, and there was a new pressure on ICRC officials. In a reprise of the previous August, Dutch and Scandinavian Red Cross societies were again furious with the ICRC for its dilatory approach as starvation rose in Biafra. There was an added element this year, setting a deadline for the ICRC. The quadrennial meeting of the International Red Cross was to begin in Istanbul September 6. All national societies as well as the League of Red Cross Societies and the ICRC would be in attendance. ICRC officials feared a serious confrontation unless they could come up with some positive result from their "daylight flight negotiations" by the time the Red Cross societies arrived in Istanbul.

Bignami was given new instructions. The day before, Freymond had met again with Sylvanus Cookey and again obtained from him agreement on the technical terms. Two weeks earlier, the ICRC had received from Ojukwu written agreement to the Red Cross proposal—in principle. ICRC officials felt there was significance in the fact that Ojukwu's letter did not mention the need for a third-party guarantee. They did not see how they were going to get this, though they had assured Cookey during the first round of negotiations in early August that they would explore the possibility of obtaining such a guarantee from countries in the Hague Group. Freymond hoped he might satisfy this Biafran requirement with the control commission contained in the Red Cross proposal. This provided for a representative of a neutral nation proposed by the Biafrans and one proposed by the Nigerians.

This was not, however, sufficient for Cookey to sign an agreement to the technical modalities. He could only agree, again, en principe. The Biafrans were particularly apprehensive that once the air defenses were down and obstructions removed from the airfield during the day, the Nigerians would in some way take advantage of this to destroy or capture Uli. As they put it: their "air traffic control chaps" told them they could not guarantee the security of Uli.

These fears were heightened by a report that reached Hugh Fraser, a former minister for air. Earlier in the summer, he told the House of Commons, "I know that there are aircraft being dressed up to look like Red Cross aircraft. There are at least three Sabena Dakotas (transport aircraft) being fitted with bomb racks and machine guns—I regret of

British Ministry of Defense design—and these could be placed into a column of other aircraft without much difficulty."

Like the report Mojekwu had heard earlier, there is no way of ascertaining whether this was accurate. It could have been planted by the British Foreign Office with an M.P. friendly to the Biafrans in order to heighten their fears so as to harden their resistance to daylight flights into Uli.

Cookey, meeting with Freymond, asked for only one change, requested by Foreign Minister Godwin Onyegbula, one of the hard-liners in the Biafran government. To the article that gave the Nigerian government the right to order "at any requested time" any aircraft flying in or out of Uli to land at Lagos "for supplementary control," the Biafrans wanted added: "Biafra reserves the right for security reasons to order such aircraft to return to bases." They could thus turn back any planes taking off from Lagos, to foil any such scheme as that reported by Fraser. Freymond accepted this, as the ICRC believed the Biafrans already had—implicit in another article—the right to turn back aircraft.

The same day Cookey and Freymond were conferring in Geneva, Marcel Naville traveled to Paris to meet with the French foreign minister, seeking the support of France to get Biafran acceptance of the ICRC proposal. As the Biafrans had agreed to the proposal in detail, except for their insistence on a "guarantee," while the Nigerians had thus far agreed to nothing, this might seem a bit strange. But an ICRC plan was afoot, for which Bignami had been recalled to meet with the committee.

Some members of the committee felt it was time to stop trying to negotiate, time to get out of Nigeria altogether. There was only little more than a week before the start of the Red Cross conference. They felt the ICRC had to go to Istanbul either with an agreement for daylight flights or with a decision to withdraw entirely. Naville wanted to force the issue of daylight flights; he had a personal stake in succeeding with the proposal, given the public humiliation and the loss of confidence within the committee he had suffered after falling into the trap laid for him in Lagos.

The plan was this: Bignami would return to Lagos and try to get agreement *en principe* from the Nigerian government for the ICRC proposal. Enahoro was still insisting that flights must originate in Lagos or elsewhere in Nigeria, but Ferguson was in Geneva and the U.S. was prepared to press the FMG to allow Red Cross planes to start outside Nigeria. The control commission inspecting cargoes and the right to order aircraft to land at Lagos for "random inspection" gave the Nigerians, in fact, what they pretended to want in the way of inspection and control over relief cargoes. However, it did not give Enahoro and other "hawks" what they really wanted—a negotiating proposal they could be absolutely certain the Biafrans would reject. Enahoro was no longer so sure the Biafrans would continue to refuse daylight flights into Uli, so he was reluctant to give up the second condition, known to be unacceptable to the Biafrans.

As the ICRC already had Biafran concurrence, once Bignami obtained in principle agreement from the Nigerians as well, the plan was to put this to the test. Red Cross planes would fly in daylight from Cotonou and Santa Isabel to Uli, then circle over the airfield, seeking Biafran permission to land. It would be a dramatic moment. If the Biafrans allowed the planes to land, the ICRC would have overcome their insistence for a guarantee. It would also begin a daylight airlift into Uli, something that the Nigerians had been saying they accepted but that Red Cross officials knew they did not want at all.

ICRC officials thought they would make both the Nigerians and the Biafrans allow something they did not want. They intended to force the Biafrans to let flights land at Uli in daylight and to force the Nigerians to accept relief by flying in daylight to Uli on the basis of agreements entered into only *en principe*. It was a desperate plan. They were under tremendous pressure to succeed before the Istanbul conference and, as one put it later, there was "a strong element of fatigue."

Committee members agreed to the plan. Bignami was sent back to Lagos with instructions to get FMG agreement at the earliest possible date, preferably by September 1, so there would be time to put the scheme to the test before the conference began. The U.S. began urging Gowon to get Enahoro to accept the Red Cross proposal. He was in no mood to do any such thing. In Lagos, Bignami was finding it difficult to arrange a meeting. He was being put off day by day: Gowon was not there, then Enahoro was not there. He could not get to anyone until September 4.

"The Federal Military Government has served notice that it will not deviate from its policy of prior inspection on Nigerian soil of relief supplies bound for rebel territory." Though he made this announcement after meeting with Bignami, Enahoro soon had his mind changed for him. There were new pressures on the Nigerians too. The annual OAU conference was about to open in Addis Ababa, and FMG representatives sent off to other African countries were finding a change in attitude. As the publication close to the Nigerians and British, *West Africa*, commented: "At the Algiers summit meeting of the OAU last year the Federal Government had an easy passage: Biafran resistance seemed to have been broken. . . . Now . . . there are many in Africa who say that a resistance which has lasted this long entitles at any rate the Ibos to 'nationhood.' . . . "

The British pointed out that there was no need for the Nigerians to seem obdurate in public to the Red Cross proposal when it was possible to appear reasonable, then tie up negotiations later by adding new conditions. So the OAU meeting, American urging, and British counsel helped Gowon persuade Enahoro to make what other governments would view as a "great concession"—to have relief flights take off from Cotonou instead of from Lagos.

It was not obvious to those not privy to the details of Red Cross negotiations that this was hardly any substantive change at all, since planes inspected at Cotonou could then be called down for a second inspection at Lagos. Instructions went out to make the most of this. The Nigerian ambassador to the United States, for example, went to the office of an editorial writer of the *Washington Post* the following Monday morning, who wrote: "Now, however, Nigeria has magnanimously abandoned its earlier inspection demand. General Gowon, its leader, says Nigeria will allow food planes to fly to Biafra direct from Dahomey; he claims only a right to call the planes down for inspection. Biafra, however, is still balking. . . ."

Sylvanus Cookey was leaving Geneva that day, to return to Biafra. An ICRC official who had been in negotiations with him and Freymond rushed to the airport to tell him they had just heard from Bignami in Lagos. An agreement had been reached, but the technical modalities would be worked out by the Nigerian Air Force. The official asked Cookey if Biafra would have any objection to signing an agreement with the ICRC separate from the one Nigeria would sign. The two would be the same, based on the August 4 technical modalities, but with some slight differences in phraseology. Cookey said there would be no objection if the substance was the same. There was nothing new in the Nigerians accepting daylight flights in principle, he pointed out; this had been their position all along.

That evening, in Paris, Cookey heard a report on the radio: the Nigerian government had agreed to daylight flights. There was no mention that the Biafrans had already accepted the same agreement. This puzzled Cookey.

The ICRC gave orders to the crews of the Red Cross planes to be ready to take off on relief flights without delay. Heinrich Jaggi arrived in Istanbul for the start of the International Red Cross conference. Freymond told him of the plan: We will fly in daylight anyway and see what the Biafrans do, he said.

Jaggi, alarmed, remarked: "This is dangerous. The Biafrans won't accept it. They will be so angry that our seventy people in Biafra will be in danger. So will the church people."

So the start of the relief flights was held up. Naville arrived in Istanbul, back from a week's trip to Yemen. He asked: Why haven't we begun flying in daylight? Jaggi explained his concern. Naville was angry and upset.

In Lagos, Bignami continued negotiating. Luke Obi, who had been in the negotiations with Cookey and Freymond, was suddenly asked to come to Geneva, urgently. The ICRC gave him a copy of the agreement Bignami had worked out with the Nigerian government. He was furious when he read the technical details. The Red Cross officials said they would continue trying to reconcile the differences between the Nigerian and Biafran versions. On the way to the airport, Obi said to the ICRC official who accompanied him, "I cannot send *this* to my government."

The conditions the Nigerians had added were calculated to make the technical modalities unacceptable to the Biafrans:

• Instead of Red Cross relief planes taking off from both Cotonou and Santa Isabel, only Cotonou could be used. This would cut the airlift by half; what is more, Cotonou was more than three times the distance to Biafra than Santa Isabel, so planes could not make as many flights each day flying from that base alone.

• Instead of the control commission being composed of neutral nations proposed by both Nigerians and Biafrans, it would have representatives from the Nigerian and Dahomean governments and the ICRC—none chosen by Biafra. Aware that the Nigerians had intimidated Dahomey into giving the FMG control over flights from Cotonou, the Biafrans regarded the control commission, so constituted, as providing the Nigerian government with a veto. This was compounded by another change: instead of a standard list of relief materials being agreed upon in advance, the commission would decide for each flight what could be carried as cargo.

• Instead of the time for relief flights being 9:00 A.M. to 6:00 P.M. each day, it was now to be 9:00 A.M. to 5:00 P.M. This not only shortened the time in which flights would be made but, the Biafrans felt, left Uli unobstructed for one hour before nightfall, so that it could be bombed and damaged just before the night flights would be coming in.

• Instead of the relief flight route passing "abeam of Lagos," as originally proposed, it would now pass directly over Lagos and Benin, both of which had airports from which Nigerian military or other aircraft could take off. The Biafrans charged that this made it easy "for Nigeria to misuse the route."

• The ICRC had not obtained the "third party guarantee" the Biafrans insisted upon as necessary if they were to open up Uli during the day. Instead the Nigerians had gotten the ICRC to add: "This agreement shall be without prejudice to military operations by the Federal Government."

• While the clause "Any aircraft flying into and out of Uli may be ordered to land for supplementary control in Lagos by the FMG at any requested time" was retained, the version presented to Obi did not include the one addition the Biafrans had requested, that Biafra reserved the right to order such aircraft to return to base.

The ICRC officials did not really think the differences very great. The Biafrans did. They found particularly ominous the phrase "This agreement shall be without prejudice to military operations by the Federal Government." Its vagueness held a portent of the worst imaginable.

The Red Cross had only six planes at Cotonou. Besides the shorter hours and greater distance, the planes could be tied up endlessly by being recalled at any time for inspection at Lagos. To make the proposal acceptable to the Nigerians, the ICRC had agreed to a trial period of only three weeks. So the Biafrans were being asked to accept a plan they felt would jeopardize the security of Uli for a relief operation that would get in little food.

Further, it would jeopardize the food already getting into Biafra. Joint Church Aid, with fourteen aircraft at São Tomé, was rapidly building up to a level of relief the ICRC and JCA together had been able to attain earlier in the year, and the Biafrans knew they could count on the church relief agency officials to continue trying to fly no matter how they were threatened by the Nigerians or pressured by governments. They had no such confidence in or trust of ICRC officials. Also some donor governments were beginning to say, in an echo of the British Foreign Office, the war has gone on too long, the airlift is costing too much, relief cannot be supported for long at this level (a level infinitesimal compared to later operations in the Bangladesh, Sahel, Kampuchean, and Ethiopian and Africa famine emergencies).

Joint Church Aid officials were themselves feeling considerable pressure from governments for daylight flights. If the Red Cross started flying in daylight, there was every reason to expect that the JCA airlift would have its food and funds cut off by governments unless it put itself under the ICRC. The Biafrans had everything to lose, nothing to gain, in the ICRC proposal as now reconstituted with the Nigerian conditions.

Though ICRC officials had encountered less criticism at the Istanbul conference than they had expected, they still hoped to produce an agreement before the session concluded. Bignami was instructed to press ahead. Thinking that the differences between the Nigerian and Biafran versions were not so great, the ICRC officials decided to *assumer* the differences—that is, to take upon themselves the differences. They instructed their pilots in Cotonou to continue on standby, ready to take off on relief flights.

Chief Enahoro had begun to see the propaganda benefits following the announcement of the Nigerian conditions, so on September 13, he signed an agreement with Bignami. The next day, Biafra rejected it. Much was made of this. There was scarcely any mention of Biafran acceptance of the original Red Cross proposal or of Nigerian refusal to negotiate for many weeks. No one knew the technical details of the Red Cross proposal or the conditions added by the Nigerian government. Hardly anyone was aware that the agreement the Biafrans rejected was for three weeks only and would have moved only a small amount of food.

Governments were quick to condemn the Biafrans, even those whose citizens were deeply committed to providing humanitarian relief. The Dutch foreign minister commented, " . . . For several months now the flow of foodstuffs and medical supplies has stagnated. Ways have been sought, in particular through the International Red Cross, to resume relief flights. It is most regrettable that the local authorities in the Eastern Region have seen fit to withhold, at the last moment, their consent to an arrangement for the resumption of such flights. . . . " And the Swedish foreign minister said, "In view of the very critical food situation in Biafra I find it hard to understand that the Biafran leaders can reject the agreement, thus preventing the effective relief of the suffering civilian population. . . ."

September 1969—January 1970

Chapter 24

"After the great propaganda triumph the Nigerians have had with the Red Cross negotiations, they're in no mood to agree to anything," Clyde Ferguson remarked to me a few weeks later. We were talking about a proposal that had just been made by a group of prominent Americans with which I had become associated after leaving the United Nations.

Hubert Humphrey, Coretta Scott King, and General William Tunner announced the plan to use helicopters from an aircraft carrier offshore to fly food into Biafra. It overcame all the objections either side ostensibly had to the airlift by cargo planes, using, as it did, helicopters that could fly in daylight but would not need to land at Uli.

As far back as March, when Ferguson had first gone to Biafra, the Biafrans had told him they would accept relief by helicopter from "a ship anchored in mid-ocean." This was at the time Ferguson's deputy, Gene Dewey, was exploring the use of helicopters from a ship but had considered using the "Flying Crane," the helicopter that looks like a giant grasshopper. He concluded that it could not carry a sufficient load a great enough distance, and there was a problem about the kind of ship to fly from.

Tunner learned from executives of the Sikorsky Corporation of a new, much faster cargo helicopter that could transport a load of seven or eight tons. Only six would be needed to carry as much tonnage each day as both airlifts had been averaging during May. That would be with the agreement of the Nigerian government. Without agreement, ten would be required, as they would have to take off from a ship outside Nigerian territorial waters. But they were less vulnerable than relief planes: they could fly at night at treetop level below radar (having, as they did, advanced avionics) and would not have to land at a fixed location. The problem of Uli airstrip would be overcome.

Canadian Prime Minister Trudeau's assistant, Ivan Head, had taken up this proposal with General Gowon on behalf of our private American group in June. At first Gowon threw up his hands and exclaimed, Oh, we have so many relief proposals already. The following day, however, he informed Head that his government would be willing to explore this proposal, as it met two conditions: 1) helicopters could be easily inspected as shipments would not originate on foreign soil, and 2) helicopters could be distinguished as not being the airplanes flying in arms and ammunition.

Head expressed his willingness to our group to carry this exploration forward, but his meeting with Gowon had been a few days before the shooting down of the Red Cross plane, the ascendance of the hawks in Lagos, and Gowon's displacement in humanitarian matters by Chief Enahoro.

Ferguson and Dewey at first asked us to hold up on the helicopter proposal so as not to jeopardize their negotiations on the Cross River corridor. Later, during the summer, they urged us not to do anything that might "jeopardize the Red Cross daylight flight negotiations."

Tunner wrote a number of letters to Henry Kissinger in the White House and conferred at the Pentagon with top officials of the air force. Our group sent letters to Secretary William Rogers and Undersecretary Elliot Richardson, asking that a "hold" be placed on delivery of some of the Sikorsky helicopters that had not yet been delivered to the marines. From his own experience Tunner knew that the military would insist it needed all of the helicopters: no general could admit he did not have to have every last piece of equipment he had requested. Tunner believed some of the helicopters could be diverted to this relief operation if the decision were made at a higher level of government.

We informed Rogers and Richardson that in organizing the committee of prominent American citizens we "sought to provide the United States Government with a non-governmental framework through which it can act more effectively than in the past to provide humanitarian relief. . . ." Given the gravity of the situation in Biafra, we asked their "concurrence in proceeding now as if the helicopter foodlift will be needed and has the support, in principle, of the United States Government. . . .

"Should both the upriver corridor and the airlift begin operating, all that will have been lost by beginning action to organize the helicopter operation on a contingency basis will be some dollars. Should either barges or planes not begin operating what will be lost for each day's delay now in preparing a stand-by alternative will be tens of thousands of lives."

Later that month, August Lindt told me in New York that the Nigerians had adopted a policy of starvation and were prepared to turn down all proposals that would actually get food into Biafra in sufficient quantity. (He did not think the Nigerians had acquired a night fighter capability.) He counseled me on how to proceed with the helicopter plan: "You must first get agreement, in principle, between the Nigerians and the Biafrans, then announce the plan and state that, if there is not agreement within two weeks, it will fly anyway. Then build up public opinion behind it so that the Nigerians will not be able to refuse."

He urged that a group comparable to ours be formed in Europe to organize public support in both places and recommended Prince Bernhard of the Netherlands as the best person to provide leadership in doing so. Weeks later, after the Dutch Foreign Ministry had conferred with the State Department, Bernhard had to turn down our request, saying, "The Government was in fact most emphatic about their advice so that I really have no choice in the matter as I could not do this job without their backing."

At this same time a Biafran representative, Pius Okigbo, informed Elliot Richardson about the acceptability of this proposal: " . . . As you know, large helicopters would make it possible to pick up supplies directly from a ship anchored at sea or from Santa Isabel and deliver them directly to agreed centers in Biafra. You know also that Biafra accepts the principle that the cargo can be inspected at the original point of loading of the helicopters, and Nigeria, if she so desires, can participate in this inspection. There would be no danger of confusing helicopters with other aircraft nor would there be any necessity for the helicopters to use Uli airport."

Okigbo went on: "In view of the enormous need to immediately expand relief operations and the current crisis over relief flights, Biafra asks the United States to do what is required to get large helicopters into immediate service for relief purposes."

After three weeks, Richardson replied to our committee: "I am sure you will agree that the first step is to confirm the logistic feasibility of incorporating the CH-53 in a relief transport system. Assurance of this feasibility is necessary before attempting to divert helicopters from what are likely to be higher priority requirements."

The CH-53 had, in fact, been designed to fly from a helicopter carrier and was doing so even then off the shores of Vietnam. (Later this method would be used to provide relief to earthquake victims in northern Peru.) However, Tunner went through the exercise of proving the logistics feasibility of this cargo helicopter for relief; a team of experts at the Sikorsky plant in Connecticut gave up part of their vacations to prepare a complete operations analysis.

Some weeks later, when Tunner and I took the analysis to Ferguson,

Colonel Dewey informed us that they now agreed the helicopter plan was a workable proposal, but the Defense Department said the helicopters could not be available without diverting them from "high priority military requirements." The letter they had obtained from Defense stated that the Sikorsky helicopters "are scheduled for delivery this summer to the Marines and Air Force for support of Southeast Asia requirements." I told Dewey this was a wonderful reason, and I looked forward to taking a full-page ad in the *New York Times* saying that the U.S. government refused to make helicopters available to fly food to the children of Biafra because they were needed to fight the war in Vietnam. He looked startled.

Ferguson was delayed an hour-and-a-half, tied up with the Africa bureau. One of his assistants remarked that they spoke of their relations with the bureau staff as "the civil war." When he finally arrived, exhausted, and asked us what we wanted him to do, we told him we wanted what we had wanted for the past six weeks: for the U.S. government to quietly help put together the helicopter plan, because it was now clear from the course of the daylight flight negotiations that it would be needed.

Ferguson said, "Look, the Department of State knows that the Nigerians aren't going to agree to any proposal, so I don't feel like taking on one more battle with them about this."

Getting the helicopters would not be easy but, then, where would we get an aircraft carrier? I telephoned Ivan Head and said we would like to borrow one from the Canadian government. He said he would have to get back to me on that. A couple of days later he responded, "Listen, let me give you some advice. When you want to borrow an aircraft carrier from a government, don't ask them first, because that gives them time to think up reasons why they can't let you have it. Come right out and ask for it publicly."

Red Cross daylight flight negotiations had run their course, and the ICRC announced it would "examine with donors" what to do with relief stocks at Santa Isabel and Cotonou. So when Hubert Humphrey, Mrs. King, and General Tunner announced the helicopter plan, governments could no longer claim that negotiations were in progress. Their statement called upon others, in other countries, to join in forming an International Committee of Conscience: "We ask each of you, as citizens of your nation, to call upon your own government to help, insisting that millions more not be allowed to starve." It would prove important later that the *Times* of London reported the story across five columns at the top of page one.

The Biafran government urged that our committee "take immediate steps to implement" the plan. The only Nigerian response was a vituperative broadcast by Lagos radio saying "Humphrey should have known better" than to think that the Nigerian government would permit a foreign warship off her shores.

When we met again, Clyde Ferguson told me that, because of the people who had announced the proposal, there was new political respect for it within the administration. "Previously," he said, "when I tried to bring it up, Richardson all but threw me out of his office."

The Defense Department had now done complete studies of the proposal, he said, and had come up with five ways it could be made to work. One plan envisaged using three helicopter carriers that were being taken out of service, running them in relay out of Norfolk—one on station with the helicopters off the Nigerian coast, another returning to the U.S. for resupply, the third headed back across the Atlantic from Norfolk with new food and fuel.

The United States would be prepared to sell the carriers to such an international relief operation for only slightly more than a million dollars for all three. There was one problem, Ferguson said: the government would take absolutely no initiative on behalf of this plan. It was up to our committee to work it out and negotiate agreement.

The Biafrans again announced acceptance of the plan in principle. We counted on Ivan Head's returning to Lagos to negotiate with the Nigerians on our behalf, but the Canadian cabinet took the decision not to allow him to do so, giving as the reason they did not wish to use up Canada's credit with Nigeria attempting to negotiate something the Biafrans might later turn down.

A few days later, responding to a question from former prime minister John Diefenbaker "regarding the hideous increase in inhumanity in Biafra and the potential starvation that faces tens of thousands of children," Trudeau commented, " . . . The right honorable gentleman should know that the difficulty with the relief flights is based on the fact that the Biafran authorities do not permit daylight flights, that they are using the night flights of relief supplies in order to screen shipments of arms. The Biafran authorities apparently have followed a course directed at making sure that they receive arms rather than food or other medical supplies for the starving people through the air space controlled by them."

Trudeau went on: "In these circumstances we can only continue to make our appeals, such as those made by the Red Cross and which I believe the opposition should also make, to Colonel Ojukwu to be a little more humane and to think of the starving people to whom the right honorable gentleman properly made reference." Only members of the cabinet knew that the prime minister had just declined to allow his assistant to negotiate with the Nigerian government the proposal already accepted by the Biafrans.

"Daylight flights" had proved so useful in managing the situation that the British wanted to keep the negotiations going. The British high commissioner in Lagos urged the ICRC to continue trying to negotiate. So an ICRC mission flew into Biafra, a month after announcement of the Nigerian agreement on daylight flights, which the Biafrans had rejected, and weeks after the Red Cross indicated it was disposing of relief supplies at its two airbases.

An end to ICRC negotiations would leave the British government without the cover-up that had worked so well. And now there was an alternative to daylight flights: "Last week a plan was put forward by Mr. Hubert Humphrey, Mrs. Martin Luther King and General William Tunner (the director of the 1948 Berlin airlift) to send food into Biafra by helicopter from a neutral aircraft carrier offshore," *The Economist* commented. "It would be a further tragedy in a long line of tragedies if this proposal—which neither side can have good reason for rejecting—failed through lack of foreign support or for reasons of American party politics."

Even *West Africa* pointed out the attractiveness of the alternative, its editor commenting: "Far more important, I think . . . is the proposal, now associated with former Vice-President Humphrey, to use helicopters based on aircraft carriers to take relief into Biafra. There is no doubt that helicopters could operate far more effectively than ordinary aircraft, particularly as they need not land at Uli but can deliver their loads directly to distribution points. This would put an end to the Biafran allegation that daytime relief flights would be used by the Federal Government as a cover for military operations against Uli airstrip. The Federal Government has already agreed to neutral inspection of relief aircraft in Dahomey and would, presumably, agree to such an inspection on the neutral territory afforded by an aircraft carrier. . . ."

So restarting Red Cross negotiations was important to the British government, as this exchange in the House of Commons makes clear:

Question: "Almost all the talks involving both sides are phony in the sense that the object is to maneuver the other party into an intransigent position. Since the humanitarian need is so great, could not the Government seek to break the deadlock by putting forward some such proposal as that put forward by Mr. Hubert Humphrey . . . ?"

The reply for the government by Undersecretary Maurice Foley: "I hope that the deadlock might be broken in the next few days. I understand that a high level mission of the ICRC will be flying in to talk to Colonel Ojukwu and to argue agreement on daylight flights . . . "

The ICRC mission was carried out in conjunction with an effort by Clyde Ferguson to meet the Biafran demand for a "guarantee" of Uli if they agreed to daylight flights into that airfield. Biafran insistence on a "guarantee" of their principal airport was genuine enough, but it is difficult to see how it could have been provided, short of a major power such as the United States stationing troops at Uli to repel a Nigerian attack. Providing a guarantee, according to Ferguson, was "the one thing we could not do" under terms of the policy "imposed from the Seventh Floor [Secretary Rogers]."

Ferguson traveled to Libreville in Gabon to meet a Biafran representative, bringing with him the statement: "The Federal Military Government has assured the United States Government, as well as the international community, that during the specified daylight hours of ICRC relief operations, no hostile military action will be taken against the ICRC relief aircraft. The United States government understands and accepts that this undertaking by the Federal Military Government as to the inviolability of the ICRC daylight relief flights has been made in good faith. . . . "

Assurance from the Nigerians that they would not attack Red Cross planes "during the specified daylight hours" was not the guarantee the Biafrans were seeking. Their fear was not that the Nigerians would again interfere with the ICRC airlift but that they would try to capture Uli airstrip or put it out of action for a crucial time once its defenses were removed during the day.

"No country or international organization of a political nature has been willing to give any effective guarantee against Nigeria's possible abuse of daylight flights for military ends," Ojukwu commented. "All they want us to accept, as a guarantee, is Nigeria's good faith and possible world reaction to any breach by Nigeria. We are in the best position to know what that means and cannot be deceived. World probable reaction to a breach by Nigeria? My answer is that Biafra saw what that meant when Nigeria committed its crime of the fifth of June [the shooting down of the Red Cross plane]."

The commander of the Nigerian Air Force had told reporters, a short time before, that his planes had increased the number of attacks on Biafra from twenty-eight to fifty each day. In addition, there were now two "Intruders" harassing Uli airfield at night, and Nigeria claimed that as a result of "attrition missions" the Biafrans were finding it increasingly difficult to repair damaged runways.

Within the U.S. government the "assurance" was given the operation name "Nettle I." There was to be a "Nettle II" but, as it happened, it came up for approval just when Secretary of State Rogers came back from Capitol Hill one day where he had been given a bad time by a Senate subcommittee looking into commitments and guarantees the United States had already made around the world. Rogers was angered at the proposal to give any new "assurances" to the Biafrans and "chewed out" Ferguson and the new assistant secretary for African affairs, David Newsom, for suggesting it.

The Biafrans again announced their acceptance of the Cross River route. By now it was the dry season. There was probably not enough water in the Cross River for the barges to navigate it, turn around and return. This was largely academic, as the proposal had already run aground on the issue of inspection. The Nigerians took the position that the Cross River lagoon was part of their territorial waters and they had the right to inspect every cargo. The Biafrans insisted that these were *their* territorial waters and suggested the place of inspection could be internationalized or the United States should be guarantor of the river route.

The State Department had the secretary put out a statement: "Even if the plan could be promptly implemented the capacity of the river route will be greatly reduced by a low water level for several more months. . . . Nevertheless, our Relief Coordinator is continuing his efforts to bring about agreement on the Cross River proposal. Daylight flights under agreed procedures therefore remain the only practicable scheme for an immediate and substantial expansion of relief operation. We believe that the ICRC proposal is such a realistic and reasonable scheme. We consider that the Federal Government, in agreeing to the ICRC proposal, has acted constructively and in accordance with its humanitarian responsibilities. We also believe that the proposed arrangements for daylight flights meet in a reasonable manner the legitimate security concerns of the Biafran authorities. . . . "

No mention of helicopters.

There was no longer even the pretense of negotiations. With the mission to Biafra over, the ICRC began disbanding its airfleet, retaining only three planes at Cotonou. But the British wanted the war ended, and they had the backing of governments in Europe and North America. They went on talking, talking about daylight flights as though something might happen.

By this time the Biafrans had lost out to British and Nigerian propaganda. Even some of Ferguson's staff and some Red Cross officials became convinced that the Biafrans did not want relief coming in by day because they needed flights at night to provide cover for arms shipments into Uli. These were staff new on the job who had not watched the Nigerian negotiating proposal evolve over the previous year. If even they were misled, how could the public discern what was behind the incessant call for daylight flights, especially since crucial pieces of the puzzle were concealed? Night flights as a cover, however, would not stand up to close scrutiny.

The Nigerians did not have the capability of shooting down planes at night. Prior to the start of the airlifts, there were few relief planes, and for some weeks following the shooting down of the Red Cross plane, there were few relief flights. During these periods when there was no "cover," the Nigerians were not able to prevent arms flights from landing at Uli.

They had continued to attempt to shoot down all planes, even after the two airlifts began, using fake radio beacons to lure planes off course into antiaircraft fire, and "the Intruder's" bombs were intended for relief planes quite as much as for those unloading arms and ammunition.

It could not be contended, from June 5 on, that the Nigerians were concerned they might mistake a relief plane for an arms flight in the night: they had already deliberately shot down a Red Cross plane in daylight.

From the time Chief Enahoro had ended the ICRC role, the transition had dragged on through July, August, September; the Nigerian government insisting that its National Rehabilitation Commission be in charge, the Red Cross and donor governments resisting the FMG's takeover of food, funds, and equipment, as well as responsibility for relief.

Finally Lagos gave in to the pressure and permitted the transition from the ICRC to the Nigerian Red Cross, stating that the National Rehabilitation Commission "will not interfere in any way with the recruitment of the personnel, and the management of the funds or materials of the Nigerian Red Cross."

The long uncertainty left the relief operation in bad shape. The president of the Nigerian Red Cross made an appeal: " . . . The Nigerian Red Cross needs more money, more materials and more of the human resources which it lacks very badly. We need food. We need clothes. We need money." It did not get them. Donor governments still were not satisfied with the arrangement.

The number of people being fed on the Federal side had to be reduced drastically—five hundred thousand dropped immediately and others later cut off without food supplements, " . . . owing to increased selectivity in feeding made necessary by financial and logistical limitations coupled with the need to conserve stocks," according to the Nigerian Red Cross president.

At the beginning of October, the ICRC had turned over more than 103 trucks and other vehicles, in addition to vans, jeeps, and motorcycles. Nonetheless, there was a serious shortage of transport. The two landing barges chartered by Clyde Ferguson in hopes of getting the Cross River route started—the *Doña María* and the *Doña Mercedes*—were pressed into service instead moving food along the coast. The shortage of funds became so grave that Nigerian relief personnel had to donate 5 percent of their salaries for three months.

The FMG did not make up the shortfall resulting from this drying up of contributions from outside the country. A. U.S. government report stated: ".... The Nigerian Government's financial support for the relief effort has been somewhat sporadic and piecemeal."

The editor of *West Africa*, customarily friendly to Lagos, wrote: "... Although everyone must hope for a good response to the NRC's international appeal for help, it seems the most urgently needed action must come from within Nigeria, where despite the war, there is plenty of money around. I cannot understand why, when such a high proportion of food distribution does not call for foreign currency, immediately at any rate, the Federal Government and its agencies, including the army, firms and individuals, cannot see to it that the food which is available goes to those who so desperately need it. . . . "

While the Nigerian Red Cross was forced to cut back on those it could feed, the numbers in need grew as people inside the enclave made their way across the lines seeking food in the Federal areas. Finally, after more than two months of worsening malnutrition in Nigeria, the FMG "decided that the Nigerian Red Cross Society [would] be exempted from the provisions of the National Commission for Rehabilitation. . . . " At last the impasse was ended, and national Red Cross societies of other countries began providing support. But this breakdown of relief on the Nigerian side and the government's apparent indifference to it did not bode well for what would happen should Biafra collapse and the FMG take over relief for the gravely weakened people who would then come under its control.

Richard Baxter of Harvard Law School, a leading authority on the Geneva Conventions, advised our committee that the Nigerian government had an obligation, as a signatory to the Conventions, to allow impartial humanitarian relief to reach the sick and wounded, women and children and the aged who would die without it, under provisions of Article 3 that "persons taking no active part in the hostilities shall in all circumstances be treated humanely." Baxter commented: "It's the thin edge of the wedge."

So the committee, aware that the Nigerians were not going to agree to anything, took the position there was no need to seek further agreement between the two belligerents given "the obligations resting on the Nigerian government as a contracting party to the Geneva Conventions." Baxter's interpretation of the Geneva Conventions was the position governments could have been taking all along.

Releasing a statement setting forth this position, our committee commented: "It must be the concern of the entire civilized world that the Geneva Conventions not be diminished by their non-observance. We believe that the other 125 nations that have signed the Conventions should uphold them. We urge them to call upon the Nigerian Government to give full effect to the Geneva Conventions."

Governments following the lead of the British chose to ignore the helicopter proposal, however, hoping no doubt it would go away, which it was not destined to do.

At this time church relief officials began feeling what Viggo Mollerup characterized as "structured pressure." For some time Reverend Edward Johnson of Canairelief had been observing a progressive buildup in the propaganda line organized against JCA: the church relief agencies are prolonging the war; by paying landing fees at Uli airfield they are supporting the Biafran war effort; church relief food is going to Biafran troops; the church relief flights carry arms; JCA relief planes provide cover for arms flights.

Even before the Nigerians shot down the Red Cross plane, church relief agency officials had begun feeling pressure from their governments to get Ojukwu to agree to daylight flights, suggesting that as long as they continued flying at night, they were keeping the Biafrans from agreeing to the Red Cross proposal for daylight flights. The pressure grew in intensity until executives of JCA decided they had to try to negotiate agreement for daylight flights.

American agencies were especially vulnerable; U.S. food, channeled through Catholic Relief Service and Church World Service, also provided funds as reimbursement for freight to fly the food into Biafra. This gave the State Department leverage upon them and upon Joint Church Aid in turn. Some American church officials felt they must try to seek agreement on daylight flights, however unlikely it was that they could succeed where the ICRC had failed. It was a necessary exercise so they would be able to go back to the State Department and say that they had tried.

Joint Church Aid officials invited Biafran and Nigerian representatives to a hotel in Lausanne, just down the lake from Geneva, an easy commute but out of sight of the large press corps at the Palais des Nations. The Nigerians had always taken the position with the church relief agencies that the agencies had to agree first that Lagos could authorize flights, then the Nigerians would tell them how many they could fly. JCA officials in turn said they would agree to daylight flights only if they did not diminish the volume of the airlift. Among other questions, they wanted to know if the air corridor would be open in altitude or limited so as to constrict the number of flights and reduce the tonnage flown in.

At Lausanne, JCA put forward its own guidelines for daylight relief. Flights could operate from the airbases at Cotonou, Santa Isabel, and São Tomé from six in the morning until six in the evening (so Uli would not be left open at the beginning and end of the day). Security of relief planes in the air corridors would be internationally guaranteed, with neither Nigerian nor Biafran aircraft allowed in them during relief flight hours. Inspection of cargoes would be with international guarantees. Both inspection and security would be assured by representatives of countries designated by the Nigerians, the Biafrans, and the church relief agencies.

Nothing came of this. The JCA officials went back and forth between the Biafran representatives in one room and the Nigerian representatives in another. Ambassador Sule Kolo insisted on the conditions for daylight flights added by the Nigerians in September, which had proved unacceptable to the Biafrans then.

This necessary, fruitless exercise out of the way, church relief officials got back to the business of building up the airlift. They were getting in more protein, but the problem now was a shortage of carbohydrates; the carbohydrate starvation foreseen a year before had taken longer in coming than anticipated. This meant not just kwashiorkor among the children and the elderly but marasmus—plain starvation—threatening everyone.

Chapter 25

General Gowon asked Jacques Beaumont to get the World Council of Churches to halt the Joint Church Aid airlift on the grounds that it was prolonging the war. Beaumont had been active in France since the previous autumn, when the Nigerian government had approached him to set up a group to counter de Gaulle's support for Biafra.

A Protestant minister, Beaumont had political experience with a French non-Communist left group working for liberation of peoples in developing countries, such as the Kurds, and with movements such as SWAPO. He also had a long relationship with the World Council of Churches. Shortly after de Gaulle began supplying arms to Biafra, Beaumont met with Gowon in Lagos for four hours, at a time when the French ambassador could not even get to see the general. The Nigerians provided funds with which Beaumont returned to Paris and set up the Association France-Nigéria.

Foreign Office professionals at the Quai d'Orsay welcomed this, as did French businessmen who feared that de Gaulle's support for Biafra would jeopardize long-term relations with Nigeria. They supported the pro-Nigerian group as a counter to the pro-Biafran committee established by de Gaulle's former ambassador to Lagos, Raymond Offroy.

Beaumont and his group had done what they could over the next year to counteract the overwhelming sympathy and support for Biafra in France. The Nigerians were annoyed about the role of the church relief agencies in Biafra, seeing it as church intervention in the conflict. Beaumont continued to work with the World Council of Churches and on a regular basis fed information representing the Nigerian point of view to officials of its Commission for International Affairs.

Those within the WCC bureaucracy concerned with development and international affairs, like their counterparts in the Vatican, were worried about the effects the airlift and other church relief activities might have on their acceptability in Nigeria after the war. Inevitably a split developed between them and the churchmen primarily involved with humanitarian relief.

Though, at its meeting in July 1968, the WCC had encouraged the mounting of "a continuous and effective airlift," its bureaucrats never approved of flights made without Nigerian permission once they began in earnest. Purchase of aircraft with funds from the West German government, however, had freed the church organizations from WCC influence. Eventually this had evolved into Joint Church Aid, combining the efforts of thirty-three church relief agencies. It had no headquarters: its flight operations were based on São Tomé, its secretariat in Copenhagen, its logistics administration in Stuttgart, its press office in Geneva. Its executives met in Frankfurt, Rome, Lucerne, New York, Amsterdam, Paris, Oslo.

JCA existed as planes flying into Biafra at night. The Nigerians would have liked to find a way to get control over Joint Church Aid, but it was as difficult to locate and hit as one of its planes in the dark. For over a year, the churchmen who ran the international relief agencies had been resisting pressures from governments. The shooting down of the Red Cross plane, the warnings about MiGs with a night fighter capability, threats that the Nigerians had the "will" to use them against relief planes, the ousting of the Red Cross—all were palpable events for the ministers, priests, and other executives running JCA. They were not intimidated, but proceeded with new caution.

They adopted regulations restricting the kinds of cargoes and personnel carried on JCA planes; if one should be forced to land, the Nigerians would not be able to say there was anything but relief supplies and personnel on board. It was no longer easy for journalists or others to fly in and out of Biafra, though the passenger committee set up to oversee the new regulations allowed a few *bona fide* reporters passage on church flights.*

Even though JCA executives and the pilots flying for them gradually felt reassured that the Nigerians did not have a night fighter capability, there was greater air activity: a noticeable step-up of strafing along the highways, interfering with trucks distributing relief, as well as intensified attacks upon civilian centers. There was also "a big new operation against

---

*One who did manage to fly in during this period of restricted access was Renata Adler who commented, in a "Letter from Biafra" (*The New Yorker*, October 4, 1969), "Editorial writers for the Western press, unlike reporters on the spot, often treat the Biafran position as morally ambiguous, as though the years from 1939 to 1945 had never existed, and as though killing and dying existed on a single plane of atrocity. It is possible that another ethnic population will be decimated before modern intelligence completes its debate about the extent to which the greatest crimes can be said to be the fault of the victims of them."

Uli airstrip." Those under the bombings believed that "The Intruder" must now be two aircraft, harassing planes coming into the Biafran airfield more than ever.

One night three bombs set on fire a Nordchurchaid plane, carrying five tons of baby food and six tons of stockfish, just as it reached the parking platform. The Norwegian pilot and copilot escaped through the front door, but flames forced back the British flight engineer and two relief workers—Irish and Italian priests. They suffered burns before they could make their escape through the rear door. The DC-6 was destroyed. Four other planes in that night's first shuttle had to return to São Tomé without landing to unload their food.

Months earlier, two other JCA planes had been destroyed on the ground at Uli by MiGs in daylight, after having been damaged while landing the night before. "The Intruder" eventually destroyed two more planes as they were unloading, bringing to nine the number of Joint Church Aid aircraft lost, with twelve crew members killed in crashes while approaching Uli at night without lights. More than 40 percent of the 245 flights that had to be aborted during the May–January period were unable to land because of a bomber in the area, bombing under way, or as a result of the airport's being unusable due to bomb damage.

In an attack on Benin airport in the Mid-West Region of Nigeria, the miniplanes of the Biafran Air Force destroyed a MiG fighter as well as one of the aircraft believed used by "The Intruder." As they swept in low over the field during the raid, one of the Biafran pilots recognized a familiar figure running on the airstrip amid a group of men, who were then hit by a rocket—the tall figure of the commander of the Nigerian Air Force. A few days later the Nigerian government announced that the air force commander had been killed while piloting a private aircraft that ran out of fuel in bad weather and crashed trying to land on a football field.

The small Biafran planes were now concentrating on the oil installations in the midwest. The raids threatened to halt production; should this happen, it would be a blow to Nigeria's economy. In Britain, pro-Biafran activists distributed bumper stickers reading "PUT A DEAD BIAFRAN IN YOUR TANK—By filling it with Shell or BP."

Though State Department officials continued resisting any measures that would anger the Nigerians, Clyde Ferguson and his staff were working in every quiet way they could to build up the airlift. Two of the planes lost had been C-97s, so at last the United States allowed Joint Church Aid to purchase the two C-97s it had been requesting since the previous March. Now, though, rather than augmenting the capacity of the airlift, they only replaced the planes that had been lost. Ferguson also provided JCA with twenty-five spare engines, which eased maintenance problems.

While in Gabon, Ferguson had set about to assist the airlifts flying out of Libreville, those operated by the French Red Cross and the Irish group, "Africa Concern." Governments always regarded the Libreville airlifts as tainted, flying as they did from the same airfield as the arms flights (though, of course, all planes, from whatever point of origin, landed at the same field in Biafra). As a result, they had not obtained enough support to carry in more than limited quantities of relief. By now, however, the ICRC was using the French Red Cross airlift clandestinely to supply its medical personnel, and Ferguson was equally prepared to use any channel to increase the tonnage of food and medicine.

Ferguson's activities to strengthen the airlift helped Joint Church Aid build up until it was flying in as much as JCA and ICRC together had been averaging in the months before the Nigerians shot down the Red Cross plane. During September, JCA planes managed to land 404 times, carrying in 5,139 metric tons. But during October, bombing of the airfield reduced the landings to 363, so that only 4,510 tons arrived. The number of flights rose in November to 423 and in December to 543, so that JCA got in 5,399 tons during November and 7,119 tons in the last month of 1969.

The estimate of monthly need, however, had risen to 18,000 tons. By this time the Catholic and Protestant relief networks had taken over some of the Red Cross centers and were trying to care for 1,222,000 refugees housed in 1,491 camps, another 300,000 refugees not in camps but getting regular food supplies, 427,000 others receiving food through 1,139 feeding centers, 7,300 patients in 97 sick bays, plus another 9,000 patients in 23 hospitals that the church agencies were helping support. It was a massive effort, but the overall condition of the people in Biafra was going down in spite of it.

Those in charge of the Protestant relief operation reported "significant deterioration." They could not give accurate statistics about the number of deaths but cited as an example: "In one hospital which is superbly staffed and in which very accurate records are maintained the death rate among new pediatric admissions had doubled in three months; from sixteen to thirty-three per cent. In a single refugee camp located in another area and populated by recently displaced persons, the total deaths increased from thirty-five in June to one-hundred-forty in August. . . . "

Though the airlift was inadequate to meet the rapidly growing need, its buildup nonetheless threatened to undercut the British-Nigerian strategy. In the *Manchester Guardian*, correspondent Walter Schwarz, an authority on the Nigerian situation, wrote about the airlift: "British officials have made no secret of the fact that this effort, too, is displeasing to Britain. Churchmen have been told at a high level that their effort 'only serves to prolong the war and therefore the suffering of the Biafrans.' "

Hugh Fraser questioned the foreign secretary about this in Commons, commenting, "Surely the right honorable Gentleman knows that he is assisting what has become genocide by starvation . . . " and saying to Michael Stewart: "He surely ought to do something about it now. Will he confirm or deny the truth of the article in the *Guardian* last week which said that he is trying to put pressure on the churches to stop it?" To which Stewart responded: "Of course that article was not true. It is surprising that it should even have been published."

Through much of the war, governments had tended to discount reports from the relief agencies as unreliable and claimed they needed an official survey to provide them with hard, factual information. Now at last they got one. Clyde Ferguson organized nine studies covering all aspects of the relief problem. One was a medical survey carried out in Biafra by a team of three American doctors headed by Dr. Karl Western of the Communicable Disease Center in Atlanta (since renamed the Center for Disease Control).

Western and his colleagues went in "to assess the nutritional status of the civilian population in as many representative areas as possible." They came away with an impression of "slow, creeping starvation of almost the entire population. . . . " Edema (the swelling of the joints and belly that is one of the signs of advanced protein starvation) was found in almost a third of the population (31.4 percent). But the effects of the prolonged famine were far graver on both the very young and the elderly, with edema in 42.2 percent of the children under four and in 52.1 percent of those over forty-five years of age. The Western survey (as it came to be called) found that "no segment of the population has been spared significant edema rates. School-age children and young adults had edema rates of 28.2% and 17.0% respectively."

These findings showed that the effects of the blockade and famine in Biafra were worse than any ever before medically recorded—three times greater than those during the siege of Leningrad or the "hunger winter" in the western Netherlands toward the end of World War II. The U.S. government did not, however, at this time make these findings known to the public. It also did not convey them to Nigerian officials to make them aware of the gravity of the situation; this would become a source of controversy later.

Western's team, by noting the percentage of scars from earlier smallpox vaccinations, estimated the civilian population inside the Biafran enclave at 3,240,000. While Western warned that the technique used in arriving at this estimate "makes several assumptions which people familiar with the situation know are not entirely valid," some State Department officials derived satisfaction from this quantification suggesting there were far fewer people in the besieged area than heretofore thought. If accurate, even as an approximation, it meant either that greater numbers had already died from starvation or that many were now outside the blockade, under Federal control. Even the latter possibility was not reassuring, given the breakdown of relief distribution taking place in Nigerian areas.

When Ferguson and his assistants completed the nine-part report in early December 1969, they concluded that the collapse of Biafra would occur within thirty to ninety days. (The logistics section showed that the trucks were being held together with pieces of wire.) This estimate was conveyed to Maurice Foley and Donald Tebbit in the British government, and a copy of the report went to Henry Kissinger in the White House.

Ferguson called a meeting of senior officials of American nongovernmental relief agencies. He needed to learn from them what they were prepared to do when Biafra collapsed. He and his staff had begun contingency planning within the U.S. government, including helicopters to replace the trucks, but distribution would depend on the agencies with their feeding stations already in place.

Ferguson could not get the relief officials to accept his own sense of urgency. (One of his staff had seen for the first time, a few weeks before, Biafran soldiers trying to get fed in the relief lines, taking off their uniforms and donning civilian clothes in order to receive food.) They had heard all this before. Periodically the FMG announced the start of the "final offensive," and they had become immunized against reports that Biafra was about to be overrun by Nigerian troops; it had never happened yet. Ferguson felt there was real resistance to his assessment that Biafra was about to collapse.

The pressures on the church relief officials had just reached their peak; they had reason to be suspicious of almost any government estimates or requests. The effort to bring the church airlift to a halt had surfaced. In addition to the long-term contacts of Jacques Beaumont, the Nigerians had sent other emissaries to pressure both the World Council of Churches and the Vatican—churchmen from African countries who were close to their own governments and the ruling group in their countries and willing to do the work of Lagos. (When Beaumont asked Viggo Mollerup to halt Joint Church Aid flights, Mollerup regarded him as a fellow pastor with whom he had long worked through the World Council of Churches and was unaware he was acting on behalf of the Nigerian government.)

At a November meeting of the WCC's division concerned with development assistance and emergency relief, known familiarly as "Dickers," Mollerup and Monseigneur Carlo Bayer of Caritas succeeded in moderating somewhat a resolution aimed at bringing an end to the airlift. So it came as no surprise to JCA executives when in early December "Dickers" asked publicly whether the churches and their relief agencies "should prolong the massive airlift in its present form." The statement expressed "deep distress at the ambiguous position in which the tremendous effort has put Christian people, churches and agencies because of its political side-effects." The WCC division suggested that these side effects exposed the churches "to the charge of prolonging the war and adding to the suffering of the people."

That same day, in the British Parliament, Prime Minister Wilson commented in a philosophical rumination on "this dilemma—this choice between ends and evils" that "has arisen for the World Council of Churches." He saw as "the agony of choosing between ends" the fact that the WCC "could even consider suggesting cutting off the food program to Biafra as a means of shortening the war. . . ."

Wilson went on that ". . . once again, the parties to the fighting, and their peoples, and we here in Britain face a situation where every decision of policy is a choice of evils, where what is right—indeed, what to some honorable Members seems to be an overriding bounden duty—means a denial of what to other honorable Members will seem a categorical imperative which cannot be laid aside. That is the essence of the problem."

Returning to the WCC's dilemma, Wilson said: " . . . When press reports and the television screens bring to our own homes the tragic picture of hunger and malnutrition, of children dying, no one, whether in the World Council of Churches or anywhere else, would choose this moment to relax in their efforts. And yet even they have set this undeniable, compelling suffering in a context in which they have to ask whether there is not a danger of still greater suffering, through a prolongation of the war, and therefore, of the starvation itself. . . .

"History may well say," Wilson went on, "that if the Federal Government had hardened their heart against our pressure and the pressure of other governments and of civilized organizations the whole world over, this war might have ended a good deal earlier, perhaps with far less suffering, fewer casualties, and fewer deaths from starvation. I do not know, but the fact that this can be argued shows the nature of the dilemma that Nigeria, and we, and this House, have to face, and are facing, the dilemma now made newly articulate by the World Council of Churches."

It was, of course, an elevated presentation of "the quick kill theory," about which there had been an uproar a year before, and it was the culmination of a policy the British and Nigerians had set in motion six months earlier. The *Guardian* commented on Wilson's reflections on the dilemma facing the World Council of Churches: ". . . If Mr. Wilson were to tell the whole truth could he be sure that the question asked by the World Council was not prompted by the British Government itself? Has it not put to church leaders precisely the point raised at Geneva last week—that their relief airlift was prolonging the war? It is somewhat disingenuous then to quote the question as passed on by the World Council. . . ."

The argument that the church airlift was prolonging the war had validity only if the Nigerians intended to bring the war to an end by starving the Biafrans into submission, something the British and other governments continued to deny.

There was widespread alarm among those still concerned about Biafran relief who were not aware that the World Council of Churches did not control Joint Church Aid. JCA executives received many expressions of concern and encouragement that they should not discontinue the airlift. They responded to the WCC declaration: "To stop the airlift now would not only have political consequences, but also result in the death of millions of innocent civilians. It would establish starvation not only as a legitimate weapon of war but also as a partisan tool in the hands of groups pursuing their own motives."

JCA called upon governments to bring both sides to the negotiating table: "We will support them in all attempts they might take to achieve this difficult but most vital goal, provided they, in their attempts, will not tamper with the integrity of serious relief operations, as we reject everything that will mix relief work with politics."

The churchmen running Joint Church Aid expressed their concern that they must "follow the divine law which commands that above all we serve our neighbor in need," and concluded, "We have no alternative but to continue the relief work for as long as it is an effective means of alleviating the present suffering."

Chapter 26

The day after Prime Minister Wilson spoke to Parliament about the dilemma facing the World Council of Churches, the Conservative party divorced itself from responsibility for starvation in Biafra—out of genuine revulsion, for political advantage, or both. Sir Alec Douglas-Home proposed that Britain take the lead in organizing an international humanitarian relief operation using helicopters from aircraft carriers. He told the Commons: "The advantages will be apparent to the House. Helicopters do not have to land to deliver their supplies. Uli airstrip which is a military target and is of military significance to Biafra would not be involved at all. The supplies could be dropped in other designated areas. Neither side possesses helicopters, so there would be no difficulty about identification . . . neutral observers could supervise the distribution and the Federal inspection could take place as easily on an aircraft carrier as at an airport outside Nigeria."

There was more of an ultimatum to the government behind this than was obvious from Douglas-Home's words. Conservative leaders had teams of foreign affairs and defense experts research the proposal for weeks; they had consulted British admirals and the U.S. Navy. The carefully prepared plan "almost alone will provide the basis on which the Conservative Party is willing to continue to support the policy of supplying British arms to Federal Nigeria . . . ," the political editor of *Times* wrote the next day. "Sir Alec and his colleagues believe that the plan provides the only escape from the moral dilemma of those British politicians who continue to believe that Britain should supply arms to the Nigerian Government but who cannot any longer tolerate the thought that they are being made parties to the starvation of untold numbers of Biafran women and children."

The proposal came at a bad time for Wilson's government. Labour's backbenchers were threatening to defect on the issues of British support for U.S. involvement in Vietnam and the supply of arms to Nigeria.

Earlier, at their party conference at Brighton, they had passed a resolution calling upon the government to halt arms shipments to Nigeria. Wilson responded, on television: "If I thought I had been doing wrong all this time, I would not have been doing it. I understand feelings. I understand the resolution. I have been out to Nigeria. I discussed it with them. I have been to Addis Ababa. I have asked Ojukwu to meet me to settle it. But as I say, if you have been doing something you passionately believe to be right, however unpopular, you don't just change because other people say it's wrong."

Until now, only a few Conservatives had displayed concern about the mass starvation; many more were closely involved with the FMG and British business interests in Nigeria. Sir Alec Douglas-Home, when approached about matters of relief, had always shown less interest in the humanitarian aspects of the conflict than what he viewed as the Soviet threat to West Africa. The defection of such major journals of opinion as the *Times* and *The Economist*, however, suggested that this was a good time for the Conservative party to take a position independent of the government's policy.

The Tories sent Lord Carrington, the Opposition leader in the House of Lords, to Biafra and to Lagos. He explored the helicopter proposal. Ojukwu indicated it was entirely acceptable, saying, "We've accepted a number of times already; no one seems to do anything about it." It was not, however, received with enthusiasm in Nigeria; the Lagos *Daily Sketch* quoted General Gowon: "I am not going to accept any proposal that may likely endanger the security of the state. Dropping food by helicopter to the rebels is Sir Alec's idea, but we have our own ideas."

The British government began a feasibility study of the proposal, seeking reasons, it seemed, why the helicopter plan was not feasible. Washington was asked how much it would cost. Glimmerings of this search for a negative response began appearing within days, from an unattributed source in the government: "Serious doubts were expressed in London yesterday about the possibility of speeding relief supplies to Biafra by using helicopters operating from aircraft carriers," according to the *Sunday Telegraph*. "It was said that several hundred helicopters would be needed and there would be considerable difficulty in arranging carriers to cope with such a fleet."

"The cost of the helicopter airlift proposed last Tuesday by Sir Alec Douglas-Home to take food to Biafra would be utterly prohibitive . . . ," the *Sunday Times* cited experts as saying. "The probable verdict is that the proposal is a non-starter." And *The Observer* commented that "inquiries into the feasibility of Sir Alec Douglas-Home's proposal for an Anglo-American helicopter food-lift into Biafra produce an uncomfortable impression that Whitehall is looking harder at the difficulties than at a way to get over them."

"Nonstarter" seemed to be the vogue word at the Foreign Office. Having no good argument for turning down the helicopter plan, the government had to stall. British officials had Clyde Ferguson's estimate that Biafra would soon collapse. On the evidence of Colonel Robert Scott's report from Lagos, this assessment was not necessarily shared by the High Commissioner's Office. Whatever divided counsel Whitehall may have been receiving, there was need to put off the inevitable negative reply to the Conservative party's ultimatum as long as possible.

There was another "nonstarter" under way at this time. Since the last OAU meeting three months before in Addis Ababa, Haile Selassie had been attempting to get peace negotiations going once again. Earlier attempts at Kampala, Niamey, Addis, Monrovia, and at the Commonwealth Conference and OAU meeting had all failed.

For some months now, however, there had been concentrated efforts to bring about a settlement of the conflict. The U.S. and Canada had been active; the Swiss government had just responded to a Biafran request by consulting with other neutrals—Sweden, Austria, Yugoslavia—to see if they might join in a mediation effort. Sierra Leone warned that if Nigeria did not accept a cease-fire and begin peace talks soon, it and a number of other West African nations would extend recognition to Biafra.

The Nigerians always insisted that negotiations had to be conducted under the auspices of the OAU (which they were able to dominate) and on the basis of "Nigerian unity," i.e., Biafra giving up its claim to independence and accepting reintegration into Nigeria. This was unacceptable to the Biafrans: it meant capitulation in advance. They insisted, instead, on negotiations without preconditions. (At times they sought a cease-fire before peace talks could begin.)

The Federal Military Government had had the principle of "Nigerian unity" enshrined in an OAU resolution. Governments continued to say that negotiations should take place "within an African framework," by which they meant the OAU. It was, by now, a well-established impasse out of which nothing could be expected to come.

Haile Selassie, however, had now invited both belligerents to his capital, and the Biafrans understood it was on his own initiative, not under OAU auspices. There was a moment of renewed hope, long enough for Michael Stewart to say during the Commons debate: "There is a chance now of the two sides meeting face to face in an African framework. I think that the whole House will agree that it is a good thing that the Nigerian government have agreed to send representatives there. I think that the whole House will also agree that it would be right for Colonel Ojukwu to send representatives there. . . . "

He also said, "I hope most earnestly, as I am sure will all honorable Members, that he [Ojukwu] will agree; and the House will be bound to judge that, if he is not willing to do so, then the blame for the continuance of the strife and the impossibility of reaching agreement cannot be laid at the door of the Nigerian government, and certainly not at the door of Her Majesty's Government."

The Biafran delegation arrived in Addis, but no Nigerian delegation showed up. In Lagos, Chief Enahoro and Okoi Arikpo stated that their nation would enter into talks only on the basis of Nigerian unity. "Why did we go to war?" Arikpo asked rhetorically. "It was to maintain territorial integrity and national unity." The Nigerians insisted that Selassie had to be "acting in his capacity as Chairman of the O.A.U. Consultative Committee on Nigeria." Still no Nigerian representatives arrived in Addis. The Biafran delegation left.

For some weeks a Nigerian offensive had been under way on the northern and southern fronts of Biafra. This time Lagos did not announce the launching of a "final offensive." There had been reports in the press that the Soviet Union had supplied the Nigerian army with eight new 122-millimeter guns for each of its three divisions. (The reports were correct. The defense adviser to the British high commissioner in Lagos wrote that each division had recently received "a six-gun battery of Soviet 122-mm. gun Howitzers with a range in excess of 13 miles.") The First Division was supposed to move from the north and the Third Marine Commando Division from the south to bring Uli airstrip within shooting distance of these long-range artillery pieces.

In addition, shipment of regular arms and ammunition to the Nigerian army had been stepped up for this offensive. During the debate in Commons on British arms supply, Michael Stewart said, "I was asked yesterday what that supply was. There has been the suggestion that the Government have been trying to camouflage from the House what the supply was. That is untrue. It remains, as I have informed the House, about 15 per cent by value of the total purchases by Nigeria. It comprises, overwhelmingly, ammunition, spares, anti-aircraft equipment, and a small number of armored vehicles. . . . " When, a few weeks later, a critic of government policy discovered that the chief statistician of the Nigerian government had been publishing in the *Nigerian Trade Summary*, throughout the war, the arms imported into Nigeria by country of origin, it was revealed that the British had greatly stepped up their supply of ammunition and other ordnance during October and November.

The Nigerian forces met stiff resistance: the Biafrans also had improved firepower. The report of the British defense adviser set forth one of the tasks of the First Division—"to advance southward on two axes . . . both aimed at securing the high ground overlooking Nnewe as a prelude to securing Uli airstrip"—and among the tasks of the Third Marine Commando Division: "On reaching the southern shore of the Oguta Lake, to occupy a defensive position and harass the Uli airstrip with medium artillery."

In London, the government continued seeking some reasonable excuse for turning down the Tory proposal for organizing an international relief operation. Early reports indicated that the British officials were chiefly considering very small helicopters that could carry only a ton-and-a-half or less, thereby requiring more than a hundred helicopters to move, at considerable cost, less than an adequate amount of food. Our committee in the United States provided Douglas-Home with details of the plan to use Sikorsky helicopters that could carry a seven-ton payload at much faster speeds, so that only twelve or fifteen could fly in the total required tonnage each day. We also informed him that the U.S. government had developed five different plans of operation. Sir Alec handed this information to Foreign Secretary Stewart publicly, in Commons, so there could be no question that it was known to the British government. Still, *The Economist* reported on December 20: "Starvation continues, and there are few signs of further British Government action to bring aid to the victims of the war. That government has not yet completed its feasibility study of Sir Alec Douglas-Home's plan to send in relief by helicopters, nor can it say when it will have done so. . . . "

British newspapers were filled with accounts of a terrible massacre. Eighteen months earlier an American infantry company had wantonly killed a hundred or more civilians in a village of Vietnam that would become known as My Lai. Many times that number of civilians were dying each day in Biafra as a result of a calculated government policy; three or four thousand more would starve that day, three or four thousand more the day after that.

While, for the British government, Christmas holidays provided a distraction, many Britons fasted for Biafra instead of feasting on Christmas, and the Archbishop of Canterbury asked that church bells be rung for an hour throughout the land.

. . .

Christmas for the Biafrans was somber. On Christmas Eve, Nigerian troops made the breakthrough they had long sought. Their troops were able to rush up the highway from Ikot Ekpene to Umuahia, dividing the Biafran enclave and cutting off a major food-producing area east of the Imo River. Its loss, a third of what remained of Biafra, was not one the Biafrans could withstand.

By this time General Ojukwu was so mentally exhausted he could barely think. His Christmas message to his people had a tone of despondency: "For the third year in succession we are spending Christmas in the midst of war, suffering and death. For the third year in succession our homes are going to be without cheer, without the joy, without the laughter and without the merriment of Christmas. For the third year in succession we are spending Christmas in fear of air raids and other forms of enemy action. As I address you, therefore, on this occasion my mind goes particularly to all those who are in terrible suffering, those in hospitals, those in the throes of death, our fighting forces exposed to vicious elements.

"I think of those behind enemy lines, those separated from their families and loved ones, and those who are in great anxiety about the fate of their friends and relatives of whom they have heard nothing," Ojukwu continued. "All these are terrible thoughts, particularly when one remembers the traditional mood with which the people of this part of the Christian world would normally spend their Christmas—the exchange of gifts and visits, dancing and drumming in the streets, children in attractive new dresses going to church, merriment of all sorts, laughter and joy in every home."

The Biafran leader concluded: "Let us think of the future and having experienced grief and suffering ourselves, let us pray for ourselves and for others in other parts of the world who may be facing situations similar to what we are facing in Biafra."

The world, insofar as it was embodied in the United Nations, was not so generous in spirit, for the General Assembly had just adjourned, once again having done nothing about Biafra. When prime ministers or foreign ministers were queried about this in their parliaments, their answers were similar to that of the Swedish foreign minister: ". . . . The requisite support is not forthcoming for this issue to be taken up for consideration by the UN. In particular, discussions have been opposed by the African states, which are of especial importance in this connection. . . . "

The African states were not unaware of the various human rights and humanitarian conventions. They had succeeded in having a number of resolutions passed during this session of the General Assembly deploring abrogations of human rights in the territories of southern Africa and calling upon governments to ensure that the Geneva Conventions be observed in Southern Rhodesia, as it was then called. The application of the conventions was political and selective rather than universal, however; Nigeria was never an object of this concern. Nigerian diplomats continued to insist that the conflict remain an internal affair, to be dealt with only by the OAU, not the UN.

Not all Africans were indifferent to the horror that continued in Nigeria. The president of the General Assembly, Angie Brooks of Liberia, said in her closing address, "I cannot close my heart to innocent victims. It is the women and children who are suffering most. It is our impression that the situation of these children is deteriorating and for many the damage is now irreversible." She made a moving appeal for a cease-fire, if only for a limited time, to allow food and medicine to go to those in need on both sides of the conflict.

U Thant left on a trip to Africa. A number of times, as he traveled from country to country, he spoke out urging Ojukwu to "show enough magnanimity" to conform to the OAU resolution that called upon the two sides to accept the unity of Nigeria. Thant said that the United Nations would never accept secession in one of its member states.

Finally, a month after Sir Alec Douglas-Home had put forward the helicopter proposal, the British government responded. In a letter to the Shadow Cabinet foreign secretary, Michael Stewart turned down the plan, saying it would cost over £1 million a week. "The hard fact is that, over the sort of distance which the helicopters would have to fly from a carrier, the most which one of our Wessex helicopters would be able to lift in one flight is rather less than one ton," Stewart wrote, disregarding the information provided him three weeks before about the larger, faster helicopters.

"I have never contemplated that the helicopter lift would be a purely British operation," Sir Alec replied. "I had it in mind that the Americans, the Swedes and others with helicopters that can carry heavier loads would be asked to cooperate. It would certainly be expensive but that ought not to be a decisive factor."

Stewart in his letter commented that "it would be wrong to give the impression that there is an adequate and readily available substitute for daylight flights."

Reports coming out from relief workers indicated it was only a matter of days before the enclave collapsed. The Third Marine Commando Division, pushing up from the south, unexpectedly encountered little resistance. Biafran soldiers had eaten only a few times a week for weeks, and then only spoonfuls of cassava. Ojukwu encountered troops near Owerri withdrawing from the battlefield "with eyes glazed with hunger." "The inner man was still there," Ojukwu said, "but there was no strength left to fight." They laid down their rifles and faded away.

The southern front gave way. Nigerian troops rushed in. Uli fell. Biafra collapsed. The policy of starvation had succeeded.

January–June 1970

Chapter 27

"**W**e won't get in there for weeks," grim-faced officials at the United Nations Children's Fund said that Monday morning, January 12, 1970. News reports had been coming in since Saturday that Biafra's defenses had given way. For any who thought, "At last those people will be fed," it soon proved a moment of naïveté. Senior officials of international relief agencies who had known since June that "the hawks are in the ascendance in Lagos" had no expectation that the Nigerian government would soon allow relief to begin to the weakened—now conquered—people.

Joint Church Aid executives held an emergency meeting in Stuttgart that weekend. They had no illusions about the Nigerians allowing them to help, but felt they had to try. "According to reports from medical staff," they stated publicly, "the physical resistance of the civil population in the afflicted areas is at such a low ebb that if supplies are cut back even for less than a week a high percentage of the population might not survive." Warning that " . . . unless immediate action is taken to bring massive relief supplies an indescribable toll of lives of innocent victims will result," they flew to São Tomé. They had JCA planes fly back and forth along the coast of Nigeria, radioing Lagos their offer of so many tons of food, so many planes, so many personnel.

That Sunday, during his regular benediction to the crowd in St. Peter's Square, Pope Paul said, "the war seems to be reaching its conclusion, with the terror of possible reprisals and massacres against defenseless people worn out by deprivations, by hunger and by the loss of all they possess. The news this morning is very alarming. . . . One fear torments public opinion. The fear that the victory of arms may carry with it the killing of numberless people. There are those who actually fear a kind of genocide. We wish to exclude such a horrendous hypothesis for the honor of the African people and of their leaders who have themselves excluded it with many explicit assurances."

His statement infuriated Nigerians. Students celebrating victory in the streets carried signs such as "Hottest Part of Hell for the Pope." The Nigerians had by now become quite xenophobic. It did not help matters that the British defense adviser's report appeared in the London *Sunday Telegraph* that weekend with its depreciation of the fighting prowess of the Nigerian troops and its appreciation of the qualities of the Ibos. There is no telling what its impact might have been on Nigerian-British relations had it been published at some time earlier than the moment of triumph; as it was, Colonel Scott was immediately expelled from Nigeria.

The Pope's concern was also the chief worry of a group of men in nearby Yaounde. Gathered there to help Cameroon celebrate its tenth anniversary were U Thant, British Undersecretary Maurice Foley, and American Assistant Secretary of State David Newsom. They moved quickly to make sure that General Gowon sent the international observers team to monitor Nigerian troops, now overrunning Biafran areas. Thant did the same with the United Nations observer. General Gowon ordered Federal troops to shoot "only if they encounter resistance" and to continue to observe the Code of Conduct they had been given. He declared that "all field commanders will take all necessary measures to give full protection to surrendering troops. . . . "

When word reached London that the collapse had begun, Harold Wilson presided over an emergency meeting of government ministers preparing British participation in a large-scale relief operation. Wilson conferred by telephone that Saturday evening with President Nixon and the next morning cabled him a British assessment of the situation.

Relief officials in Lagos had been concerned since November about reports that the FMG might not allow relief teams in the "secessionist area" to remain and continue to work after the war. There had been alarm about the report that in one area food was being withheld from people regarded as "rebels." Just two weeks before the collapse, some relief officials warned the U.S. Embassy that the FMG had a policy of genocidal intent toward the Ibos.

These fears were heightened by the way Lagos had allowed conditions to deteriorate in Nigerian areas during October and November, following takeover from the ICRC. The Nigerian Red Cross report of November 20 showed a steady worsening of the situation: as food distribution had to be cut back, week by week, the numbers of those suffering kwashiorkor and malnutrition increased proportionately.

Stockpiles of food in the forward areas had fallen, and the overall amount of relief food in the country had been sharply reduced during the months of indecision about Nigerian takeover from the ICRC. Food had not been imported in the quantities needed: while the ICRC, the relief center of the NRC, and the major food-importing agencies had agreed the previous May that the minimum acceptable stockpile level for the entire Federal area was close to 30,000 tons, the actual amount on hand at war's end was 13,000 tons. Only slightly more than half of this was warehoused at the forward depots in Enugu, Port Harcourt, Uyo, and Calabar, within effective logistical proximity to the people in need. The numbers of people on the Federal side had been increasing in recent weeks; as starvation inside the enclave grew sharply worse, refugees flocked out to the Nigerian side.

There had been talk in Lagos of contingency planning. At one of the regular meetings of relief agencies, a representative "pointed out the need for—and apparent absence of—a contingency plan to be prepared by the Nigerian Red Cross for presentation (should need and opportunity arise) to the Government." One of those present at the meeting reported: "The NRC does not presently feel itself to be in a position to offer such plans to the Government (in absence even of authority to maintain the present operation). . . . "

The notes of a senior relief official who attended Clyde Ferguson's mid-December meeting anticipated the new situation: "If the enclave were overrun . . . it was noted from experience on the Federal side that delays in reestablishing relief distribution after 'liberation' were almost disastrous. For Biafra, a delay in food distribution of 20 or 30 days would be catastrophic—the present state of malnutrition would bring about mortality on a colossal scale. Air drops, helicopter lifts, and the use of river traffic to the maximum would need to be expeditiously organized. The need for some international sponsorship of such relief planning was again stressed. The real problem would not lie so much in logistics as the attitude of the Federal authorities and the behavior of the military forces. . . . "

Within the U.S. government, once Ferguson and his staff concluded that Biafra's fall was imminent, contingency planning went forward within an interagency working group. There was hesitation, however, about asking Secretary of State Rogers to approve contingency plans, given his earlier anger about providing further assurances to the Biafrans. The U.S. Embassy in Lagos also was reluctant to approach the FMG about formulating plans for postwar relief once the enclave came under Nigerian control. So, while planning went on within the U.S. government for a month before the war ended, its only end result was to get more food shipments at sea, on their way to Nigeria, to meet the contingency now full upon governments that had assured the Red Cross: once the war ends, we will rush in massive humanitarian relief and save all those people.

News photographers took pictures of 20,000 pounds of medical supplies being loaded onto a Royal Air Force plane. Other photos in the morning papers showed a Red Cross DC-4 loaded with supplies at Cotonou airport. Nixon's press secretary announced that the president had ordered eight C-130s and four helicopters placed on "ready alert." Planes seemed to be taking off from everywhere, laden with food and medicine, to begin the long-promised "massive humanitarian relief." But the planes did not take off.

On the day the collapse of Biafra began, General Gowon made clear the attitude of the Federal government, warning "all foreign governments, organizations and persons to desist forthwith from meddling in the internal affairs of Nigeria." The Nigerians, always proud, now felt prouder than ever. They had won the war. They had never accepted reports of grave starvation, and now did not believe that Biafran troops had given way because they were half-starved. They had deeply resented the relief flown into Biafra in defiance of the FMG, resented the criticism from Europeans and North Americans, resented the presence of outside relief workers—"white faces"—resented the warnings they were now getting not to commit genocide, resented pressures from governments wanting to help provide relief.

If government officials really wanted relief to begin, there were a number of ways this could be done:

• Recognizing the magnitude of the problem, they could welcome the offers of assistance made by Britain, the United States, Canada, and numerous other countries. Customarily, in major disasters—earthquakes, hurricanes, floods—the international community marshals its resources and comes rushing to the aid of a stricken country. While the national government or national Red Cross society may be the titular head of the relief operation, assistance comes from Red Cross societies and other governments all over the world—much of it military personnel and equipment, on military aircraft. These were, in fact, the kind of preparations the British, U.S., and other countries had under way that weekend, the British planning to use the Royal Army Medical Corps hospital and ambulance units, and the Royal Engineers for repairing roads, airfields, and bridges that were down everywhere. Such a relief force could be organized under Commonwealth auspices, to make it more acceptable to the Nigerians.

Lagos announced that military personnel from other countries would be unacceptable for relief operations, that no military aircraft would be allowed to land in Nigeria. The drugs that had been loaded onto the

Royal Air Force aircraft had to be unloaded—without photographers present—and the C-130s and helicopters the U.S. Air Force had on "ready alert" stayed that way. Governments began seeking civilian airplanes to charter to fly relief supplies to Nigeria.

• The airlifts from São Tomé, Fernando Po, and Cotonou could have flown for a time. The Red Cross still had planes there and was seeking permission to use them. JCA informed the FMG it could fly in 600 tons of food a day. The airlift stopped flying January 10; given the condition of the people in the stricken area, any delay in organizing a new relief operation meant the certain death of large numbers. The food distribution system of 3,194 feeding centers could be used; many of the Red Cross and church relief personnel had left Biafra on the last planes out, but some missionaries remained. Even if they were unacceptable to the Nigerian government, the quickest way to get food distributed again would be to reactivate as much of the existing relief system as possible, replacing foreign personnel with local workers.

"Do you think that Nigeria would really accept such people who have been party to the lives we have lost in this country?" General Gowon said in a radio interview about the relief agencies. "Let them keep their blood money. Let them keep their blood relief supplies. We don't want it. We will do it ourselves, and I want to assure you this. We will do it. Nigerians: this is a challenge to us, and we will do it."

• Even if JCA and the ICRC were unacceptable to the FMG, the quickest way to get food in would be to fly it to Uli. All around the stricken area were torn-up, cratered roads; destroyed bridges; roads jammed with refugees moving in all directions, trying to get back to their former homes, seeking food; roadblocks maintained by Nigerian soldiers—sometimes for their own purposes; and, it soon became known, Nigerian troops who seized trucks to carry off the loot they were confiscating as the spoils of victory. At first, it was said that Uli had been destroyed by bombardment from the long-range artillery during the final three days of the war, but a photograph soon appeared showing Nigerian troops running triumphantly along the airstrip. The following week, Lord Hunt and Henry Labouisse each drove the length of the airstrip and found it intact, in serviceable condition.

The FMG said Uli could not be used for relief. British and U.S. spokesmen explained that, for the Nigerians, Uli was a symbol of the rebellion. There were other airfields in the area: one southeast of Orlu was only a dirt strip but could be used by some cargo planes; the one at Uga needed only generators to make it fully serviceable night and day. Then there was the paved strip at Obilagu, constructed and neutralized for the Red Cross, captured by the Nigerians a few weeks later. The

C-130s the U.S. was offering could have flown to any of them; a thousand tons or more of food could have been delivered each day, then distributed by helicopters to the feeding stations. But the Nigerian said they wanted no planes or helicopters flying into the area: trucks could do the job. Over the coming weeks Uli became a symbol also for those demanding a major relief effort. The Nigerians plowed up the airstrip.

• The Nigerian Army had thousands of trucks, some of which could be pressed into service. The north-south railroad was damaged and the rivers too low in the dry season for barges. The commercial trucks were tied up at that time of year moving the crops to ships in Lagos harbor, but the magnitude and efficiency with which these truck movements were carried out—one million tons or more of peanuts, 300,000 to 400,000 tons of cocoa—indicated that the Nigerians had the capacity for organizing trucks for relief.

There were few trucks available where relief was needed. The Biafran relief fleet had largely fallen apart. Some trucks had been taken off into the bush by their drivers, but they reemerged with them once the area settled down again, prepared to move food. Most of the vehicles eventually used by the Nigerian Red Cross for relief distribution had to be imported.

• The Nigerian Red Cross could be used as a channel for relief from all the national Red Cross societies, as well as governments who wished to help through their own Red Cross. As Biafra was collapsing, the Nigerian Red Cross sent out an urgent appeal, worldwide, for at least 100 doctors and nurses and, the next morning, requested from Britain £10,000 worth of medical supplies. The National Rehabilitation Commission immediately put out a statement warning foreign governments that all relief must be channeled through it rather than through the Red Cross. *The Economist* wrote of this "first snag" in the relief effort as "an old row between the government-sponsored National Commission for Rehabilitation and the Nigerian Red Cross." For those familiar with the "old row" that had caused governments and Red Cross societies to withhold aid on the Nigerian side from the previous July until early December—thus leading to the breakdown of relief in the Federal areas and a sharp cutback in food distribution—it was a worrisome incident. The FMG resolved the controversy later in the week by putting the Ministry of Economic Development in charge—adding to its title "and Reconstruction"—making Allison Ayida the responsible minister. Thus, the government itself took over relief.

As the signs, one by one, became ominous, statements of reassurance issued from governments, day by day. On that first Sunday, as the officials gathered in Yaounde were anxious that Nigerian troops overunning the enclave might commit mass slaughter, Foreign Secretary Stewart said: "While there will be great distress and disorder, I think it would be quite wrong to assume that this will be an opportunity for genocide." (For British officials and the observers team they had created, genocide was always confined to violent killing, as by shooting, never by other means, as provided against in the Convention for the Prevention and Punishment of Genocide.)

The international observers left Lagos and briefly visited the northern and southern fronts, conferring with the officers in command of the First and Third divisions. Four stayed one day; the other four, two days. They explained that their decision not to follow the troops into the Biafran areas was based on the urgent need to get back to Lagos to make a report. It stated: "The observers neither saw nor heard of any evidence of genocide in the newly liberated areas visited." This was headlined around the world.

The observers went beyond their mandate in reporting on the condition of refugees they had seen: "With the exception of those in Owerri and environs, they appeared to be in good physical shape." Their report went on: "Refugees seen in Owerri and walking down the Owerri-Aba road were not in such good physical condition. There were signs of malnutrition amongst some of the children, but not extreme." Later in the week, pressed for details of this by reporters, one observer shook his head and replied slowly: "We are not doctors. . . . There were some children who seemed to have malnutrition, with their big bellies"—made a gesture suggestive of a swollen stomach—"but they were walking, so they could not have been so badly off."

Other reporters quoted another observer as saying that there was "a lot of food" in the area, but that frightened villagers had run away: "If they are stupid enough to go away from the food, they're going to get hungry."

The people in the enclave were hiding from the advancing troops. Doctors, nurses, and medical personnel fled from hospitals. One medical adviser to the Nigerian Red Cross described the situation: "Many of the hospitals were looted and/or abandoned. Doctors and nurses had run into the bush leaving patients behind without medical care, food, and in a few instances water. Most ambulatory patients also deserted the hospitals, leaving behind those with lower-extremity injuries or with incapacitating medical conditions. The mortality within hospitals was understandably very high and in a few cases the initial Red Cross responsibility was to bury the dead."

Brigadier Said-Uddin Khan, the secretary general's observer, had just returned from the United Nations; he commented on the fact that the international observers had rushed back to Lagos to issue a report without going north of Owerri. This robbed their findings of significance, he said; "as it is not based on visits to areas liberated by the surrender, there is no point in the report now."

At the State Department, officials were disagreeing with predictions of dire starvation. Thirteen thousand tons of food were stockpiled on the fringes of the Biafran enclave, they noted, with more available on short notice. "But it was acknowledged here," the *New York Times* reported from State, "that the truly awesome problem was to bring the former Eastern Region of Nigeria out of a condition that hovers between dangerous malnutrition and semi-starvation. As many as two million people are known to require feeding for an indefinite period, and assistance is needed for a large percentage of the balance of about 10 million."

This news story revealed what was uppermost in the minds of officials in the Bureau of African Affairs: "A new political situation is certain to develop in Nigeria, United States officials believe, and a contest with the Soviet Union for influence is not to be excluded."

In Moscow, a spokesman for the Ministry of Foreign Affairs said that humanitarian assistance should be given only through the Federal government and upon its request: "We think that so-called relief for the rebels from Western agencies is nothing but interference in the internal affairs of Nigeria," he declared.

Under Secretary of State Elliot Richardson held a reassuring news briefing; responding to a question whether the Nigerian government might be sensitive about offers of help: ". . . . They are sensitive in the sense that they believe that they have accepted the responsibility which they are prepared to carry out; and certainly they could understandably be sensitive to the impression of any outsider that they not be completely sincere about this or completely capable of carrying it out." Richardson assured the journalists: ". . . . Our experience in dealing with them, and particularly with the Nigerian Red Cross in connection with relief operations conducted for areas that have been regained by the Federal Military Government in the past, is that they do take their responsibilities very seriously in carrying them out very competently."

Asked whether he believed Lagos was unduly delaying acceptance of offers of help, the under secretary replied, "No, I don't think it would be fair to draw any such inference at this point." Assistant Secretary of State David Newsom was then in Lagos meeting with the Nigerian head of state. "We will know more about what the Nigerian Government believes to be needed in the form of help from us when we get a report from Ambassador Newsom after his talk with General Gowon today," Richardson said.

Gowon expressed appreciation to Newsom for Nixon's offer of assistance. Newsom had conveyed to Gowon the president's interest, offering the Nigerian government the fullest U.S. aid for relief and rehabilitation, including facilities for a helicopter airlift into the stricken area. The message also expressed the president's feeling that in Nigeria's own interest, the observer team should be beefed up so that the world would have a clear picture of what was happening. Gowon told Newsom that the Nigerian government would let the United States know if it required assistance; for now, he said, he wanted to be certain that requests for relief were based on genuine need and were coordinated.

In London, Clyde Ferguson and American Ambassador Walter Annenberg met with Prime Minister Harold Wilson. In the course of their discussion, Wilson remarked that if a million Ibos had had to die to preserve the unity of Nigeria, well, that was not too high a price to pay.

Chapter 28

In New York, I had been worrying since the day before, after hearing the comment at UNICEF: "We won't get in there for weeks." I caught Dick Heyward, the deputy executive director, just before he left for lunch: "I'm going to do something, and I'm going to tell you what it is, but not to get your permission, just so you will be informed."

After telling him, I returned to my office and phoned others associated with the group I had been working with that past year. Jean Mayer telephoned the White House and Roger Fisher of Harvard Law School called Elliot Richardson's office. I got in touch with Clyde Ferguson's staff and later the prime minister's office in Ottawa. Our proposal: one international relief agency had been working on the Federal side in Nigeria, with written agreement to do so, and had never operated directly in Biafra. It had been carrying on a small helicopter operation that could be expanded. Three of its helicopters, in fact, were still at Calabar. This was the United Nations Children's Fund.

The plan was for the United States, Britain, and Canada to use UNICEF as a channel and pour all their relief in through the UN agency already there. These governments, which had always said during the war that once the conflict ended they would send in massive humanitarian relief, should now insist that the Federal Military Government allow relief on a scale needed "to save all those people."

Planes loaded with helicopters, relief supplies, and personnel would head toward airfields close to Nigeria; shortly before their arrival, an announcement would be made that a massive relief program was beginning through UNICEF. The personnel would wear blue armbands and function on behalf of UNICEF. The Nigerian government would find it awkward to expel UNICEF, already on the scene and operating. How could the FMG object to the United Nations agency concerned with children expanding its emergency assistance to children?

Crucial to success of the plan was the use of helicopters to move relief directly into the former Biafran area: those who knew the events of the past seven months felt it was absolutely essential to get foreign personnel in to make sure food was actually being distributed to those in need. The helicopters were also necessary to overcome the serious physical obstacles of broken roads and downed bridges.

That evening the White House phoned back: "O.K. We're ready to go on this. You can have anything you want—planes, helicopters, personnel, anything. Just get us a complete list by midnight."

George Orick and Dick Heyward worked up a list of food and medicines while I telephoned Sikorsky experts at their homes in Connecticut about the kinds of helicopters that could best be used: those that would fit inside U.S. cargo planes for the long flight to West Africa. By ten o'clock we got back to the National Security Council staff with a list, the crucial element of which was eighteen cargo helicopters, CH-3Ds and CH-46s. The U.S. and other countries might provide the Nigerians with trucks and food, but the trucks might never move the food. Helicopters would not only insure food distribution but would bring a UN presence into the area as well.

The next morning Heyward suggested to Labouisse that he see Gowon in Lagos. The UNICEF executive director conferred with the Nigerian ambassador. It was important that State Department officials would read in the *Washington Post* the next morning: "Nigeria's representative to the United Nations warmly endorsed humanitarian help through the U.N. Children's Fund today and exempted it from his government's criticism of aid agencies."

In Lagos, the FMG was barring relief from France, Portugal, South Africa, and Rhodesia (a grouping presumably intended to pain the French) or from any other country or relief agency that had been "studiously hostile" toward Nigeria. The announcement on Nigeria Radio also declared that all relief personnel who had flown into Biafra, violating Nigerian airspace, would not be allowed into Nigeria, thereby excluding a considerable portion of the international relief community that customarily provides aid in disaster situations. Among the various relief agencies the FMG listed as unacceptable: the Red Cross societies of the Scandinavian countries, some of whom had helped organize and train the Nigerian Red Cross in recent years. At the UN, however, Nigerian Ambassador Ogbu was telling reporters that UNICEF had provided "invaluable service and assistance" and was encouraged to continue. Henry Labouisse began making plans to leave the next day for Lagos.

But at one o'clock Heyward received a phone call from Jack Foley,

Clyde Ferguson's chief of staff. Africa bureau officials had set about to block the plan to channel relief through UNICEF. They said that there was a statutory upper limit on the amount of money the United States could provide UNICEF in any fiscal year. Foley asked Heyward whether this was true and, if so, whether there was any way around it.

Africa bureau officials had been briefed in November on the preliminary conclusion of Dr. Karl Western's survey and had received the short memo in December that began: "Slow, creeping starvation of almost the entire population is the key impression today in Biafra. . . . " So that there would be no mistaking the meaning of the findings in the survey, the White House that day asked Dr. Western to prepare a brief memo estimating food needs, and this information was given to the Africa bureau the next day.

In Geneva, Ferguson gave the Western survey to Nigerian ambassador Sule Kolo, but he was among those in the Nigerian government not greatly concerned about humanitarian relief. When he met the press, Kolo intimated that President Nixon's offer of C-130s and helicopters would not be accepted and Uli could not be used; he categorically rejected the assistance of Joint Church Aid, Caritas, or the French Red Cross; and he said that "the gravity of the situation is being generally exaggerated." He warned against "wild figures and guesses" and, according to the London *Times*, stated: "We appreciate there is a problem, but it is not as bad as it is made out to be. The Nigerian Rehabilitation Commission is capable of coping with the situation."

Foley and Heyward were exploring ways of getting around the legal obstacle the Africa bureau had set up. Finally they hit upon it: create a trust and put the money in it, UNICEF would administer the funds on behalf of the children in Nigeria; they would not pass through its regular budget or constitute a U.S. contribution above the annual limit to the UN agency. The next day the State Department spokesman announced, as one more example of the ways the United States was helping provide relief, that it had told UNICEF it was prepared to make a special contribution up to $2 million to establish a "fund-in-trust" for the Nigerian emergency.

Food distribution had now been disrupted for five days. General Ojukwu, somewhere in exile, released a statement from Geneva, stating in part: "From all indications it is clear that Nigeria will not feed our people. They have said so often enough and their past records clearly underline this fact. There is no food whatsoever in Biafra, and unless food can get into Biafran mouths in the next 72 hours it will be too late. Nigeria's insistence to control the distribution of relief is both to insure that Biafrans get no such relief and also to shut out outsiders who might witness and expose the enormous crimes she plans to commit against our people."

Newspapers that day quoted the State Department spokesman as stating that General Gowon had declared "he would not hesitate" to make use of United States assistance if it was needed. The spokesman took issue with what he said "appears to be an impression in some quarters" that if the aid that is offered is not immediately used, there is no relief effort. "That is not the case," he said. "There is a relatively large effort underway, and it appears to be having some impact." The *New York Times* quoted another State Department official, who asked not to be identified, as saying: "We know food is moving. We know relief teams are operating."

The *Times* reported: "Privately, United States officials explained that the American Government was anxious to counter an impression that there is a serious danger of deliberate starvation and reprisals. 'We don't want to be criticized for not taking action about a situation that doesn't exist,' one official said. 'And we don't want to be under pressure to take action.' "

Elliot Richardson met with editors and broadcasters attending a foreign policy conference at the State Department. He reiterated what he had said two days before about the Nigerian leaders: "They are sensitive because they recognize the responsibility they have at the bar of world opinion. They are also sensitive because they realize that they are dealing with fellow Nigerians, and they believe that it is essential to the healing of the scars of this civil war that the help that is extended to the people of the Biafran enclave be extended by Nigerians."

Responding to a question, ". . . If there is any alternative policy . . . we might be developing possibly to bring pressure so that the patient policy . . . you outlined . . . might be speeded so that starvation and famine be avoided . . . ," Richardson displayed some annoyance: "I would remind you that the Federal Military Government has already announced that it will not accept assistance from the Government of France. I would ask you to consider—and I won't pause to develop the point—what the so-called pressures to which you refer might be and what you think they would accomplish. These, I think, are points perhaps sufficient to emphasize the fact that we are concerned with results and not with exhibiting to the American public as flashy as possible an approach to the matter."

Back in his office, Richardson met with staff members of the National Security Council, Ambassador Ferguson's office and the Africa bureau. The alignment of battle: Kissinger's and Ferguson's staffs on one side, the Bureau of African Affairs on the other. The bureau won, one final time, persuading Richardson that:

1) There was no mass starvation.

2) The problem was much smaller than anyone had thought: there were only 1.3 million people in need.

3) The Nigerian Red Cross had the situation well in hand.

4) UNICEF did not have the capability of carrying out such an operation.

This seemed to say that the Nigerian Red Cross alone could handle the job but that UNICEF, which could draw upon other UN agencies and governments for assistance, could not help the Nigerian Red Cross do the job. Of course, the State Department had no direct reports from the stricken area providing an evaluation of the condition of the people or the extent of the relief effort; no relief officials had gotten out and reported back as yet. At that point, practically no food was being distributed, but Africa bureau officials persuaded Richardson to postpone any decision about channeling relief through UNICEF.

Upon learning that evening that the Africa bureau had blocked the plan before Labouisse had even reached Lagos, I telephoned a number of people. One was Roger Fisher. I asked him to call Richardson.

"Look," he said, "I have a better idea. I have Tom Winship here at dinner—the editor of the *Boston Globe*. Why don't we have him call Richardson about this. What should he say?"

I suggested: "Why don't you have him ask: 'Say, Elliot, I understand UNICEF had requested eighteen CH-3D and CH-46 helicopters to fly food to those children starving in Biafra, and you've just turned them down. Why?' "

It seemed that one way of alerting people to what was actually going on was to get this story, revealing as it was, out to the press. The next morning I walked into the office of the foreign affairs editor of *Time*. He was standing at his desk looking down at the stack of the week's copy he had to edit for the deadline. I told him I had a story to tell him. He looked harried and asked, "Can't I give you a correspondent?" I said, "No. I want ten minutes of your time." Then he started taking notes. Later that day I gave the story to six other major newspapers and television correspondents.

Only the *Globe* carried a story, with a front-page banner headline, the following day:

Nixon's Biafran Plan:
U.S. Copters for Aid

The article was accurate in all particulars but one: it did not mention that the plan had in effect been blocked two days before. The other news media were remarkably silent about what must have been, at least, an intriguing news lead. Editors said later they had been unable to confirm the story. Christopher Beal of the Ripon Society found the press officer assigned to the Africa bureau in a state verging on nervous collapse, the following week, from his efforts to keep news stories out of the papers.

Beal, Orick, and two Irish priests who had just flown out of Biafra—the Fathers Kevin and Michael Doheney—met with officials of the Bureau of African Affairs. The Doheney brothers sought to persuade them to make use of the feeding system that they and others had been running in Biafra. In his own parish of 22,000 people, plus 16,000 refugees, Father Kevin had been feeding 5,000 children every morning and bringing subsistence-rations to 950 destitute families. When Dr. Western had been making his survey, Doheney had asked him to let him know in what condition he found the people in his parish. Western later wrote him: "Your ordinary people, the people that you are not even bringing any relief to, who are walking around the roads, who are carrying on their work, I surveyed those people for you, and 62.3 percent of your parishioners to whom you are giving no relief are suffering from famine edema."

This was only one parish—one of the worst—and the Doheney brothers feared that those who had not already died soon would, if food did not start reaching them quickly. They urged that Uli be used to fly food into the heart of the stricken area and pointed out that they and other relief workers in Biafra had been operating more than three thousand food distribution centers that could quickly be reactivated.

Orick, who had been angry with the Africa bureau diplomats for more than a year-and-a-half, was less gentle with them than the Irish priests. He asked why they, who had never been into Biafra, always questioned the information of those who had; why they implied that people like himself and others who brought reports out of Biafra were in some way lying, while the bureau's own information was superior. Ending the meeting on a rancorous note, Orick told the Africa bureau officials: "What you are doing is murderous—murderous."

In Lagos, Henry Labouisse met with Gowon. A day earlier, the Nigerian leader had accepted surrender from a Biafran major general. He was conciliatory to the Biafrans, saying, "We have been reunited with our brothers," and "We have never considered them our enemies . . . " (suggesting they had been misled by Ojukwu). Encouraged by the British and Americans to assume a Lincolnesque tone, he urged his people to adopt a spirit of reconciliation so "that all those dead shall not have died in vain."

British and American spokesmen began portraying him as binding up his nation's wounds.

At about the same time, Chief Anthony Enahoro told a press conference that "the relief situation is well under control"; that the Nigerian relief administration was working in all the main towns and that the problem would be "overcome this month." He said that there was no need for immediate airlifting of food into Nigeria, that the principal relief requirement was trucks. Maurice Foley had gotten Gowon to request fifty four-ton trucks, thirty ten-ton trucks, and fifty Land Rovers. Some of the four-ton Bedfords were now beginning to arrive by air, the British having chartered commercial cargo planes to transport them. Lord Hunt, sent out once again to Lagos, emphasized this aspect of the problem: "It is very much a question of how to get that food into those starving mouths." And: "A good deal of transport is already there, and it is being used."

Gowon told Labouisse much the same thing: it was chiefly a problem of trucks—there was no need for helicopters. He gave a response similar to the one Assistant Secretary David Newsom had received a few days before: UNICEF's offer of assistance was appreciated; the government would let Labouisse know if anything was required. Labouisse did not press to have UNICEF play a major role in providing emergency relief but turned, instead, to concentrating on long-term rehabilitation of children.

U Thant arrived in Lagos, talked with Gowon, then lunched with his humanitarian representative, Said-Uddin Khan, and Labouisse. That evening, at a state dinner, Gowon offered a toast to Thant: "I have found you to be a true friend and wise counselor. Your vision of world order, based on peace and justice, and your unimpeachable integrity enabled you to resist pressures from powerful interests that threatened to destroy Nigeria."

The next morning, Thant breakfasted with Labouisse and Henrik Beer, the secretary general of the League of Red Cross Societies. Beer had just returned from a brief trip to the stricken area. After meeting again with Gowon, Thant spoke with correspondents at the airport, prior to his departure. "I am convinced the process of national reconciliation has started auspiciously," he told the journalists. He mentioned having talked with Gowon, Khan, Labouisse, and Beer. "As you know, Mr. Beer came back from the afflicted areas only yesterday. According to him, the atmosphere was very congenial. There was no hint, or even the slightest or remotest evidence of violence or ill treatment of the civilian population in the area by the Federal forces. He saw the people fraternizing as brothers, and according to his judgment, the climate, the psychological climate in the area was much more congenial than the psychological climate in Europe immediately after World War II. Mr. Beer was also in Europe at that time."

Henrik Beer was very angry when he learned of this. He cabled Thant: "I am worried exaggerated reports Nigerian press today of U.N. Secretary-General's quoting me at departure. My impressions based on two-day visit and should not be interpreted as press says here as blanket guarantee that no violence or ill treatment has taken place. I said while general impressions being very positive some violence and looting from both sides was bound to happen. I hope further reference to briefing in Lagos would give more nuanced picture."

Journalists at the airport were waiting to get out to the former Biafran area. They were among close to two hundred reporters, photographers, radio and television newsmen who had flown into Lagos when news started coming out that Biafra was collapsing. They had been kept in Lagos nearly a week, being told that the relief effort was gathering momentum; that Nigerian Red Cross trucks were rolling into the center of the stricken area carrying large quantities of food; that it would take a few more days to gauge the size of the problem but, except for those suffering advanced malnutrition, the problem seemed far less acute than at first feared; that of the 1.5 million needing relief, only a fifth required full rations—supplementary feeding would do for the rest. There was ample food in Nigeria, the reporters were told, with stocks in depots close to the distressed areas, so there was no need to import large quantities of food.

The correspondents, of course, wanted to check these reports for themselves. Four London reporters tried to travel to the area on their own and got as far as Onitsha. Back in Lagos, they were roused out of their beds at five o'clock in the morning, had their belongings searched and all their notes read, were questioned for an hour-and-a-half, then escorted to the airport and expelled from Nigeria. Others were warned that any attempt to enter the recaptured area without authorization would be dealt with severely.

They kept the pressure on. Finally a large group of them was given permission to travel in the eastern part of Nigeria. There was one last holdup, however; the first planeload had taken off from Lagos airport, then circled and returned. The reporters had to disembark. The plane had been commandeered for a wedding party that now began to arrive, escorted by motorcycle police. Military officers and their ladies, in elegant dress, were soon on board the plane, bound for Port Harcourt and the wedding of the military governor of that state, Lieutenant Commander Diete-Spiff.

Although two other planes were available, the journalists were now told that because of the wedding there would be no room for them in the Port Harcourt hotels. Angry and sweltering, they staged a demonstration of sorts, advancing in single file across the airfield to the international side where Gowon was awaiting the arrival of U Thant. Police and Gowon's military aides halted them, but they made their protest felt. After seven hours, some of them finally departed for Port Harcourt with the remainder promised they would be flown out the next day, the beginning of what was soon to become one of the worst examples of press relations in the history of governments.

In Washington, Secretary of State William Rogers was saying on a television show that "the Nigerian Red Cross has been very active." He commented: "On the whole, I think we feel by working through the Federal Government in Nigeria that the United States can do the best possible job in providing food and medicine to those in need. . . .

"The reconciliation process in Nigeria has to be effected by the people in Nigeria," Rogers explained. "I think Americans have to keep in mind that the Nigerians are a proud people, and General Gowon says he has the ability and his government has the ability to effect a reconciliation and to provide the food and medicine, and I think we should recognize that he is their leader and they obviously have pride in their country, so I think it is important for us to work through them."

However, Richard Nixon got a very different sense of the situation when he met with Rogers and officials of the Africa bureau. Following their briefing, he telephoned his national security adviser and said: "They're going to let them starve, aren't they, Henry."

Chapter 29

E dward Kennedy called a meeting of his Senate subcommittee. "The civil war in Nigeria has ended and the moral imperative to act in behalf of a suffering people can no longer be questioned," he said in opening the hearing. "But getting food and medicine to the sick and dying is as difficult today as it ever was—perhaps more so."

Kennedy asked Assistant Secretary of State David Newsom, now back from Lagos, and Clyde Ferguson to appear before the committee. By now the embassy in Lagos had managed to get a request from the Nigerian Red Cross for fifty jeeps, three portable hospitals, a 200-bed hospital, and two 50-bed hospitals. The U.S. had also taken over the option for fifty trucks ordered by UNICEF, though the Nigerian government showed no interest in them and, in fact, most would never get out to where they were needed.

Newsom told the subcommittee: "Observers have reported favorably . . . on the present relief operation under the general direction of the Nigerian Red Cross and have found that the reports that large numbers of refugees having taken to the bush and still not found seem so far to have been exaggerated."

Ferguson now began sounding more like the Bureau of African Affairs than the independent humanitarian coordinator he had been. (At war's end, the State Department reasserted direct control over relief by placing it under an interdepartmental working group, directed by William Brubeck.) He stated that the FMG was the controlling authority for all relief and assured the senators "from the various reports reaching Washington we feel that Government is carrying out its responsibilities and the relief effort is gaining momentum."

Citing the estimates of Dr. Western and other doctors, based on their earlier survey, Ferguson reported "that to treat the severely malnourished will require a consumption of 17,000 tons a month. To supplement the diet of the remaining population—2.2 million—at 250 grams a day, approximately one-half pound, will require an additional 18,000 tons."

He summed up: "Thus a total feeding program would require a consumption of 38,000 tons a month; 3,000 for the former federally occupied area, 17,000 for the severely malnourished, and 18,000 for the remainder on half rations."

This estimate of need was cabled to the embassy in Lagos with the instruction that it be presented to the Nigerian Ministry of Health. The United States offered to make the food required available to the FMG, emphasizing that the relief action should aim at distributing at least 10,000 tons a week for several months. Nigerian reaction was hostile: who do you think you are? Why do you think you know more about our problems than we do?

The Western survey had not been made available to Lagos at the time it was completed, so the medical basis for the estimates of need were not appreciated within the FMG. This now became a focus for controversy in Washington, with Roger Morris in the White House pressing to have the Lagos embassy place before FMG officials a full understanding of the survey. It was not easy for a layman to grasp; even a doctor who was not a nutritionist might not comprehend its full implications. So one of the physicians from the Communicable Disease Center was sent to Lagos to brief the ambassador and embassy staff and to discuss the problem with the Ministry of Health.

Senator Kennedy was distressed that the Western survey had never been released and placed it in the hearing record. He and Senator Charles Goodell questioned Newsom and Ferguson closely about what was being done to meet the need the survey clearly disclosed. Goodell commented to Newsom at one point: "You mentioned genocide, calculated genocide, and the feeling that this was not the policy of the Nigerian Government. I don't believe it is the policy of General Gowon. I spent some time with him. I did spend time with some other Nigerian leaders who expressed hostility in such vehemence toward the Ibos and the Biafrans that I don't doubt many of them would embrace a policy of genocide if they could get away with it. I am not sure they could get away with it within their own population, but I think now we have the danger of genocide by neglect, not a calculated direct policy, not a shooting, not mass destruction, but simply letting former Biafrans die, and this is what we must concern ourselves with."

Newsom and Ferguson were asked to testify further the following day, but overnight two things happened: journalists filed stories on the conditions they found when they finally got out among the stricken population, and a cable arrived from Ferguson's deputy, Colonel Dewey, reporting his own findings in the former Biafran area—a cable that found its way to Senator Kennedy within hours of its arrival at the State Department.

Another cable, this one from the UN representative in London, warned the Secretariat of what was about to happen: "If first despatch from British correspondent Owerri proves typical can expect strong press reaction tomorrow. *Times* correspondent Wolfers just broadcast BBC Owerri refugees have not eaten eight to ten days." The UN official went on to report an account of inadequate medical care in one hospital, then: "Correspondent's despatch says that the phrase that conditions were 'under control' which he claims was used by Foley and International Observers is 'not true.' He reports bulk food exists but many children are dying for lack of food as people are confined to villages and few get food and transport deficiency holding up distribution." The cable to the Secretariat continued: "He admitted Nigerian Red Cross working hard in small numbers but on immediate medical problems and not food distribution. He concluded Nigeria must admit it requires immediate crash aid from every available source including missionaries who know the region."

The journalists, many of whom had never been in Biafra before, were shaken by what they found. Everywhere people told them they had not eaten for more than a week. "Skeletal men and women, children with swollen bellies and malnutrition scabs, pathetic wrecks of humanity" were awaiting food that did not come. When food was spilled, people "clutching, clawing, screaming" fought to get a little of it. The few Nigerian Red Cross personnel were preoccupied trying to care for patients in hospitals from which foreign doctors had been evacuated and whose Ibo doctors and nurses had fled to the bush. They had little time for distributing food. Most remaining missionaries had by now been taken to Port Harcourt, pending deportation.

There were few trucks left in the area; soldiers were using them to carry off loot. The troops, at least in the south where the journalists traveled, were out of control, raping women, carrying girls off for concubinage, stealing from refugees. Occasionally an officer would shoot a soldier for rape, but officers were not everywhere. Some correspondents intervened to prevent soldiers from taking an Ibo man's wife. Others nearly came to blows with members of the international observers team who had reassured them in Lagos about conditions in the reconquered area.

Even where traders had brought in canned food to sell, the people had only worthless Biafran currency for buying food. There was no coherent relief plan. The correspondents found Uli airstrip in good shape but, of course, relief flights were banned. Near Owerri people were too weak to bury their dead. All this contrasted with what the reporters had seen at Port Harcourt, only sixty miles away: the marriage of the military governor, officers impeccably dressed with sabers and golden epaulettes, waiters from Lagos offering canapés and champagne to the 500 guests, goats turning on spits, suckling pigs roasting, twenty-pound turkeys being served.

In London, Prime Minister Wilson was asked whether he thought that press and television broadcasters had been unduly biased in favor of Biafra during the Nigerian civil war. He replied, as if in anticipation of the storm about to break around his government and other governments: "Over a considerable part of the field, yes. I think that there has been on television and radio, and in some parts of the press, a failure to reach the usual level of detachment and neutrality which I always find in British political affairs in all the newspapers I read—even more so." He added: "I do not think it has been conscious or organized."

The correspondents in eastern Nigeria had not yet filed their stories. They were having trouble doing so. Upon their arrival back in Port Harcourt, the military detained them. Some were already aboard a plane about to taxi along the runway when an army lieutenant came aboard and said, "Everybody must get off. That is a military command." All aircraft were needed for military purposes, they were told. This resulted in exposing them to a horror most of them up till now had not witnessed: more than five hundred children had been brought to Port Harcourt by Dr. Kenneth Diete-Spiff and Panayotsis Stanissis of the League of Red Cross Societies. Diete-Spiff had been on the Biafran side during the war. Perhaps he thought if he could get the children to Port Harcourt, he would be able to get help for them from his brother on the Nigerian side. But Commander Diete-Spiff was busy getting married.

The "Biafran babies" were lying there on the ground or just sitting or standing with their swollen bellies. Photographers, unable to depart for Lagos, took many pictures. Oil construction workers were doing what they could to care for the children. Correspondents who until now had been covering the Nigerian conflict from the vantage point of foreign offices, experienced what had been the familiar day-to-day sight for relief workers and others in Biafra. The diplomatic correspondent of the London *Sunday Times* wrote: "I was more affected by the sight of those babies than I liked to admit. I had never before seen a prolapse of a child's rectum, protruding three or four inches from between the tiny buttocks. I asked a doctor about it. 'You can push it back quite easily,' he said, and proceeded to do so. But it immediately began bulging out again when the child started whimpering. 'The muscles are too weak to keep it in place,' the doctor explained. The last time I saw that little boy he was squatting on the ground, his prolapsed rectum smeared with earth and the diarrhea that lay in pools all over the yard of the improvised hospital."

The reporters managed to get word to Lagos that they were being held in Port Harcourt. Their respective ambassadors spoke to the government. After one more night on the floor of the airport lounge or of the lounges and bars of the local hotel, the journalists were allowed to fly back to Lagos. They began filing their stories:

"Death, Not Food, Is Awaiting Many Biafran Refugees"

"Starvation and Looting in Biafra—Gowon's Soldiers Steal Ambulances"

"Press Sees the Rape of Biafra"

"Rape, hunger, lootings—this is Biafra   THE AWFUL TRUTH"

"Biafra Peace No Help to the Starving"

Newsom and Ferguson returned to testify before the Kennedy subcommittee. Kennedy and Goodell questioned them about the use of helicopters. Newsom acknowledged he had been instructed to offer Gowon full facilities for a helicopter airlift, but the Nigerian government did not want foreign military personnel operating in their country. He and Ferguson stressed the technical difficulties of using helicopters; such an operation must be carried out by the military. Kennedy expressed some skepticism about this, pointing out that there were American helicopter operations in Laos using civilian crews: "I think the American people would want to know why we are able to carry in guns and supplies to Southeast Asia and we have difficulty in supplying food if requested in this part of the world."

Kennedy asked, "Has UNICEF made a request to our Government for helicopters?"

Ferguson replied, "No, sir. To the best of my knowledge there has been no such request. There have been discussions. In fact, there have been discussions which have been proceeding the last three months revolving around the use of helicopters in the various patterns."

What all this was leading up to was the cable that had arrived the afternoon before from Colonel Dewey, describing conditions in the former Biafran area. Dewey warned: "A disaster of major proportions appears to be developing here. At least one million people are in acute need now, and the situation grows worse daily." The problem was "particularly explosive because press have seen just enough during recent escorted visit to realize how inadequate relief effort is. . . ." Dewey's report emphasized the chaotic conditions caused by the rampaging Third Marine Commando Division, stating that until that problem was brought under control any plan to distribute food by trucks was "academic."

After discussing the possibilities of helicopters, the senators asked Newsom and Ferguson: ". . .Have you received any later reports about the situation in the enclave as of today? I mean do you have anything current? Have you heard anything at all, say in the last week, or within the last eight to ten hours from the enclave as to the condition over there?"

"We have received some word," Ferguson said. "It is still fragmentary but it does tend to confirm that the major problem, as has been pointed out over the last forty-eight hours, is, in fact, that of transportation for various reasons developing in the enclave. The transportation situation is a major stricture on the distibution of food which, in fact, is in the area."

Kennedy became more specific: "Have you heard anything about the Nigerian Third Division recently—say, in the last eight or nine hours?" Ferguson and Newsom began getting the drift of the questioning. "We have reports, Mr. Chairman, of troops of Nigerian units, the Third Division is one that has been mentioned, carrying out undisciplined acts," Newsom stated. The evening before there had been a meeting of the interagency group, under the chairmanship of Elliot Richardson. "As a result, we have placed in the hands of our ambassador out there some additional instructions urging that he take up on an urgent basis with the Nigerian government these problems. . . . We are stressing in our conversations with the Nigerians that nothing can be done to meet the massive relief problem if security problems intervene, and we are doing everything we can to get to them the seriousness of the relationship between any act of indiscipline and the ability of the world community to provide relief."

Pressed further about the cable, Newsom finally commented: "We want to cooperate fully with the Committee in providing an evaluation of the situation. But at the same time we are in an extremely sensitive situation with the Nigerian Government, and our access, which we both want information of what is going on in the enclave could be seriously jeopardized . . . by the characterizations which might flow from observers, official observers, who have been in the enclave."

To which Goodell rejoined: "Are you saying that we can't tell the world the truth about what is going on there for fear we will no longer know what is going on there?"*

In London, Harold Wilson was once again facing the Commons. Over the past ten days he had reassured Parliament a number of times that relief was going well. He had sent Lord Hunt out to check on the situation, to confer with the Nigerian authorities, and Hunt had just returned, reporting to Wilson for over an hour the previous evening. But now the newspapers were filled with horror stories of conditions in the stricken area and reports that people had not eaten for a week.

The prime minister set about once again to reassure the House: "I am in no doubt that the Nigerian Government and the Nigerian Red Cross are coming to grips with the situation, and this is the view that has been taken by Lord Hunt, and his colleagues. . . . Not enough even now is where it is most urgently needed. While the reports I have are that the situation is changing hour by hour, the movement is gathering momentum. The condition of the roads is generally good, bridges have in most cases been repaired already and the distances involved are not great. . . ."

The M.P.s were no longer willing to accept this. Edward Heath spoke of the "anxiety among so many in this House" and asked the prime minister how "the very detailed accounts . . . we read in the press this morning" could be reconciled with the more reassuring reports.

Wilson responded, "The Right Honorable Gentleman expresses what is in the minds of many honorable Members—the confusion in the minds perhaps of all of us after seeing the reports in the press and the photographs and the reports on television, and after the reports which we have had, for example, from Lord Hunt and his mission and also from the International Observers. I believe that the reports which we have read have been honest, but I believe that, inevitably, both newspaper accounts and newspaper photographs tend to be episodic and to deal with individual cases. They naturally do not present a general view of the whole panorama in the sense that we have been able to have from Lord Hunt and his mission, all of whom are highly experienced and expert in the relief field. They have been working closely with the Nigerian Red Cross on these visits. I do not think that there is conflict between these reports. I have tried to give the general panoramic view. I know that the press feels strongly about the matter, but the press inevitably—and I understand it—

*Ten days later, Colonel Dewey was awakened in his hotel room in Lagos, escorted to the airport, and expelled from Nigeria.

has dealt with individual cases of rape and atrocities. It was right that these things should be reported, but that does not mean that they are necessarily taking place on a total scale. All the evidence is to the contrary."

There were further news stories the next day, and Lord Hunt told a press conference at the Foreign Office: "I am horrified at the tone and slant of British press coverage." His own report, he asserted, was more reliable: "I think it is a matter of whether we are concerned with the truth, or simply with half truths—whether one is concerned with describing a developing situation or simply recording an aftermath." He said that the numbers said to be starving "have been wildly exaggerated and gullibly accepted."

The day before, Heath had asked why Uli airport was not being used, and another M.P. queried whether it was not true that the Nigerian government was opposing use of Uli "on purely political grounds which have nothing to do with the urgent humanitarian situation." Lord Hunt stated at the press conference that he had tried to get relief flights into Uli: "I did my best to persuade the Nigerian Government to open the strip. It was a political decision. I do not think it was necessarily the right decision."

Henry Labouisse was encountering the same conditions the journalists and Colonel Dewey had reported: broken roads, refugees walking south without food or money, loot being carried away in commandeered trucks. A man shot by a Federal soldier when he would not hand over a basket of yams belonging to his mother had lain by the side of the road for hours— Labouisse took him to the hospital. He also provided Dr. Diete-Spiff with funds and equipment for the infants at Port Harcourt, cabling the UNICEF warehouse in Copenhagen to airfreight fifteen tons of the formula food used to treat kwashiorkor.

The former head of the Biafran Red Cross complained to Labouisse about the looting and the molesting of young women. The Canadian and British military observers told him they had witnessed looting and abductions of young women; they had apprehended several soldiers, but a Nigerian officer threatened to use his pistol if they interfered with the looting.

The international observers had been sent back into the area by the Nigerian government to produce an interim report on relief measures. They were about to turn in a reassuring account. Labouisse told them if they did that and large numbers of people died, he would inform the world about the source of the information. The international observers then asked to have the relief situation explained to them. The UNICEF officials gave them a frank appraisal:

- There was an urgent need to allow an airlift into Uli airstrip, on a temporary basis, to alleviate the immediate situation.
- Trucks and other transport must be made available to overcome the present relief bottleneck.
- Law and order must be established: people were being molested by marauding soldiers and young women especially felt endangered. Nigerian Red Cross trucks were being stolen, and drivers were frightened; this was reducing the relief capacity. There was need for military escorts of trucks and guards for storage warehouses, hospitals, clinics, etc. This would encourage nurses to come out of hiding,
- The basic foods were available or on route, the drug supply was all right, but the above factors were interfering with relief work.

The Canadian observer said that law and order must have first priority—which meant getting the soldiers back into barracks as quickly as possible—but he doubted the capacity of the Nigerian Red Cross to handle the job.

This was also the view expressed by the secretary general's representative, Brigadier Khan. He did not think transport was the problem; there was enough available, but it was being used ineffectively by the Nigerian Red Cross. He was critical of the general lack of organization of the NRC, and thought that the military should distribute food.

In Washington, Senator Goodell was talking with Jean Mayer, planning a press conference for the following Monday, when suddenly it struck him he was not going about it in the best way. Instead he telephoned the White House. Though Goodell was opposing the president on Vietnam and a Supreme Court nomination, Nixon returned the call within a few minutes. Goodell explained in detail what the State Department was doing in the Biafran situation. Nixon asked what Goodell thought he should do, and the senator suggested he call Mayer to the White House and take up the matter with the British prime minister when Harold Wilson was in Washington the following week.

That Sunday evening, Henry Kissinger had Jean Mayer and Dr. Davida Taylor come to his apartment to talk with Elliot Richardson. Taylor was a pediatrician and nutritionist who had worked with Mayer at Harvard, had been in Biafra, and had flown out of Uli on one of the last planes. She had just told the Kennedy subcommittee: "I think a false impression is often given when people drive along the roads in Biafra and see people that look quite healthy. Often as we went to our refugee camps, as we arrived at the camp, the clinic, our first impression was things did not look so bad. But this is because it is the healthier portion of the population who are standing along the roads and who are the first seen when one goes to a refugee camp. The critically ill people are in their houses, and are in the bush. They are not in sight. Only when people heard that a doctor was there did they bring out their very ill people for us to see, and then the impression we had was far, far different."

Taylor and Mayer now explained the Western survey's findings to Richardson. Mayer provided a thorough briefing on the logistical situation, not omitting the political factors that were causing delays in organizing relief. The two set forth what the survey meant in layman's terms: in brief, that the nutritional condition of many people was such that great numbers were dying—and were going to die, if food did not reach them soon.

Richardson seemed shaken by their exposition. Apparently he had never thoroughly understood what was at stake in Nigerian insistence on controlling relief and the Africa bureau/British cover-up of the fact that this Nigerian insistence was actually to block effective relief from ever commencing. As he left, walking along the corridor, Kissinger looked after him, shook his head, and said: "And he's supposed to be the most aggressive one at State."

On the first day of Harold Wilson's visit, President Nixon asked him: What are we going to do about Biafra? Wilson became very emotional, exclaiming: Oh, it's all Ojukwu's fault. If he hadn't done what he did last year, those people wouldn't be in the shape they're in now. Wilson went on this way excitedly for a couple of minutes, and Nixon, not wishing to cause difficulties at the outset of their talks, dropped the subject.

The next day, however, he brought it up again: Now, Harold, what are we going to do about Biafra? Again Wilson became excited, shouting: Oh, it's all Ojukwu's fault. If he hadn't done those things he did last year, all those people wouldn't be in the condition they're in now. Ojukwu did this, and he's going to have to pay in world history for what's happening now, etc. This time, Nixon waited until the prime minister calmed down, then said: Look, Harold. Two months from now, all those people are going to be dead, and no one is going to blame Ojukwu—they're going to blame *you*. Now here's what I think we must do. . . .

Nixon got Wilson to join him in sending a cable to their respective ambassadors in Lagos, instructing them to insist to the Nigerian government that it must allow relief to go through. Foreign Secretary Stewart and Secretary of State Rogers sought to moderate the wording of the cable, but Kissinger insisted it take a strong position.

At the same time, at the United Nations, Dick Heyward coordinated with the United States an approach to the Nigerian government. He spoke with Undersecretary General Ralph Bunche who then talked with U Thant, persuading him that the UN should join the U.S. in pressing Lagos to accept four points:

1) Helicopters should operate out of Enugu, Port Harcourt, and Calabar.

2) Uli and Obilagu airfields should be reactivated for planes bringing in food.

3) Officers and men of the First Division should be used to organize a food transport and distribution system in the northern sector.

4) The Federal Government should ask Nigerian businesses to make personnel available to administer the relief operation.

U Thant had just received a report from his representative that was not reassuring. After five days of traveling in the various areas, Said-Uddin Khan reported that the Nigerian Red Cross was providing food in some refugee camps and from roadside kitchens for those people walking to their former homes; " . . . their condition is bad. Many months of malnutrition and the present physical strain is visible on their faces. These people will soon reach their homes, but will still need assistance for a long time." Khan also found that people who had run into the bush out of fear had had very little access to food. The men were now beginning to come out and "as they shed their fear they will bring out the womenfolk."

The largest group in need were those living in the former Biafran area, Khan found: "Many months of privation and constant movement of troops by both sides over their land have left them completely destitute. They are undernourished, and without money or even seedlings to plant for their next crop." He reported that on January 21 the Nigerian Red Cross "had distributed enough CSM [corn, soya, and powdered milk] to provide one cup per head of 18,000 people and were not sure when they would reach the same people again. This obviously is not adequate."

That day, Anthony Lewis of the *New York Times*, who had continued traveling about the former Biafran area after the other journalists returned to Lagos, wrote in his column: "The Secretary-General of the United Nations, U Thant, flew into Nigeria the other day for what was described as a look at the relief situation after the war. He was tired, so he spent the afternoon resting in Lagos. That night he attended a dinner. The next day he was supposed to visit Port Harcourt, which would have put him only fifty miles from the area of real damage and suffering, but

he canceled the trip and, after some morning meetings with relief officials, he flew to Paris. At the airport he told the press that the relief
situation was well in hand and that Nigeria was doing a fine job."

Lewis then recounted some of the horrors U Thant would have seen
if he had traveled in the former Biafran area. He concluded: "Of course
U Thant does not know about any of this, because he saw nothing. The
only question is why he bothered to come to Nigeria. Perhaps he thought
it politic to say a good word for the winning side in a civil war—the side
favored by most U.N. members. Perhaps he thinks things will be wonderful if he says they are. . . . There are times to be angry. One of them
is when an international civil servant uses his position to suggest that there
is nothing to worry us in a situation actually stinking of human misery."

The United Nations spokesman, responding to this, stated that Thant
had made no assessment of the relief situation, he had only been quoting
Henrik Beer of the League of Red Cross Societies. Later, when Lewis
elaborated on his charge in a longer article in the *New York Times Magazine*, Thant had a UN undersecretary general write a letter to the *Times*
explaining that he had only been quoting what Henrik Beer had told him.

Chapter 30

After the briefing by Jean Mayer and Davida Taylor, Elliot Richardson asked Dr. Taylor to go to Nigeria and make an up-to-date survey of present conditions. Roger Morris had been in contention with State Department officials for days about the Western survey, Morris pressing to have its findings conveyed, with greatest urgency, to the top levels of the Nigerian government. This might appear quixotic, given State's knowledge that many within the FMG were either indifferent or vindictively committed to starving the Ibos. Morris reasoned that a true understanding of the gravity of starvation based on findings of an authoritative U.S. survey would arm General Gowon with facts to help him prevail over the hard-liners.

Only negligible amounts of food had been distributed during the two weeks following the collapse. Richardson told Taylor: We have conflicting reports: the AID team in Lagos reports there is no massive starvation; you say that a million people will die within a month. She agreed to go and was joined by Dr. George Lythcott, associate dean of Columbia Medical School, and Dr. Michael Latham of Cornell Medical School.

At the embassy in Lagos they found the staff proceeding at a casual pace, not taking seriously the gravity of the situation. They met with Ambassador William Truehart. Edward Marks and others of the AID team who had gone into the former Biafran area described the results of their observations. They had driven three hundred miles, stopping only once, and had seen no massive starvation. There were no vultures, and the children looked fat. Taylor told them of her own experience in Biafra, that the starving people were not out where they could be seen, that the people who would at first flock around the medical team would be the healthy-looking; only after a half-hour did they bring out of the houses in the bush those too weak to move by themselves.

There would be no vultures, she explained, because the Biafrans buried their dead within a few hours. The AID officials said: Well, of course, they were not familiar with Biafran customs and not qualified to make medical judgments. But you *have* been making medical judgments, the doctors exclaimed. After further discussion, Truehart broke off the meeting and cabled the State Department to disregard the earlier report.

Truehart had been under pressure for days to bring the Western survey to the attention of the Nigerian government and to push in other ways for action on relief. Not only were the Nigerians growing increasingly hostile because of these pressures but Truehart could not even get to meet with Gowon. He was caught between the hammer of White House insistence and the anvil of Nigerian resistance. A few days earlier, one of Richardson's assistants had been dispatched to lean on Truehart. Now, an army colonel from the National Security Council staff who accompanied the doctors—faced with delay, hesitation, and reluctance—pounded the table and exclaimed: "The president of the United States has ordered that this survey be done."

So it was done. Lythcott and Latham organized medical teams from the Nigerian Ministry of Health and got out into the field as quickly as possible. Taylor could not participate, however. She thought it best to inform the government she had been in Biafra; as soon as she did, her permission to travel in the area was revoked, and she departed for the United States. When security police came to the hotel the following morning to expel Colonel Dewey, they were also looking for Dr. Taylor to expel her, but she had already left.

By the third week after the fall of Biafra, a limited relief effort began getting under way. The Nigerian Red Cross was doing its best to provide food to those in need. Much of this, however, was being given to those walking back to their homes—one meal from a roadside kitchen, perhaps with an additional dry ration to carry with them. This did not represent relief organized on a continuing basis, assuring people of a daily ration. The 1,565 tons of food distributed during this last week of January compares with the average of 2,124 tons reaching people weekly on both sides of the conflict during the last month of the war, when relief had broken down on the Federal side.

British trucks were beginning to arrive—ninety-six four-ton Bedfords and forty-five Land Rovers, plus another thirty-two ten-ton trucks purchased in Nigeria. Some were shipped directly to Port Harcourt, but those flown to Lagos and driven overland were delayed by heavy congestion at the ferry crossing of the Niger River. (Permission had been denied to fly the trucks to Enugu or Port Harcourt, let alone to Uli, Uga or Obilagu.) The downed bridge across the Niger River at Onitsha could have been replaced in a few days with a temporary span by the British Royal Engineers the FMG had refused to admit.

Once the new trucks reached the area, the Nigerian Red Cross was able to step up its food distribution: during the first week in February, 2,307 tons were distributed. However, the U.S. trucks that had by now arrived in Lagos never would join the relief action. Some were just taken over outright by the National Rehabilitation Commission. (Later, when the U.S. General Accounting Office sought to investigate what had become of American contributions to relief, the Nigerian government refused its personnel entry into the country.) Other trucks were still standing at Lagos airport months later, loaded with blankets and generators, the holdup attributed to the need to "service" and "license" them.

Numerous efforts to move food within the country were resisted by Nigerian authorities. UNICEF chartered two DC-6s in Europe and tried to get them accepted for food distribution inside Nigeria before having to cancel the charter. Washington sought to persuade the Nigerian government to accept planes or helicopters, even offering to turn the C-97Gs over to the Nigerians themselves to operate. (Two of them flew to Enugu and Port Harcourt airports as a test and found that those airfields could not take the weight of a loaded C-97G; Uli, of course, could have.)

There was no problem keeping foodstocks up, given the limited distribution. Adequate quantities were arriving in the country, and small coastal vessels provided by UNICEF, governments, and Red Cross societies began carrying supplies from Lagos to Port Harcourt.

Relief was better in the northern sector, where the First Division was more disciplined and where some of its officers and men were beginning to help. The chaos created in the southern sector by Third Division troops—now being brought under better control—was compounded by the fact that this area had been fought over in seesaw battles, frequently cutting people off from food for long periods. All observers reported: Owerri and the area north toward Orlu was the sector with the largest number of people in the worst shape.

Efforts were being made to restore the old sick bays, as well as hospitals that had been abandoned and plundered. The Nigerian Red Cross teams in the area all along were being augmented. Some sixty Ibo doctors and three hundred Ibo nurses were now back in the hospitals, but not all former Biafran medical personnel presenting themselves at Enugu were being put to work. Since the end of the war, twenty doctors and twenty-nine nurses had arrived from abroad. Medical teams had been provided by the Red Cross societies of Australia, Austria, Japan, and Switzerland. The British sent doctors and nurses through the British Red Cross and Save the Children Fund.

After the government overruled the Nigerian Red Cross appeal for doctors and nurses and warned that all such requests must come from the FMG, it had only once acceded to a request to send personnel, when Maurice Foley was in Lagos. There were now 96 foreign and 337 Nigerian Red Cross personnel operating in the southern sector. This was entirely inadequate, but the government ruled that no field organizers, warehousemen, transport supervisors, or other administrative personnel would be admitted to the country from abroad. While the FMG had said it would allow in medical staff, it was now refusing to do so.

This was a cause of great concern among the international relief agencies still trying to work under the aegis of the Nigerian Red Cross and still meeting every week in Lagos as they had during the war. They discussed the need for building up the medical and relief teams; though previous requests for relief workers had been turned down by the government, they wondered whether they should not ask again. The Nigerian Red Cross was still pressing for an additional fifteen doctors and thirty nurses from overseas, but Lagos was now taking the position that the emergency would be over by the end of the following month and the Red Cross should turn its relief action over to rehabilitation commissions at the state level on March 31.

Lythcott and Latham returned from the field with the five survey teams organized through the health ministry and the Nigerian Red Cross. The doctors had visited sixty localities, examining a total of 3,000 persons. They had also looked into houses to find sick persons, checked food stocks on hand in households, and sought to ascertain the ability of each family to purchase food. They aimed at a representative sampling of the affected area.

Out of an estimated population of 5,810,000, the American and Nigerian doctors found that some 970,000 were suffering edema, marasmus, or kwashiorkor. As always, the highest rate was among children under five, 31.4 percent of them showing signs of severe malnutrition. This represented 480,000 small children, plus an additional 180,000 under the age of fourteen with such symptoms. The other age group seriously affected, the elderly, had a malnutrition rate of 22 percent, which meant that some 170,000 were in need of feeding and special care.

These figures were somewhat lower than the findings of the Western survey three-and-a-half months earlier. Statistics tend to mislead; it is necessary to keep in mind that the 31.4 percent of the children under five found suffering edema, marasmus, or kwashiorkor in early February 1970 were not the same children as the 42.2 percent under four in that condition the previous October. Many of the latter had died, their statistical numbers being replaced by those who slipped from moderate to severe malnutrition, then into death, and so on.

This changing condition of the population was shown in a report, "New Cases of Severe and Moderate Malnutrition," prepared by the Nigerian Red Cross medical adviser in the northern sector during the period January 10 to February 21. There was a sharp rise in malnutrition during the four weeks following the end of the war—from about 800 new cases of severe and moderate malnutrition each week to a peak of about 4,100 a week by February 7. Then there was a leveling off at around 3,500 new cases a week. (Very likely, there was a higher rate of new cases in the southern sector.)

The report of the survey teams finally made a difference in Lagos, having been carried out by the Ministry of Health and Nigerian doctors. General Gowon was able to accept the helicopters the United States had been pressing upon his government since the day of Biafra's collapse. One German and four U.S. helicopters started delivering food in mid-February, though the original point in offering them had largely been lost. Now that the trucks had reached the field, food was moving even if the overall relief operation was insufficient.

The doctors who conducted the nutritional survey estimated the total tonnage needed each week at 4,155 tons. This would provide full feedings for the 60,000 people in hospitals, sick bays, orphanages, and refugee camps and the 660,000 children identified as malnourished; plus supplemental, partial feeding for the malnourished adults, pregnant women, nursing mothers, and those children one to four who did not show symptoms of malnutrition—a total of some 2,160,000. In making this estimate the doctors warned: "It is recognized that the caloric intake for the outpatient malnourished population is insufficient to meet full caloric need and will require supplementation with equal quantities of local food."

This estimate was only what was required for the malnourished population surveyed, however, as the doctors made clear: "The above estimate provides no food however for the 1½ million hungry people currently receiving food to supplement limited supplies of locally available food or the population in unsurveyed war-affected areas. Without more information on the availability or non-availability of local food supplies, the food requirements in excess of the 4,000 tons calculated above cannot be estimated." Their report stated: "At this time it is estimated that feeding will be required till the fall harvest."

This level of feeding was never to be attained. By the second week of February, the Nigerian Red Cross managed to distribute 3,086 tons; by the week ending February 21, 3,266.5 tons; and by the end of the month,

3,219 tons. There was a slight falling off in distribution during the first week in March; then the relief effort attained its peak, distributing 3,775.1 tons of food during the week ending March 14; 3,994.2 tons in the week ending March 21; and 3,403.9 tons during the last week of the month.

Thus the relief operation never managed to achieve food distribution at the minimum the February survey estimated as needed. Nor did it reach the target set by the Nigerian Red Cross, variously spoken of as 4,200 or 4,500 tons a week. And it fell far short of the 38,000 tons a month earlier called for by Dr. Karl Western and his colleagues.

The relief effort, such as it was, had no sooner gotten under way than the hard-liners in the Nigerian government set about to bring it to an end. By early February they were telling the Nigerian Red Cross to conclude its role by March 31; it was within the framework of the NRC that the various relief agencies were managing to organize what limited relief there was. In his press conference the day after Biafra's surrender, Chief Enahoro had said that the urgent relief problem would be ended that month, and within three months relief would give way to rehabilitation.

With the government now telling relief agencies that the NRC must turn over relief to the state rehabilitation commissions by the end of March, long-term planning became impossible. Requests for delivery of food during the months ahead could not go forward. As the doctors said in their survey, feeding would be required until the fall harvest—September at the earliest—but no one could now be sure there would be a relief organizational structure through which to continue distribution.

By this time, the public had turned away from the Biafran problem. The Nigerian government, following the initial press reaction, was allowing no journalists into the area. Relief agencies knew what was going on, however, as did governments. Officials who traveled there were dismayed at what they found, in contrast to the reassuring briefings they received in Lagos. The senior nutritionist of UNICEF made a tour at the end of February and beginning of March. He saw considerable starvation among adults in sick bays and kwashiorkor among the children. Food deliveries were on a more or less hand-to-mouth basis, and he estimated that at least twice the amount of food being distributed was needed. Relief teams were trying to select for feeding those most seriously in need. Deliveries of locally purchased food were lagging. (In fact, while there was considerable talk of buying food in Nigeria, only a quarter came from "local purchase" during the postwar period; the rest had to be imported by relief agencies.)

The UNICEF nutrition expert found that there was simply not

enough food moving into the area. There were not enough trucks. The National Rehabilitation Commission had "requisitioned" Nigerian Red Cross trucks, and those that had arrived in Lagos in late January were still there. Some twenty-five or thirty, plus other, lighter vehicles, were being held at the docks at Apapa harbor (Lagos), ostensibly for customs clearance. The UNICEF nutritionist found personnel for supervisory relief operations "thin at all points" and heard reports of one hundred or more Ibo doctors sitting around in Enugu waiting to be assigned work, though there were not sufficient medical personnel in the area. Other relief officials brought out similar reports, but not for the public: they feared they might suffer the fate of Colonel Dewey and the journalists. A curtain of silence had descended over the eastern area of Nigeria.

Odumegwu Ojukwu, in exile in the Ivory Coast, believed that what the Nigerians were doing was intended "to devitalize the Ibos."

Secretary of State William Rogers paid a visit to Lagos. There was much fence-mending to do, as the Nigerians were very angry over the pressure they had received from the White House. State Department officials did everything they could to placate the FMG. There were, for example, more than five hundred Ibo students studying at universities in the United States who were suddenly cut off from what funds they had been receiving from home. Many were in desperate straits, some eating only once a day. The Nigerian government told them to return home—"to help rebuild the nation." Most were skeptical of this, even terrified. Obviously, to break off in the middle of their studies was not going to benefit their "nation"; presumably there were people in the Nigerian government who did not want Ibos getting any more education.

The Ibo students knew generally of conditions in their homeland, but were not at all sure of the fate of their families and friends. Rumors flew among them, such as one that fourteen students had returned, had boarded a truck in Lagos bound for Iboland, but never arrived. They had no intention of returning to an uncertain future or, they feared at the time, death.

U.S. Assistant Secretary for Educational and Cultural Affairs John Richardson had been active, while still in private life, in support of humanitarian relief for Biafra. As it happened, there was as much as a million dollars in his State Department budget that could have been made available to help these students continue their education. But since the Nigerian government had ordered them to return home, the Bureau of African Affairs—trying harder than ever not to offend Lagos—blocked the use of any State Department funds for this purpose.

The Africa bureau's dogged stand did little good. A copy of the Lythcott-Latham nutritional survey was leaked to the *Washington Star*. As the FMG had authorized it only after the U.S. promised the results would never be released, its publication nearly brought a break between Lagos and Washington. This, added to anger over American support for relief and White House pressures following the war, created bad relations between the United States and Nigeria for years afterward.

Pressures from the U.S. and other governments did keep the Nigerian government from ending the role of the Nigerian Red Cross on March 31. But the lack of forward planning and needed medical personnel caused a falling off in the relief effort from its peak during the last three weeks in March. The NRC was next put on notice that it should bring its activities to an end by April 30. More alarm, more pressures from governments. The Red Cross was allowed to continue with the understanding that it would phase out its operations and turn relief over to the state rehabilitation commissions by June 30.

In order to phase out, the Nigerian Red Cross made a drastic cutback on May 9 in the amount of food being distributed and the numbers being fed, switching over to "very selective feeding for the vulnerable groups and a milk program for children." The situation was so grave that relief workers of the other agencies working in the country under the aegis of the Red Cross issued a "Declaration of Conscience." Gowon suggested to the hard-liners, Look, we won't be bothered by these governments if we allow some relief to go in. So, at the beginning of June, the FMG began saying: Why don't you get in 1,100 tons of food a week (which would have been twice the amount by then being distributed)?

But it was too late to build up again. The Nigerian Red Cross finally ended its role on June 30. Those being fed by the relief action were suddenly without food. Malnutrition had been on the rise, people were still starving in what had been Biafra until six months before. Many were still without money with which to purchase food. (Though the government had called in all Biafran currency, announcing that Federal currency would replace it, a maximum payment of twenty pounds was finally decreed. In Nigeria, the money paid an official to get anything done is known as "dash"; when people went to pick up their twenty pounds, they found some of it already gone, as they had to pay "dash" to get the payment.)

When food distribution was cut off, the harvest was still two months away. Jessie Zimmerman was in the area, working with the International Union of Child Welfare, preparing the repatriation of some five thousand children who had been taken from Biafra to other countries during the war. She had a million Swiss francs to draw upon, so she began hiring commercial trucks to move food. Later, when she was about to be declared persona non grata and expelled, supposedly for a minor infraction, she was summoned before the Supreme Military Council.

General Gowon wanted to know what she had done. When it came out that "this woman" had gone out and hired trucks, without authorization, and had begun distributing food, Gowon rebuked the representatives of state governments present for not having made adequate provision for taking over relief. She was not declared persona non grata.

Malnutrition and starvation continued for the remainder of that year.

How many died?

Writing a retrospective piece a year later, a correspondent of the *Washington Post* summed up the whole episode, presumably after checking with officials, in the internally contradictory statement: "No one knows how many persons died from starvation as a result of the Nigerian Civil War that ended in January 1970, but current estimates place the total at closer to 1 million than the 2 million once feared. Many of these were children. . . ."

Epilogue

A decade-and-a-half later, starvation affected millions of people in many countries of Africa, and governments and the public responded with a massive outpouring of humanitarian aid and compassion. The international community is now better organized to meet such emergencies and has done so—in Bangladesh, the Sahel, Ethiopia, Kampuchea (Cambodia), and now Africa—on a scale far beyond anything that would have been needed during the Nigerian-Biafran war.

Drought, desertification, and deforestation all contributed to the African famine of the 1980s, but underlying this vast tragedy are structural defects within many sub-Saharan African countries. United Nations agencies are attempting to assist governments to overcome problems that threaten further deterioration of their economies and prolonged suffering of their people.

Reform is not likely for one of the most fundamental of these problems: most of the African nations shaped by colonial interests, with boundaries cutting across tribal lines, are proving nonviable. In many countries where famine has been worst, those most seriously affected have been peoples with whom the central government in the capital has long been at war—for example, in Eritrea and Tigre province in the north of Ethiopia or in the southern Sudan, where war went on for fifteen years and has now begun again.

Ironically, one economically verdant area of Africa is to be found in the east of Nigeria, now known as Anambra and Imo states. Their capital cities of Enugu and Owerri are more than twice as large as they were before the Biafran secession. It took the Ibos awhile to recover and restore their countryside to the economically prosperous corner of Africa it has now become. General Gowon did insist upon a reconciliation following the end of the war in 1970. Not everyone in the Nigerian government agreed, and for a long time the former Biafrans felt deprived and inclined to think it was Federal policy not to give them their fair share of the revenues flowing from the growing oil wealth. They turned in upon themselves, resolved to make the most of their difficult situation, determined to rebuild the war-stricken area, and did so with their usual industriousness and ingenuity. Few ventured out of Iboland to other tribal regions as they had before the war. Gowon's reconciliation policy, however, allowed some to take up roles as executives with foreign companies, and a number of lower-ranking military officers were even reintegrated back into the army.

As the former Biafrans concentrated upon reconstructing their homeland, however, they had to do so within the federation, and Nigeria has proved an uneasy national structure within which to work. In 1975, General Murtala Mohammed (who had commanded the First Division on the northern front during the war) became head of state following a coup d'état that sent Gowon into exile, to study at Warwick University in England.

The following year, Mohammed was assassinated in another—aborted—coup, following which General Olusegun Obasanjo (who had commanded the Third Division on the southern front during the latter part of the war) took over. The government charged Gowon with complicity in the plot and sought his extradition from England. Britain declined, but Gowon had to go into hiding.

Finally, in 1979, the military made good on its long-delayed promise to return the country to civilian rule, and a government modeled on the United States system was elected. On the last day of 1983, Major General Mohammed Buhari ended the civilian administration of President Shehu Shagari with a coup aimed at eliminating, once and for all, the corruption that has plagued Nigeria. (Corruption, it will be remembered, had been the issue that precipitated the first coup d'état in 1966 that brought to an end the first civilian government.)

Corruption had become epidemic after the war as oil revenues began flowing in; many military officers and others acquired fortunes. The most notable instance: government purchasing agents went around the world entering into contracts (presumably from which they profited), and when 20 million tons of cement began arriving, hundreds of ships tied up Apapa harbor for months, running up huge demurrage fees and paralyzing commerce in the Lagos port.

General Buhari organized a puritan administration whose first act was to round up many of the old politicians and lock them up for a time. One of those caught up in the sweep was Odumegwu Ojukwu, whom President Shagari had pardoned and allowed to return from exile in the

Ivory Coast, presumably to benefit Shagari among the Ibos in his bid for reelection.

The austere regime also brought repression, including curtailment of the press as well as a ban on criticism of the government, and in August 1985 army officers ousted Buhari in a coup led by General Ibrahim Babangida.

What of the British, who had so staunchly gone down the line in support of Nigeria throughout the war? The pride and xenophobia that seized the Nigerians in the days following the war's conclusion led to what they called "indigenization" of business. Increasing "Nigerianization" led finally to the government nationalizing of the operations of British Petroleum in July 1979.

Meanwhile, Harold Wilson became Lord Wilson of Rievaulx; Michael Stewart, Lord Stewart of Fulham; and George Thomson, Lord Thomson of Monifieth.

Oil production rose following the war till it approached 2.5 million barrels a day. When OPEC, of which Nigeria is a member, greatly boosted oil prices in the mid-seventies, the revenues rolled into the central treasury. Some were disbursed to the states, and when the government increased the number of states from twelve (the division that had precipitated Biafra's decision to secede) to nineteen, thereby breaking up Iboland into Anambra and Imo states, some Ibos felt that they benefited by receiving an added share of the revenue.

Not all of the petrol dollars that made up 90 percent of Nigeria's foreign exchange earnings were diverted by corruption; a large portion, indeed, was turned to the development of the whole nation—united Nigeria. Most notably, an ambitious program to get all the children in the country into primary education was undertaken, and the goal has been largely attained.

As a petroleum-exporting country Nigeria benefited from the higher prices of fuel and fertilizers that damaged the economic development of the many nations that had to import oil. Its revenues in the seventies led to extravagant imports, however; though Nigeria embarked on a number of drives to increase food production (President Shagari called his the "Green Revolution"), the country in fact imported more and more—even frozen chickens from Alabama.

As a result, in the 1980s the government has been beset by some of the same problems afflicting other nations in Africa and throughout the world affected by the global recession. As oil glutted the world market and OPEC had to cut production and prices a number of times, Nigeria has found itself overextended.

Like many other developing countries it had concentrated on the big projects intended to bring instant industrialization. Modernization of the few cities, while the rural areas remained to a large extent neglected, resulted in a flight from the villages by young people attracted to the false promise of urban living.

Shantytowns have given their inhabitants not the good life but unemployment, malnutrition, sewage, disease, violence, and crime. In Nigeria crime has become so serious that the government at times has resorted to public executions in an attempt to curb the organized bands of highwaymen and the pirates preying upon crews of ships in Lagos harbor.

As one Nigerian publication commented, "In the cities where they found themselves, thousands of jobless young men and women live in squalid, overcrowded slums. . . . The slums quickly became hotbeds for criminal hoodlums and organized thuggery. The scale of petty and organized crime in Nigerian cities beggars the imagination. Extortion and protection rackets, ritual murders, kidnapping and arson make newspaper headlines almost every week. Mention the name 'armed robbers' and Nigerian city dwellers visibly shake with fear."

As oil prices declined in the early 1980s, Nigeria, like many developing countries with a brief boom in commodity prices, borrowed heavily to keep projects going; the debt burden has now curtailed development.

The human consequences were dramatized in 1983 and again in 1985 by the expulsion of hundreds of thousands of illegal workers forced to return home to neighboring countries. The effect on Nigerians may be less obvious to the world but, as UNICEF's "State of the World's Children" reported at the end of 1984: ". . . despite the massive oil wealth that poured into Nigeria in the 1970s, it is now clear that many sections of the population, particularly the poorer and more vulnerable groups, did not receive the social benefits that might have been expected to accrue."

To reform the unbalanced development that stressed industrial projects, while neglecting rural people, the World Bank has set in motion a program of action encouraged by special funds to help African nations with programs of health, education, population control, and agricultural research to improve local farming.

It is an interesting turn of history that the necessity for the Ibos to rely largely upon themselves to rebuild their land during the postwar period has resulted in the former Biafran area being one of the economically bustling parts of Nigeria and Africa. To indulge in the historical subjunctive: what would Biafra have become as an independent nation? It would be more populous than twenty-nine of the thirty-eight countries of sub-Saharan Africa, but how prosperous it would be would depend on how much of the oil it had been able to secede with.

What is to be learned from the Biafran experience? The response to the African famine emergency might suggest that the world will no longer stand by while millions face starvation. Yet there have been a number of situations since Biafra in which political problems caused long delays before the international agencies could begin humanitarian relief, only after large numbers had starved.

Many months passed as the Pakistani Army carried out its mopping-up operations in East Pakistan, before the outpouring of some ten million refugees from what was to become Bangladesh finally provoked India into war with Pakistan. Only then did the United Nations begin the huge relief operation that might have forestalled the conflict if it had started earlier.

As Haile Selassie was one of the few statesmen who had actively sought to do something about starvation in Biafra, it is ironic that his downfall a few years later came about through his government's attempt to cover up famine in Ethiopia so it would not reflect upon the emperor. More than six months went by before international agencies could begin aiding people in Wollo and Tigre provinces. At the same time, governments across the Sahel of Africa delayed relief for months because they had no concern about the nomadic Tuaregs—a people different from their own, who were dying along with their cattle.

In 1979, it fell to Jacques Beaumont to play quite a different role from the one he had undertaken on behalf of the Nigerian government a decade earlier. By this time he had become head of UNICEF's Indochina operations. Long before others were aware of the problem, he sought to find a way to get the UN involved in providing food to the people of Kampuchea (Cambodia), half-starved already from the period of genocide under Pol Pot and now facing total starvation as a result of disruption of the country following invasion by the Vietnamese Army.

Beaumont went to Phnom Penh with an ICRC delegate seeking to gain access to the Khmer people in the stricken countryside. He remained in the Cambodian capital for fifty days, singlehandedly organizing teams of Khmer students to unload the occasional Red Cross plane. UNICEF and the ICRC had to insist on providing food impartially to victims on both sides of the conflict; the regime in Phnom Penh did not want relief going to people under Pol Pot, with whom they and the Vietnamese Army were still fighting. Not till hundreds of thousands of emaciated people stumbled or were carried across the border into Thailand did the break-through finally come that allowed relief to begin on the scale needed.

In the autumn of 1983, Beaumont, by then director of emergency operations for UNICEF, began attempting within the UN to get relief organized to meet the overwhelming famine in Africa, which only came to public attention a year later. His initiatives in both Kampuchea and the Africa famine, contrasted with his earlier role during Nigeria-Biafra, make the point that institutional behavior is not the same as personal behavior. The same men who carried on the cover-up about relief in Biafra, given a different institutional role, would in all likelihood have acted with equal determination to get food into the beleaguered enclave.

The ambassadors in Lagos and diplomats in foreign offices making these decisions were not evil men. On the contrary, they were, if anything, more ethically sensitive and morally responsible than most people. Most were under pressure from colleagues, friends, and even their own families to do something about the starvation. They were obeying not their own personal standard of morality but that of the institutional framework within which they were operating. They felt compelled to carry out acts on behalf of what they saw as their nation's interest that went contrary to their own personal ethics.

As a result, they did not wholly believe the reports of starvation, preferring to regard them as greatly exaggerated Biafran propaganda. They came to believe their own propaganda, that it was Ojukwu who was refusing to agree to reasonable proposals acceptable to the Nigerians, as the Biafrans needed the starvation to evoke world sympathy for their political cause. And they came to indulge in a defense mechanism to deny their own guilt by becoming very excited when the subject came up, blaming Ojukwu in an angry way for what he was doing—when in fact it was they who were doing it.

Thus, the propaganda line they propagated to mislead others became internalized and misled them as well. As George Orwell wrote in *1984*: ". . . To know and not to know, to be conscious of complete truthfulness while telling carefully constructed lies, to hold simultaneously two opinions which cancelled out, knowing them to be contradictory and believing in both of them, to use logic against logic, to repudiate morality while laying claim to it . . ."

Those making policy for their nations in this situation took only a short-term, day-to-day view of their "nation's interest." At the working level, it seemed all-important to them not to lose influence with Nigeria, the largest nation in Africa, with great potential for business and trade. They feared that the Soviet Union would gain entrance to West Africa through its supply of arms. Those in Lagos had to meet every day with government ministers who were angered by any assistance going to "the rebels." This was the crucible of day-to-day reality that formed their policy decisions. They disregarded the emotional concern of citizens and legislators in their own country, rooted in traditional morality, as irrelevant to the reality with which they had to grapple.

The public in Europe and North America reacted in an exemplary way when they became aware that large numbers of children were starving and even greater numbers faced death if food did not soon reach them in massive quantities. The ad hoc groups that came into being in many countries were remarkable in their number, the intensity of their commitment, and the fact that they extended across the breadth of the political spectrum. They concentrated, however, on the government of their own country. The diplomats, on the other hand, in regular touch with each other internationally, colluded to manage this pressure, which pushed them to do what they could not or did not want to attempt.

When massive starvation began, those responsible for foreign policy of their governments did not see this changed situation as requiring of them a different response. In the long term, their nation had an interest in seeking observance of the Geneva Conventions, gaining support for the Red Cross and other humanitarian agencies, and helping move the world a bit farther along toward a more humane civilization. The long view of what might be in the interest of their nation or of humankind did not, however, figure prominently in their thinking: within bureaucracies there is an inner dynamic that impedes reexamining policies once they have been set in motion. The decision makers at the working level would have had to be overruled by the political leaders, and this seldom happened.

Fragmented as the efforts of private citizens and groups were from country to country—pressing only their own government to act, never fully comprehending the concerted effort being mounted to keep their appeals ineffective—they succeeded for a time, in a limited way, before being defeated by the diplomatic-propaganda campaign.

Only the large international relief agencies had organization enough to act and then because the priests, ministers, and others had the courage to defy governments and fly an airlift that diplomats denounced as "illegal." In doing so they surprised themselves with the ecumenical spirit in which they worked and were emboldened to persevere in the face of great pressures from governments, something they might have been reluctant or unable to do if they had attempted to act separately and not under the umbrella of Joint Church Aid.

JCA suggests an analogy for what is needed on an ongoing basis to sustain the drive for human rights and humanitarian action and to bring governments back to a position of rectitude to their obligations under the existing conventions.

Alone, no one of the many international organizations is a match for governments. They can do good work but, separately, they do not have the impact necessary to restrain nations from gross violations of human rights. Most are specialized, having a specific mission to perform that often must be given priority over their commitment to human rights or humanitarian action. Frequently they are dependent on the goodwill or support of governments. They do not possess the resources of information comparable to those available to governments through diplomatic and intelligence-gathering services. It is difficult for private agencies or individuals to counter the propaganda organized by governments. They cannot command the attention of the media as readily as governments, nor are they accorded the same credibility as foreign office spokesmen. The information produced by one organization may not be picked up and given wider dissemination by others. They do not coordinate their actions in support of human rights or draw upon one another for support as fully as they might in situations where humanitarian action is urgently needed.

The relief agencies lack the financial resources to mount an effort large enough or sustain it long enough to have an effective impact. They have not established a common goal of working to implement the humanitarian and human rights conventions. Most protest activities take place within each country, directed by its citizens against their own government, with little contact, exchange of information, coordination, or mutual support between them and people in other countries. Governments, frequently acting in concert, make short work of this fragmented activity.

Yet the basis for action exists in the impressive body of humanitarian and human rights law that has been created over the past four decades: the United Nations Charter, the Geneva Conventions and their Protocols, the Universal Declaration of Human Rights, the Convention on the Prevention and Punishment of Genocide, and the International Covenants on Human Rights.

The potential of these conventions is great. To cite only a few of their provisions is to remind ourselves how far the world is from implementing them but how great are their possibilities:

• Article 5 of the Declaration of Human Rights provides that "no one shall be subjected to torture or cruel, inhuman or degrading treatment or punishment."

• The Genocide Convention prohibits "deliberately inflicting on the group conditions of life calculated to bring about its physical destruction in whole or in part."

- Article 3 of the Geneva Conventions requires that in civil wars "persons taking no active part in the hostilities . . . shall in all circumstances be treated humanely . . ."
- The International Covenant on Civil and Political Rights says that "everyone shall have the right to freedom of expression; this right shall include freedom to seek, receive and impart information and ideas of all kinds, regardless of frontiers, either orally, in writing or in print, in the form of art, or through any media of his choice."
- Article 7 of the International Covenant on Economic, Social and Cultural Rights insures "fair wages and equal remuneration for work of equal value without distinction of any kind, in particular women being guaranteed conditions of work not inferior to those enjoyed by men, with equal pay for equal work."
- Article 54 of the first Protocol to the Geneva Conventions states: "Starvation of civilians as a method of warfare is prohibited."

This body of law might be likened to the Magna Carta: mankind has set about to place restraints upon the sovereign. The Magna Carta did not become effective the day it was signed at Runnymede; centuries of effort were required before limits were finally imposed upon the powers of the king. Today's sovereigns—nations—are no more willing to accept restraints upon themselves.

There is a natural complicity among governments to preserve the sovereignty of nations. As the International Conference on Human Rights observed at the time of Biafra, nations parties to the Geneva Conventions "sometimes fail to appreciate their responsibility to take steps to insure the respect of these humanitarian rules in all circumstances by other States, even if they are not themselves directly involved in an armed conflict."

The interests of governments, as we have seen in the Biafran situation, are not always the interests of the human beings caught up in some man-made catastrophe. All of us, as human beings, have an interest in supporting the human rights and humanitarian conventions. Those of us who have the good fortune to live in democratic countries with representative governments can insist to a greater degree on strengthening human rights and humanitarian law and upon its observance by other nations as well as our own. However, something more is needed.

There is now emerging in the world a human rights movement. It needs strengthening with funds, a secretariat, a working coalition that can act in situations beyond the capacity of any of the separate participants. Individuals can play a role as well as organizations; neutral governments should provide diplomatic support, and other countries committed to human rights and humanitarian action should contribute funds and assist politically.

Such a coalition of individuals and private organizations with government support could sustain the long-term action needed. The humanitarian and human rights conventions are sometimes spoken of as "the public conscience." For the most part, however, the public conscience has yet to be created. That this can be done is suggested by the success of the International Red Cross in diffusing, over more than a century, the principles of the Geneva Conventions. Today, public outrage at the bombing of hospitals, the abuse of prisoners of war, or the killing of innocent civilians reflects this century of work, of educating people to the idea that such acts are "illegal." The new conventions provide a basis on which to extend the effort of creating a public conscience that will increasingly restrain governments and others from excesses. It may well be the work of another century.

What happened to the children of Biafra—how it was done—reveals the need for a human-rights and humanitarian-action coalition to prevent such brutality and suffering in man-made disasters of the future.

Notes, Acknowledgments, and Index

Notes

Prologue

4   **correct bureaucratic behavior:** To indicate from the outset the author's own involvement, the "someone at the UN" was myself. As the person at the UN authorized to talk with the press about humanitarian relief in Nigeria-Biafra, I received a copy of the cable. When no action had been taken on it by the secretary general's office, I took it to George Orick who, like me, was a consultant to UNICEF, saying, "This is terrible. This cable has been here for days and nothing is being done about it." He said, "Well, what can we do?" And I replied, "We can leak it." He said, "How do we do that?" I suggested: "Well, we shouldn't do it here in New York, as they'll suspect us. Why don't you give it to Lloyd Garrison in Paris." Orick and Garrison had been friends in Nigeria, so George telephoned Garrison and read him the cable, then telexed it to him through the *New York Times*. Garrison dissembled so well, making it sound as though he had obtained the cable from humanitarian agency officials in Europe, that people at the United Nations never suspected it was in fact the cable that had come into the secretary general's office—which he denied receiving—that had been leaked.

6   **great resistance of government representatives:** During the meeting being held in the early 1970s by the International Committee of the Red Cross to begin revising the Geneva Conventions, the Nigerian delegate made an excited and emotional presentation about all the troubles his government had had during the Biafran war. "Our airspace was violated," one delegate who was present reports him saying. "We are an unsophisticated people. We don't have radar. Planes were flying over our territory and violating our sovereignty." He spoke with bitterness of the way other nations had allowed their relief agencies to intervene in the internal affairs of his country and warned the other government representatives against making their nations vulnerable to similar activities. At this, other delegates backed away from some of the proposals intended to strengthen the Geneva Conventions.

Chapter 1

13   **Enahoro wrote M.P.s:** Chief Enahoro had been imprisoned a few years before along with Chief Obafemi Awolowo, charged by the first Nigerian government with having plotted a coup in 1962. By this time, in 1968, Chief Enahoro had become minister of information and Chief Awolowo the minister of finance of

the Federal Military Government. They were the kind of experienced political men who surrounded General Gowon.

British military adviser: The report by Colonel Robert E. Scott, "An Appreciation of the Nigerian Conflict," appeared in the London *Sunday Telegraph* on January 11, 1970—at the moment, as it happened, that Biafra began to collapse. He analyzed thoroughly the strengths and weaknesses of both sides in the conflict, giving many details of Nigerian military capabilities—and lack thereof. Publication of the confidential document angered Nigerians. It also resulted, a year later, in a sensational Official Secrets Act trial of Jonathan Aitken (the correspondent who provided the "Scott report" to the newspaper), the editor of the *Sunday Telegraph,* and a hapless colonel who would seem to have been indicted in lieu of the general who Aitken claimed had passed the report on to him. (Presumably the Crown did not wish to bring him to trial since he had been one of the government's strongest supporters on Nigeria.) The government did not succeed in persuading the jurors that these three were guilty. The trial, however, revealed a great deal about the British system of secrecy, as well as much about Britain's involvement in the Nigerian-Biafran war. Aitken has written about this in his book *Officially Secret* (Weidenfeld and Nicolson, 1971).

one of the government's critics: George Knapp discovered the Nigerian arms statistics. Suzanne Cronje, in her book *The World and Nigeria* (Sidgwick & Jackson, 1972), appendix 2, provides a breakdown of the value of these imports of ground weapons from 1967 through 1969.

14 **prepared a policy statement:** Michael Stewart later told me he had assumed responsibility for the government's position during this debate when George Thomson had not been able to be present. He said the statement had been prepared beforehand and was not just something he stated in the course of the debate.

Stewart had not had great experience in international affairs (he had been in education), having become foreign secretary when Patrick Gordon-Walker lost his seat in Parliament. It seems likely that at this time he did not play a major role in formulating policy.

During this initial, crucial period, policy would appear to have arisen, first, through the energetic initiatives of Sir David Hunt, the British high commissioner, in close collaboration with ministers of the Nigerian government; and, back in London, with Donald Tebbit in the Commonwealth Office. It is an interesting question at what point Prime Minister Harold Wilson and Stewart became fully cognizant of the Nigerian situation. Hunt initially briefed the prime minister in early August 1967 and assumed that this would have been the first time Wilson became personally involved.

15 **four African nations:** Tanzania, Gabon, the Ivory Coast, and Zambia.

16 **the wording of the government's note is revealing:** This April 10, 1968 note, on which ICRC officials based the legality for their relief flights into Biafra until June 5, 1969 (though at least some officials of the Nigerian government apparently did not agree with their interpretation of its continuing validity), is to be found in *Face au blocus,* originally a doctoral dissertation, by Thierry Hentsch (Institut Universitaire de Hautes Etudes Internationales, 1973). Hentsch served as an assistant to the ICRC president in 1969. He was later given access to the

ICRC archives (not customarily provided scholars or others outside the ICRC) for purposes of writing this dissertation. He reproduces the April 10, 1968, note in footnote 90, pp. 74–75.

former ICRC delegate: Georg Hoffmann, who went to the Kampala conference on behalf of the International Committee of the Red Cross, had been withdrawn as Red Cross West Africa delegate in Lagos, according to his own account, in January 1968 because ICRC officials in Geneva had come to regard him as too "pro-Gowon."

Chapter 2

18–
19
a dynamic, progressive, and ambitious people: Their education and abilities did not endear them to those among whom they lived. Even during British rule there had been massacres of Ibos in Northern Nigeria: in Jos in 1945 and in Kano in 1953. The Ibos acquired the sobriquet "The Jews of Africa."

19
potential civil war: The Biafran head of state, Odumegwu Ojukwu, addressing the Addis Ababa conference on August 5, 1968, provided the delegates with an extended historical account of the troubles leading up to and precipitating the Nigerian-Biafran conflict. He quoted the late premier of Northern Nigeria, Sir Ahmadu Bello, as having stated: "Politicians always delight in talking loosely about the unity of Nigeria. Sixty years ago there was no country called Nigeria. What is now Nigeria consisted of a number of large and small communities all of which were different in their outlooks and beliefs. The advent of the British and of Western education has not materially altered the situation and these many and varied communities have not knit themselves into a complete unit."

government asked Ironsi: In a detailed account of the January and July 1966 coups, Robin Luckham explores whether General Ironsi had any foreknowledge or part in the January coup and concludes: "There is little evidence as to whether he favored the coup to start with, though his actions at Police HQ and Ikeja do not seem to suggest he did." Luckham states: "At the second meeting Ironsi asked that power be handed over to the armed forces. The ministers were by now divided and demoralized, and they abdicated authority without too much argument. . . . Apparently Ironsi insisted he could only deal with the situation if he were given complete power and the constitution abrogated." Ironsi appointed Lieutenant Colonel C. Odumegwu Ojukwu military governor of the Eastern Region, and another young lieutenant colonel, Yakubu Gowon, became chief of staff of the army. Robin Luckham, *The Nigerian Military* (Cambridge University Press, 1971), pp. 24–25.

one million Ibos must die: According to George Orick, an American businessman in Nigeria at the time. He reports that one could hear on Northern Nigeria radio the reading of long lists of names of Ibos who were targeted for extinction. Similarly, Heinrich Jaggi, a Swiss businessman in Nigeria who later became the chief Red Cross delegate in Biafra, reports seeing one of the circular letters in the Northern Region which stated that every Ibo down to the age of six would be killed. Orick believes that once the one million Ibos had been killed, the Hausa, with the Sardauna of Sokoto's death thus avenged, would have been ready to end the war.

20 **"we are the former colonial power"**: Maurice Foley to Commons, *Parliamentary Debates* (Hansard), 13 March 1969.
"a difficulty facing many African states": *Ibid.*, 12 June 1968.
"African statesmanship has been right": *Ibid.*

21 **"it is a thing of my conscience"**: This quote and others later in this section from Ojukwu and Gowon come from the transcript of the Aburi Report on the meeting of the Supreme Military Council of Nigeria held in Aburi, Ghana, on January 4–5, 1967, as reprinted in the Minutes of Proceedings and Evidence of the Standing Committee on External Affairs and National Defence, House of Commons, Parliament of Canada, no. 8, appendix M, October 17, 1968 (hereafter cited as the Aburi Report).
a journalist who witnessed them: Alan Grossman had been West Africa bureau chief of the *Time-Life* News Service in Lagos from May 1966 to June 1968. He was Ottawa bureau chief of *Time* when, as a Canadian citizen, he testified before the external affairs committee of the Canadian House of Commons on October 16, 1968, about the events he had witnessed in Nigeria and Biafra; see Minutes of Proceedings no. 7, pp. 239–40.

22 **a young lieutenant colonel:** Some of the biographical material about Ojukwu that follows is derived from Frederick Forsyth's *The Biafra Story* (Penguin Books, 1969), which he wrote while in Biafra as a correspondent, with access to Biafran sources. (Forsyth later became better known as the author of such novels as *Day of the Jackal* and *Dogs of War*. The latter opens on the closing scene of Biafra when a fictional general, presumably based on Ojukwu, flies out of a besieged African redoubt on the point of collapse.) Some of the material is from conversations with Ojukwu in 1977.

23 **joined to keep province peaceful:** The account of the two coups and the events that flowed from them is based on Ojukwu's statements at both Aburi (Aburi Report) and the Addis Ababa conference and also on Frederick Forsyth's *The Biafra Story* and Suzanne Cronje's *The World and Nigeria*.

24 **Gowon broadcast to nation:** Both Cronje and Forsyth attribute this last-minute change in the speech to the intervention of the British high commissioner (at that time, Sir Francis Cumming-Bruce), who persuaded Gowon not to announce the breakup of Nigeria along North-South lines. Cronje reports that Cumming-Bruce told this to Sir Louis Mbanefo, a former member of the World Court who became Biafra's chief justice, and to Dr. Eni Njoku, the former vice-chancellor of Lagos University.

27 **"We were now thoroughly convinced"**: Ojukwu to OAU consultative committee, Addis Ababa, August 5, 1968, Ministry of Information, Republic of Biafra, p. 22.
"shall henceforth be an independent sovereign state": Proclamation of the Republic of Biafra, *West Africa*, June 3, 1967, p. 716.

Chapter 3

28 **only one airfield in Biafra:** The Swedish Embassy, in its cable from Lagos to the Foreign Office in Stockholm, had commented upon the summary of the Federal

Military Government's statement of May 28, 1968: "In fact, this means that the Federal Government is not ready to give permission for flights to the airport under Biafran control, which is the rebels' only remaining way of importing arms and therefore constitutes a primary target that cannot be exempted from military attack. Furthermore, they do not want to allow humanitarian relief in any way that would place other limits upon warfare." (My translation from the white paper released by the Swedish Foreign Office, which included many documents about humanitarian relief in the Nigerian-Biafran conflict: *Sverige och Konflikton i Nigeria, 1967–1970, En documentsamling*, Utrikesdepartementet, Stockholm, 1970, hereafter cited as Swedish White Paper.)

29 **Michael Leapman:** Leapman later wrote: "Here there is another myth that needs exploding; that Colonel Ojukwu exploited and indeed even encouraged the starvation of his people to gain world sympathy. I was one of the first reporters to write about the Biafran food crisis and on my first visit the authorities tried to discourage me from visiting the worst affected areas because they thought the existence of the problem reflected on their competence to govern." Michael Leapman, "Nigerian Civil War in Retrospect," *Venture*, April 1970.
David Robison: The quotes that follow are from Robison's story in the *New York Times* of Sunday, June 30, 1968. It brought the first alarming predictions of massive starvation to American readers, though people in Britain and Ireland had been aware of the developing situation for some weeks.

30 **British diplomats to Red Cross:** According to senior ICRC officials. See also note for p. 69.

31 **"a legitimate weapon of war":** Chief Anthony Enahoro press conference at United Nations, July 8, 1968; Chief Obafemi Awolowo statement, June 26, 1969. See note for p. 189.

32 **British seized upon it:** George Thomson, during Question Period in House of Commons, *Parliamentary Debates* (Hansard), 26 June 1968.
Nigerians first proposed: Thierry Hentsch notes (*Face au blocus*, p. 67) that the route proposed by the FMG on February 29 would have had to go through the front in a sector in which combat was especially intense. It was difficult for the Red Cross to ask the Biafrans to open a breach in their defenses, he points out; further, not only would this have been unacceptable to the Biafrans but would have confronted those taking convoys through with far greater risks than would an air corridor.
"perhaps my honorable Friend did not hear . . .": Thomson during Question Period in Commons, *Parliamentary Debates* (Hansard), 26 June 1968.
" 'pincer movement' ": *West Africa* of June 15, 1968 reported: "Federal forces in the Enugu sector are reported unofficially to be planning an advance southwards from Agbani, 12 miles south of Enugu, to Awgu. Our correspondent says it is pointed out in Lagos that the capture of Awgu would help a 'pincer movement' on Umuahia from Afikpo (in Federal hands for several weeks) and Awgu, if it were decided to attack Umuahia."
A week later (June 22), *West Africa* reported: "Nigerian forces have captured Awgu, it was announced on June 18. Unofficial reports say forces under Col. Shuwa captured it intact after a brief resistance, and also seized an airstrip near

the town. The advance southwards from Agbani began a few days before, and at one point the Biafrans claimed to have halted it in a big battle; but then, according to Biafran reports, thousands of people fled the town and neighboring villages as shelling began. . . ."

33 **areas of greatest need not accessible:** Christian Council of Nigeria emergency relief report, Earle Roberts, Christian Social Action Secretary, July 8, 1968.
the *Guardian* finally did: *Manchester Guardian,* July 15, 1968.
"Because it was preposterous": According to a Biafran official with major responsibility for negotiating relief.
had, in fact, been poisoned: The report of the Goodell-Mayer study mission (entered into the Congressional Record of February 25, 1969, by Senator Charles Goodell) stated: "Deliberate poisoning of food supplies was first suspected in 1967 when several deaths were thought to have resulted from the ingestion of toxic foods. . . . The most tangible evidence of poisoning seems to be in salt, which is also the principal item being smuggled in. Of 1,487 samples tested during the last part of 1968, 20 samples contained toxic quantities of arsenic, 50 samples contained cyanide; and all others were non-toxic and non-infectious. . . ." (p. S1979). Senator Goodell later told me that the Jean Mayer team purposely arrived unexpectedly at the Biafran laboratory in order to check on the allegation of poisoning and that at the time of our conversation (March 1971) Goodell still had in his possession five bottles of the poisoned food which the team had picked up at the laboratory.

34 **prime minister's reply:** The *Times,* July 8, 1968.
"seek and destroy all aircraft": The *Daily Times* of Lagos the next day reported the government's statement under the headline: "Air Force Gets the Green Light—Clamp Down on Private Planes." Later, when Canadian Secretary of State for External Affairs Mitchell Sharp testified before his Parliament's Committee on External Affairs, he cited this Nigerian statement to indicate the attitude of the Federal Military Government (Minutes of Proceedings, October 10, 1968, p. 124).

Chapter 4

35 **"should move through the ICRC":** The note given U Thant by ICRC officials on July 8, 1968 in Geneva stated, in part: ". . . According to last minute information from the ICRC delegation in Lagos, the Federal Government has decided that all non-governmental relief should move through the ICRC." In *Face au blocus* (footnote 58, p. 98), Thierry Hentsch quotes from a message in the ICRC archives sent by its delegate in Lagos on July 8: "The FMG having decided that all relief by non-governmental organizations must be channeled through the ICRC, our delegation in Lagos is confronted with numerous long- and short-term problems."
DEAL WITH MEDDLERS: *Daily Times,* Lagos, July 8, 1968.
an act of hostility: Department of State Disaster Memo No. 2 on Nigeria, July 24, 1968.

36 **characteristics of ICRC:** The International Committee of the Red Cross carried out a self-appraisal in the early 1970s, largely as a result of its experience during

the Nigerian-Biafran war. One of its observations: "One of the most persistent criticisms heard during the Re-appraisal, often from the strongest supporters of the ICRC, concerned the institution's operating style. The ICRC operates, it is said, as a closed system: it is not open about what it is doing and why. It is not open to ideas and information from outside. . . .

"On the whole, the ICRC seems to have blurred the differences between the discretion which their work requires and an obsession with needless secrecy. Secrecy on some matters is harmful to protection and assistance efforts. If others do not know what you are doing, they cannot possibly support you, and they may distrust you as well. . . .

"The closed nature of the ICRC is particularly evident in its relations with other Red Cross organs and with other organizations at the international level. Relations are scrupulously maintained, but often the relations seem more a matter of form than substance. The polite and formal atmosphere serves to keep other agencies at their distance and discourages free and open discussion of common problems. This attitude of remoteness and unwillingness to share information and ideas manifests itself in the ICRC's relations with UN agencies and international non-governmental agencies. A common complaint from other agencies is that their relationship with the ICRC is one-sided—cooperation occurs only when the ICRC is seeking information and assistance. . . ." Donald D. Tansley, *Final Report: An Agenda for Red Cross*, Re-appraisal of the Role of the Red Cross, Geneva, 1975, p. 114.

confined itself to using Swiss: Thierry Hentsch, who had been assistant to the president of the ICRC in 1969, remarked upon this problem in *Face au blocus* (p. 98): The ICRC did not have enough qualified people in sufficient numbers to build up a large relief operation quickly; when personnel were borrowed from other organizations in the public or private sector, they could leave their regular jobs for only a limited time, resulting in discontinuity in the operation.

According to the ICRC's director of operations in 1981, as a result of its self-appraisal following the Nigerian-Biafran experience, the ICRC has since set about to build up its professional staff.

37 **permission of Nigerian authorities:** In contrast to this, the then director for operational activities, Jean-Pierre Hocké, told me in 1981 that the ICRC now proceeds on the following working assumption: wherever there is need to provide humanitarian assistance, the Red Cross has a working right to do so. Where a people in need during a civil conflict can be reached, the ICRC does not ask the government's permission but says, "You must allow us to assist." Hocké said that the ICRC bases this doctrine on Articles 5, 6, and 9—as well as Article 3— of the Geneva Conventions. Had this been the doctrine being followed at the time of the Nigerian-Biafran conflict, the situation would, conceivably, have evolved differently. That it does not always work, however, is evident from such situations as Afghanistan, where the Red Cross is not able to gain access directly to civilian populations in need of humanitarian relief.

Hank Warton: The State Department had set about to curb Warton's activities in support of Biafra six days before the Nigerian attack that began the war on July 6, 1967. According to a document released to me under the Freedom of Information Act, Elbert Mathews, the ambassador to Nigeria, cabled the U.S. Embassy in Paris (and other relevant embassies) on August 11, 1967, informing them that the Department had issued instructions June 30, 1967 to lift his passport and the FAA to suspend his airmen's certificate. (See note, p. 119.) Mathew's cable asked the other embassies to inform local police and aviation authorities and to request that "they act to prevent movement of plane and/or Warton."

38 **British persuaded FMG:** The day the FMG invited the ICRC to coordinate all relief, George Thomson indicated in Commons that the idea had originated with the British: ". . . The Prime Minister emphasized—in his answer given over the weekend to Oxfam's anxieties—our belief that the International Red Cross is the best instrument for coordinating this operation. Indeed we have been supported in this view by a message from Lord Hunt this morning. . . . The International Red Cross has been accepted by the Federal Government as the most effective coordinating organization and I am sure that, if this were done, it would greatly help to create the sort of atmosphere which would allow the relief work to go forward." *Parliamentary Debates* (Hansard), 8 July 1968.

ICRC deeply concerned: The note of the ICRC to Secretary General Thant of July 8, 1968 read, in part: "The only practical way to move substantial quantities of relief would be through a land corridor. An alternative procedure would be to obtain neutralization under the ICRC flag of an airstrip in the Biafran territories. The International Committee of the Red Cross is negotiating for acceptance by both parties of either or both such measures which involve partial lifting of the blockade for humanitarian reasons, under the provisions of the 4th Geneva Convention of 1949, under Article 23.

"The ICRC is deeply concerned with the difficulties it is meeting to obtain such facilities, which are indispensable to provide the victims with urgently needed relief, and it respectfully requests the assistance of the Secretary-General of the United Nations in order to obtain from the belligerent parties full recognition and implementation of the 4th Geneva convention of 1949 relative to the protection of civilian persons in time of war. . . ."

39 **Article 3:** Some portions of Article 3 that might have been relevant in the Biafran situation: ". . . each Party to the conflict shall be bound to apply, as a minimum, the following provisions:

"1) Persons taking no active part in the hostilities, including members of armed forces who have laid down their arms and those placed *hors de combat* by sickness, wounds, detention, or any other cause, shall in all circumstances be treated humanely, without any adverse distinction founded on race, color, religion or faith, sex, birth or wealth, or any other similar criteria.

"To this end the following acts are and shall remain prohibited at any time and in any place whatsoever with respect to the above mentioned persons:

"a) violence to life and person, in particular murder of all kinds, mutilation, cruel treatment and torture; . . .

"c) outrages upon personal dignity, in particular humiliating and degrading treatment; . . .

"2) The wounded and sick shall be collected and cared for.

"An impartial humanitarian body, such as the International Committee of the Red Cross, may offer its services to the parties to the conflict.

"The Parties to the conflict should further endeavor to bring into force, by

PAGE

means of special agreements, all or part of the other provisions of the present
Conventions. . . ."

40   **briefed the secretary general:** Letter of a UNICEF representative in Lagos to
the UNICEF deputy executive director in New York, July 17, 1968.

The newspaper account stated: "The Nigerian crisis will not be discussed at
the resumed session of the U.N. General Assembly. Amb. Ogbu . . . said he
personally met the U.N. Secretary-General U Thant and briefed him about the
correct situation in Nigeria, adding that he also told him that the Federal Military Government still regarded the crisis as her internal affair. . . ." Lagos *Daily
Times,* June 12, 1968.

43   **One of those present:** This note of naïveté was injected by myself, participating
for the first time in an official discussion of the relief problem. In this and
subsequent discussions with top officials of other relief agencies it was clear that
they all regarded the obstacle to their efforts as the Nigerian government,
the exact opposite of what the Nigerian and British governments were
contending—that Biafran leaders were blocking relief agencies to starve their
own people deliberately so as to gain political advantage. While relief agency
officials knew the FMG sought to obstruct their access to the people in the
besieged enclave, they did not speak out in public, as they believed (no doubt
correctly) that to do so would cause the Nigerians to throw them out for good
and all.

A million are going to die: This view was shared at the time by others
knowledgeable about the situation. George Orick, an American who had been a
businessman in Nigeria from 1961 to 1967, was the fourth person present at
that meeting; later, in a memo to Heyward, he explained why the people in
Biafra were prepared to starve "rather than submit again to the Northern-
dominated Nigerian government": "The Ibo acceptance of at least a measure of
the disastrous consequences of their fight for independence from what they
consider to be recessive domination is matched in Lagos by an acceptance
among the Hausas and Yorubas who run the government now that large
numbers of Ibos must die to placate the Northerners for the loss of their
spiritual leader and for the affront to their dignity implied in the Ibo rebellion.
Your own man in Lagos, Dr. Kyarusi, told me that it is generally agreed that a
ceasefire will be possible when, and not before, at least one million Ibos have
died."

survey by pediatrician: Ifekwunigwe found in March 1968 that, during this
early period of starvation, 89 percent of those affected were children under five
years of age, while the remaining 11 percent were children five to fifteen. This
resulted from a shortage of protein foods, as small children need proportionately more protein for their growing bodies than do adults. Later, however, the
elderly would be affected, and the following year, when carbohydrates would be
in short supply as well, all age groups would suffer malnutrition and starvation.

44   **Thant cable to Gowon:** UN press release SG/SM/976, July 15, 1968. This communication was perhaps U Thant's most forceful expression of concern regarding the situation in Nigeria and Biafra. He may well have felt he was being
even-handed in pressing both sides for a solution to the problem. Overall,
however, throughout the more than twenty months of starvation, he did not go

beyond this initial message of concern but consistently accepted the position of the Nigerian government without attempting to use the resources available to a secretary general to seek a solution to the humanitarian problem.

Ogbu agitated: This account was reported to UNICEF headquarters in New York by a UNICEF representative in Lagos on July 17, 1968, the day after Ambassador Ogbu consulted him.

Chapter 5

46   **Mathews had flown to Enugu:** Palmer stated this in his testimony to the Senate Foreign Relations Committee, September 11, 1968: ". . . When negotiations broke down, we counseled against secession through our Consul in Enugu and Ambassador Mathews flew to that city to try to dissuade Colonel Ojukwu from this course."

47   **"losing West Africa to communism":** Ambassador Mathews, who died in November 1977, confirmed the foregoing interpretation to me in February 1972.
"political integrity of Nigeria": Suzanne Cronje quotes Mathews as stating, in July 1967: "My Government recognizes the Federal Military Government of Nigeria. We have repeatedly made known our complete support of the political integrity of Nigeria. Many times we have expressed our hopes that Nigeria would continue to remain a united country. This is not only an official view, but one that is also felt by American businessmen engaged in the rapidly growing trade between our two countries." *The World and Nigeria* p. 225.
Palmer and Katzenbach: This exchange was reported by Roger Morris who, from 1968 to 1970, was the National Security Council staff member concerned with Nigeria-Biafra.

48   **President Johnson statement:** July 11, 1968.
gave statement a new direction: *Baltimore Sun,* July 12, 1968; Reuters, July 11, 1968; *New York Times,* July 12, 1968.

49   **Dr. Howard Rusk:** *New York Times,* September 22, 1968, p. 49.

50   **"consort with the Devil himself":** Byrne would later comment about this period in his Annual Report to Caritas Internationalis: "The conditions of Captain Warton's planes and the instability of his crews hindered the progress of the operation. These planes carried ammunition when chartered by the Biafrans and relief supplies when chartered by Caritas and the Red Cross. Naturally the Biafrans regarded ammunition more important than food and Captain Warton preferred Lisbon-Biafra flights to the short and dangerous São Tomé–Biafra shuttles. At times it was very difficult to engage these planes and it was suggested that planes be purchased for this program . . ." *Annual Report of the Relief Program to Biafra* (Annex 17), Caritas Internationalis, Rome, April 27, 1969.

     The quotes from Father Byrne in this and the next paragraph were made in private to me and others following the press conference mentioned, which was held in New York City on July 18, 1968.

51   **meeting with Rusk:** This account was provided by one of those present at the meeting.

WCC resolution: World Council of Churches fourth assembly, Uppsala, July 15, 1968 (Gen. Doc. 62).

51–2 **Pope and "Vatican Smuggles . . .":** The two newspaper clippings from which these quotes are taken were not dated. However, the Nordchurchaid report indicates that the first of the planes purchased by the West German Protestant and Catholic relief agencies landed at Uli on the night of July 26; they did not become fully operational till mid-August. Hugh G. Lloyd, Mona L. Mollerup, and Carl A. Bratved, *The Nordchurchaid Airlift to Biafra, 1968–1970: An Operations Report* (Folkekirkens Nodhjaelp, Copenhagen, 1972), pp. 6–7, 23.

52 **"another 49 days formal warfare":** This report, from correspondents in Lagos and Owerri, appeared in the *Sunday Times* of London on July 28, 1968. After the event it is difficult to establish whether any ICRC officials accepted a September 15 "confidential target date . . . for the start of full-scale relief." It would seem likely that it reflects a diplomatic or government source in Lagos, while not providing proof of ICRC collusion in a deliberate holdup on starting relief, as officials of other agencies attending the meeting were by this time ready to believe.

Chapter 6

54 **"Build up stockpiles of food":** According to senior ICRC officials. It was known to us at UNICEF headquarters in late July–early August 1968 that the Red Cross had begun positioning food stocks at Enugu, Asaba, and Calabar on the periphery of the enclave. August Lindt so informed Henry Labouisse in Lagos on July 22; he stated as the two objectives at that time: "to press for a break somehow in order to reach the East Central state; meanwhile to start relief wherever possible in liberated territories." Internal UNICEF record of Labouisse visit to Nigeria, July 20–31, 1968, p. 7.

However, it was not till after the conflict that I learned that British diplomats had been counseling ICRC officials in this manner (see next source note). Of course, ultimately, the Red Cross did not accept this counsel but began an airlift without authorization of the Nigerian government.

top ICRC officials kept their own counsel: One ICRC official later made the point to me that the element of time entered into this as well. Under great pressure as they were, the few top executives could not keep others informed about everything they knew. It seems likely, though, that British pressures upon them to hold up on starting relief is not something they would have informed others about even had they had the time.

55 **misnaming and mistitling him:** George Thomson, Question Period in Commons, *Parliamentary Debates* (Hansard), 26 June 1968.
"The important thing to bear in mind": *Ibid.*
if they spoke out: In response to my comment that none of those who knew at the time what was actually happening ever spoke out and informed the public, a top ICRC official remarked that the public could not make all that much difference, that people like himself might better work in traditional ways with governments to gain and keep their support. The melodramatic gesture, he thought, would only have had long-term bad consequences with governments.

This may have been true for the ICRC, which is dependent upon governments for resources, goodwill, and access to military prisoners or civilians in need of humanitarian assistance. However, in nearly every major human catastrophe of recent years it was not possible to aid distressed civilians until after the public became aroused and put pressure upon their own governments to act.

In the Biafran situation, the disinclination of the few officials who knew what was happening to speak out made possible the prolonged British cover-up of Nigerian intransigence toward the relief organizations.

55–6 **Dutch Red Cross:** *de Tijd,* October 11, 1968.

56 **"hopes . . . faded cruelly yesterday":** This report in *The Observer* of London on July 14, 1968, was by-lined "By Our Commonwealth Staff" and presumably, therefore, reflects the way British officials in the Commonwealth Office were talking with newsmen. It would appear that the pure version is contained in the opening paragraphs of a *New York Times* report from London on July 9: "The British Government, under intense public criticism for its support and arming of Nigeria against the Biafran rebels, contends that it is the Biafran leaders who are obstructing peace and relief operations. Informed quarters here charge that Lieut. Col. Odumegwu Ojukwu, the Biafran rebel chief, is using his starving people as political pawns in the hope of gaining world sympathy. . . ."
"these discussions are . . . extremely delicate": George Thomson in Commons, *Parliamentary Debates* (Hansard), 8 July 1968.

This would be the pattern of British government response throughout the Nigerian-Biafran war: whenever the subject was scheduled for debate in Parliament, an important official from London would be sent to Lagos to confer or another action would be taken to create a sense of expectation that something was about to happen so that the Commons would not be pressed to a vote on continuing the supply of arms to Nigeria.

56–7 **prime minister to Commons:** *Parliamentary Debates* (Hansard), 18 July 1968.

57 **"this particular Lord cannot be our Shepherd":** Even in moments of horror, there can be levity. The Biafrans began getting a very bad press when they refused to admit Lord Hunt to discuss the British offer of relief. What they needed was food, and the British had sent a national hero instead. The Biafran representative in New York nearly fell out of his chair laughing when it was suggested to him that the Biafrans would do better, instead of appearing so inflexible and ungrateful, to announce: "We shall welcome Lord Hunt and his mission and, when they get here, we shall eat them."
"Biafra is grateful . . . cannot understand . . .": Biafran government statement, the *Times,* July 5, 1968, and *New York Times,* July 6, 1968.
British wanted the war ended: Numerous peace initiatives would be taken throughout the course of the war, by the British and through the Commonwealth Secretariat, as well as by many individuals, including Emperor Haile Selassie and Pope Paul. These negotiations at Kampala, Niamey, Addis Ababa, Monrovia, and elsewhere always foundered on the basic, irreconcilable fact that the Nigerian government sought to retain within the Nigerian Federation the territory seceding as Biafra, while the Biafrans did not feel their lives could be secure within Nigeria. Customarily, in the formal negotiations, the Nigerian

government would insist on the renunciation of secession as a precondition and the Biafrans would not agree to this.

58 **"can roll easily into our homeland":** Press conference of Odumegwu Ojukwu, July 18, 1968 (Biafran press release 242).

"misguided humanitarian rubbish": The quote from Colonel Adekunle was widely reported. *New York Times* News of the Week in Review, July 14, 1968.

"Ankrah was completely isolated": *New York Times,* July 18, 1968.

communiqué already agreed upon: Ojukwu told me that Diallo Telli, the secretary general of the Organization of African Unity, was preparing the final communiqué before the Biafran head of state arrived in Niamey. Diallo Telli played an active role in support of the Nigerian government. Ironically, if an account published in *Jeune Afrique* (November 8, 1978) is correct, Telli was himself later deliberately starved as a method of political execution. According to this report, having been reassured and encouraged to return to his own country, Guinea, Diallo Telli was imprisoned in July 1976 on a charge of leading a plot to assassinate President Sekou Touré. He and his fellow political prisoners, after torture, confessed and on February 17, 1977, were placed on the "black diet" (no food, no water). By February 25, according to this *Jeune Afrique* account, Diallo Telli was dead.

59 **"Sir Colin Thornley himself drove down the road":** *Parliamentary Debates* (Hansard), 22 July 1968.

"The callousness of it beggars description": *Newsweek,* July 22, 1968, p. 42.

Chapter 7

60 **relief agencies were resented:** The mood in Lagos at the time Henry Labouisse and August Lindt arrived and met with Nigerian government officials is suggested by an article in the *Morning Post* of July 30, 1968: "In recent months, some foreign relief organizations, notably CARITAS, OXFAM and the World Council of Churches, have been meddling quite distastefully in the Nigerian crisis. They have got themselves deeply involved in the crisis on the pretext that they are seriously concerned about the sufferings of the people in areas still being forcibly held by the rebels. These so-called humanitarian organizations have for some time openly identified themselves with the secessionist cause. They have not only danced to the tune of the rebels' vicious propaganda but have also helped the rebels in spreading their falsehood in foreign countries. The result of their criminal activities is that almost all foreign relief agencies, no matter their sincerity of purpose, are now looked at with suspicious eyes."

62 **UNICEF works only with governments:** By contrast, however, eleven years later, when UNICEF began negotiating to gain access to the people of Kampuchea (Cambodia), it did so (again in concert with the ICRC) with the government that the Vietnamese Army had installed in Phnom Penh, though the former regime of Pol Pot was still recognized internationally and continued as a member of the United Nations.

While Labouisse went to Lagos to negotiate access to Biafra, he sent at the same time another UNICEF official, Willy Meyer, into the besieged enclave and contemplated going himself, but missed the opportunity to do so when Ambassador Lindt informed him that he had told the Federal Military Government only Red Cross personnel would be on board the first flight of the new ICRC plane. Labouisse left Lagos before another flight from Fernando Po might have taken him in. Meyer did get into Biafra, but was stricken with a grave illness soon after coming out and died a short time later. A draft of the report he had been writing, found among his papers, did not reach UNICEF officials until months after it would have been of use.

63   **arms in planes carrying relief:** This, of course, was the opposite of what had been happening during the initial months of the relief effort. Planes chartered by Biafra to fly in arms and ammunition sometimes had space available into which church agencies put food and medical supplies, a practice some church relief officials later regretted. The agencies on numerous occasions offered the Nigerian government the right to inspect relief shipments, but the FMG did not take up these offers.

64   **"I blink my eyes at the night flights":** Labouisse's meeting with Gowon took place July 24, nineteen days after the Nigerian government issued its statement warning relief agencies that instructions had been issued to the Nigerian Air Force "to seek and destroy all aircraft which enter into Nigeria on missions not expressly authorized and cleared by the FMG. . . ." The air force did not possess a night fighter capability at any time during the war.
"I think ICRC now does recognize": First report from UNICEF executive director to secretary general on his visit to Nigeria, July 26, 1968, p. 7.
"Trying to get the ICRC to delay": While Katzenbach made this remark more than three years later, in January 1972, he did so as if it were not a new thought but reflected what his attitude had been in 1968.

66   **"Guestimates":** While news coverage and books such as this focus on the more dramatic aspects of an emergency situation, it should be kept in mind that relief agency officials must be occupied day by day, urgently, with the more mundane problems of organizing the logistics of a relief action: what kinds of food are acceptable to the people, how many trucks will be needed and where they can be procured most rapidly and how shipped, what are the numbers of people actually at risk and how many will it be possible to reach and when, what personnel are available and how qualified are they for these particular conditions, what specific medicines are required and is their procurement being duplicated by a number of agencies, what will be the situation next month, where are the funds to come from? The fact that Heyward of UNICEF titled his working paper "Guestimates" suggests how uncertain are the factors on which planning of logistics must go forward, even before factoring in the political obstacles that inevitably arise.

67   **a demilitarized, neutralized airfield:** It was July 22 when Gowon reaffirmed to Lindt that the Nigerian government would allow relief flights into a demilitarized, neutralized airfield, as it did not want them going into Uli airfield, where planes with arms were landing; further that it did not want daylight flights at all because they would interfere with military operations of the Nigerian Air Force. It is important to keep these positions in mind as events unfold over the coming weeks; the FMG completely reverses itself, refusing (on August 15) to authorize

flights into a neutralized airfield under the control of the Red Cross and later (in the weeks following September 3) insisting that only daylight flights into Uli will be acceptable.

Chapter 8

68 **"it is not the case that there are large numbers of Saladins":** The central issue in Britain, the supply of arms to Nigeria, was, of course, cloaked in official secrecy and was a subject about which the government was not entirely candid with members of Parliament. Lord Shepherd, official spokesman for the government in the House of Lords, perhaps tripped up at the beginning of the year in saying: ". . . while we deplore the tragic and sad civil war in Nigeria, we have been supplying Nigeria with pretty well all its military equipment, and in the present circumstances we think that we should continue to supply reasonable quantities of arms to the legal Government of Nigeria." *Parliamentary Debates* (Hansard), 29 January 1968.

A few months later, as the issue heated up, Prime Minister Wilson told the Commons: "The position about arms supplies is exactly as I and my right honorable Friend the Secretary of State have described it on a number of occasions. We have continued the supply—not the Government; I mean that we have allowed the continuance of supply of arms by private manufacturers in this country exactly on the basis that it has been in the past, but there has been no special provision for the needs of the war. As I have said, we have refused to supply arms of a kind, such as bombs and other things which we were asked for, which were required, or considered to be required, for this war. . . ." *Ibid.,* 16 May 1968.

"quickest way to save starving Biafrans": This argument came to be known as the "quick kill theory." Later a conservative Congressman, Donald Lukens of Ohio, would create controversy by charging that this had been the theory advanced to him by the American ambassador in Lagos as the best way to get food to the starving.

In the debate during which Michael Barnes made this comment, the Commonwealth secretary had informed the Commons that Lord Hunt had just made his report expressing the view that the land route would be the most effective way to get relief into the "Ibo area" and that General Gowon had confirmed the Nigerian government's willingness to open up a relief corridor from Enugu to Awgu and then to an agreed point on the Okigwe road, where "Colonel Ojukwu's authorities could take over." *Ibid.,* 22 July 1968.

69 **D-notices:** At that time, the secretary of the Services, Press and Broadcasting Committee had only to issue a D- (or Defense) Notice, warning a newspaper editor that publication would contravene the Official Secrets Act, to prevent the printing of information the government wished to suppress.

Jonathan Aitken, who would be prosecuted (unsuccessfully) in 1971 for violating the Official Secrets Act by providing a copy of the British defense adviser's report about the Nigerian civil war to the *Sunday Telegraph,* later commented: "Today D-notices are a compulsory extension of the Official Secrets Acts, and all available evidence suggest that they are used just as unfairly as the

Act itself in suppressing non-secret information which may prove embarrassing to the Government of the day."

Aitken pointed out that the most damage to press freedom was done not by prosecution of editors and journalists but by intimidation of government civil servants who were made to take a vow of silence. He commented: "The overall effect of having the Official Secrets Act dangling like a sword of Damocles above the head of every minor bureaucrat is that Britain today has the most closed government in the free world, a situation which seriously hinders the legitimate activities of a free press." Aitken, *Officially Secret*, p. 45.

By way of contrast, at the time Aitken was writing, the United States Supreme Court refused (in the Pentagon Papers case) to accede to the government any right of "prior restraint" of what a newspaper might publish.

"the old boy unofficial network": *Ibid.*, pp. 187–88.

"letting a few thousand die now": An extract of the BBC interview with Charles Ammann, January 15, 1969, is printed by Cronje in *The World and Nigeria* (pp. 136–7), and it is significant that Thierry Hentsch reprints it in *Face au blocus* (pp. 121–2), as he was an ICRC official concerned with Nigeria–Biafra in 1969.

70 **"No, the road coming down from the north":** The land corridor proposal had a plausibility that bemused not only the public but even government officials who were not themselves familiar with the geography or the military situation on the ground between Enugu and Awgu. Edward Hamilton of the National Security Council staff (characterized at the time by his former boss McGeorge Bundy—not one given to easy praise—as "the ablest bureaucrat in the United States Government") tried energetically that summer, apparently with the best intentions in the world, to find some way to open the land corridor. He and some lower-level officials in the Bureau of African Affairs wanted to find a way to break through the humanitarian impasse, but they sought to find a solution only within the terms of the proposal made by the Nigerian government. It would appear not to have occurred to them that the land corridor had been put forward precisely because the Nigerians knew it could not be accepted by the Biafrans, as it would make their defenses highly vulnerable.

"The Red Cross accepts this as a genuine offer": Subcommittee on Africa, House Committee on Foreign Affairs, July 23, 1968.

71 **naturally follow diplomatic channels:** At the time, I shared the growing conviction of other relief agency officials that the ICRC was in some way deliberately participating in what appeared to be complicity with governments to frustrate humanitarian relief attempts. Research after the war persuaded me, however, that the customary and reflexive legalistic, diplomatic approach of the ICRC, concerned with maintaining good long-term relations of the Red Cross with governments, lent itself to the diplomatic/propaganda campaign British diplomats had set in motion to get through the next two months. The ICRC became the victim, rather than the accomplice, of governments. This cautious approach had the effect, however, of doing great damage to the Red Cross in its relations with others in the international community, not to mention its effect upon efforts to begin relief to Biafra.

73 **the worst conditions they had ever seen:** The *Times* of London more than three weeks earlier (July 9, 1968) reported a visit to the same area by an administrator

for the Save the Children Fund describing the conditions Labouisse observed. Nearly a month had gone by and no effective relief had yet been organized, though no blockade prevented aid to victims on the Nigerian side.
"6,000 deaths a day greatly exaggerated": Disaster Memo Number Four, State/AID Office of Private Resources, Voluntary Agencies Division, Washington, D.C., August 7, 1968.

74 **mail at twice the volume:** According to State Department officials in a meeting with heads of voluntary agencies in midsummer 1968.
rejected in Nigeria for ten years: A paraphrase of the account provided me by an assistant to the undersecretary of the dialogue between Katzenbach and his staff and Palmer and some of his top officials in the Bureau of African Affairs.
$1 million "drawing rights": Statement of July 18, 1968, Department of State Bulletin, August 5, 1968.
Nixon statement: July 18, 1968, Nixon for President Committee, New York City.
TV crews into Biafra: It is significant that in this (as in a number of subsequent human disasters) the public came to put pressure upon their governments to act only after television crews got into the area and started sending back film of the children and adults suffering. Until this happened, governments—though aware of the calamity—have usually not begun to act to provide relief because political obstacles stood in their way. When TV camera crews have not gotten in—in Southern Sudan, Eritrea, Afghanistan—governments have not been pressured by their citizens, impelling them to act.

75 **"first demonstration . . . in sympathy with":** This remark was made while I was observing the late-night vigil.
"mandatory relief airlift": *New York Times*, August 3, 1968.
"prompt, risk-taking initiatives": This letter of the vice-president's, sent to nongovernmental relief agencies on August 9, 1968, indicated an attitude developing in international circles (apart from the inner diplomatic community with direct responsibility for Nigeria) that the caution of the ICRC was obstructing the start of relief.

Chapter 9

76 **Ojukwu to correspondents:** News release, July 19, 1968, Biafran Overseas Press Division.

77 **to try to start an airlift:** A good account of how the church relief agencies sought to begin an airlift, including this incident, is contained in *The Nordchurchaid Airlift to Biafra*, pp. 2–21.

77–8 **"What are we doing? What are you doing?":** The transcript of this meeting on August 14, 1968 of Lindt and Roger Gallopin of the ICRC with national Red Cross societies and other relief agencies made available to me identifies the questioner only as "Délégation du conseil Oecumenique des Églises (Délégué du Liberia)." Other representatives of relief agencies were equally emotional and angry with the ICRC; their patience was at an end. Lindt's responses were mild and unargumentative. My translation.

79–
80   **not inclined to go out looking for adventure:** At least this is what von Rosen said in conversations with me in 1971 and 1972, but later, in 1977, he organized a humanitarian relief airlift in the Ogadan Region of Ethiopia and was killed in July 1977 when guerrillas attacked the house of a local administrator in which von Rosen was spending the night. The information here is based on conversations with von Rosen during and after the Nigeria-Biafra war and also on his book *Biafra—Som jag ser det* (Wahlstrom & Widstrand, 1969), translated from Swedish into French by Raymond Albeck as *Le Ghetto Biafrais—tel que je l'ai vu* (B. Arthaud, 1969).

81   **Reverend Edward Johnson:** Johnson would play an important role as one of the executives of Joint Church Aid; in organizing Canairelief, which provided planes for the airlift; and in attempting to create a second airfield in Biafra for relief flights. His involvement, like that of many of the churchmen who organized the humanitarian relief operation, was based on long acquaintance with Nigeria. He was as knowledgeable as an outsider might be about the internal politics of the country. As secretary for overseas missions of the Presbyterian Church in Canada and a representative of the World Council of Churches, he had made ten extensive visits to Nigeria over the previous twelve years and knew well such officials as Okoi Arikpo, the Nigerian foreign minister, and N. V. Akpan, the chief secretary of the Biafran government. (Both men were elders of the Presbyterian Church.)

82–5   **Lindt press conference:** The following account of Ambassador Lindt's press conference of August 14, 1968 is taken from a tape recording of the conference made by the ICRC.

85   **formal response from Nigerian government:** Reuters reported that the Nigerian government, in rejecting the ICRC plan for relief flights into a neutralized airstrip, stated that the suggestion that "any portion of Nigeria should be internationalized and handed over to a foreign agency was unacceptable . . . The Federal Government, as already indicated, will only permit supplies to Enugu, from whence they will be carried southward by road." *New York Times,* August 16, 1968.

    The day Lindt had Gowon reaffirm that the Nigerian government would accept relief flights into a neutralized airstrip, George Thomson had told Parliament: ". . . Colonel Gowon confirmed to Lord Hunt that he would seriously consider the possibility of direct flights to a neutralized airstrip in Biafra if the International Red Cross were able to make arrangements with Col. Ojukwu by which the IRC assumes full control of this. I have just heard—a short time ago—that the IRC has now asked the Biafrans for the use of an airstrip under the control of International Red Cross for use day and night.

    "The Biafrans have not so far replied, but the International Red Cross says that even if daylight flights only can be arranged it will still insist that the airstrip should be under its complete control. I very much hope that this offer, which seems to unlock what has been a particularly difficult door, will be accepted swiftly by Col. Ojukwu on behalf of the people who are suffering in the territories which he controls. . . ." *Parliamentary Debates* (Hansard), 22 July 1968.

Chapter 10

87   **ICRC announcement:** Press release no. 898b, August 16, 1968, International Committee of the Red Cross, Geneva.

88   **Lagos newspaper:** Lagos *Daily Times,* August 18, 1968.

89   **second stage from Douala:** This second stage, of flying from Cameroon, was projected not only because the airport at Douala could handle twenty to thirty planes, while the airfield at Santa Isabel on the island of Fernando Po had a capacity limited to five, but because it was expected that, in October, Fernando Po (along with Rio Muni on the mainland) would become an independent nation. Lindt correctly anticipated that this might cause difficulties for Red Cross relief operations into Biafra. He believed in mid-August that agreement to fly from Douala could be obtained from the government of Cameroon, as it had up till that time taken a neutral position on the war between Nigeria and Biafra. This never came to pass, however, so that stage 2 of Operation INALWA was never implemented.

90   **Enahoro and British officials:** *New York Times,* August 21, 1968. The Associated Press also reported that same day, August 20, from London that "Chief Anthony Enahoro . . . conferred today with Minister of State Lord Shepherd at the Commonwealth Office." *Washington Post,* August 21, 1968.
     four elements unacceptable: *The Financial Times,* August 23, 1968.

91–8 **Commons debate:** This and subsequent quotations from the debate in the House of Commons are from *Parliamentary Debates* (Hansard), 27 August 1968.

92   **"final push":** While Gowon appeared on the BBC the evening before the August 27 Commons debate on Nigeria, the final offensive had actually begun three days earlier, on August 24.
     That the Nigerian "final offensive" had in fact begun was not unknown to officials of the British government. Presumably their only surprise came when General Gowon said it had—and said it on the BBC. John de St. Jorre reports: "The first news that the offensive was underway came on a British television interview with Gowon himself which was shown in the United Kingdom on the eve of a parliamentary debate on the Nigerian crisis. It caught most people, especially the British Government and its High Commission in Lagos, on the hop. 'The trouble with Jack Gowon,' a diplomat told me in Lagos, 'is that he can't help but blurt out the truth in front of a camera.' " John de St. Jorre, *The Nigerian Civil War* (Hodder and Stoughton, 1972), pp. 228–29.

94   **public relations firm Markpress:** The British government was quite successful in persuading many people, including some journalists, that the Biafrans were carrying on a clever propaganda campaign through Markpress. In all my research, I never came across a news report that appeared to have been based upon a Biafran press release issued by Markpress in Geneva.
     The impact of starvation in Biafra on readers and television viewers in Europe and North America came from stories filed by reputable journalists and photographers on the scene and filmed by camera crews of national television networks who flew into Biafra. Journalists and news organizations are reflexive in rejecting press releases, especially those given out by a public relations firm.

At the same time, the British government and Foreign Office favored certain "insider" correspondents; as Anthony Lewis, then the *New York Times* London bureau chief commented in 1967: "I think the central mechanism of political reporting in your newspapers has gone wrong. I refer to the Lobby system. That a selected group of trusted correspondents should have access to the leaders of Government on a confidential basis sounds wise, but all too often the result is only to make captives of the reporters." Quoted by Jonathan Aitken in *Officially Secret*, p. 51.

Chapter 11

99   **Lindt notified Nigerian Government:** The Nigerian government on September 2, 1968, characterized Lindt's note to the FMG as "a peremptory message." More than a week before, Lindt had informed Chief Anthony Enahoro about the ICRC plan when Enahoro attempted to persuade Lindt to come to London during the period when the British and Nigerians were making efforts to tie the ICRC up in further negotiations. Thierry Hentsch in his book *Face au blocus* (in the writing of which he had access to the customarily secret archives of the ICRC) reports on page 120: "See the Archive, the note addressed personally by Mr. Lindt to General Gowon, dated Geneva, 30 August 1968. The sending of this note had been preceded by an interview which the High Commissioner [Lindt] had with the Federal Minister of Information in Geneva on the 24th of August (see *Le Monde* of 27th August 1968), in the course of which Mr. Lindt set forth to the Nigerian Government representative the plan of the ICRC." My translation.

99–   **Arikpo to Nordic representatives:** The White Paper released by the Swedish
100   Foreign Office following the war contains a cable from its ambassador in Lagos reporting the meeting with the Nigerian foreign minister on August 29, 1968, after the FMG had been formally informed that day by the ICRC that it would begin daylight flights the next day into the neutralized airstrip: "The Swedish, Danish and Norwegian embassy representatives were summoned to Foreign Minister Arikpo today at 3 o'clock. The Foreign Minister was disturbed that four Nordic planes placed at the disposal of the ICRC for relief flights from Fernando Po into Biafra were (according to a statement just received), going to start flying the next morning, 30 August. Arikpo said that this was especially unfortunate in view of the compromise solution that seemed possible in Addis Ababa. General Gowon had instructed the Foreign Ministry to say that the FMG would not be able to take responsibility for what might happen to unauthorized flights." Swedish White Paper, document 15. My translation.

While this report by the Swedish ambassador states that the ICRC would start flying August 30, Red Cross flights did not actually begin until four days later. The delay resulted from Lindt's having to travel first to Addis Ababa and later to Lagos, as well as from the time it was taking to make the Obilagu airstrip operational.

100   **Nordic appeal:** Press release, August 31, 1968, *Documents on Swedish Foreign Policy 1968* (Royal Ministry for Foreign Affairs, Stockholm, 1969), document 78. **ICRC announces airlift:** Statement by ICRC, press release no. 905, International Committee of the Red Cross, Geneva, September 2, 1968.

PAGE

101   **Swedish prime minister cabled:** This is in paraphrase as released to the press by the Swedish government on September 3, 1968, but we may suppose follows the wording of the prime minister's note. *Documents on Swedish Foreign Policy 1968,* document 79. The Danish and Norwegian prime ministers telegraphed similar appeals to General Gowon.

     not to Obilagu, to Uli instead: Thierry Hentsch reports from the ICRC archives the exact conditions of the Nigerian proposal, *Face au blocus,* pp. 125–26.

     Lindt-Gowon: The joint communiqué released at 1700 hours in Lagos, September 3, 1968, is contained in press release no. 906, International Committee of the Red Cross, Geneva, September 3, 1968.

102   **Onyegbula and Ojukwu:** According to senior ICRC officials interviewed after the war.

103   **reserved the right to fly over Uli:** The Nigerian government was less than candid about this condition being added. For example, a report on relief put out ten days later stated: ". . . It was agreed that the bigger of the two airstrips, at Uli-Ihiala, should be used. The flights were to operate on a trial basis for ten days, which the Red Cross considered adequate for evacuating the accumulated supplies [i.e., 3,500 tons on Fernando Po]. The Federal Government undertook to ensure that air force and military activity would not be conducted there during this period, if the Red Cross would give a guarantee that no other use would be made of the airstrip during the period. . . ." *Relief Problems in Nigeria: Effective Measures Taken by the Federal Government,* press release, Sept. 13, 1968, Embassy of Nigeria, Washington, D.C.

     "we *must* fly": According to senior ICRC officials interviewed after the war.

     Nigerians had learned: The complete turnabout that the Nigerian government took in insisting from this time forward upon "daylight flights into Uli" as the only acceptable negotiating proposal can be seen not only in the FMG insisting on daylight flights but in making Uli the only acceptable airfield. As the Swedish Embassy in Lagos commented to its Foreign Office in Stockholm three months earlier when reporting on the FMG statement criticizing the ICRC demarche at Kampala: "In fact, this means that the Federal Government does not intend to give authorization for flights to airfields under Biafran control, since these are the rebels' only remaining possibility for importing weapons and therefore are primary targets which cannot be exempted from military action. . . ." Swedish White Paper, document 6. My translation.

Chapter 12

107   **relief agencies estranged from ICRC:** The ill will felt, by this time, by officials of other relief agencies toward ICRC officials had come to color their thinking about everything the Red Cross did. George Orick, for example, reflected this bitterness in a report from São Tomé to UNICEF headquarters. He spoke of the Red Cross as "very definitely planning on the collapse of Biafra," saying it "can hardly wait to see all those people lined up in refugee camps, in orderly rows of tents . . . receiving Red Cross rations, as defeated people." He reported the ICRC as setting up a parallel operation in Biafra, "parallel that is to the church groups and other existing operations," and commented that the Red Cross was becoming "separated and almost totally isolated from the other groups."

108   **numbers of those starving:** The estimate of those who had died up to that time in the Vietnam War is based on the record of casualties in Indochina being kept by the *New York Times*. The reference to "all four Arab-Israeli wars" was written before the Israeli invasion of Lebanon in 1982 and does not therefore include an estimate of casualties as a result of that later conflict. The numbers "killed during the entire Spanish Civil War" is based on Hugh Thomas's estimate of 410,000 violent deaths in that conflict, in his book *The Spanish Civil War* (Harper Colophon Books, 1963), appendix 2, "The Casualties of the War."

Statistics about the numbers starving were a subject of considerable controversy during the Nigerian-Biafran war. My own observation both during the conflict and in my interviews and research following the war is that those attempting to maintain some record of these deaths—such as Dr. Clyne Shepherd, Dr. Herman Middelkoop, and Heinrich Jaggi—were men of great integrity. I have given credence in this passage to the numbers they were reporting at the time. Diplomats, on the other hand—British, American, or others—who sought to downplay the numbers starving, were motivated to do so by the need to take the pressure off their governments to do something about the starvation. Significantly, unlike Shepherd and Middelkoop and the Red Cross delegate in Biafra, who had networks of relief workers making weekly reports to them, the diplomats did so with no on-the-spot reporting in Biafra.

Without wishing to join in the past controversy, my own estimate was that considerably more than two million died of starvation and that something like 70 percent of these were children under the age of five. Whatever the actual number, it is important to keep in mind something that might be forgotten after the fact: at the time the war was on and events were unfolding, the diplomats who sought to diminish the numbers could not know how many would die in the future if conditions persisted or grew worse, as seemed entirely possible. For all they knew at the time, the final number could have become the entire population of Biafra.

108– **Clyne Shepherd on statistics:** Minutes of Proceedings no. 10, Standing Com-
9   mittee on External Affairs and National Defence, House of Commons, Parliament of Canada, October 21, 1968, p. 401.

110   **air dropping:** As first one airfield then the other was threatened, the relief agencies began exploring with a sense of urgency the various possibilities for dropping supplies without landing the plane. UNICEF, for example, had experts develop proposals for using a technique known as LAPES (Low Altitude Parachute Extraction System) and another using large numbers of C-119s (the "Flying Boxcar"), which were available in quantity in the United States.

According to an internal paper of Oxfam, reviewing efforts to provide relief: ". . . However, in September 1968, Oxfam's Director attended a meeting at the Commonwealth Office which was specifically concerned with an airdrop of relief supplies into Biafra. At this meeting Mr. George Thomson, the Minister concerned, emphasized that the British Government would like no action without the approval of the Lagos Government. He also requested that there should be no public pressure for an airdrop as the matter was being examined by the Commonwealth Office."

Obilagu goes uphill and downhill: The relief official was George Orick of UNICEF.

327

111 **Swedish Air Force Hercules:** Interestingly, in view of the reluctance of other governments to make their aircraft available to the ICRC without an agree ment by Nigeria and Biafra, an official of the Swedish Foreign Ministry later informed me that his government "did not get any adverse reaction from the Nigerian Government" for having turned an air force C-130 over to the Red Cross.

"at the moment hypothetical": Mitchell Sharp remarked about the ICRC's request for C-130s: "Unfortunately for all of us, after agreement has been reached with the Nigerian government the Biafran authorities refused to agree to the airlift. In these circumstances the question whether we should supply Hercules planes is at the moment hypothetical. However, just as soon as arrangements are made for the use of an airstrip we shall be glad to provide additional aircraft. . . ." Canadian Parliamentary debate, September 13, 1968, p. 14.

112– **Uli Airport:** Five days after Red Cross flights would have begun into Uli Airport
13 under the proposal made by Gowon to Lindt, the Nigerian Third Marine Commando Division had advanced up from the southwest (using boats across Lake Oguta) and was threatening to capture the Biafran airstrip. By September 10, as a consequence, Uli was out of action and Biafran authorities had to rescind their agreement with the ICRC that had demilitarized Obilagu airstrip so that arms flights could begin landing there.

Lindt protested this vigorously, but for the Biafrans it was a life-or-death situation. The ICRC continued to fly into Obilagu September 11 and until midnight on September 12; then the Biafrans stopped relief flights entirely on September 13, 14, and 15 so that arms flights from Libreville could fly in the desperately needed ammunition.

Ojukwu led a counterattack and drove the marine commandos back at Oguta, making it possible for flights to begin landing again at Uli Airport on September 16. Both the ICRC and church airlifts started flying by night into Uli, though for a time the Biafrans had to limit the number of relief flights to ten a night. A few continued to land at Obilagu, but within a week the Nigerian First Division, driving down from the north, was fighting with the Biafrans over that area, and Obilagu ceased being operational. From that time forward, relief as well as arms flights came into Uli, the only airport left in Biafra capable of handling large aircraft.

113 **Orick as UN representative:** After passing on his request to Ojukwu, the chief of the Biafran cabinet responded in this way, according to Orick, explaining: "You have been traveling around Biafra at large, but you do not understand, we are a state."

114 **Orick's assessment:** *Conclusions of George T. Orick from Visit to Biafran Enclave as UNICEF Consultant,* UNICEF internal paper, October 1968, pp. 3–4.

Chapter 13

115 **annual OAU meeting:** At the meeting in Kinshasa the year before, the FMG had succeeded in keeping the OAU from taking up a mediating role, insisting that the conflict be regarded as an internal matter of Nigeria. According to John Stremlau, based on his interviews with General Gowon and especially with Chief

Obafemi Awolowo, who headed the FMG delegation to the African summit held in Zaire, the Nigerians took a very tough line with other African governments, threatening to walk out of the conference if the subject were brought up, and even to raise issues of other nations' problems of secession (Stremlau, *The International Politics of Nigeria*, pp. 85–96). However, the concern of a number of heads of state, including Haile Selassie of Ethiopia, Ankrah of Ghana, Kaunda of Zambia, Tubman of Liberia, and Nyerere of Tanzania finally led to a compromise of setting up a "Consultative Committee." This had no mediating role, however, and the resolution forming it proved a strong bulwark against further attempts to take up the Nigerian-Biafran conflict, particularly within the United Nations.

As we have seen, by July and August of 1968, the consultative committee had taken on a much more active role than envisaged for it in the OAU resolution, and Selassie, especially, had begun attempting to mediate both the conflict and the humanitarian situation. The firm line pressed upon other African governments by the Nigerian delegation at Kinshasa, however, showed the importance the FMG attached to preventing the OAU (or, later, the UN) from internationalizing the conflict.

". . . il a droit à disposer de lui-même": Statement issued by the minister of information following a meeting of French Council of Ministers, July 31, 1968. *New York Times,* August 1, 1968, and *West Africa,* August 3, 1968.

". . . preoccupies and moves the French Government": *Ibid.*

116 **State urged French diplomats:** Those of us at the United Nations concerned with Nigeria-Biafra heard a report in September 1968 that the State Department made a request to the French government, through the U.S. Mission to the UN, that it halt arms shipments to Biafra, but I have not confirmed that this channel was used.

French businessmen and Foreign Ministry: According to Jacques Beaumont, Sam Ikoku (an Ibo in the Federal Military Government) came to Paris, seeking to find out from the diplomats at the Quai d'Orsay what could be done to counter de Gaulle and the rising emotions in France favoring Biafra. Beaumont, a Protestant pastor who had been active with a group in France working for liberation of minority peoples (such as the Kurds and SWAPO), was asked to visit Lagos. He met with General Gowon for four hours, then returned to France and helped set up a pro-Nigerian group, Association France-Nigéria. It was funded mainly by the Nigerian government, though some funds may also have come from French businesses with commercial interests in Nigeria. Beaumont served as secretary general; Association France-Nigéria became the pro-Nigerian counterpart in France to the pro-Biafran group Comité pour la Biafra, headed by Raymond Offroy, a deputy close to de Gaulle who had been the French ambassador to Nigeria during the first year of its independence.

Most French people sympathized with Biafra, while Association France-Nigéria had support mainly from professional diplomats and businessmen with interests in Nigeria. The principal purpose of the association, according to Beaumont, was to keep Nigerian government officials from feeling that all France was against them. The fact that the Quai d'Orsay helped the Nigerian government to set up this pro-Nigerian group in France suggests the depths of the split within the French government.

France was prolonging the war: This was what we were hearing at the United Nations at the time. Later, a U.S. diplomat who had held a senior position in London during the war remarked to me that those in State principally concerned with the problem felt that if there had not been so much meddling from intruders, the war would not have been prolonged. He did not mean humanitarian relief, he said, but the French and other arms support.

arms supply faltered: It was never entirely clear to the Biafrans why the French supply of arms halted for a time at this crucial moment, shrouded as it was in the secrecy surrounding Foccart's clandestine operations in Africa on behalf of the Elysée Palace. It may have represented a brief triumph for those pressing to counter de Gaulle's policy of supporting Biafra. The Nigerian government sent an official to Paris (see previous note), and a deputy with business interests there raised questions in the National Assembly about the use of airbases in Chad for the transit of arms to Gabon (and thence, from Libreville, into Biafra). According to Beaumont, a meeting in Paris "at the highest level"—by which he meant de Gaulle—took a decision to stop the arms shipments. There was a shift in policy in September, then a reversal later, when Foccart was able to reestablish the supply of arms. What lay behind this decision and its reversal remains, at least for this writer, obscured by the secrecy of clandestine operations and de Gaulle's personal operating style.

118   **von Rosen concluded:** Von Rosen wrote of this in his book published some months later. C. G. von Rosen, *Biafra Som jag ser det,* translated into French as *Le Ghetto Biafrais, tel que je l'ai vu,* p. 55.

It should be remembered that von Rosen had a close personal relationship with Emperor Haile Selassie, who presided over the Addis Ababa negotiations during August and early September. (In appreciation of his humanitarian assistance to Ethiopia during the Italian invasion in the thirties and his having helped organize the Ethiopian Air Force, 1946–56, the emperor had given von Rosen a plantation in Ethiopia where he spent a part of each year.)

119   **Warton's passport:** A cable from Ambassador Elbert Mathews stated on August 11, 1967: "Warton's arms smuggling and illegal international air activities led Dept to issue instructions June 30 [1967] to lift his passport and FAA to suspend his airmen's certificate."

Lloyd Garrison saw Warton pleading with the U.S. consular official in Enugu to retrieve his passport so he could go to Miami (where Warton's air charter operation was based) to get airplanes. Garrison later wrote: ". . . The airlift, the only real link with the world for the secessionist former Eastern Region of Nigeria, is the project of Henry Arthur Warton, a German-born pilot who became a United States citizen and who has now become virtually a man without a country. . . . The flights have made trouble for Mr. Warton with the State Department in Washington because the United States has proclaimed a policy of neutrality in the war while supporting the principle of Nigerian unity. Mr. Warton's United States passport has been confiscated because of his unorthodox activities. Without it he cannot work, at least officially, or travel freely." *New York Times,* July 30, 1968.

PAGE

> **C-46 made two flights:** George Orick provided me with this account of his and von Rosen's effort to get the ammunition at the São Tomé airfield airlifted in to Uli.
>
> **Mollerup–von Rosen heated exchange:** Nordchurchaid published, after the war, what was ostensibly "An Operations Report"; it included, laconically, accounts of some political issues: "Capt. von Rosen, on his return from his second trip to Addis Ababa (September 6th–13th) started daily press conferences at noon to answer questions. The conferences often developed into discussions of the political and military situation in and around Biafra, and were the source of much unfortunate publicity for Nordchurchaid. This even reached the point of accusations of weapon-smuggling on the relief airlift which were absolutely unfounded.
>
> "After discussions with Pastor Mollerup and Capt. Orner who arrived on September 24th, Capt. von Rosen asked to be relieved of his duties as Chief of Operations on September 26th, and was succeeded by Capt. Axel Duch. . . ." Lloyd, Mollerup, and Bratved, *The Nordchurchaid Airlift to Biafra*, pp. 14–15.

120   **Code of Conduct:** It should be kept in mind that the idea of the Red Cross and an understanding of the Geneva Conventions did not have the long tradition in Nigeria that they had in Europe. It had taken years of education by the Red Cross in Europe, following adoption of the First Geneva Convention in 1864, to diffuse an understanding of their observance in time of war. Nigeria had been independent only seven years when the Code of Conduct was issued to its soldiers; while the officers (many of them trained at Sandhurst) no doubt fully understood the Geneva Conventions, it is doubtful that many of the hastily trained troops did.

121   **"troops we can hear clanking up the hill":** George Orick provided this account of his and Jaggi's visit to the Red Cross medical station at Okigwe.

> **ICRC described what had happened:** Press release 915b, International Committee of the Red Cross, Geneva, October 4, 1968.
>
> **secretary general's representative:** "Report of Incident at Okigwe, Nigeria," press release SG/1716, United Nations, October 9, 1968.

122   **Biafrans were bitter:** The Biafran commissioner for information, Dr. Ifegwu Eke, issued a statement, saying, in part: "If the ICRC feels that protests with the vandal regime in Lagos have any use, it should not just investigate and protest against the killing of four persons because they happened to be white. . . . It should also investigate and protest against the coldblooded murder at the same time of over 100 Biafran civilians, all of them non-combatant men and helpless women and children, and all of them, white and black, victims of the same killers in the same army. . . ." Biafran Overseas Press Division press release, Umuahia, October 8, 1968.

Chapter 14

123   **Arnold Smith on genocide:** Smith testified before the External Affairs and National Defence Committee of the House of Commons, Parliament of Canada, Minutes of Proceedings and Evidence, no. 2, October 8, 1968, p. 56.

> **no policy of genocide:** However, one U.S. presidential candidate said what British diplomats had been trying to discourage anyone from thinking: ". . .

Genocide is what is taking place right now—and starvation is the grim reaper." Richard Nixon stated: "If adequate food is not delivered to these people in the immediate future, hundreds of thousands of human beings will die of hunger."

This break with the official line put officials in the State Department on notice. In a few months Nixon might be president; they would have to begin taking this possibility into account. The other candidate, Vice-President Hubert Humphrey, had already issued two statements in support of humanitarian relief for Biafra. The Nixon statement also said: "This is not the time to stand on ceremony or to 'go through channels' or to observe the diplomatic niceties. . . . The destruction of an entire people is an immoral objective, even in the most moral of wars. It can never be justified; it can never be condoned."

And further: "The time is long past for the wringing of hands about what is going on. While America is not the world's policeman, let us at least act as the world's conscience in this matter of life and death for millions." News release, Nixon for President Committee, September 10, 1968.

124 **Investigation of Crimes of Genocide:** The committee, which met in Paris, March 22–23, 1969, included a number of the main religious leaders of France, as well as René Cassin, winner of the Nobel Peace Prize for his work on human rights. The committee resolved that "there was a prima-facie evidence of genocide against the Biafrans."

Onya-Onianwah: The account that follows is a portion of one of the numerous depositions appended to the report of the International Committee on the Investigation of Crimes of Genocide. It is not entirely clear how these depositions were gathered, though the introduction to the report states that Dr. Mensah, a Ghanaian appointed by the committee to travel to Nigeria and Biafra, "met a wide range of people" in Biafra in December 1968 and "a number of affidavits were collected. . . ." This, apparently, is one of them.

125 *Newsweek* **account:** *Newsweek,* September 9, 1968.

125– **British suggested observers:** While I had been told that the idea of interna-
6 tional observers had been Sir David Hunt's, John Stremlau gives an account that leaves precise authorship of the proposal less clear (based upon an interview with Lord Shepherd): "The next morning [following the Commons debate] Wilson's minister of state in the Commonwealth Office, Lord Shepherd, was scheduled to see Chief Enahoro to counteract Biafra's successful penetration of British politics. Shepherd recalls preparing for the meeting in light of recent 'nasty incidents,' and was determined to 'get the heat off.' The result was a suggestion that the federal government invite a team of international observers to serve as 'umpires,' overseeing the conduct of battle for the purpose of dis-crediting the Biafran lobby in Britain.

"The proposal for international observers was not new, but in the past it had been associated with policing a cease-fire. When Shepherd met Enahoro later in the morning, August 28, he claims to have told him bluntly: 'Look, your pro-paganda machine is bloody awful. You know what we're up against. What do you think of inviting observers, military men who would report publicly on the situation?' Enahoro agreed to pass along the proposal, and within forty-eight hours Gowon sent his approval. . . ." Stremlau, *The International Politics of the Nigerian Civil War,* pp. 265–6.

126 **letter requesting observers:** The letter from the FMG to the Canadian government was printed as Appendix N of the Minutes of Proceedings and Evidence
of the Standing Committee on External Affairs and National Defence, House of
Commons, Parliament of Canada, October 23, 1968, p. 530.
director of oil shipping company: "Observations on the Observers" by Suzanne
Cronje, *Peace News*, London, November 14, 1969.
Aitken on Alexander: Aitken, *Officially Secret*, p. 102.

127 **observers' first report:** *News from Nigeria*, issued by the Embassy of Nigeria,
Washington, 1968.
secretary general's representative: As quoted in Nigerian press release issued
by the Embassy of Nigeria, Washington, 1968. (The original is in UN press
release SG/1715, October 9, 1968.)

128 **Canadian M.P.:** Mr. Stewart (Cochrane), Minutes of Proceedings and Evidence
of the Standing Committee on External Affairs and National Defence, House of
Commons, Parliament of Canada, October 8, 1968, p. 10.
British M.P.: Frank Allaun, oral answers by Foreign Secretary Michael Stewart,
House of Commons, October 22, 1968 *Parliamentary Debates* (Hansard, col. 1076).
only FMG propaganda success: Scott report, para. 80.

129– **Scandinavian foreign ministers:** *Documents on Swedish Foreign Policy 1968*, doc-
30 ument 80.

130 **Pastor Mollerup:** *Scandinavian Times*, May 1970.

131 **Thant under pressure:** A top UN official later informed me that the secretary
general had been under constant pressure from the Soviet Union during the
1960s aimed at inhibiting his initiatives.

Also, Thant's successor as secretary general, Kurt Waldheim, commented in
a similar vein: "The Secretary-General cannot force issues," Waldheim said. "He
has to be neutral. He has to be as objective as possible. I will tell you frankly, you
know what happened during the Congo crisis: Dag Hammarskjöld was very
active in this dispute and he involved the United Nations deeply in that conflict
and the result was, of course, a deep crisis.

"I don't know what would have happened to him if he had survived. As a
result of Mr. Hammarskjöld's action we have had a financial crisis at the United
Nations that has lasted to this day." *New York Times*, April 27, 1972.

132 **U Thant to OAU:** Press release SG/SM/998, United Nations, September 13,
1968, pp. 3–5.
Senator Edward Kennedy: He spoke in the U.S. Senate. Kennedy became involved as chairman of the Subcommittee on Refugees of the Senate Judiciary
Committee.

In America, as in Europe, the humanitarian situation in Biafra evoked concern of people, surprisingly, across the political spectrum. Senator Richard
Russell, leader of the Southern senators, for example, joined Senator Kennedy
in deploring what he characterized as "this mass murder or attempted genocide," expressing his sense of guilt at being so completely helpless and unable to
do something about it: ". . . I do not favor military intervention in Nigeria, but
I cannot understand why our Government has acted so casually about what is a

great world tragedy—the elimination of a whole people. I feel a sense of guilt. I feel it individually, and I feel it even greater for my country, the most powerful nation in the world. This nation has satisfied itself with a few sanctimonious words of regret. Many thousands, even millions, of people are being murdered either by arms or by starvation, without our making a truly active and vigorous protest in undertaking to get some of our associates, such as the British, who have great authority and influence in that area, to take steps to attempt to stop the tragedy before the last of the Ibos are killed." *Congressional Record—Senate,* September 23, 1968, S-11227-8.

132– **Thant initiative:** Press release SG/SM/1009, September 23, 1968, United Na-
3   tions, pp. 5–6, 15, and 16.

133   **Thant on Nigeria-Biafra:** *Ibid.,* pp. 3, 15, 16.

134   **international law expert:** The dean of the University of Toronto Law School, Ronald St. John MacDonald, made his comment in a memorandum submitted to the Committee on External Affairs and National Defence, Canadian House of Commons (Minutes Proceedings, no. 13, appendix P, October 31, 1968).
       Ojukwu to UN: Ojukwu's letter was sent October 3, 1968. Biafran Overseas Press Division news release Gen. 333.

135   **Mitchell Sharp distressed:** Alan Grossman, the correspondent of *Time* maga-zine in Ottawa at the time (who had just returned from being the correspondent in Nigeria), recounted this experience with Sharp a short time later in conver-sation with the author and others. It suggests the conflict some diplomats and government officials felt between their humanitarian instincts and the official role they were being called upon to perform.
       Thant warning to Mitchell Sharp: At the time, the acting assistant secretary of state for African affairs, C. Robert Moore (Joseph Palmer was in Lagos), testified to the Senate Subcommittee on African Affairs (chaired by Senator Eugene McCarthy): "To be perfectly frank, there is not sufficient support at the present time among the U.N. membership for a useful consideration of this question there. . . . In a recent exchange of letters between the Canadian Foreign Min-ister and the Secretary-General of the United Nations on the subject, the Secretary-General expressed the view that to raise the Nigerian question in the General Assembly could be divisive, particularly in the light of the resolutions adopted by the heads of state of the OAU." Statement of C. Robert Moore, acting assistant secretary of state for African Affairs, Subcommittee on African Affairs, Committee on Foreign Relations, U.S. Senate, October 4, 1968, p. 7.
       Arikpo and Thant to Labouisse: Some years later Henry Labouisse professed not to recall Thant speaking to him in this way. However, those of us working with him at the time were aware he had been so admonished. I hesitated to use this information without further corroboration. Then, in conversation and with-out prompting, General William Tunner remarked to me, "Harry Labouisse told me that U Thant had warned him to stop meddling in the Nigerian situa-tion." It was Ambassador Clyde Ferguson who commented to me, in 1969, that Arikpo had "read the riot act to Labouisse—not once, but a number of times." I was present when Labouisse responded in this agitated manner.

Chapter 15

136   **Nigerian government statement:** "Relief Problems in Nigeria," press release of September 13, 1968, Nigerian Embassy, Washington, D.C. This nine-page statement, subtitled "Effective Measures Taken by the Federal Government," summarizes the FMG's position on relief and provides a particularly full account of the Nigerian version of events surrounding the start of the Red Cross airlift.

137   **Yewande Oyediran:** Mrs. Oyediran was chairwoman of the National Advisory Committee of Voluntary Agencies (NACVA) in Lagos.

138   **"World opinion left in the dark":** This quote as well as the other information in this paragraph is based on an interview I had with the diplomat of another nation about his conversation with Ambassador Mathews just after Palmer's meeting with Gowon. He read the quote to me from a report he had made to his own government at the time.

     "You are a correct institution": According to the Red Cross official who provided this quote, Gowon in his meeting with Gallopin wanted ICRC planes to first make a touchdown in Lagos, so the Nigerians could check the cargo. While ICRC field staff feared any checking by the Nigerians could obstruct the airlift, Gallopin's own view differed: the ICRC should have taken the risk, he felt, as it would have provided security to Red Cross flights. But Gallopin believed a touchdown at Lagos was unacceptable to Ojukwu. This was, of course, the case; presumably Gowon was proposing it for Red Cross flights because the Nigerians had learned the previous November, when the Biafrans refused to accept an ICRC flight direct from Lagos Airport, that it would be unacceptable to them.

139   **the "Lagos mentality":** This thinking affected, of course, the thinking and planning of officials and diplomats back in governments and foreign offices who believed that the information from their embassies in the Nigerian capital was superior to that reaching the public and members of parliaments and the Congress from journalists and relief agency officials reporting from Biafra. The hubris of diplomats in this regard persisted throughout the conflict and following the collapse of Biafra in spite of the many instances in which events proved the information from Lagos incorrect.

     The planning paper mentioned in the next paragraph provides two examples: Biafra was not conquered by mid-September, as expected, nor did it later collapse before March 1, 1969, as the paper presumed for purposes of planning relief. The "Lagos mentality" was an important factor standing in the way of overcoming government reluctance to support relief agencies.

     "D-day": The AID paper from the U.S. Embassy in Lagos stated that as of March 1, 1969, ". . . we estimate there will be 3,000,000 persons requiring assistance in what was formerly Biafra and 1,500,000 in the rest of Eastern Nigeria." Of course, when the collapse of Biafra finally did come more than ten months later than "D-day," after January 10, 1970, political factors got in the way of such earlier planning assumptions, as we shall see.

139–
40   **ICRC meeting with governments:** This account of Gonard's and Lindt's remarks to the representatives of donor governments at the meeting the ICRC

held in Geneva, November 8, 1968, is based on notes taken by one of the relief agency representatives present.

140 **Lindt: remarkable improvement:** As of that date, November 8, 1968, when the ICRC was meeting with representatives of governments, appealing to them for the funds necessary to continue the relief operation, the Red Cross had made 414 relief flights into Biafra, and the church relief airlift a total of 587 (including the limited number each had made before the airlifts began in early September). The number of flights each night varied, depending on various factors, as can be seen in these figures for the number of flights by each of the airlifts over the week prior to the meeting:

Night	ICRC flights	Church flights
Nov. 1–2	10	10
2–3	10	7
3–4	8	8
4–5	6	–
5–6	6	5
6–7	–	2
7–8	2	6

request to Canada for C-130s: Wrinch provided an account of the ICRC's deliberations and his own requests to the Canadian government for Hercules aircraft to the External Affairs Committee of the Canadian House of Commons.

141 **Canadian M.P.s:** The two members of Canada's Parliament, Andrew Brewin and David MacDonald, have given their own account of their efforts to change the Canadian government's policy in their book *Canada and the Biafran Tragedy* (James Lewis & Samuel, 1970).

Sharp approached Arikpo: Mitchell Sharp to Standing Committee on External Affairs and National Defence, House of Commons, Parliament of Canada, October 10, 1968, p. 124.

142 **Ivan Head to Lagos:** Trudeau gave an account of his assistant's visit to Lagos to the House of Commons a few days later. Canadian Parliamentary Debates, November 4, 1965, pp. 2345, 2363–64.

daylight flights: The note of the Nigerian External Affairs Ministry of November 4, 1968, withdrawing authorization for the ICRC to fly at its own risk stated: ". . . Owing to the difficulty of identifying ICRC flights at night it has now been decided that all ICRC flights should take place in daylight hours. The ICRC is therefore invited to enter discussions with the Federal Military authorities about the arrangements for flights in daylight hours. The agreement [*sic*] whereby the ICRC was authorized to fly to the rebel-held areas at its own risk is hereby withdrawn with effect from the date of this note."

That this was a complete reversal of the Nigerian opposition to daylight flights prior to September 3 is reflected in the testimony of Assistant Secretary of State Joseph Palmer to the Senate Committee on Foreign Relations on September 11, 1968, when he said: "The Federal Government, for its part has been generally opposed to mercy air corridors, which Biafra favors, because of concern that they will be infiltrated during daylight hours—as they now are at night—by clandestine arms shipments into Biafra or otherwise give a military advantage to the Biafrans. . . ."

Trudeau: Statement by prime minister respecting Biafra and discussion with U Thant, Canadian Parliamentary Debates, November 4, 1968, p. 2345 *et seq.*

formal note to ICRC: November 4, 1968, previously cited in note above, "daylight flights."

Chapter 16

145 **Middelkoop cable to Thant:** See p. 3.

Orick's assessment: Upon his return from Biafra, Orick reported to UNICEF: "My guess (which is also the guess of relief personnel in Biafra) is that total crop exhaustion will occur at the end of this year. . . . At best, the airlift has reduced or possibly stabilised the *rate of increase* of deaths, and has not, insofar as I could determine, reduced the death rate itself. There are plans to double the airlift capacity. As the carbohydrate deficit increases, the airlift tonnage of an enlarged airlift can probably, for a period of a few weeks, continue to create the illusion of controlled starvation, but I believe that by December it will be apparent that depletion of food stocks in the enclave will have rendered the airlift incapable of meeting even 10% of the need at that time." *Conclusions of George T. Orick from Visit to Biafran Enclave as UNICEF Consultant,* UNICEF internal paper, October 1968, pp. 3, 5.

146 **Opinion of AID counsel:** August 15, 1968.

Van Hoogstraten rose in great wrath: While I have taken this account from the minutes of the meeting, held July 30, 1968, at the American council of Voluntary Agencies for Foreign Service in New York City, I was present and remember the emotion and tension quite vividly.

147 **". . . everything in its power to block them":** Orick's telephone conversation took place in my presence.

***Washington Post* editorial:** November 18, 1968.

147– **Senator Edward Kennedy:** Press release of November 17, 1968: "Senator
8 Kennedy appeals to America's leaders for greater humanitarian aid to Nigeria-Biafra and efforts to end the civil war."

148 **"deluge of mail":** Benjamin Welles reported in the *New York Times,* October 30, 1968, that ". . . The White House, State Department and Congressional and relief sources report a deluge of mail, telegrams and phone calls from across the country. These inquiries are said to reflect increasing disquiet over the Administration's apparent inability, or unwillingness, to slash through red tape and feed the victims of the 16-month-old Nigerian war. . . ."

Soviet trade agreement: The "high-ranking British diplomat" was quoted in a *New York Times* story, datelined Lagos, November 21, 1968, which reported on the reaction in Nigeria: "What is generally known and admired is the promptness with which the Soviet Union moved to take sides in the civil war while Nigeria's 'traditional friends' in the West vacillated. 'Ironically enough,' said a commentator on the government-owned radio recently, 'it was one of the nations which Nigeria used to treat with fear and suspicion that has turned out to be her greatest friend in her most trying hours. This nation is the Soviet Union.' "

task force at State: Welles, in the *New York Times,* reported about creation of the new emergency task force: "It is said to reflect a growing belief in high Government circles that officials both in the United States Embassy in Lagos, the Nigerian federal capital, and in the State Department's Bureau of African Affairs are committed both professionally and emotionally to a quick victory by the Nigerian Government as the only true solution to Biafran starvation.

"These officials are said to see little useful purpose in deliberately risking the displeasure of the Nigerian Government—and United States influence at a time when Soviet influence is growing—by too great an involvement, even to aid starving civilians, in a 'rebellious' territory." *New York Times,* November 27, 1968.

149   **Katzenbach speech:** Department of State press release no. 267, December 3, 1968.

149– **State corrects Katzenbach:** The department spokesman's briefing of news cor-
50   respondents on December 5 and 6 are reprinted in the Department of State Bulletin of December 23, 1968.

150   **State Department proposal:** A news story setting forth the details appeared on the front page of the *New York Times,* December 15, 1968, headlined "U.S., in shift, maps $20 million plan to relieve Biafra."

Chapter 17

151   **Catholic connections:** Whatever feeling did exist within the Foreign Office and the Department of State that opposition to Britain's support for Nigeria came particularly from Catholics (I was told this by a top official of the American Embassy in London) was mistaken. The response was remarkably ecumenical and across the political spectrum as well, to a degree seldom seen in any international situation. That such a view was held at all (and it is difficult to judge how widespread it was) suggests how out of touch some British and American diplomats became, besieged as they were in a diplomatic enclave of their own making.

a sense of stalemate: Anthony Lewis reported in the *New York Times* from London: "British expectations of an early total military victory for federal forces in Nigeria—a belief that has persisted for many months—shows signs of changing. The military situation in the bloody civil war is now appraised here as a stalemate. . . . This is a significant change in the prevailing London view. Until recently the operative feeling has been that an early federal victory would be the most humane way to end the fighting and reestablish internal order and food supplies." *New York Times,* December 4, 1968.

152   **tax riots in the West:** *West Africa* reported: "Troops opened fire in Ibadan, killing eleven people, when a crowd of about 2,000 stormed offices to protest against tax

measures on Nov. 26. The previous day people protesting for the same reason had burned down the palace and car of the traditional ruler of Ishara, about 35 miles southwest of Ibadan. . . ." *West Africa*, November 30, 1968.

152   **cost of war to Nigeria:** *West Africa* comment "the thought still nags" was in *West Africa* of January 18, 1969, while the reports on oil production appeared in *West Africa* of November 23, and December 7, 1968.
Foreign Secretary Stewart: *Parliamentary Debate* (Hansard), December 12, 1968, cols. 599–600.
"great tragedy looming up": This comment—"already there is a great tragedy occurring and an even greater one looming up in the months ahead"—indicates that Her Majesty's Government was aware of the possibility of carbohydrate starvation affecting the entire population of Biafra. This did not, however, result in a change of policy.

153   **Gowon to emperor:** Reuters, Lagos, *New York Times,* December 25, 1968.
Ojukwu anger at Lindt pressure: A top official of the ICRC informed me that Ojukwu had warned he would throw the Red Cross out of Biafra if Lindt did not stop pressing for daylight flights, but the official was vague about the exact time this occurred. Analysis has persuaded me it would have been about this time, at the end of 1968, but I have not received confirmation of the exact date.

153– **Stewart on night flights:** The argument that Ojukwu wanted relief at night
4   as cover for arms shipments, therefore would not agree to flights during the day, by this time had become a part of the campaign for daylight flights into Uli.

154   **Ojukwu Christmas message:** Biafran Overseas Press Division press release Gen-459, Umuahia, December 22, 1968.
Biafra on daylight flights: Biafran Overseas Press Division press release Gen-471, Umuahia, December 29, 1968.
Ojukwu on second airfield: Biafran Overseas Press Division press release Gen-459, Umuahia, December 22, 1968.

155   **C-97 crews:** A reference to the recruitment of the pilots and crews from Air National Guard units in the United States appears in an "Evaluation of C-97G Operation on São Tomé" by Col. Arthur E. Dewey (July 3, 1969), deputy to the U.S. coordinator for humanitarian relief in Nigeria. Reprinted in Lloyd, Mollerup, and Bratved, *The Nordchurchaid Airlift to Biafra*, pp. 184–85.
Gowon warning and FMG statement: Associated Press, Lagos, in *New York Times,* December 31, 1968.
U.S. Embassy statement: *New York Times,* January 1, 1969.
Ibadan professors: The letter of the six professors at Ibadan University appeared in the Lagos *Sunday Times* of December 29, 1968.

157   **identifying himself as "Genocide":** A tape recording of this flight was made by one of the pilots, describing the events, including a recording of the conversations with "Genocide"—from which this account is taken.

339

PAGE

157–8 **UN observer's report:** "Fourth Interim Report by Representative of Secretary-General to Nigeria on Humanitarian Activities," UN press release SG/1725, January 17, 1969.

158 **Secretary General Thant:** "Transcript of Press Conference by Secretary-General, U Thant, held at Headquarters on 28 Jan. 1969," UN press release SG/SM/1062, January 28, 1969, p. 13.

U Thant went on to state, as a principle that would appear to be more a political expedient for the occupant of the post of secretary general: "Another important principle from the United Nations point of view, and for that matter from my point of view, is that the United Nations as such cannot endorse or support any action or any movement for the secession of a particular part of a Member State. . . .

"As you know, there are secessionist movements in many parts of the world. I would say that more than half of the Member States of the United Nations are beset with that problem. Of course, it is a purely internal problem. If the United Nations were to give endorsement to the principle of secession, there would be no end to the problems besetting many Member States." Ibid., p. 14.

Chapter 18

159 **a vigorous, energetic policy:** While the Nixon administration set about to establish a new policy, giving priority to humanitarian relief, the reluctance of anonymous "experts" in the State Department to implement such a policy was indicated in a report by Benjamin Welles in the *New York Times* about the new initiative: " 'Congress and the public don't realize that the facilities to handle relief inside Biafra are almost at the saturation point,' one expert said. 'There's one airstrip with limited parking and warehousing facilities. Biafra allows only night flights, which are risky. You can put all you want into the big end of a funnel—but it's what comes out at the small end that matters.'

" 'There's a shooting war going on between Nigeria and Biafra,' one official said. 'That's where the decision lies, not here. Until they stop fighting, there's very little relief we can get into Biafra.' "

A change had just taken place in the United States on the part of those groups and individuals concerned about starvation in Biafra, a change that antagonized officials in State with responsibility for Nigeria even more than pressures for relief. As Welles reported in the *Times*: "Another factor affecting Washington's policy is that full-page newspaper advertisements in the United States press last week began calling not merely for more aid to Biafra but for political recognition. This call has added to the mood of war weariness in Federal Nigeria the suspicion that United States humanitarian interest in Biafra conceals growing political support.

" 'What does recognition of a landlocked African area fighting for its life mean?' asked one expert. 'Would it mean United States military and financial guarantees of Biafra's territory? Of its political existence? Of its economy? We ought to think this through pretty thoroughly.' " *New York Times*, January 27, 1969.

Thant: "earnest hope": From a statement released as a *Note to Correspondents* at the United Nations, UN Press Services, note no. 3505, January 23, 1969. This is an extremely brief account of the activity that went on in the international diplomatic community during the last half of January 1969 in an attempt to gain reestablishment of Red Cross relief flights from Fernando Po. It was one instance during the lugubrious history of interference with the relief agencies when those who publicly extolled the role of the International Committee of the Red Cross, such as Secretary General Thant, actually took seriously their responsibility to intervene and support the efforts of the ICRC.

160   **Congressional Resolution:** S. Con. Res. 3 and H. Con. Res. 96, 91st Cong., 1st sess.

160–   **Nixon letter to Gowon:** This paraphrase of the letter was set forth to me by a
1   White House official well acquainted with its content. At the time it was considered highly confidential, involving as it did a communication between the president and another head of state on an extremely sensitive subject. While I have not since obtained the original text, I believe the paraphrase contains accurately the gist of the message from President Nixon to General Gowon.

161   **Richardson testimony:** The undersecretary of state himself made reference to this delay in an opening apology to the committee: " . . . Let me say first of all that I'm personally chargeable with the delinquency you noted in the timely submission of these statements. I simply felt that my own statement required a significant amount of revision in order to cover a point which seemed to me to be within the purview of the Committee. . . ." Hearings, Subcommittee on Refugees, U.S. Senate Committee on the Judiciary, July 15, 1969, p. 8.

162–   **Goodell team report:** Senator Goodell placed the report of the Biafra study
3   mission he headed in the Congressional Record of February 25, 1969 (pp. S1976-7). The team was composed of a nutritionist, Professor Jean Mayer of Harvard School of Public Health; a pediatrician, Dr. Roy Brown of Tufts University; an expert on agriculture in Nigeria, Dr. George Axinn of Michigan State University; a logistics and transport expert, George Orick, who had gone into Biafra the previous fall as a consultant to UNICEF; and the senator's administrative assistant, Charles Dunn. While this was a responsible, experienced, authoritative group, it would appear that their extensive report was largely disregarded within the State Department, for when Elliot Richardson and Ferguson testified before Senator Edward Kennedy's subcommittee in July they emphasized the difficulty of getting reliable estimates of the situation in Biafra.

163   **assurance to Goodell:** Goodell announced in February and later stated in testimony submitted to the Senate Subcommittee on Refugees: "On my return from Biafra in February of this year, the Administration gave me, and I announced, the assurance that: 'The United States Government will make available to relief agencies on a feasible and emergency basis such cargo planes, ships, maintenance personnel, and parts as are found to be necessary to perform the humanitarian mission of getting food and medical supplies to the starving people in Nigeria and Biafra.' "

Later (1971), Goodell informed me that, after he had made a similar statement in a speech to the National Press Club in February 1969, the State Department spokesman stated that United States policy had not changed. Goodell said that the Bureau of African Affairs thereby went counter to what the secretary of state and the secretary of defense had told him; that the wording he had used had been cleared with the president in the National Security Council meeting.

no "rinky-dink politician": Allard Lowenstein had been one of the principal organizers of the "Dump Johnson" movement which led to Eugene McCarthy's presidential primary campaign that helped bring about President Johnson's decision in March 1968 not to run for reelection. Lowenstein himself became a candidate for Congress and was elected in November 1968. His first trip to Biafra was in December 1968, and his second coincided with the arrival in Lagos and Biafra of the Goodell-Mayer team in February 1969.

164–5   **Lowenstein plan:** Lowenstein provided me with his side of the experience of attempting to negotiate a second airstrip in two conversations, April 1971 and March 1972. At that time he still was not entirely clear what had happened to his proposal. He was killed by a former associate on March 14, 1980.

165   **Ojukwu letter to congressmen:** The letter, to Senators Edward Kennedy and Charles Goodell and Congressmen Allard Lowenstein and Donald Lukens, was released March 24, 1969, in the Biafran Overseas Press Division press release Gen-544.

166   **pressure on Reverend Johnson:** Johnson informed me about this in 1972 when he provided me with his side of the attempt to build a second relief airfield in Biafra. It is worth noting that Johnson was a man of acute political sagacity who understood the Nigerian situation well and had had a long personal acquaintance with some top leaders of the FMG.

167–8   **"The Hague Group":** The group, which held its first meeting at the Hague on February 28, 1969, was composed of diplomats from Austria, Belgium, Canada, Denmark, the Federal Republic of Germany, Ireland, Italy, the Netherlands, Norway, Sweden, Switzerland, and the United States. Britain was not included. Clyde Ferguson had only been appointed six days before; though a quick learner, he could hardly have understood the situation in depth in less than a week. That the Hague Group agreed to concentrate negotiations on two proposals that all should have known in advance could not be accepted by Biafra for military reasons need not be viewed as calculating or sinister. Rather, it manifests the way in which diplomats—even of countries and governments committed to humanitarian relief—had come to think about this problem. They would do only what was acceptable to the Nigerian government. The Hague Group essentially formalized a working approach the participating diplomats had already evolved among themselves while to the public it gave a false impression of being primarily concerned with getting humanitarian relief in more effectively.

Chapter 19

169   **Jean Mayer on bombing:** The report of the Goodell team had described the bombing of civilians in Biafra: ". . . It is particularly significant that children as young as 16 months of age were observed by us running into the bunkers when

they hear the first warning shots (substitutes for air raid sirens) and the bombs fall. . . ."

Mayer, who headed the team, wrote the letter from which this quote is taken to *The New Republic* in March 1969 in response to an earlier comment in the magazine deprecating reports of federal atrocities as "pure fabrication fed to reporters."

Churchill in the *Times*: The articles by Churchill appeared in The *Times* on March 3, 4, 5, and 6, 1969.

169–
70

Churchill and Garrison: Garrison described this experience to me.

170

discredit Churchill: The *Times*, in its leader of March 12, 1969, defended Winston Churchill III against these attacks: ". . . The attempt to discredit Mr. Churchill, which we believe to be officially inspired, is an attempt to cover over the facts of starvation, bombing and death by resorting to personalities."

The other journalist who wrote to the *Times* (letter, March 13, 1969) was Michael Leapman, who at the time he first reported from Biafra was a correspondent for the *Sun* and later joined the *Times*.

What was worrying government officials is indicated in the report by the *Times* political correspondent on March 6: "Party managers on both sides of the Commons warily recognize the increasing disquiet and restiveness of many of their backbenchers about the impotence of the Government to prevent Nigerian bombing of non-military targets in Biafran territory. . . ."

Spectator comment: This leader appeared in the *Spectator* of March 14, 1969. Nigel Lawson, then editor, and Auberon Waugh, who wrote for it, consistently took a strong position critical of government policy on Nigeria and Biafra. Waugh not only wrote a book, with Suzanne Cronje, *Biafra, Britain's Shame*, but named his daughter, born at the time, "Biafra."

171

James Griffiths: His account of his own experience in Biafra appears in the debate held in the House of Commons, *Parliamentary Debates* (Hansard), 13 March 1969, cols. 1591–93.

Heath and Sir Alec: Edward Heath's question appears in col. 1558 and Sir Alec Douglas-Home's comment in col. 1589 of the House of Commons debate, Parliamentary Debates (Hansard), 13 March 1969. It should be said that while the leader of the Conservative party, Heath, and its Shadow Cabinet foreign minister, Douglas-Home, enjoyed having a bit of fun at the Labour prime minister's expense, the Conservative party was not a critic of the government's Nigeria policy. Not until December 1969, shortly before the end of the war, would the Tories break with Labour and insist on a plan for humanitarian relief. Throughout the war, the Conservatives backed the supply of arms to Nigeria. Critics in Parliament of Britain's policy were individuals in all three parties.

172

"stage-managing" destruction: R. W. Apple, Jr. reported to the *New York Times* from Lagos on March 31: "Maj. Gen. Yakubu Gowon said that the federal Government's air strikes on Biafra, in which a large number of civilians have been killed, would continue as long as the raids were militarily useful. General Gowon . . . conceded at a news conference that some civilian targets had been hit by error, but he argued that this was impossible to prevent while bombing troop concentrations, railroads and supply dumps.

" 'They are nothing deliberate,' the 34-year-old general said of the attacks on markets and hospitals. 'I can swear to that by Almighty God.' He accused Colonel Ojukwu of 'stage-managing many of the scenes' of destruction witnessed by correspondents in rebel-held territory. He asserted that many alleged bomb craters had been faked by Biafran demolition teams with dynamite." *New York Times*, April 1, 1969.

172– **recapture of Owerri:** Ferguson spoke of the situation of people who had been
3   trapped in the fighting around Owerri in his testimony at the July 15, 1969 hearing of Senator Kennedy's Subcommittee on Refugees, p. 11: "When Owerri was finally liberated in April, these people were in the most deplorable condition. The ICRC could not even count the number of persons who died in the immediate weeks after." The ICRC reported: "On 3 May, ICRC teams were able to penetrate into areas which had been, until then, entirely deprived of relief, because communications had been cut by one or the other of the belligerents. Here, they found people, especially in the region south and south-west of Owerri, in an alarming state of distress." *1969 Annual Report,* International Committee of the Red Cross, p. 15.

173   **real objectives of Nigerian offensive:** See *West Africa*, April 12, 1969, p. 425. **Nigerians despair of winning militarily:** A U.S. official with a central role in Nigeria policy informed me of this, and accounts written at the time reflect this attitude in Lagos. Richard Kershaw, after reporting on the military situation, concluded: ". . . Now it is obvious to Nigerians that the fall of Umuahia is not ending the war. Year Three is starting, and that obscene talk of a 'quick kill' which far too many British voices echoed is dying down. There is still unlimited serious fighting to come. It is distinctly possible that neither side will be the winner before the seams begin to give in this sad and tortured country. . . ." *New Statesman,* June 6, 1969.

174   **mercenary pilots:** John de St. Jorre in his book *The Nigerian Civil War* (p. 318) suggested that the mercenary pilots flying for Nigeria were not inclined to shoot down relief planes: "Uli presented the mercenaries with a double-edged dilemma: if they knocked it out, the war would quickly come to an end and they all would be out of a most lucrative job; and then, to close the airport and keep it closed they would have had to shoot down a number of the relief and arms planes thus killing their mercenary comrades on the other side. Since they wished to do neither of these things, they decided, not unnaturally, that Uli should not close—at least not through their own efforts. . . ."
Colonel Dewey: "Evaluation of C-97G Operation on São Tomé," Report by Arthur E. Dewey for Ambassador Ferguson, Department of State, Washington, July 3, 1969 (reprinted in *The Nordchurchaid Airlift to Biafra*, appendix 32).
airlift tonnages: These tonnages, from the ICRC and Joint Church Aid, are drawn from the table compiled by Hentsch for *Face au blocus*, annex 8, p. 278.

175 **ICRC to French Red Cross:** Letter of Jacques Freymond, acting president of the ICRC, to M. Carraud, vice-president of Croix-Rouges Française, May 4, 1969.

Ferguson on food tonnages: Testimony to Senator Kennedy's Subcommittee on Refugees, July 15, 1969, p. 11.

176 **one thing they don't want to look at:** A *Life* editor told me this at the time.

Ojukwu resentment: Ojukwu expressed this vitriolic response to European concern about the oilworkers in the course of an impassioned address to his countrymen on "Thanksgiving Day, June 1, 1969," which became known as the "Ahiara Declaration—setting forth the principles of the Biafran revolution."

177 **Alexander reflected gloomy assessment:** *Sunday Telegraph,* May 11, 1969.

178 **mercenary pilots:** David Robison, who had been a correspondent in Biafra and later did considerable research and interviews on the war, informed me in 1973 that in May–June 1969 the chief of staff of the Nigerian Air Force had warned the mercenaries flying for Nigeria that they had to shoot down planes or the Nigerians would bring in Russian pilots. Ironically, the head of the Nigerian Air Force was later killed in a Biafran miniplane attack on Benin airport. Count von Rosen told me in 1971 that one of the Biafran pilots, formerly in the Nigerian Air Force, recognized the lanky figure of the commander among a group of men who came out onto the airfield and were running toward their aircraft when the group was hit by a rocket from a miniplane.

Lindt arrested: The Red Cross announced: "August Lindt . . . was detained by the airport authorities at Lagos from 6.30 yesterday evening, Tuesday, until 10.25 this morning, 28 May. Apparently the incident occurred due to a misunderstanding of the control tower's instructions to the pilot. The ICRC immediately took the matter up with the Nigerian authorities." ICRC press release 978b, May 28, 1969.

Newsweek: While the story, " 'Operation Biafra Baby,' " about von Rosen's mini-air force appeared in the issue of *Newsweek* dated June 9, 1969, the lack of mention of the shooting down of the Red Cross relief plane indicates that it had been written before that incident took place on June 5.

Chapter 20

181 **FMG statement:** The Nigerian government's statement implies that the Red Cross plane was shot down because it was flying at night and therefore could not be distinguished from one of "Ojukwu's arms planes." That it was still daylight when the attack took place was known to the Nigerians. The following week External Affairs Minister Okoi Arikpo indicated as much by responding to a question at a press conference that when the Nigerian fighter plane instructed the Red Cross aircraft to land at a Federal field, the relief plane sought to escape into the cover of a cloud. Excerpt from a cable of the Swedish ambassador in Lagos providing account of Arikpo press conference, June 14, 1969, Swedish White Paper, document 65.

Also, a note from the Nigerian government to the ICRC, June 20, 1969, stated that it was twilight with thick cloud cover at the time of the incident. *Ibid.*, document 69.

John Stremlau states that in early June Gowon "ordered one of his pilots, an Englishman, to interdict a transport plane destined for Biafra." He reports that a defense attaché at the U.S. Embassy "claims to have had two days prior notice of the interdiction and first-hand knowledge of the monitored radio exchanges." Stremlau cites him as saying that ". . . the MIG first buzzed the relief plane as the Englishman ordered the Swede to land at Port Harcourt for inspection. The latter refused and headed for cloud cover. The MIG made another pass and fired warning shots across the wing tips of the relief plane. When this also failed to move the Swede toward Port Harcourt, the English flier made a third pass and shot off the whole wing." Stremlau, *The International Politics of the Nigerian Civil War,* p. 334.

Stemlau also reports (on pp. 334–35) that the Federal MiG-17 first tailed the Joint Church Aid plane, then chose the Red Cross plane instead, explaining this preference by quoting from his interview with S. Z. Mohammed, whom he identifies as director of Relief and Rehabilitation (Mohammed was chief administrator of the Nigerian Red Cross): "If we had shot down a JCA plane they were under no legal obligation to announce it and would just go on flying. The Red Cross was obliged to announce the shooting of any of its planes and that was important. . . ."

182   **JCA plane attacked:** The two reports cited are from the records of Joint Church Aid. The attack, on June 2, indicates MiG activity at Uli three nights before the shooting down of the Red Cross plane and at about the same time, 1845 hours. It is consistent with reports that the Nigerian government had begun pressing mercenaries flying for its air force to shoot down planes.

    Red Cross ordered out of Lagos airport: The quote from the senior security officer at Lagos International Airport is from the *Sunday Times* of Lagos, June 8, 1969.

183   **London *Observer*:** This report, by Nicholas Carroll, the diplomatic correspondent, appeared in the *Observer* of July 6, 1969. He went on to write that the British government was primarily concerned about getting relations between Lagos and the ICRC on a proper working basis and stated that Maurice Foley in his visit to ICRC president Marcel Naville the previous week had suggested that he send out another "ambassador-type overseer of Red Cross activities under Federal control."

184   **U Thant:** This statement by the secretary general was issued as a *Note to Correspondents,* UN Press Services, note no. 3537, June 7, 1969, United Nations.

    State Department: Statement read to news correspondents by department spokesman on June 6, 1969.

185   **Nigerian Red Cross president:** Chief Adetokunbo Ademola was so quoted in the *Daily Times* of Lagos on June 12, 1969.

    Lindt letter of resignation: Lindt attributed some of his troubles to the Nigerian reaction against the attacks by the miniplanes: "When Count von Rosen intervened, his exploits considerably changed the situation. First a campaign was

185   launched against me in the Nigerian press; then an ICRC aircraft was shot down without any notification to anybody by the Nigerian Government of a change of policy. These events resulted in the Nigerian Federal Government's decision to declare me *persona non grata*. . . ." Lindt's letter to ICRC president, June 19, 1969, ICRC press release 987b. In my opinion, the miniplane attacks served merely as a pretext for the Nigerian government to do what it wanted to do.

ICRC felt compelled: ICRC press release 982b, Geneva, June 11, 1969.

185–   **British military adviser:** Colonel Scott's report contained these references to
6   Uli airfield as the prime objective of the Nigerians in paragraphs 53, 75, 77, 27.

186   **"highly placed British sources":** Christopher Mojekwu revealed this information in Copenhagen on June 15, 1969. Biafran Overseas Press Division press release Gen-657.

daylight flights: On June 10, a few days after the shooting down of the Red Cross plane, Major General Henry T. Alexander wrote a letter to the *Times* in response to a remark made on radio by Hugh Fraser, M.P., which, he stated, " . . . implied that the air war was now entering a stage advocated by me personally."

The general commented: ". . . I have long consistently pointed out that the Federal Air Force has been waging the war under considerable handicap. The Federal Government for a long time now has wished Red Cross mercy flights to take place by day, in order that their Air Force might have free rein to attack arms planes flying in by night. General Ojukwu has insisted on night flights only, presumably because he can then mix the arms flights with Red Cross planes. The very thing which the Federal Government warned might occur, has now happened, namely a Red Cross plane has been shot down. As the efficiency of the Federal Air Force increases, so will their capacity to shoot down aircraft flying by night improve. Even so, in darkness accidents will occur.

"To my mind, General Gowon has been extremely patient over this issue, thus inhibiting the proper prosecution of the war in a very important field.

"The solution is, of course, quite simple. Mercy flights should take place by day, leaving the night air free for arms flights and the Federal Air Force." *Times*, June 12, 1969.

187   **"interdicting Uli by night":** While Scott wrote his report originally in March 1969, the version that became available when published in the *Sunday Telegraph* of January 11, 1970, had been revised in December 1969. Presumably the British defense adviser would have corrected this sentence if the Nigerian Air Force had in the interim acquired the capability of interdicting Uli airfield by night. If they had, they surely would have used it, but Uli remained operational up to the collapse of Biafra.

Biafran affirmative response: The Biafran statement was released June 18, 1969, Biafran Overseas Press Division press release Gen-664.

Ferguson's "one shot": The statement by Ferguson, June 18, 1969, opened: "The United States Government is pleased to note that the Federal Military Government and the Biafran authorities have agreed to a surface relief route into Biafra." Ferguson did not have a *de facto* signed agreement, and his "one shot" announcement was quickly overtaken by events.

Chapter 21

196   **ICRC proposals:** Naville referred to proposals made the week before: "Following its plenary meeting on 19 June, the ICRC has contacted the Nigerian and Biafran authorities in order to work out arrangements for the continuation of its relief action. This should be by air in daylight and by a water-way corridor on the Cross River, as suggested by the U.S. Government. . . . The ICRC emphasizes that its aircraft are ready to resume operations immediately and that the special craft chartered to ply on the Cross River is already available." ICRC press release 991b, June 25, 1969.

197   *The Economist:* July 5, 1969.

198   **three top relief officials:** While Pastor Viggo Mollerup, who ran Joint Church Aid, and Reverend Edward Johnson, who headed Canairelief, were well aware that the Nigerians stood in the way of the relief agencies working effectively and that British government officials and diplomats were staunchly backing them, they never fully understood—throughout the war—just how the British were managing the diplomatic/propaganda cover-up. They suspected something like this, but ICRC secrecy concealed crucial details of the negotiations. Even if diplomats and government officials always did present themselves to the public as deeply concerned about trying to find ways to get relief in to the Biafrans, JCA executives had few illusions about the deep involvement of the British. It is significant, though, that insiders as knowledgeable as Mollerup and Johnson could never get to the bottom of just how the British were doing what they were indeed doing.

199   **the *Times:*** July 7, 1969.

       foreign secretary to Commons: *Parliamentary Debates* (Hansard), 7 July 1969, col. 952.

       question to foreign secretary: Frank Allaun was the Labour M.P. who asked the question. *Ibid.,* col. 955. Of course the use of the term "agreement" was misleading. As Michael Stewart responded, " . . . Of course, there was no written agreement." An agreement that would have allowed the Red Cross to fly in daylight into Uli would have had to include the Biafrans.

       ICRC reaction: While the reaction of Red Cross officials at headquarters was one of "furious anger" (as one of them later told me), one would not learn this from the press release put out in response to the British announcement of agreement. As was its custom, the ICRC released a mild statement, not suggesting any criticism of a government. ICRC press release 995b, July 8, 1969.

       "inaccuracies in reporting": The ICRC statement in response to Sule Kolo's protest included: ". . . The allusion to armaments manufacturers was intended uniquely to serve as a reminder that even the activities of the ICRC, an important humanitarian organization, cannot morally atone for the suffering engendered by the production of weapons of death. . . . " ICRC press release 994b, July 5, 1969.

200   **Stewart to Commons:** *Parliamentary Debates* (Hansard), 10 July 1969, col. 1595.

       communiqué: The communiqué was signed by Enahoro and Naville on July 12, 1969. One diplomat present at the meeting told me that Enahoro was very tough and Naville had to give in; he commented: "I don't know what he could do."

PAGE

201   **"M. Naville has fallen into the trap":** This shrewd as well as witty remark was made by Jan Eggink, who by this time had begun serving as UNICEF's liaison to the ICRC on Nigeria-Biafra relief. He should also receive credit for the comment quoted earlier, when representatives were summoned to the Red Cross "Maison" late on the day that Chief Enahoro had met with the relief agencies in Lagos and taken the coordinating role away from the ICRC: " . . . the Hill is shaking terribly and they are seeking comfort everywhere." Eggink was not on the staff of UNICEF but rather headed the Netherlands Committee for UNICEF.

Chapter 22

202   **Mayer, *Washington Post*:** *Washington Post,* July 2, 1969. The *Post* editorial anticipated "a worldwide demand that Nigeria not interrupt the flow of food," but unlike the previous July and August the public did not, over the next two months, become aroused, though the intention of the Nigerians to starve the Biafrans into capitulation was blatant, acknowledged by Nigerian officials, and pointed out by such influential journals as the *Post,* the *Times* of London, and *The Economist.*

203   **Secretary of State Rogers:** The press conference and the statement put out in his name later in the day by the Bureau of African Affairs were both printed in the *Department of State Bulletin* of July 21, 1969, p. 48 and p. 51.
  Norman Cousins: He had begun through his magazine *Saturday Review* a project to support sending American doctors into Biafra, called Aid to Biafran Children. This led him to his efforts to find a way of negotiating peace in the Nigeria-Biafra conflict. He brought back from his trip a letter from Odumegwu Ojukwu to President Nixon (July 17, 1969) in which the Biafran head of state reaffirmed acceptance of Ferguson's proposal for an upriver relief corridor and asked the assistance of the American president in bringing about a negotiated end to the conflict.
    Cousins wrote about his encounter with the old man in Biafra in the August 2, 1969, *Saturday Review* in an editorial titled "Moon Over Owerri."

204   **five aircraft shot down:** Chief Enahoro made these statements when he was in London July 18; there is no reason to believe that five planes had been shot down. Colin Legum's story appeared in *The Observer* July 19, 1969.
  pilots decide to fly; staff in Biafra protest Naville statement: To put these incidents in chronological perspective: Marcel Naville signed the communiqué with Chief Enahoro in Lagos on July 13, stating that "the ICRC will not penetrate into Nigerian airspace without the authority and consent of the Federal Government." Three days later the pilots decided to fly without authorization if they did not get a countermanding order from ICRC headquarters in Geneva. On July 17, Naville made his statement that the nutritional situation in Biafra was serious but not yet catastrophic. It was the next day that the pilots at Cotonou in a telegram to Naville called upon the Red Cross to relinquish its control of the airlift and to turn them and their planes over to an independent organization willing to fly without the permission of the Federal Military Government. (They

had by this time learned that Joint Church Aid had quietly resumed flying at night from São Tomé into Uli without interception.) If ICRC did not do so within the next two weeks, the pilots warned, they would go home (see London *Times* story from Cotonou, July 19, 1969). The Red Cross staff members in Biafra radioed their message to ICRC Geneva July 21, provoked by Naville's statement that the situation was serious but not catastrophic.

205   **Jaggi statement:** The statement from Jaggi and all other Red Cross staff in Biafra was addressed to ICRC executives; the statement the ICRC had Jaggi put out (which began, "In view of the recent apparent controversy about the food situation in Biafra, some clarification seems appropriate") was released to the public, ICRC press release 1006b, August 2, 1969.

public criticism of Naville: *The Economist,* for example: "In Lagos M. Naville gave the impression that he had come too soon, before he had really got into his new job, and that he should have left things to one of his officials. The fact that his English is halting appeared to create mistrust; and he does not know Africa. Some of the people who met him in Lagos formed the impression that he was, as one of them put it, 'a little wide-eyed.' " *The Economist,* July 19, 1969, p. 37.

205–   **ICRC air corridor proposal:** This proposal of August 1, 1969, contained in
6   notes to General Gowon and General Ojukwu, set forth only the four principles stated here. They have been published in the Swedish White Paper (doc. 80, p. 119, in Swedish) and by Thierry Hentsch (*Face au blocus,* p. 202, in French). The ten technical modalities, mentioned later, were not proposed by the ICRC till August 4.

206   **Nigerian astonishment:** The message from Gowon to Naville of August 4, 1969, was published in the Swedish White Paper, doc. 81, pp. 120–21. My translation. Presumably this represented the new "hard line" of official policy and not necessarily an expression of Gowon's personal sentiments.

ICRC new plan: The ICRC sent the technical modalities to the Nigerians and Biafrans on August 4, 1969 (the ten points will be found in Hentsch, *Face au blocus,* pp. 202–3).

206–   **Arikpo to ambassadors:** The written reply of the Nigerian government to the
7   ICRC's proposal for daylight flights, presented by Foreign Minister Arikpo to ambassadors of donor governments in Lagos on August 5, 1969, was reproduced in the Swedish White Paper, doc. 82, pp. 121–23. My translation.

207   **Article 23:** The ICRC response to Arikpo's remark that nothing in Article 23 authorizes any authority other than the power permitting free passage to make the technical arrangements is reproduced in *ICRC Information Notes* no. 122 of August 22, 1969.

208   **Father Doran's report:** Father Dermot Doran's report on his fact-finding mission into Biafra during the week ending July 28, 1969 (during which he interviewed forty-three relief workers and twenty-three Biafran government officials) is reproduced as Exhibit 2 in the hearings of the U.S. Senate Subcommittee on Refugees, July 15, 1969, pp. 54–57 (which would have been printed after the date of the hearings, hence the later date of the report.).

PAGE

Chapter 23

210   *Washington Post:* The editorial, "Biafrans Are Still Starving," appeared September 9, 1969.

211   **U Thant support:** Chronologically, this represents a slight flashback, as Lindt was at the United Nations toward the end of July. The secretary general's statement was released July 30 (UN press release SG/SM/1139).
         Red Cross emergency flight: The two planes flew on the night of August 4/5 with a cargo of thirty tons of medical supplies and doctors for the Red Cross group in Biafra. *ICRC Information Notes* no. 122, August 22, 1969.

212   **Enahoro adamant:** A few days later the Lagos *Sunday Times* (August 10, 1969) reported: "Relief organizations operating in Nigeria have been given one more warning. . . . Chief Anthony Enahoro said at a press conference in Lagos yesterday the 'one flight operation' agreed upon by the Federal government and ICRC President M. Naville had been completed and the ICRC had made no fresh proposals. . . . He rejected M. Naville's reported proposals that relief aircraft be inspected at a base outside Nigeria recalling that the ICRC President during his three-day talks with Nigerian Government officials in Lagos, had made no mention of his demand for inspection outside Nigeria even though he had all the opportunity to do so. . . . "
         government warning: This advice not to do anything that "would jeopardize daylight flight negotiations" was made to me by Colonel Arthur Eugene Dewey, Ambassador Clyde Ferguson's deputy, when General William Tunner and I (as executive director of the Committee for Nigeria-Biafra Relief) were exploring ways to begin an alternate relief operation, using cargo helicopters from an aircraft carrier. We observed this advice (which had later been seconded by Ferguson) for a couple of months until it had become clear that daylight flight negotiations were not progressing at all. We could not proceed without Washington's support, as it was necessary to use the kind of large cargo helicopters that could be obtained only from the United States government. (More about this in the next chapter.)

213–   **Sabena Dakotas:** Fraser made this statement during debate on Nigeria in the
14   House of Commons on July 10, 1969. *Parliamentary Debates* (Hansard), cols. 608–9. Reverend Edward Johnson of Canairelief remarked to me, in regard to the fear the Biafrans had of the daylight flight negotiations and the danger that Nigerian aircraft might tailgate relief planes into Uli, that antiaircraft gunners at Uli could not be communicated with easily. If they were halted from firing, a bicyclist would have to be sent out to tell them to begin firing again.

215   **Enahoro statement:** From the *Nigerian Observer* of September 5, 1969.
         OAU: The commentary of *West Africa* cited appeared on the front page (p. 945) of the August 16, 1969, issue and went on to remark: "The Federal forces may have returned to the attack when the OAU meeting takes place; but this time it will be hard to convince anybody that Biafran resistance is breaking." This represents a gloomy view that—considering its source—reflected considerable discouragement in Lagos and Whitehall.

216 **Nigerian ambassador:** As it happened, that day (September 8, 1969) I was having lunch with the editorial writer of the *Washington Post* who regularly wrote about Nigeria-Biafra, and he told me he had just been visited in his office by Joseph Iyalla, the Nigerian ambassador. During lunch, I filled him in on what I understood to be going on in the daylight flight negotiations from my contacts with officials of relief agencies and such negotiators as Lindt and Ferguson, both of whom had informed me that the Nigerians, having halted the Red Cross airlift, had no intention of letting relief flights start again.

That evening, when I purchased the early edition of the *Post* and read the next day's editorial, I was disheartened to see that the writer had written that "Nigeria has magnanimously abandoned its earlier inspection demand" and gone on to shift the burden of blame: "Biafra, however, is still balking. The Biafran chief, Colonel Ojukwu, evidently is willing to accede to even more suffering and death, rather than accept the new Nigeria stand. The world's humanitarians, if they are to be fair, ought immediately to turn their appeals from General Gowon to Colonel Ojukwu." *Washington Post,* September 9, 1969.

218 **JCA feeling considerable pressure:** According to a number of Joint Church Aid executives.

219 **Dutch foreign minister:** This comment placing the blame for a failure in the negotiations for daylight relief flights upon the Biafrans was prepared for J. M. A. H. Luns to deliver in the general debate of the UN General Assembly on October 1, 1969, text from the Delegation of the Kingdom of the Netherlands, p. 2.

Swedish foreign minister: The press release of September 16, 1969, setting forth the statement made by the Swedish foreign minister in New York following Biafran rejection of the agreement the ICRC had signed was reprinted as document 74 of *Documents on Swedish Foreign Policy 1969* (Royal Ministry for Foreign Affairs, Stockholm, 1970), p. 175.

Chapter 24

223 **helicopter plan:** Some fifteen people had agreed to serve on the committee but, when the time came to announce the helicopter plan, it proved difficult to gain approval of the proposal from all of them at the same time. So the announcement was made by Humphrey, King, and Tunner. This proved, by chance, advantageous, for each represented a constituency or expertise that made the proposal difficult to attack.

224 **Secretary of State:** This letter from the committee requesting that a "hold" be placed on the delivery of twelve helicopters at the Sikorsky plant, destined for the military but not yet delivered, was sent July 2, 1969.

224– **August Lindt:** Lindt and I discussed the helicopter plan July 22. Two days later,
5   the deputy executive director of UNICEF, E. J. R. Heyward, informed me that he and Lindt had discussed the proposal the previous day and believed that, if carried out in the right way, it was the only one that stood any chance of success

in breaking the impasse over relief flights and that it should be pushed with all speed.

225 **Pius Okigbo:** Letter of Pius N. C. Okigbo for the government of Biafra, dated July 22, 1969.
Undersecretary Richardson: Richardson's letter of reply to our committee's request of July 2 that a "hold" be placed on the twelve helicopters at the Sikorsky plant was sent July 23.

226 **Ferguson and State:** Tunner and I met with Ferguson and his staff August 20, 1969. We know now that at that point the Nigerian government was not negotiating about either daylight flights or the Cross River proposal.
helicopter plan announcement: While it was the Committee for Nigeria-Biafra Relief that announced the helicopter proposal, it was done in the name of "The International Committee of Conscience" (press release of October 5, 1969) with the intention of internationalizing the effort. This began to happen when Sir Alec Douglas-Home and the Conservative party in Britain took up the proposal and pressed for the Labour government to adopt it; at about that time, our committee also began getting a favorable response from the opposition party in Canada to do the same. (Hubert Humphrey had, of course, been the Democratic presidential nominee the year before.) If the Netherlands government had not barred Prince Bernhard from organizing people of equal stature in Europe, the proposal would have been launched with greater impact and this organizing effort of opposition parties in each country could have begun sooner and with greater effect.

227 **Trudeau to Diefenbaker:** Canadian Commons Debates, November 14, 1969, p. 824.

228 *The Economist:* This comment appeared in *The Economist* of October 11, 1969. *West Africa* **on helicopters:** This comment, in "Matchet's Diary," is from *West Africa* of October 11, 1969, p. 1211.

228– **exchange in Commons:** Michael Barnes, M.P., asked the question of Maurice
9 Foley, from excerpts of the debate in Commons reprinted in the *Times*, October 14, 1969.

229 **U.S. assurance:** The statement which Ferguson provided a Biafran representative was quoted by Odumegwu Ojukwu in an address to the Biafran Consultative Assembly on October 31, 1969. Biafran Overseas Press Division press release Gen-746, p. 6.
Ojukwu comment: *Ibid.,* p. 6.

230 **secretary of state:** Press release 339, *Department of State Bulletin,* December 1, 1969.

231 **Red Cross transition:** This undertaking on the part of the FMG not to interfere with the Nigerian Red Cross did not extend, however, to other relief agencies. FMG Press Release 981, September 9, 1969, reprinted in annex 2, "Nigerian Relief Action: Report of the Nigerian Red Cross Society 1966–1970," p. 24. The agreement of transition between the ICRC and the Nigerian Red Cross was not signed until three weeks later: "Agreement of 30th September 1969," contained in annex 3, *ibid.,* p. 25. However, this did not sufficiently reassure donor gov-

231   ernments and, as we shall see, it was not until December 9, 1969, that the FMG finally exempted the Nigerian Red Cross from provisions of the National Commission for Rehabilitation Decree of 1969 "with immediate effect." During the intervening two months the relief operation on the Federal side of the conflict suffered gravely as a result and also weakened it so that it was ill prepared to take on the greatly enlarged task following the collapse of Biafra a month later.

Nigerian Red Cross president: Second International Appeal of the Nigerian Red Cross Society, October 2, 1969: "To All Men of Goodwill," by Sir Adetokunbo Ademola, contained in annex 4, *ibid.,* p. 28.

number fed reduced drastically: Statement by Ademola, on the "Phase-out Plan of the Nigerian Red Cross Relief Operation," May 2, 1970.

232   **U.S. government report:** The report, "Assistance to Victims of the Nigerian War," stated (p. 8): "NRC's [Nigerian Red Cross's] main problem is financial. ICRC costs on the Federal side have been about $700,000 per month. NRC's estimated monthly budget, reduced to a minimum, is reported to be $308,000 needed per month, or $3.6 million for one year. No final action has been taken on this request and the Nigerian Government's financial support for the relief effort has been somewhat sporadic and piecemeal. Although the NRC has appealed for outside help, insufficient contributions have been received to date. NRC has had to operate from month to month and at one point, from week to week in covering current expenses."

West Africa: November 8, 1969, p. 1331.

NRC exempted: The letter from the secretary to the cabinet of the FMG to the president of the Nigerian Red Cross was dated December 9, 1969.

233   **"thin edge of the wedge":** International Committee of Conscience statement, New York City, December 12, 1969.

obligations of a contracting party: Today the ICRC takes a position similar to that which Baxter advised in 1969. Wherever there is need to provide humanitarian assistance, the ICRC now insists it has a right to do so, based on Articles 5, 6, and 9 of the Geneva Conventions.

234   **JCA guidelines:** The "Proposed Guidelines for Daylight Relief Flights" were published as appendix 42 of *The Nordchurchaid Airlift to Biafra,* p. 212.

Chapter 25

236   **JCA regulations:** Appendix 31, *The Nordchurchaid Airlift to Biafra,* pp. 177–78.

237   **plane destroyed by bombs:** This incident, November 1, 1969, was reported in Jointchurchaid press release 109, November 3, 1969.

aborted flights: *The Nordchurchaid Airlift to Biafra,* pp. 78–79.

"Put a dead Biafran in your tank": Among those who addressed a rally in Trafalgar Square: Conservative M.P. Hugh Fraser, Liberal M.P. Jo Grimond, Labour M.P. Michael Barnes. The following month, in another form of protest,

John Lennon returned his OBE (member of the Order of the British Empire) to the Queen.

238   **JCA relief flights and tonnages:** Joint Church Aid published these statistics on numbers of flights and tons flown in in its press releases nos. 109 (November 3, 1969), 117 (December 2, 1969), and 125 (January 8, 1970).
church relief effort: The estimate of need at the end of 1969 comes from JCA press release no. 125 of January 8, 1970, while the other statistics on numbers the Catholic and Protestant relief networks were trying to feed and help care for during September to December 1969 appear in the table published as appendix 37 of *The Nordchurchaid Airlift to Biafra,* p. 199.
"significant deterioration": This Protestant relief operation report was made as of October 1, 1969. (See *The Nordchurchaid Airlift to Biafra,* p. 89.)

239   *Guardian* **and the foreign secretary:** The article by Walter Schwarz appeared in the *Guardian* of November 14, 1969. The exchange about it between Hugh Fraser and Michael Stewart took place November 17, 1969. *Parliamentary Debates* (Hansard), col. 823.

239–   **Western survey:** Western's medical team carried out its nutritional health sur-
40   vey of the Biafran population between October 17 and 28, 1969. Their report was not released when completed in December but was later printed in hearings of the Senate Subcommittee on Refugees, January 21–22, 1970, p. 212 *et seq.*

240   **Ferguson called meeting:** One rather thorough account of this meeting was made by G. Fred Hamilton who, during 1969, was chairman of UNICEF's Nigeria/Biafra Emergency Standing Committee. "Meeting of participating relief groups with Ambassador Ferguson, at Washington 15 December 1969," internal paper, UNICEF, New York. However, the real purpose of the meeting—to get the relief agencies to begin contingency planning—and Ferguson's disappointment at the reluctance of relief officials to think that collapse of Biafra might be imminent, come from Ferguson's own comments to me.

240–   **Beaumont asked halt to JCA flights:** For the opposite role played by
1   Beaumont, ten years later, during the Kampuchea emergency, see epilogue. Also, William Shawcross describes Beaumont's negotiations in Phnom Penh in *The Quality of Mercy: Cambodia, Holocaust and Modern Conscience* (Simon and Schuster, 1984).

241   **"Dickers" statement:** The four-point statement, presented by the deputy director of the World Council of Churches Division of Inter-Church Aid, Refugee and World Service to the meeting of JCA executives at Sandefjord, Norway, on December 8, 1969 was printed in Jointchurchaid press release 120, December 12, 1969.

241–   **philosophical rumination:** The prime minister's remarks, from which these
2   brief excerpts are taken, will be found in *Parliamentary Debates* for December 8, 1969, cols. 41, 47, 48, and 50. While he quoted the *Times* of two days earlier as the source of information about the suggestion by the World Council of Churches that the airlift might be wound up as a way of cutting off the food

program as a means of shortening the war, he also remarked that "there may be further controversy over this today when Joint Church Aid meets." *Ibid.,* col. 41.

242 **Guardian comment:** The leader appeared in the *Guardian* December 9, 1969, the day after the prime minister's remarks in Commons. A few weeks earlier the *Guardian* had commented on Foreign Secretary Michael Stewart's statement in Commons of November 17, 1969: " . . . But he also failed to dispel the impression that Britain opposes the night flights organized by the churches which manage to get a minimal amount of food in and which urgently need to be enlarged." *Manchester Guardian,* November 18, 1969.
JCA executives respond: The full statement of the plenary meeting of the Joint Church Aid executives was published along with the WCC statement in Jointchurchaid press release 120, December 12, 1969.

Chapter 26

243 **Douglas-Home's proposal:** See *Parliamentary Debates* (Hansard), 8 December 1969, cols. 257–59.
the *Times* political editor: His account gave some of the background of the Conservative party's proposal: "I learn that the plan has been thoroughly researched during the past few weeks by Conservative leaders and a team of back-bencher specialists in foreign affairs and defense. They have informally consulted British admirals to make sure that it would work, but have also checked the details with the United States Navy, who apparently would be more than willing to take part." The *Times,* December 10, 1969.

244 **Harold Wilson on TV:** Quoted in *West Africa,* October 11, 1969, p. 1229.
Gowon on helicopter plan: This comment by General Gowon on Sir Alec's proposal appeared in a story headlined "Gowon rejects Home's plea," which appeared in the *Daily Sketch* of Lagos, December 19, 1969.

244– **search for a negative response:** The news stories all appeared the same day,
5 December 14, 1969: the *Sunday Telegraph,* by John Michael, the Commonwealth affairs correspondent; the *Sunday Times,* by Nicholas Carroll, the diplomatic correspondent; and *The Observer,* by Andrew Wilson, the defense correspondent.

245– **Michael Stewart on Addis:** The quotes from Stewart's statement during the
6 debate on Nigeria in Commons will be found in *Parliamentary Debates* (Hansard), 9 December 1969, cols. 274–75 and 271.

246 **Okoi Arikpo:** His statement was quoted by John Michael, the Commonwealth affairs correspondent of the London *Sunday Telegraph,* December 14, 1969, and reprinted in *West Africa,* December 20, 1969, p. 1565.
Soviet 122-mm. Howitzers: Colonel Scott's report, para. 12.
Michael Stewart to Commons: *Parliamentary Debates* (Hansard), 9 December 1969, col. 276. The British defense adviser in Lagos, writing at the same time

(his report was dated December 13, 1969), stated: "This perennial shortage of ammunition has been aggravated by the decision of many countries in Western Europe to place an embargo on the supply of arms to the FMG. In consequence, the major suppliers of arms and ammunition are the U.K., Spain and the Soviet Union." Colonel Scott's report, para. 70.

"15 per cent by value": Later *The Economist* questioned this perennial claim of the government that the British throughout the war supplied an unchanging, modest quantity of arms and ammunition to the Nigerian armed forces. *The Economist,* January 31, 1970, p. 32.

246– **Nigerian Trade Summary:** See note p. 13.

7

247 **British defense adviser:** Colonel Scott's report, para. 13, b, (1), and para. 15, b, (4).

The Economist: December 20, 1969, p. 28.

248 **Ojukwu's Christmas message:** Biafran Overseas Press Division press release Gen-777.

Swedish foreign minister: Reply in the Second Chamber of the Riksdag, November 20, 1969, printed as document 75 of *Swedish Foreign Policy 1969,* p. 175.

249 **UN resolutions:** For example, the General Assembly approved Resolution 2547, which

• called upon "the Government of the United Kingdom . . . to reconsider its deplorable refusal to intervene in Southern Rhodesia by force and to restore the human rights and fundamental freedoms of the people of Zimbabwe . . .";

• called upon "the Government of Portugal to observe the terms of the Geneva Conventions relative to the Protection of Civilian Persons in Time of War" (the resolution recalled an earlier resolution "by which it reaffirmed the inalienable right of the people of the Territories under Portuguese domination to self-determination, freedom and independence. . . ." Res. 2547 (24), part A, December 11, 1969.

Further, in the same resolution, in a second part adopted later, applying to South Africa, the General Assembly recalled an earlier resolution "in which it invited the Economic and Social Council and the Commission on Human Rights to give urgent consideration to ways and means of improving the capacity of the United Nations to put a stop to violations of human rights wherever they may be. . . ."

This selective application ignored the universality of the Universal Declaration of Human Rights and the fact that it and the Geneva Conventions were obligatory international humanitarian law applying to all people everywhere.

Angie Brooks: Quoted in *West Africa,* December 27, 1969, p. 1593.

U Thant: The secretary general stated in Dakar that Biafran secession was unacceptable to the United Nations, that the world organization would never accept the principle of secession in one of its member states. He repeated this at a number of other stops in his African tour. Agence France Presse in the *Times* of London, January 5, 1970. He also asked General Ojukwu "to show enough magnanimity and vision to conform to the resolution of O.A.U. heads of state." Reuters in the *New York Times*, January 5, 1970.

Stewart and Douglas-Home: The rejection of the Conservative party's plan for using helicopters to fly in relief did not come till January 6 (see the *Times*, January 7, 1970, and the *Daily Telegraph*, January 7, 1970).

250 **"... eyes glazed with hunger. ... The inner man was still there, but ... no strength left to fight":** Odumegwu Ojukwu later used these words in describing to me the troops he encountered as he approached Owerri shortly before the collapse of Biafra.

Chapter 27

253 **a moment of naïveté:** "At last those people will be fed" was my own reaction on that weekend of January 10–11. I was quickly disabused of this expectation in the headquarters of the United Nations Children's Fund on Monday morning when François Remy, a medical doctor and senior planner of UNICEF, grimly said: "We won't get in there for weeks." As soon as he said it, I knew he was right, and it proved to be the case.

JCA executives: They met in Stuttgart on Sunday, January 11, as soon as word reached them that Biafra was, in fact, finally collapsing (see Jointchurchaid press release 126, January 11, 1970). The paraphrase of the message they had their planes radio to the government of Nigeria was told to me by one of the Joint Church Aid executives.

Pope Paul VI: Quoted in the *New York Times*, January 12, 1970.

254 **"Hottest Part of Hell for the Pope":** *New York Times*, January 14, 1970.

British defense adviser's report: Scott's report, "An Appreciation of the Nigerian Conflict," had apparently already been set as the main news story of the *Sunday Telegraph* (January 11, 1970) before word began coming out of Biafra that the collapse had begun, so the major headline of the paper read: "Secret British report on Biafra leaked: Muddle, corruption, waste by Federals."

Gen. Gowon order to troops: *New York Times*, January 14, 1970, p. 16.

NRC report: The Nigerian Red Cross reported on November 20, 1969 ("NRC Relief Action Activities Report for Federal Nigeria") the numbers of people receiving rations in Federally-occupied territories at weeks ending:

Oct. 25th	445,919
Nov. 1st	338,767
Nov. 8th	254,363

while the cases of kwashiorkor reported in treatment programs went up during this period:

Oct. 25th	34,108
Nov. 1st	46,196
Nov. 8th	50,503

254– **food stockpiles:** The Nigerian Red Cross report of November 20, 1969 con-
5 tained three graphs that charted the consumption, replenishment, and stock

PAGE

levels for the forward field areas during July–November 1969, "all of which," the report stated, "have been subject to certain difficulties in the maintenance of the quantities of food reaching them each month from Lagos, Koko Port and Port Harcourt." The second graph, giving the actual level of stocks in the warehouses at Enugu, Agbor, and Uyo, indicated that "this has been falling slowly from a level which, even at the beginning of August, must be considered as lower than desirable." *Ibid.*

255 **tons on hand at war's end:** UNICEF's resident director in Nigeria reported to headquarters on January 2, 1970, that "as of last weekend (27 December 1969) the stock levels within Nigeria are approximately as follows:

Enugu	3,300 tons
Uyo/Calabar	1,300
Port Harcourt	2,800
Mid-West	300
Lagos	400
Koko	4,500

for a total of 12,600, with another 400 tons in transit to Enugu."

Ferguson's mid-December meeting: From "Meeting of participating relief groups with Ambassador Ferguson, at Washington 15 December 1969," internal paper, UNICEF, p. 3.

256 **"desist forthwith from meddling":** The *Times* (London), January 12, 1970, p. 1.

No military: The *Times* of London reported on January 14, 1970: "One restriction imposed by the Nigerian Federal Government caused the hold-up on Monday of an R.A.F. Hercules loaded with medical supplies: no military aircraft are to be used, and civilian helpers rather than soldiers will be accepted in the relief operation. This has meant the transfer of medical supplies to a civilian aircraft and the abandonment of the plan to send out field hospital teams from the Royal Army Medical Corps and units of the Royal Engineers which could have been used on road repairs, bridge building and the repair of airfields."

257 **"Let them keep their blood money":** General Gowon quoted in the *New York Times,* January 14, 1970. While "We will do it ourselves . . ." and "Nigerians: this is a challenge to us, and we will do it" reflected the newfound pride in victory and the xenophobia that now gripped Nigerians in the days following Biafra's collapse, the relief teams eventually operating under the aegis of the Nigerian Red Cross were, in fact, made up of medical and other personnel from many countries, including Ireland, Italy, Britain, America, Austria, Japan, Australia, Switzerland, Sweden, and India. See Medical Relief Teams (annex 7) and Administration Staff (annex 8) of *Nigerian Relief Action,* Report of the Nigerian Red Cross Society 1966–1970.

258 **helicopter distribution:** UNICEF still had three helicopters at Calabar. These were not military aircraft but operated by a civilian charterer. The FMG did not allow them to be used for distribution.

trucks imported: The Nigerian Red Cross did begin requesting relief assistance immediately, and vehicles were high on the list. Panayotsis Stanissis of the League of Red Cross Societies cabled his headquarters on January 14: "Road transport immediate urgent needs are: 60 trucks, 7–10 tons capacity; 40 Landrovers; maritime transport immediate needs: one vessel 5, to 7, tons capacity. No, repeat, No aircraft required."
The Economist: January 17, 1970.

259   **Michael Stewart:** *New York Times,* January 12, 1970. The *Times* of London, January 12, 1970, quoted the foreign secretary: "Speaking on BBC radio yesterday, Mr. Stewart was asked if he thought British Government policies had now been vindicated: 'I do believe they have.'

      "Mr. Stewart commented," the *Times* continued, "that he had often said that if Britain had pursued a different policy it could only have prolonged the war and suffering. On the future prospects of the Ibos, he said: 'All the evidence is that there is the prospect for them of a peaceful and honorable place in a united Nigeria.' "

international observers: The headline, "Observers Find No Sign of Genocide in Biafra," appeared in the *Times* of London, January 17, 1970. The headline in the *New York Times* was more precisely worded: "Biafra Observers in One Area Find No Mistreatment." The text of the report by the international observers team was printed in its entirety by the *New York Times,* January 17, 1970.

      The *New York Times* account of their press conference in Lagos noted that "the team of eight observers began its tour last Saturday [January 10] by flying from Lagos to Port Harcourt. The men then headed north toward Owerri. Four members returned to Lagos Monday [January 12]. The other four returned the next day [January 13]. The team members said they had not gone north of Owerri because they wanted to return to Lagos to issue their report." *New York Times,* January 17, 1970.

doctors and nurses fled: This account of general conditions during the first two weeks following Biafra's collapse described the situation in the northern sector, generally considered less chaotic than that in the southern sector. It was included at the beginning of the longer "Report of the Area Medical Adviser, Northern Sector, Nigerian Red Cross Relief Action (Jan. 9–Mar. 7, 1970)."

259– **Brigadier Said-Uddin Khan:** The UN secretary general's representative was
60   quoted in the *New York Times* account of January 17, 1970, about the report and press conference by the international observers team.

260   **State Department:** These comments by State Department officials were made on the first working day, Monday, following the beginning of the collapse of Biafra over the weekend and appeared in the *New York Times,* January 13, 1970.

Moscow: It appeared at the time that Soviet support for Nigeria during the civil conflict had paid off. The *New York Times* reported from Moscow, January 20: "Nigeria's Ambassador said today that Soviet aid to his country was the most important factor in the defeat of the Biafran secessionists. At a news conference at his embassy, G. T. Kurubo strongly praised Moscow's extensive military aid, which included jet bombers and fighters as well as artillery.

      "He said that victory over the Biafrans was the result of the Soviet assistance: 'more than any other single thing: more than all other things together.' "

PAGE

The *Times* account of the Nigerian ambassador's news conference continued: "Nigeria is grateful 'because the Russians understand African sensitivity,' he added, explaining that 'the important thing is that the Soviet Union made no noise about the assistance it had rendered Nigeria.' . . .

"The Soviet Government has said nothing officially about the war," the article went on, "but the Soviet media have been stressing the victory of 'progressive forces.' An effort has been made to link the Western aid for the Biafrans with 'imperialist intrigues' to weaken Nigeria.

"Pravda, the Communist party newspaper, said today that 'Western powers would like to hinder the national reconciliation and postwar restoration of the country under the guise of aid to Nigeria.' " *New York Times*, January 21, 1970.

Elliot Richardson: Richardson held a news briefing on January 13, 1970. *Department of State Bulletin*, February 2, 1970, pp. 120–24.

261 **Gowon to Newsom:** Newsom told of his January 13 meeting with General Gowon at the hearing of Senator Kennedy's Subcommittee on Refugees, January 21, 1970.

prime minister: When I later asked Clyde Ferguson about this remark by the British prime minister during their meeting on January 12, 1970 he said he could not give me the exact quote but would have to check his notes. Roger Morris, the National Security Council staff man in the White House dealing with Nigeria-Biafra, later alluded to this: " . . . Prime Minister Wilson, who once told a U.S. diplomat that he would accept a million Biafran casualties if that were the price of the rebels' collapse. . . ." Roger Morris, *Washington Post*, January 24, 1975.

Chapter 28

262 **UNICEF as a channel:** UNICEF notified international new agencies three days later (January 16, 1970): "Several governments have decided to channel their aid to the children victims of the Nigerian war through UNICEF, whose Executive Director, Henry R. Labouisse, is at present in Lagos. Responding to an urgent appeal by Mr. Labouisse the Governments of the United States, Canada and Ireland have already advised they will contribute: United States $2 million, Canada $200,000 and Ireland $25,000. . . ." Memo quoting press release sent to all European national committees for UNICEF by UNICEF's Office for Europe in Paris, January 16, 1970.

263 **"O.K. We're ready to go on this":** It was Roger Morris of the National Security Council staff who phoned me back at about eight o'clock in the evening of Tuesday, January 13. It took only two hours to respond to the request with a complete list of the kinds of medicines, food, and helicopters that would be needed for the U.S. and other governments to channel relief through the United Nations Children's Fund.

Washington Post: This was the lead on the story by Robert Estabrook reporting from the United Nations on Ogbu's press conference, the *Washington Post*, January 15, 1970, p. A-14. He also quoted the Nigerian ambassador as saying, "Nigeria will not tolerate interference in her sovereign affairs," but, "by contrast," he noted, "Ogbu stressed UNICEF has provided 'invaluable service and assistance' and is encouraged to continue."

The original text of Ogbu's statement to the press at the United Nations, released by the Nigerian Mission, January 14, 1970, quoted the ambassador as saying: "The UNICEF as you all know have provided invaluable assistance to Nigeria and have continued their very good and altruistic humanitarian work which my Government welcomes and deeply appreciates."

FMG statement: Federal Government statement on Emergency Relief Operation, press release 43, January 15, 1970.

264   **Ambassador Sule Kolo:** His press conference in Geneva was reported in the *Times* of January 15, 1970, headlined: "Starvation reports rejected by Lagos as 'wild guesses.' "

264–   **Ojukwu's statement:** His statement, distributed by Reuters, was printed in its
5   entirety in both the *New York Times* and the *Times* of London, January 16, 1970. While the statement was released in Geneva, Ojukwu was actually in Abidjan, Ivory Coast. There was speculation and a certain mystery as to his whereabouts at the time.

265   **State Department spokesman and official:** Quoted in the *New York Times*, January 15, 1970, p. 14.

Richardson to editors: The complete statement to the editors and broadcasters and their questions and Richardson's answers were printed in the *Department of State Bulletin*, February 2, 1970, pp. 113–17.

266   **postpone any decision:** Another account of this meeting, emphasizing a different aspect of the relief problem (the findings of the Western survey), was later reported by Elizabeth Drew, who wrote: " . . . In any event, the State Department prevailed, not by any means so overt as disobeying or even overruling the White House, but by the more classic technique of postponement. . . ." Elizabeth B. Drew, "Reports: Washington," *The Atlantic*, May 1970.

Boston Globe: The story, by Richard M. Stewart of the *Globe*'s Washington bureau, reported: "The Nixon Administration is formulating a plan that would enable emergency food relief to be sent to Nigeria on 18 of this country's largest helicopters under the auspices of the United Nations International Children's Fund (UNICEF).

"White House and congressional sources said the White House, with the support of President Nixon, has taken the initiative in pressing for action to supply the relief because of the caution exhibited by the State Department in dealing with the problem.

"Under the plan, the helicopters would be loaded onto giant transports and flown to the island of Saotome off the Nigerian coast, where surplus food is stockpiled.

" 'We expect a break in this within the next 24-hours,' a White House aide said.

"Key to the success of the plan are the negotiations currently underway in

Lagos, Nigeria, between the Nigerian Government and Henry Labouisse, director general of UNICEF. . . ." *Boston Globe,* January 17, 1970.

267–
8   **Lincolnesque manner:** The *New York Times* reported: "General Gowon followed the formal ceremony with a midnight radio message notable for its conciliatory tone. 'Once again we have the opportunity to build a great nation,' he said, promising a general amnesty for the rebels.

"The general, a devoted student of Abraham Lincoln, spoke of the casualties of the bitter war and urged his people to show by the reconciliation 'that all those dead shall not have died in vain.' " *New York Times,* January 16, 1970, pp. 1, 13.

268   **Lord Hunt:** He made these statements upon his arrival in Lagos from London on January 15, according to the account in the *New York Times,* January 16, 1970.
Thant in Lagos: This account, including the toasts exchanged by Gowon and Thant, is based on an internal UN report about the secretary general's visit to Nigeria, January 19, 1970.
Thant at airport: UN press release (from UN Information Center, Lagos).

269   **Henrik Beer to Thant:** From Henrik Beer cable transmitted through U.S. Embassy, Lagos.

270   **secretary of state:** William Rogers was questioned about relief in Nigeria on the ABC-TV program "Issues and Answers," January 18, 1970. *Department of State Bulletin,* February 9, 1970, pp. 150–51.
Nixon to Kissinger: Nixon was quoted by Roger Morris in an article some time later: " . . . Richard Nixon was closeted in his Executive Office Building hideaway, drafting his first State of the Union message. He had little time for African problems, but he knew he was being misled when Secretary of State William Rogers and some State Department officials briefed him at midweek with an optimistic report on the gruesome conditions inside fallen Biafra." Morris in the *Washington Post,* January 24, 1975.

Chapter 29

271   **Edward Kennedy:** This quote and the subsequent testimony by Newsom and Ferguson appear in "Relief Problems in Nigeria-Biafra," Hearings of Senate Subcommittee on Refugees, January 21–22, 1970.

272   **Western survey controversy:** Christopher Beal, policy chairman of the Ripon Society (the liberal Republican study group), having been directly involved in efforts to get the findings of the Western survey understood within the U.S. government and conveyed to officials of the Nigerian government, wrote an account titled, "How the State Dept. Watched Biafra Starve" in the *Ripon Forum* of March 1970 (pp. 8–12, 17–19).

Elliot Richardson took the charges in this and an accompanying editorial in the publication of his own natural political allies with sufficient seriousness to write a full-page response in the same issue. To the charge of "insubordinate delay" by State in not carrying out the president's instruction to transmit to the Nigerian government all information it had on Biafran starvation, he responded: "The critical argument made by Mr. Beal in support of his charge of 'insubordinate delay' relates to the presentation of Dr. Western's report to the Nigerian authorities. The argument is based on a series of unsupportable premises:

"A. That the Nigerian Government was completely unaware that they had a major relief problem;

"B. That a forceful presentation of the Western Report during the first week after the war's end would, in a situation of disruption and conflicting reports, have had a critical beneficial impact on the flow of relief supplies to Eastern Nigeria; and

"C. That the subsequent presentation of the report enraged the Nigerian Government because we had lulled it into accepting its own inadequate estimates.

"In fact, the critical problem in the early weeks after the fighting stopped was not convincing the Nigerian Government that the need was very great—they were aware of this, as General Gowon publicly acknowledged—but the logistical problem of actually getting the food to the people most in need. It was to this need that the President's offer of funds, planes and equipment was directed, and it was to this need that the Nigerian Government turned its efforts, although it insisted on adherence to its previously announced policy that all relief be provided through Nigerian organizations. During the weeks following the Biafran collapse, the actual movement of food and medicine certainly fell far short of even the Nigerian Government's own estimate of the need. But this was attributable to the suddenness of the Biafran collapse, the disruption in Eastern Nigeria, the sudden need to extend Nigerian organization, and, above all, the Nigerian lack of transport. . . ." Excerpt from "A Reply From Elliot L. Richardson" (dated February 27, 1970), *Ripon Forum*, March 1970, p. 28.

274 **champagne, roast suckling pig:** Brian Silk, London *Daily Telegraph*, January 22; Andrew Borowiec, *Washington Star*, January 21; Hugh A. Mulligan, Associated Press, the *Times* (London), January 23, 1970.

"a failure to reach the usual level of detachment": Wilson's response was reported in the *Times* of January 22, 1970. The story went on to report: "In the Commons, answering Mr. Julian Snow, Labor M.P. for Lichfield and Tamworth, Mr. Wilson recalled that he had raised the question of brainwashing. He thought that professional commentators on politics were the least likely to be brainwashed in the manner he had suggested.

"But he was told," the *Times* report continued, "that some of the 'less professional people'—some of those who were called upon to 'regurgitate' at weekends and others who were invited to give their views on radio and television—were not so good at resisting the brainwashing organizations as the hardbitten members of the press who reported politics at Westminster. . . ."

274–
5
correspondent of *Sunday Times*: *Sunday Times*, January 25, 1970.

275–
6
Colonel Dewey's cable: Elizabeth Drew quoted Dewey's cable in *The Atlantic*, May 1970. Extensive questioning by Kennedy and Goodell of Newsom and

365

PAGE

Ferguson disclosed a good deal of its contents without quoting directly (see pp. 203–206 and 208–209, Hearings of Senate Subcommittee on Refugees, January 22, 1970).

277–
8

prime minister and Opposition: These excerpts appear in *Parliamentary Debates* (Hansard), 22 January 1970, cols. 707, 710, and 711.

278

Lord Hunt on press coverage: *The Financial Times,* the *Times,* and the *Daily Telegraph* of January 23, 1970.

international observers: Another account that told about encountering the international observers in the field was made by the correspondent of the *Sunday Times,* quoted earlier (pp. 274–75). After describing the conditions he and other foreign journalists had found once they had been able to get into the former Biafran area, he went on to report: "On returning to Orlu we came across the international team's gleaming convoy of half a dozen shiny Land-Rovers and cars halted at a crossroad. We stopped, jumped down from our cattletruck and clustered round the senior observer, Brigadier-General John Drewry of Canada. We told him what we had seen and heard, complaining of the apparent absence of any flow of relief along the roads, of shortages everywhere we went, of the pillage, raping and abduction.

"I jotted down some of the brigadier-general's comments, delivered from a height of about six feet four inches in a chill voice.

"As a piece of studied indifference to suffering and total failure to grasp a public relations opportunity, his performance would be hard to beat. His words fell on the ears of a bunch of American and European reporters who were keyed up emotionally by what they had seen themselves and who desperately sought information on the real relief situation.

"They had been led in Lagos to expect to find relief flowing freely everywhere; what they had in fact found in the one tiny bit of Biafra they had managed to penetrate with very little help from anyone looked like a monumental piece of mishandling.

"I suppose that the brigadier-general's 10 minutes with the Press did the Nigerian government one of its major public-relations disservices. Furthermore it undermined any confidence the journalists might have had in the international observer team's objectivity." *Sunday Times,* January 25, 1970.

280

Elliot Richardson: Interestingly, a year later, Richardson (who by then had become Secretary of Health, Education and Welfare) commented briefly on this experience when he responded, on behalf of the White House, to a *Newsweek* article appraising Richard Nixon "at midpassage in his Presidency." Richardson wrote: "We were discussing what to do about starvation in Biafra. There was a definite danger in straining our relations with Nigeria, then in the final stages of its civil war. The President weighed the problem of Nigerian displeasure against the need of the hungry Ibos; the deciding factor was the humanitarian feelings of the American people. The President owed it to his fellow citizens to make the kind of response that was rooted in the American character: the President's reaction could not be the 'correct' diplomatic reaction, it had to be the gut American reaction." Elliot Richardson, "Nixon Behind the Scenes," *Newsweek,* February 1, 1971, p. 17.

Wilson and Nixon: This account was provided by one White House official and confirmed by another.

281   **secretary general's representative:** Press release of the United Nations Information Service, New York, January 26, 1970.

281–   **Anthony Lewis:** *New York Times*, January 26, 1970. William Powell, the official
2   spokesman of the United Nations, responded that day (*New York Times*, January 27, 1970). The article by Lewis, "How Pointless It All Seems Now," appeared in *The New York Times Magazine* of February 8, 1970.

Chapter 30

284   **1,565 tons:** Dr. David Miller, chief medical adviser to the Nigerian Red Cross, provided this figure of total tonnage of food distributed during the last week of January 1970 at the meeting of voluntary agencies in Lagos on February 5, 1970 and estimated that a population of 1,323,000 had been fed during that week. "Minutes of NARCVA Meeting," February 5, 1970.

286   **Lythcott-Latham survey:** "The Malnutrition Survey of the Eastern States of Nigeria, February 1970," as it was officially titled, was completed and submitted to the Nigerian Ministry of Health and the Nigerian Red Cross on March 15, 1970.

287   **sharp rise in malnutrition:** Figure 2 (table showing new cases of severe and moderate malnutrition per week in the Northern Sector), "Report of Area Medical Adviser, Northern Sector (Orlu/Enugu), Nigerian Red Cross Relief Action, Jan. 9–Mar. 7, 1970."
      tonnage of food needed weekly: From "The Malnutrition Survey of the Eastern States of Nigeria, February 1970," March 15, 1970.

287–   **food tonnages:** These weekly tonnages of food distributed during February and
8   March were compiled by the Nigerian Red Cross (and received by the Department of State, Washington, from Agency for International Development representatives at the U.S. Embassy in Lagos).

288   **Chief Enahoro:** *The Times* of London, January 17, 1970, reported on his news conference in Lagos: "Enahoro sees no need to fly food into Nigeria."

289   **"devitalize the Ibos":** Ojukwu expressed this opinion to me later, in 1977.
      Rogers in Lagos: According to the *New York Times*: "In a chat with newsmen, Mr. Rogers said, he believed that his talks on Friday with Maj. Gen. Yakubu Gowon, Nigerian head of state, had been 'very useful and quite successful' in smoothing over tensions that had arisen with Nigeria over Western efforts to rush food and relief materials to starving victims of the Nigerian civil war. . . .

      "Mr. Roger's most delicate diplomatic task had been in Nigeria. The Nigerian military government had shown resentment because it felt the United States, private relief agencies, and other groups had been critical of Nigerian intentions and performance in getting aid to the former region of Biafra.

"It was known that Mr. Rogers had gone to considerable lengths to placate the Nigerians to assure them that the United States agreed that national reconciliation could only be reached if all rehabilitation efforts were channeled through the Nigerian Government." *New York Times*, February 23, 1970.

290   *Washington Star:* April 7, 1970.

currency: William Borders wrote in June that many could still not buy anything "because all they had to spend was worthless Biafran currency," and told of the government's plan "to give $56 to every individual who responded to a recent call by turning in the blue and green Biafran notes."

About 200,000 former Biafrans—most, heads of families—expected to receive payments, he reported from Lagos, but there were several million in the area: "Those who had no Biafran currency or who for some other reason made no deposit when the call went out, will receive no grant under present Government plans." *New York Times*, June 13, 1970.

291   *Washington Post:* Robert Estabrook wrote this retrospective article, which appeared in the *Washington Post* on February 14, 1971.

Epilogue

292–   **took Ibos awhile to recover:** William Borders, *New York Times*, November 21,
3   1971; John Darnton, *New York Times*, February 21, 1977; David Lamb, *International Herald-Tribune*, November 25–26, 1978.

293   **executives and military reintegrated:** Borders, *New York Times*, November 18, 1971.

20 million tons of cement: John Darnton, *The New York Times Magazine*, July 24, 1977.

294   **nationalizing BP:** "Nigeria said it undertook the nationalization because of BP's links with South Africa. The action, Mr. Olorunfemi [chief economist of the national petroleum company] said, was 'one of the very few times when we have used oil policy as an instrument of political policy.' " Pranay B. Gupta, *New York Times*, September 17, 1979.

Ibos felt benefited: Darnton, *New York Times*, February 21, 1977.

primary education: "The one social indicator which recorded a significant improvement was education. Nigeria was far behind the average of lower middle income countries in enrollment in 1970, but now can boast of virtually full primary enrollment except in the North. Since traditionally the enrollment rate for boys was much higher than for girls this has particularly benefitted girls . . ." *State of the World's Children 1984*, UNICEF, p. 149.

295   **public executions:** "Fourteen convicted armed robbers were executed today by an army firing squad before a cheering crowd of thousands in Port Harcourt, it was reported in Lagos. The executions brought to 171 the number of Nigerians shot since the death penalty was decreed for armed robbery two years ago." Associated Press, *New York Times*, July 23, 1972.

PAGE

"squalid slums": *Concord Weekly*, October 5, 1984.
"did not receive social benefits": *State of the World's Children 1984*, UNICEF, pp. 148–49.
World Bank special funds: "Toward Sustained Development in Sub-Saharan Africa: A Joint Program of Action," The World Bank, 1984.

297   Orwell: *1984* (Signet), p. 29.

Acknowledgments

This book is based on interviews and personal experience as much as the documentation cited. Many of those interviewed after the war still held positions in governments, international organizations, or relief agencies, so I promised them confidentiality and have used the information obtained from them for background, without attribution. It would be invidious and misleading to single out those individuals who were not granted confidentiality, so I shall express my gratitude once again to all who allowed me to interview them.

My personal experience is indicated here and there in the text and source notes. From July till early December 1968, I served as a consultant with UNICEF, working with the group concerned with emergency relief; during that period I was the person at the United Nations authorized to talk with the press about humanitarian assistance to victims of the Nigerian-Biafran conflict.

In December, my dissatisfaction with the fact that Secretary General Thant had curtailed UNICEF's efforts to assist in the emergency caused me to leave UNICEF and join with others in organizing a citizens' group to attempt to find further ways of getting food to those starving. During 1969 and early 1970, I served as executive director of the Committee for Nigeria-Biafra Relief; our proposal to use helicopters from an aircraft carrier is recounted in the book.

As I had been in close touch with many of the officials in international relief agencies and governments throughout the conflict, I thought I already knew what had happened and would write a book. In fact, as indicated in the prologue, even this close involvement did not provide a full understanding of the story set forth here.

It was only following the first round of interviews and the collection of documents, as I pulled all this material together, analyzed it, and had written two-thirds of a first draft, that the underlying story of how the British had managed the cover-up began to emerge. It then became necessary to go back for a second round of interviews with some of the officials who, it turned out, had been forthcoming the first time only up to the point of what I already knew. They were startled when I began asking the second level of questions, saying, "How did you find this out?" and "Nobody knows that!" Then, seeing that I had gotten to the bottom of what had actually happened, they responded fully so I would get the facts straight.

In addition to all who aided with interviews and in providing materials, I would like to thank those who helped in other ways, including: Irene Smirnoff, John G. Simon, Anne and Martin Peretz, Mary Kaplan, Richard Ullmann, the late Francis O. Wilcox and Robert Osborne of the Johns Hopkins School of Advanced International Studies,

ACKNOWLEDGMENTS

the Fund for Investigative Journalism, David Robison, Mona and Viggo Mollerup, Anthony Saville, Suzanne Cronje, Thierry Hentsch, Jacques Freymond, Heinrich Jaggi, Gunvor von Rosen, the late William Tunner, Fred Hamilton, E. J. R. Heyward, Sasha Bacic, Emily and George Orick, Sarah and Lloyd M. Garrison, Eric Freedman and Lloyd K. Garrison for their assistance with the Freedom of Information Act, Robert Lasky, S. William Green, and Roger Morris; and friends, for their kindness along the way: Patricia Ellsberg, Françoise de Montigny, Anne Mansfield, Deborah Appel, Constance Clodfelter, Jane Howard, Meg and William Simmons, Susan and Edward Coughlin, Joy and John Pratt, and many others—especially my patient editor, Ashbel Green.

Index

A NOTE ABOUT THE AUTHOR

Dan Jacobs has had long experience in international affairs and politics, as a speechwriter for Hubert Humphrey and other political leaders, as a political analyst with the Senate Subcommittee on Disarmament, and as a writer on social development for the UN and other organizations. He was educated at Harvard and conducted a daily interview program, "Backgrounds," on Station WGBH (Boston). He served as Executive Director of the Committee for Nigeria-Biafra Relief and recently prepared a study for UNICEF on the predicament of children in wars. He lives in New York City.